A Communicative Grammar of English

A Communicative Grammar of English

Third Edition

Geoffrey Leech and Jan Svartvik

An imprint of **Pearson Education**

London · New York · Toronto · Sydney · Tokyo · Singapore · Hong Kong · Cape Town
Madrid · Paris · Amsterdam · Munich · Milan

PEARSON EDUCATION LIMITED

Head Office:
Edinburgh Gate
Harlow CM20 2JE
Tel: +44 (0)1279 623623
Fax: +44 (0)1279 431059

London Office:
128 Long Acre
London WC2E 9AN
Tel: +44 (0)20 7447 2000
Fax: +44 (0)20 7447 2170
Website: www.pearsoneduc.com

First published 1975
Second edition 1994
Third edition first published in Great Britain 2002

© Pearson Education Limited 2002

The rights of Geoffrey Leech and Jan Svartvik to be identified as Authors
of this Work has been asserted by them in accordance with the Copyright,
Designs and Patents Act 1988.

ISBN 0 582 50633 6

British Library Cataloguing in Publication Data
A CIP catalogue record for this book can be obtained from the British Library

Library of Congress Cataloging in Publication Data
A CIP catalog record for this book can be obtained from the Library of Congress

10 9 8 7 6 5 4 3 2 1

Typeset in 9/12pt Stone Serif by Graphicraft Limited, Hong Kong
Printed and bound in Malaysia

The Publishers' policy is to use paper manufactured from sustainable forests.

Contents

CONTENTS

Based on
A Comprehensive Grammar of the English Language
by Randolph Quirk,
Sidney Greenbaum,
Geoffrey Leech,
Jan Svartvik

Preface

A Communicative Grammar of English has established itself as both an authoritative and an innovative grammar. This thoroughly revised third edition gives increased emphasis on spoken English and makes more use of real examples based on corpus data. We have also tried to make the presentation more 'pedagogical' by giving simpler explanations, in providing more corpus examples (from Longman Corpus Network), and in making clear the distinctions between major and minor points.

Another innovation is the accompanying new *Workbook* by Edward Woods and Rudy Coppieters which will help students to 'internalize' the contents of grammar.

The basic design of the book remains the same as in the second edition, including the numbering of sections. The book is divided into three parts:

- Part One: A guide to the use of this book

- Part Two: Grammar in use

- Part Three: A–Z in English grammar

This book is partly based on *A Comprehensive Grammar of the English Language* (Longman, 1985) by Randolph Quirk, Sidney Greenbaum, Geoffrey Leech and Jan Svartvik. However, it cannot be regarded as a condensed version of that larger work since its arrangement is totally different, and it contains additional material (especially in Part Two). On the other hand, the structural or formal aspect of grammar is less comprehensively treated here than in the larger work and also in *A Student's Grammar of the English Language* (Longman, 1990) by Sidney Greenbaum and Randolph Quirk. We have therefore added to each entry in Part Three a reference to the most relevant sections of *A Comprehensive Grammar of the English Language*, so that, if required, a more detailed treatment of the topic can be consulted in that book. A more recent grammar using the same general framework, which can be consulted especially on matters of frequency, language variety and conversational grammar, is *Longman Grammar of Spoken and Written English* (1999) by Douglas Biber, Stig Johansson, Geoffrey Leech, Susan Conrad and Edward Finegan.

We have attempted to simplify grammatical terminology and classifications as far as possible, so that the terms and categories treated in Part Three do not in every case correspond to the same terms in the *Comprehensive Grammar.*

Lancaster and Lund, August 2002

Symbols

( )   Items in round brackets are optional, i.e. the sentence is acceptable also if the bracketed words are left out:

> *Susan said she would call back but she didn't (do so).*

can be read either as

> *. . . but she didn't do so*   or as *. . . but she didn't*

Round brackets are also used for cross-references:

> '(*see* 408)' means 'see section 408 in this grammar'

> '(*see CGEL* 14.2)' means 'see *A Comphrehensive Grammar of the English Language*, section 14.2'

[ ]   Numerals in square brackets appear after examples when required for cross-reference:

> As in sentence [5] . . .

Square brackets are also used to separate items, such as two adverbials:

> *We go [to bed] [early].*

/   A slash indicates a choice of items, such as between *some-* or *any-* pronouns:

> *Did somebody/anybody phone?*

{ }   Braces indicate a range of choices, such as between different relative constructions:

$$\text{The film} \begin{cases} \textit{which we liked best} \\ \textit{that we liked best} \\ \textit{we liked best} \end{cases} \textit{was} \ldots$$

~   A tilde indicates 'roughly equivalent', e.g. active and passive:

> *They published this paper in 1999.*
> *~ This paper was published in 1999.*

A tilde is also used between related forms, e.g. verb forms or comparative forms:

give ~ gave ~ given

big ~ bigger ~ biggest

< > Angle brackets are used around variety labels (*see* 44–55):

<formal>, <informal>   <spoken>, <written>

<BrE>, <AmE>   <polite>, <familiar>

* An asterisk signifies that what follows is not 'good English', i.e. it is unacceptable usage:

We can say *Ann's car*, BUT NOT **the car of Ann*

// Slashes enclose phonemic transcriptions (*see* 43):

lean /liːn/   *leant* /lent/

' A stress mark is placed before the stressed syllable of a word:

'*over*   (stress on the first syllable)

temp'tation   (stress on the second syllable)

transfor'mation   (stress on the third syllable)

__ Underlined syllables carry the nuclear tone (*see* 38):

How could you do that?

` A falling tone: yes

´ A rising tone: yes

ˇ A fall-rise tone: yes

| A single vertical bar indicates tone unit boundary (*see* 37):

| I almost phoned them up and said | Come a bit later |

|| A double bar separates <BrE> from <AmE> usage:

spelling: *colour* || *color*   pronunciation: /'kʌlə || 'kʌlər/

S   subject (*see* 705)
V   verb phrase (*see* 735)
O   object (*see* 608)
C   complement (*see* 508)
A   adverbial (*see* 449)
SVO   subject + verb phrase + object
SVC   subject + verb phrase + complement
SVA   subject + verb phrase + adverbial

A guide to the use of this book

Introduction

1 It is sometimes argued that grammar is not important in a communicative approach to language. However, we take the view that communicative competence rests on a set of composite skills, one of which is grammatical:

> Communicative competence is composed minimally of grammatical competence, sociolinguistic competence, and communication strategies, or what we will refer to as strategic competence. There is no strong theoretical or empirical motivation for the view that grammatical competence is any more or less crucial to successful communication than is sociolinguistic competence or strategic competence. The primary goal of a communicative approach must be to facilitate the integration of these types of knowledge for the learner, an outcome that is not likely to result from overemphasis on one form of competence over the others throughout a second language programme. (Michael Canale and Merrill Swain, 'Theoretical Bases of Communicative Approaches to Second Language Teaching and Testing', *Applied Linguistics* 1: 27, 1980)

There are several reasons for emphasizing the communication aspects of learning English grammar as we do in this book. Here, let us consider four reasons.

A new angle

2 The type of student we have had in mind when writing this book is fairly advanced, for example a first-year student at a university or college of education. Often, such students already have grounding in the grammar of the language after several years of school English. Yet their proficiency in actually using the language may be disappointing. This, we believe, may be partly due to 'grammar fatigue'.

The student may therefore benefit from looking at grammar from another angle, where grammatical structures are systematically related to meanings, uses and situations, as we attempt to do in Part Two: 'Grammar in use'. In this way we expect students to improve and extend their range of competence and their use of communication strategies in the language. In

Part Three, called 'A-Z in English grammar', the book also supplies essential information about grammatical forms and structures, and can therefore be used as a general reference book or source book on English grammar. There we give references to relevant parts of *A Comprehensive Grammar of the English Language*, a standard grammatical description of English, where the advanced student can find extra information on topics which cannot be fully covered in this book.

A better organization

3 The conventional way of presenting English grammar in terms of structure also has a certain drawback in itself. For example, in such a grammar, notions of time may be dealt with in as many as four different places: under the tense of the verb, under time adverbs, under prepositional phrases denoting time, and under temporal conjunctions and clauses. The student who is primarily interested in making use of the language rather than in learning about its structure (and this is true for the majority of foreign students) is not likely to find such an arrangement particularly helpful. In *A Communicative Grammar of English*, the central part deals with grammar in use, which makes it possible to bring similar notions, such as those involving time, together in one place.

Spoken English

4 An important element in the communicative approach is the student's ability to use and understand the spoken language. This emphasis on speech is sometimes misunderstood, so that the communicative method is taken to imply focus on the spoken language. We do not share this view: 'communication' means communication in both speech and writing. Yet, since traditional grammar tends to concentrate on written language, we think it is important for a communicative grammar to describe and exemplify both types of language use. (On grammar in spoken and written English, *see* Sections 17–32.)

Corpus data

5 The examples given in grammars have often been made up by grammarians rather than taken from real language in actual use. A made-up example may well serve to illustrate a particular grammatical point, but it can appear stilted or 'wooden', distancing the learning of grammar from real live usage. This is no doubt one reason why grammar is often considered to be a less important part of language in the communicative approach. We take the view that the grammar of a language is indeed of central concern to students, since it describes what makes language tick – how it can carry the meanings we want to communicate. In this revised edition of our grammar we have illustrated grammatical statements with the help of hundreds of authentic examples from English language corpora, especially Longman Corpus Network. Corpora stored on computers provide access to many millions of words of spoken and written material in modern English. However, the corpus examples sometimes have to be simplified by the omission of distracting material. There can also be an advantage – for example, where precise contrasts have to be clearly indicated – in making use of made-up examples. We believe that in this book we have achieved the right balance between the use of authentic examples and the use of the clearest illustrative material.

The way this book is organized

6 The book is divided into three parts as follows:

- Part One: A guide to the use of this book (sections 1–56)
- Part Two: Grammar in use (sections 57–434)
- Part Three: A–Z in English grammar (sections 435–747)

Note that the book is organized in consecutively numbered sections (1–747), for ease of reference. At the end of the book, there is a detailed index which gives section numbers, rather than pages, as the most convenient means of looking up what you want.

We now give a brief overview of these three parts and what they contain.

Part One: A guide to the use of this book (sections 1–56)

7 In this first part, we try to explain the design of the book, and the apparatus of information you need in order to understand it, and to find what you need.

One of the major things you will need is a guide to the different labels we use for different kinds or varieties of English (44–56). Where English gives us a choice of grammatical forms or structures for a given purpose, the different structures available are often not equivalent, since they belong to different 'styles' or 'varieties'. An important part of communicative grammar is knowing the appropriate choice according to the situation you are in. For example, if you are communicating in **speech** your choices of grammar will often be different from the choices you make in **writing**. And when you are writing, if you are communicating in an **informal** situation, your choices will often be different from those that you choose in a **formal** situation. Throughout the book, therefore, we make use of 'variety labels' such as <spoken>, <written>, <informal> and <formal>, whenever we want to make a point about the appropriateness of a grammatical form for this or that situation. Remember that the **angle brackets** <. . .>, whenever they occur in this book, signal this kind of appropriate choice.

One particular purpose of Part One is to explain and illustrate the symbols used in representing features of the spoken language. Most of us are used to the conventions for representing the written language on paper – the use of spelling, punctuation, and so on. But how do we capture on paper the nature of spoken language? For this, not only do we need symbols representing vowels and consonants in speech (*see* 43) but, more important, we need symbols for representing features of stress and intonation, which are closely integrated with the grammar of spoken language (33–42). H. E. Palmer in his well-known pioneering *A Grammar of Spoken English* (first edition 1924) went to the lengths of presenting the grammar of speech through phonetic transcription of all features of the language. This brave effort was a valuable corrective to the assumption – all too common in those times – that grammar was synonymous with the study of the written language. But it increased the difficulty of using the book enormously, and paradoxically impeded the thing it was intended to promote – a widespread appreciation of the features of spoken language. Our position, in contrast to this, is that we need to reduce to a minimum the use of special symbols which students need to understand the facts of grammar. This means using phonetic symbols and symbols of stress and intonation rather sparingly, and in any case, only where they are important to understanding the use of grammar in the spoken language.

Part Two: Grammar in use (57–434)

8 Part Two is the central part and largest part of the grammar. It is also the part which justifies our title 'Communicative Grammar', by presenting grammar through the eyes of the communicator. The question it tries to answer, in as much detail as space permits, is: Given that I want to communicate certain meanings in certain situations or contexts, which grammatical forms and structures can I use?

Communication is not a simple process. It is helpful, for our purpose, to think of four circles, one inside another, representing different kinds of meaning function and the different ways of organizing such functions. The four circles in the figure below correspond to Sections A–D in Part Two.

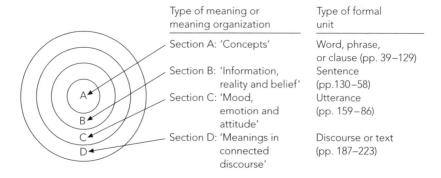

	Type of meaning or meaning organization	Type of formal unit
	Section A: 'Concepts'	Word, phrase, or clause (pp. 39–129)
	Section B: 'Information, reality and belief'	Sentence (pp. 130–58)
	Section C: 'Mood, emotion and attitude'	Utterance (pp. 159–86)
	Section D: 'Meanings in connected discourse'	Discourse or text (pp. 187–223)

The right-hand column, stating 'types of formal unit', should not be interpreted too strictly. It is useful to see the relation between the different layers of meaning and a hierarchy of grammatical units, but there is much overlap of the types of unit, and other factors are important. For example, intonation has an important role in the expression of meaning in Sections B, C and D.

Section A: Concepts (57–239)

9 The first circle is that of notional or conceptual meaning. Here we find the basic meaning categories of grammar: for example, 'number', 'definite meaning', 'amount', 'time', 'manner', 'degree'. Such terms point to aspects of our experience of the world. The structural units we deal with here are smaller than the sentence, i.e. **words**, **phrases**, and **clauses**.

Section B: Information, reality and belief (240–97)

10 The second circle represents logical aspects of communication. Here we make use of the categories of Section A, but we judge them and respond to them in the light of concepts such as truth and falsehood, which we depend on in giving and receiving information. Such categories as 'statements, questions and responses' belong here. So do 'affirmation and denial', 'possibility' and 'certainty'. The formal unit we are chiefly concerned with is the **sentence**.

Section C: Mood, emotion and attitude (298–350)

11 The third circle involves the social dimension of communication, relating grammar to the attitudes and behaviour of speaker and hearer. At the speaker's end, language expresses attitudes and emotions, and is a means of carrying out social goals. At the receiving end, language can control or influence the actions and attitudes of the hearer. This 'controlling' aspect of communication is performed through such speech acts as commanding, requesting, advising, promising. Although the logical aspect of meaning (Section B) is made use of, it is extended, or perhaps even 'distorted' to perform different kinds of social function. Thus, on a logical level, a question is a means of eliciting information – of determining what is true and what is false. But questions can be adapted 'pragmatically' for the purpose of making an offer:

Would you like some more?

or making a suggestion:

Why don't you come with me?

or expressing a strong feeling:

Wasn't it a marvellous play?

The unit of language we are mainly dealing with here is the **utterance**, which may or may not correspond to a sentence in length.

Section D: Meanings in connected discourse (351–434)

12 The fourth circle deals with the organization of communication. The question here is How shall we arrange our thoughts?, i.e. in what order shall we put them, and how shall we bind them together, in order to communicate in the most appropriate or effective way? Grammar is flexible enough to offer a considerable choice in these matters. This is the aspect of the use of grammar which takes account of 'context' in the sense of 'the preceding or following aspects of the discourse'. Looking at sentences in isolation is not sufficient: the unit here, therefore, is the **text** or **discourse**.

The four circles of the diagram represent a rational progression from the most limited and detailed aspect of meaning to the most inclusive. This design underlies Part Two, but we have not stuck to it too rigidly. To have done so would often have meant inconvenient repetitions of material in different sections. In dealing with emotive meaning (Section C), for example, we have moved directly from the **expression** of emotion to the **description** of emotion, even though it might be argued that the description of emotion belongs more naturally to conceptual meaning (Section A). The overriding consideration, in arranging the material, is that of dealing with related communicative choices together.

Part Three: A–Z in English grammar (435–747)

13 If Part Two is the main 'communicative' part of the book, Part Three is complementary to it. We need to know not only the communicative choices which grammar offers (Part Two), but the structural grammatical choices through which communication is channelled (Part Three). The two sets of choices are to a large extent independent of one another, and so are dealt with separately. The entries in Part Three are arranged alphabetically, for ease of access, and will be particularly useful in enabling students to find detailed explanations of grammatical terms (e.g. 'relative clause', 'phrasal verb') whose meaning may be unclear to them.

Cross-references and index

14 The reference apparatus is a very important part of every grammar book. In this grammar, with its innovative arrangement, it is essential to have numerous cross-references, and a comprehensive index. We have aimed to provide both. The index distinguishes between different kinds of references:

● References to individual words and phrases, e.g. *proper*, *because of*
● References to grammatical terms, e.g. PROPER NOUN
● References to functions or meanings, e.g. proportion, female person
● References to language varieties, e.g. <speech>, <American English>

In this way, multiple access is given to the information contained within the grammar.

Varieties of English

15 To use a language properly, we of course have to know the grammatical forms and structures and their meanings. These are the subjects of Parts Two and Three. But we also have to know what forms of language are appropriate for given situations, and for this purpose you will find in both those parts 'variety labels' such as <spoken>, <written>, <AmE> for American English, <BrE> for British English, <formal>, <informal>, <polite>, <familiar>. These labels are reminders that the English language is, in a sense, not a single language, but many languages, each belonging to a particular geographical area or to a particular kind of situation. The English used in formal written communication is in some ways different from the English used in informal conversation; the English used in the United States is somewhat different from the English used in Great Britain, in Australia, and so on. Obviously, in a general book of this kind we must ignore many less important differences. The purpose of this section of Part One is to explain briefly what is meant by the variety labels that you will meet, and to illustrate the varieties they refer to. If you wish to follow up a particular variety in detail, you may do so by means of the entries for variety labels in the index.

The 'common core'

16 Luckily for the learner, many of the features of English are found in all, or nearly all, varieties. We say that general features of this kind belong to the **common core** of the language. Take, for instance, the three words *children*, *offspring* and *kids*. *Children* is a 'common core' term; *offspring* is liable to occur in a rather formal situation (and is used of animals as well as human beings); *kids* is likely to occur in an informal or familiar situation. It is safest, when in doubt, to use the 'common core' term: thus *children* is the word you would want to use most often. But part of knowing English is knowing in what circumstances it would be possible to use *offspring* or *kids* instead of *children*. Let us take another example, this time from grammar:

Feeling tired, she went to bed early. <rather formal>   [1]

As she felt tired, she went to bed early.   [2]

She felt tired, *so* she went to bed early. <rather informal>   [3]

Sentence [2] is a 'common core' construction. It could, for example, be used either in speech or in writing. Sentence [1] is rather formal, and typical of written language. Sentence [3] is rather informal, and is likely to occur in relaxed conversation. In this book, you can assume that features of English given no variety label belong to the 'common core'.

Grammar in spoken and written English

Different transmission systems

17 English, like other languages, makes use of two channels: speech and writing. They have different transmission systems. Speech is transmitted by sound-waves, originated in speaking and received in hearing. Writing is transmitted by letters and other visible marks, produced in writing and received in reading. Good, all-round communicative competence involves all four skills:

● speaking and writing (production)

● hearing and reading (reception)

Spoken and written English do not have different grammars, but the shared English grammar is used differently on the two channels. For the benefit of those who want to acquire good, all-round communicative competence we will therefore indicate in this book many such differences in the use of English grammar.

What is relevant to this book is how the different systems affect the grammar of spoken and written English. We treat the two channels as of equal importance. But sometimes, when we give intonation marks (*see* 33) or present examples of dialogue, it will be clear that we are thinking of spoken English.

Transitory speech and permanent writing

18 Normal **speech** is processed in real time and is **transitory**, leaving no trace other than what we may remember. Our memory being what it is, this is often limited to just the gist of a conversation or some particularly interesting points in a lecture. Writing, on the other hand, takes longer to produce and can be read not just once but many times. **Writing** leaves a **permanent** record. Moreover, writing that is made public in some way, such as in printed books and journals, leaves a record which can be read by millions of contemporary readers, and also by later generations.

Such differences between the two channels affect our language use in several ways. One is that spoken communication requires fast, almost instantaneous production and understanding. On the other hand, when we write, we usually have time to revise, check and rewrite what we have written. Likewise, when we receive a piece of writing we can read it, reread it, ponder over it, and discuss it.

19　In spontaneous speech we have no time to prepare what to say in advance, but we must shape our message as we go along. Here is an example of such speech <in BrE> (a dash – indicates silent pause):

> Well I had some people to lunch on Sunday and – they turned up half an hour early – (laughs) – I mean you know what [g] getting up Sunday's like anyway and – I'd – I was behind in any case – and I'd said to them one o'clock – and I almost phoned them up and said come a bit later – and then I thought oh they've probably left by now – so I didn't – and – twelve thirty – now that can't be them – and it was – and they'd they'd left plenty of time for all their connections and they got all their connections at once – and it was annoying cos they came with this – child – you know who was running all over the place and they kept coming in and chatting to me and I couldn't get on with things and I I get really erm – you know when when I'm trying to cook – and people come and chat I I get terribly put off – can't get on with things at all erm – and yet you feel terribly anti-social if you you do just stay in the kitchen anyway.

On the audio-tape, this recording sounds natural and is quite easy to follow. However, when transcribed as here in written form, it looks fragmented, rambling, unstructured and is rather difficult to read. In this short extract from a conversation, we can note several features typical of informal talk:

- **silent pauses** (indicated by a dash –):

  > they've probably left by now – so I didn't – and – twelve thirty – now that can't be them – and it was – and

- **voice-filled pauses** (indicated by *erm*) indicating hesitation:

  > and I I get really erm – you know when when I'm trying to cook

- **repetitions**: *I I, when when, they'd they'd, you you*

- **false starts**: the speaker may fail to complete a sentence, or lose track of the sentence and mix up one grammatical construction with another:

  > I mean you know what [g] getting up Sunday's like anyway and – I'd – I was behind in any case

  > and I I get really erm – you know when when I'm trying to cook – and people come and chat I I get terribly put off

- **discourse markers:** When we speak we often use small words or fixed phrases (like *you know, you see, I mean, kind of, sort of, like, well, now*) that indicate our involvement in the discourse, and how we want it to continue – or just to signal that we intend to go on talking. The opening *well* in the extract is a typical in this use of 'signalling a new start' (*see* 353). Another example is *I mean* in the second line of the extract.

- **short forms** such as contractions of the negative *not* (*didn't*) and verb forms (*I'm, I'd, they've*), and *cos* for *because*.

In the next sections we will discuss why such features are so common in speaking.

Interactive and non-interactive uses of English

20 Spoken language is the most widely used form of language. Within spoken language there are many variations, but we will distinguish two main uses of spoken English. The first, and by far the most common use, is **conversation** with two or more participants taking their turns when talking to each other, either face-to-face or via some technical device such as a telephone or computer. For the foreign student of English, this is a particularly important type to learn because it is the most common everyday use of speech. Moreover, it cannot be prepared in advance: conversation is impromptu and spontaneous.

The second use of spoken English occurs with one person speaking at a time to an audience of people who do not talk back but just listen. We call this **public speaking** in contrast with conversation, which is **private speaking**. Conversation is typically **interactive**, and public speaking is less interactive, or even **not interactive** at all. Public speaking is intermediate between conversation and writing, in that a speech can be (and often is) prepared in advance in writing, and read aloud to an audience. In public speaking we include such spoken varieties as lectures, radio talks and TV news broadcasts. The figure below shows some of the different uses of English, and indicates that the relation between spoken and written English is more like a scale than a simple division. On the whole, the varieties of language towards the top of the diagram are more interactive than the varieties towards the bottom.

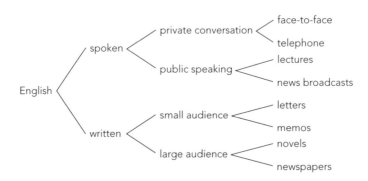

Cooperation in conversation

21 In a conversation, the speaker can check if the listener has understood by asking 'Do you see what I mean?', and the listener can ask the speaker for clarification: 'What did you mean by that?', etc. In writing we have no such direct contact between writer and reader and, in writing made public (as in newspapers, periodicals and books), we may not even have any idea who will ever read what we write. This gives speaking an advantage in providing us with an opportunity for **immediate feedback**, to find out whether our message has been properly received, or is acceptable. This feedback can be verbal (*yes, uhuh, I see*, etc.) or non-verbal (a nod, raised eyebrows, etc.).

But, usually, a conversation is not just a matter of giving and receiving information. It is also, perhaps primarily, a form of social interaction, and **participant cooperation** is indeed a basic feature of conversation. There exists **a give-and-take process** which is manifested in several ways.

22 One case of participant cooperation is **turn-taking**, which means sharing out the role of speaker in the conversation, as one speaker takes a turn, then another. In this extract from a <BrE> conversation, a young girl [A] is telling a female friend [B] about her recent very pleasant holidays in Spain (dash – indicates silent pause):

> [A] but it's so nice and relaxed down there I mean compared with London
> – I mean I I I I – I found myself – going into shops and people smiled at you and I – I was quite taken aback genuinely I mean I
>
> [B] m m
>
> [A] erm you know the feeling you you you you
>
> [B] yes one asks oneself if you're putting on this deadpan face you know
>
> [A] yes
>
> [B] yes
>
> [A] and these people smile and you – well you don't know how to react at first because it's so strange
>
> [B] yes I felt that in Scotland – yes (laughs)

A smooth conversation is characterized by a general atmosphere of co-operation and harmony. Little expressions such as *you know* and *I mean* appeal for understanding and sympathy, and *yes* and *m m* express interest and support the speaker. Multiple repetitions, such as *I I I I* and *you you you you*, signal the girl's excitement as she tries to keep the conversational 'floor' and tell her story.

23 Cooperation is largely achieved by using **discourse markers** – variously called **interactional signals, discourse particles, backchannels** and **in-serts**, which are a number of words and expressions typical of English spoken discourse. Below we list some such interactive expressions which are frequent in English conversation. We put them under three headings, indicating a scale from 'only interactive functions' (which are above all characteristics of conversation) to 'also interactive functions' (which are more grammatical and frequently used also in public speaking and writing; *see* 249):

- Only interactive: *ah, aha, gosh, hm, mhm, oh, quite, uhuh, yes, yeah, yup*
- Mainly interactive: *I see, I mean, I think, no, please, OK, that's OK, right, all right, that's right, that's all right, well, sure, you know, you see*
- Also interactive: *absolutely, actually, anyway, certainly, honestly, indeed, in fact, maybe, obviously, of course, perhaps, probably, really*

Most of these expressions are commonly used in conversations among native speakers, and it is therefore important for the foreign learner to be familiar with them and be able to use them quickly, and appropriately, in different situations. Interactive expressions may add little information, but they tell us something of the speakers' attitude to their audience and to what they are saying.

Some grammatical features of spoken English

24 *Tag questions.* A highly typical feature of speech is tag questions (*see further* 684). There are two main types:

> Positive + negative: We've **met** before, **haven't we**?
>
> Negative + positive: We **haven't met** before, **have we**?

Tag questions fit in nicely with the need for cooperation between speakers and the feature of turn-shift from one speaker to another. First the speaker asserts something (e.g. *It was a couple of years ago*), then invites the listener's response (*wasn't it?*), as in this example from the beginning of a conversation:

> [A] We've met before, haven't we?
>
> [B] Yes, we certainly have. It was a couple of years ago, wasn't it?
>
> [A] Oh yes, now I remember: at the Paris exhibition. How are you these days?

25 *Ellipsis.* In some cases part of a sentence can be omitted, for example:

Hope you're well.	~ I hope you're well.
Want a drink?	~ Do you want a drink?
Better be careful.	~ You/We'd better be careful.
Sounds fine to me.	~ That sounds fine to me.

This type of omission, which is called **initial ellipsis**, is another characteristic of informal talk. It helps to create the sort of relaxed atmosphere that we try to achieve in a cooperative social situation.

26 *Coordination and subordination.* Coordination (*see* 515) of clauses is a characteristic of speech:

> Hurt yourself? Okay, just rub it a little bit *and* then it will be okay. [1]

The *and* here expresses a condition, equivalent to *if* in a subclause (see 709):

> *If* you just rub it . . . it will be okay.

However, it is wrong to suppose that speech avoids subordination. In fact, *if*-clauses (see 207) are generally more common in conversation than in written language:

> Yeah but *if you talk to Katie and Heather* you will get a different story.
>
> [2]

Another type of subclause more common in conversation is the *that*-clause (*see* 712), especially where the *that* itself is omitted ('zero *that*'), as in [3]–[5]:

> I don't think *you can do that*. [3]
>
> I suppose *I do*. [4]
>
> I said *you can have anything on the table*, okay? [5]

In [2] above we see that the coordinator (*but* in this case) occurs at the beginning of a sentence or turn, and links to something in a previous turn. This is again very characteristic of spoken dialogue:

> A: Horses love carrots yeah . . .
>
> B: *And* horses love apples too. [6]

Again, in [6], the coordinator *And* comes at the beginning of a sentence and turn. This is very different from serious written language, where the use of a coordinator at the beginning of a sentence is often regarded as 'bad grammar', and is usually avoided. The coordinator in [6] is typical of speech, but in writing, it would be normal to make the coordinator a link between words and phrases rather than between clauses or sentences:

> Horses love *apples and carrots*.

On the whole, coordination at word level and phrase level is much more common in writing, while coordination at clause level is more common in speech.

27 *Finite clauses.* In written English we often use non-finite and verbless clauses (*see* 494) as adverbials and modifiers, as in this example:

> When fit, a Labrador is an excellent retriever. <rather formal, written>

Such constructions are unlikely in <informal speech>, where finite clauses are preferred, as in

~ A Labrador is an excellent retriever if it's fit.

~ If a Labrador's fit, it makes an excellent retriever.

Here are some other pairs of examples:

Lunch finished, the guests retired to the lounge. <rather formal, written>

~ They all went into the lounge after lunch. <more informal, spoken>

Ben, knowing that his wife was expecting, started to take a course on baby care. <rather formal, written>

~ Ben got to know his wife was expecting, so he started to take a course on baby care. <informal, spoken>

Discovered almost by accident, this substance has revolutionized medicine. <rather formal, written>

~ This stuff – it was discovered almost by accident – it's made a really big impact on medicine. <informal, spoken>

28 *Signposts.* The grammar of spoken sentences is, in general, simpler and less strictly constructed than the grammar of written sentences. In <writing> we often indicate the structure of paragraphs by such **signposts** or **linking signals** (*see* 352) as

firstly, secondly, finally, hence, to conclude, to summarize, e.g., viz.

Such expressions would not be used in informal talk where they would sound rather stilted and give the impression of a prepared talk. In a <spontaneous talk> we are more likely to introduce new points by such expressions as

the first thing is, and so, in other words, all the same

For example:

well – you know – the *first er* – *thing* that strikes me as odd about this whole business is – for example that . . .

29 *Contracted forms.* When the auxiliary verbs *do, have, be* and some modal auxiliaries occur together with *not*, they can have either uncontracted or contracted forms (*see* 582):

do not ~ don't	*does not ~ doesn't*	*did not ~ didn't*
have not ~ haven't	*has not ~ hasn't*	*had not ~ hadn't*
are not ~ aren't	*is not ~ isn't*	*could not ~ couldn't*
were not ~ weren't	*was not ~ wasn't*	*should not ~ shouldn't*

Uncontracted (or full) forms are typical of <written, especially formal> English. The contracted forms are typical of <spoken> discourse, but they also occur in <informal writing>. In some cases there is more than one contracted form available:

> I *have not* seen the film yet. <typical of writing>
>
> I *haven't* seen the film yet. <typical of speaking> OR
>
> I*'ve not* seen the film yet. <also possible in speaking>

Later on in this book we will comment on other constructions that are used differently in <spoken, informal> and <written, formal> varieties, such as the subjunctive (*see* 706) and the passive (*see* 613).

Spelling v. pronunciation

30 In <writing> we have to observe a number of spelling changes (*see* 700), when we add a suffix to a word, for example

- replacing one letter by two, e.g. when adding -*s*:

  | they *carry* | BUT: she *carries* |
  | a *lady* | BUT: several *ladies* |

- replacing two letters by one, e.g. when adding -*ing*:

  | they *lie* | BUT: they are *lying* |

- adding letters, e.g. when adding -*s* or -*er*:

one *box*	BUT: two *boxes*
they *pass*	BUT: she *passes*
a *big* spender	BUT: *bigger* spenders, the *biggest* spenders

- dropping letters, e.g. when adding -*ing* or -*ed*:

  | love | BUT: *loving, loved* |

The reason why written English has such spelling rules is often to indicate the correct pronunciation of the inflected forms with suffixes. Note, for example, the following contrasts (for phonetic symbols, *see* 43):

| *hope* /hoʊp/ | ~ *hoping* /ˈhoʊpɪŋ/ | ~ *hoped* /hoʊpt/ |
| *hop* /hɒp/ | ~ *hopping* /ˈhɒpɪŋ/ | ~ *hopped* /hɒpt/ |

There are some spelling differences between British and American English: *centre* || *center*, *levelled* || *leveled*, etc. (*see* 703). There are some differences in pronunciation, too, but these are independent of the spelling differences, for example /ˈkʌlə || ˈkʌlər/ for *colour* || *color*.

In nouns with regular plural, the written distinction between the genitive plural (*boys'*), the genitive singular (*boy's*), and also the common gender plural (*boys*) does not exist in the pronunciation /bɔɪz/ (*see* 664).

Written representation of speech

31 In some writing representing spoken English, for example comic strips and popular fiction, we can meet the form *got to* or even *gotta*, pronounced /ˈɡɒtə/, corresponding to \<standard\> *have got to*:

> You **gotta** be careful with what you say. \<non-standard in writing\>

> You**'ve got to** be careful with what you say. \<standard in writing\>

Similarly, *gonna*, pronounced /ˈɡɒnə/, is sometimes the written form for \<standard written\> (*be*) *going to*, as in

> What (are) you **gonna do** now? \<non-standard in writing\>

> What are you **going to do** now? \<standard in writing\>

These non-standard written representations of the spoken form reflect a typical phonetic reduction of vowels and omission of consonants in everyday speech. However, the written language rarely captures these simplifications. For example, in

> They could have gone early

could have is commonly pronounced /ˈkʊdə/, but even in representations of the most casual speech, the non-standard written form *coulda* rarely occurs.

Punctuation v. chunking

32 We become familiar with the structure of written language through normal education, but the way spoken language is structured is more difficult to observe and to study. In writing we work with sentences. But it is often hard to divide a spoken conversation (such as the extract from a conversation in 19) into separate sentences. Part of the reason is that the speakers rely more on the hearers' understanding of context, and on their ability to interrupt if they fail to understand. Also, in 'getting across' their message, speakers are able to rely on features of intonation which tell us a great deal that cannot be rendered in written punctuation.

- **Punctuation in writing.** The written sentence is easily recognizable, since it begins with a capital letter and ends with certain punctuation marks (. ? !). Within the sentence we can indicate clause and phrase boundaries by commas (,), dashes (–), colons (:), and semi-colons (;).

- **Chunking in speaking.** Punctuation marks cannot be pronounced or heard but, in speaking, we use other devices to indicate what belongs together in an utterance. A piece of spoken information is packaged in **tone units** (*see* 37). They are usually shorter than a sentence, averaging about 4–5 words, and have a separate intonation contour. The most heavily accented word in a tone unit contains a focal point called **nucleus** (*see* 36). There is no exact match between punctuation in writing and tone units in speaking. Speech is more variable in its structuring than writing. Chunking speech into tone units depends on such things as the speed of speaking, the emphasis given to a particular part of a message, and the length of grammatical units (*see further* 33, 397).

● **Sentence adverbials** (such as *evidently*, *naturally*, *obviously*, *see* 461) are often separated from what follows by a tone unit boundary in speech (indicated here by a vertical bar '|') or a comma in writing. Compare:

| *Obviously* | they expected us to be on time | <spoken>

Obviously, they expected us to be on time. <written>

● **Non-restrictive apposition** (*see* 471) is usually set off by a separate tone unit in speaking, and by commas in writing:

| Dr Johnson | *a neighbour of ours* | is moving to Canada | <spoken>

Dr Johnson, *a neighbour of ours*, is moving to Canada. <written>

● **Comment clauses** are often marked off from other clauses, by having a separate tone unit in speech and commas in writing (*see further* 499):

| *What's more* | we'd lost all we had | <spoken>

Moreover, we had lost all we had. <written>

As a general comment, we may note that features marked as <informal> in this book are more likely to occur in <speech>. On the other hand, <formal> features are more likely to occur in <writing> (*see further* 45).

Intonation

33 You will need some knowledge of English intonation patterns if you are to understand English grammar more fully. This is because features of intonation are important for signalling grammatical distinctions, such as that between statements and questions. For example, a sentence like *They are leaving* can be a statement when said with falling intonation, but a question with rising intonation:

| They are lèaving | [statement with falling tone]

| They are léaving | [question with rising tone]

Here we concentrate on explaining those features of stress and intonation which play a significant role in grammar, and which therefore need to be discussed and symbolized in this book. The features we want to explain in the following sections are these:

- **Stress**, symbolized by a stress mark ' (*see* 34):

'over	stress on the first syllable
an'alysis	stress on the second syllable
transfor'mation	stress on the third syllable

- **Tone units** with their boundaries marked by a vertical bar | (*see* 37):

  | The task seemed difficult |

- **Nucleus**, i.e. the focal point of a tone unit, is symbolized by underlining the syllable carrying the nucleus (*see further* 36):

  | The task seemed di̊fficult |

- **Tones** are falling, rising or combinations of rising and falling. In our grammar the most important are these three (*see further* 38):

A *falling tone* is marked:	o̊bviously
A *rising tone* is marked:	óbviously
A *fall-rise tone* is marked:	ǒbviously

Stress

34 The rhythm of English is based on stress. In connected speech, we feel the rhythm of the language in the sequence of **stressed** syllables. Between one stressed syllable and another there may occur one or more **unstressed** syllables. The stressed syllables in these examples are preceded by the stress mark ', and the unstressed syllables are unmarked:

> I'll 'ring you on the 'way to the 'airport.
>
> It went 'off 'smoothly that 'long 'meeting of the ex'ecutive com'mittee.

This means that the syllables below printed in bold are stressed:

> I'll **ring** you on the **way** to the **air**port.
>
> It went **off smoothly** that **long meet**ing of the ex**ec**utive com**mit**tee.

The normal rules for placing stress are as follows. The syllables which are stressed are:

- a one-syllable word which belongs to one of the major word-classes (*see* 744), i.e. nouns (**way**), verbs (**ring**), adjectives (**long**), adverbs (**off**).

- the accented syllables of words of more than one syllable of major word-classes, e.g. '**smoothly**, '**airport**, com'**mittee**.

The syllables which are unstressed are:

- a word belonging to one of the minor word-classes (*see* 745), e.g. prepositions (*to*), pronouns (*it*), articles (*the*).
- the unaccented syllables of words of more than one syllable, e.g. 'smoothly, 'airport, com'mittee.

35 There is no simple rule for which syllable is accented in a word which consists of more than one syllable. As we see above, accent varies from word to word, so that the accent falls on the first syllable of 'airport, but on the second syllable of com'mittee, and on the third syllable of transform'ation. The placing of stress is also variable according to sentence context, emphasis, speed of utterance, etc., and so the rules above are not without exceptions.

One point to notice is that a prepositional adverb (*see* 660) belongs to a major word-class, and is therefore stressed, whereas a one-syllable preposition is usually unstressed. Contrast:

'This 'bed has 'not been 'slept in. (*in* = preposition)

The 'injured 'man was 'carried 'in. (*in* = prepositional adverb)

The same contrast is sometimes seen between the particle of a prepositional verb (*see* 632) and the particle of a phrasal verb (*see* 630):

She's re'lying on our 'help. (**rely on** = prepositional verb)

She's 'putting 'on a 'new 'play. (**put on** = phrasal verb)

But the particle may also be unstressed:

'Make up your 'mind!

In the examples in this book, stress will be marked only where it is necessary for the point illustrated.

The nucleus

36 Not all stressed syllables are of equal importance. Some stressed syllables have greater prominence than others, and form the **nucleus**, or focal point, of an intonation pattern. We may describe a nucleus as a strongly stressed syllable which marks a major change of pitch direction, i.e. where the pitch goes up or down. Here is an example to indicate pitch direction:

She's going to the States.

The change of pitch on the nucleus is indicated by an arrow:

In this example, the nucleus marks a fall in pitch towards the end of the sentence. (The step-up in pitch before the nucleus *States* is something which will not concern us here.) As a nucleus is always stressed, there is no need to put a stress mark before it. Often in our examples, we simply indicate the nucleus by underlining without indicating the other stressed syllables:

She's going to the <u>States</u>

Tone units

37 The basic unit of intonation in English is the **tone unit**. (Other names you may meet are **intonation unit, information unit,** and **chunk.**) A tone unit is a stretch of speech which contains one nucleus. It may also contain other stressed syllables, normally preceding the nucleus. The boundaries of a tone unit are marked by a vertical bar **|** :

| She's going to the <u>States</u> |

In this example, the tone unit has the length of a whole sentence. But a sentence often contains more than one tone unit. The number of tone units depends on the length of the sentence, and the degree of emphasis given to various parts of it. This sentence

This department needs a new chairperson

would normally have one tone unit:

| This department needs a new <u>chair</u>person |

But it might be pronounced with two tone units:

| <u>This</u> department | needs a new <u>chair</u>person |

The additional nucleus on *this* here expresses an emphasis on '*this depart-ment* in contrast to other departments. The following sentence might be pronounced with either one or two or three tone units, as indicated:

| This is the kind of pressure that it's very difficult to re<u>sist</u>. |

| This is the kind of <u>pressure</u> | that it's very difficult to re<u>sist</u>. |

| This is the <u>kind</u> | of <u>pressure</u> | that it's very difficult to re<u>sist</u>. |

In general, we include tone unit boundaries in our examples only where they serve an illustrative purpose. Usually, we omit them.

Tones

38 By **tone** we mean the type of pitch change which takes place on the nucleus. The three most important tones in English, and the only ones we need distinguish here, are

falling tone:	tòwn Chàucer	| What's the name of this tòwn? |
rising tone:	tówn Cháucer	| Are you going to tówn today? |
fall-rise tone:	ťown bǐg tówn	| I can't allow you to do thǎt. |

These sentences can also be represented in the following way:

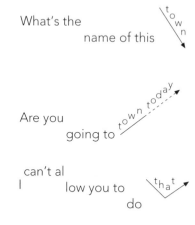

What's the

name of this

Are you

going to

can't al

low you to

do

Here are two examples of the different tones in sequences of tone units:

\| It's not like a lecture on Cháucer \| or Éliot \| or something of thàt kínd. \|
\| Our chair is very stróngly of the opínion \| that we àll ought to go on teàching \| to the end of tèrm. \|

The tone of a nucleus determines the pitch of the rest of the tone unit following it:

● After a **falling tone**, the rest of the tone unit is at a low pitch:

(Ann is getting a new job,) \| but she hasn't tòld me about it. \|

but she

hasn't

me about it

● After a **rising tone**, the rest of the tone unit moves in an upward pitch direction:

(Ann is getting a new job.) \| Has she tóld you about it? \|

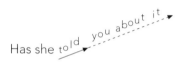

Has she told

● The **fall-rise tone** consists of a fall in pitch followed by a rise. If the nucleus is the last syllable of the tone unit, the fall and rise both take place on one syllable – the nuclear syllable. Otherwise, the rise occurs in the remainder of the tone unit. Compare the following examples:

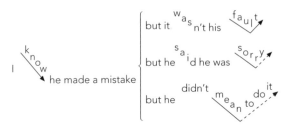

We symbolise these three tones as follows:

| but it wasn't his fǎult. |
| but he said he was sǒrry. |
| but he didn't mèan to dó it. |

Where the rise of the fall-rise extends to a stressed syllable after the nucleus, as in the last example, we signal the fall-rise tone by placing a fall on the nucleus and a rise on the later stressed syllable. This will make it easier for you to follow the intonation contour when you read the examples.

The meanings of tones

39 The meanings of the tones are difficult to specify in general terms. Roughly speaking, the **falling tone** expresses 'certainty', 'completeness', 'independence'. Thus a straightforward statement normally ends with a failing tone, since it asserts a fact of which the speaker is certain. It has an air of finality:

| In this lecture I want to enlarge on the relation between grammar and lèxis. |

40 A **rising tone**, on the other hand, expresses 'uncertainty' or 'incompleteness' or 'dependence'.

● A *yes-no* question (*see* 682) usually has a rising tone, because the speakers are uncertain of the truth of what they are asking about:

| Can I hélp you? |

Because the typical tone heard in a *yes-no* question is a rising tone, this intonation is often referred to as 'question-intonation'. However, most *wh*-questions have a falling tone (*see* 683). Compare the tones in these two questions:

| Don't you líke working here? | [*yes-no* question]
| Why are you lèaving? | [*wh*-question]

● A question put in the form of a grammatical statement depends in speech on a question-intonation with a rising tone (*see* 244, 696):

   | You got home sáfely then? |

● Making a new start in the train of thought (*see* 353) often has a rising intonation:

   | Wéll | what do you suggest we do nòw? |

● Parenthetical and subsidiary information in a statement is also often spoken with a rising tone. The reason is that this information is incomplete and dependent for its full understanding on the main assertion:

   | If you líke | we can have dinner at mỳ place tonight. |

● Encouraging or <polite> denials, commands, invitations, greetings, farewells, etc. are generally spoken with a rising tone:

   [A] | Are you búsy? |

   [B] | Nó. | ('Please interrupt me if you wish') 'Do sit dówn. |

Here a falling tone (Nò), which indicates finality, would sound <impolite>.

41 A **fall-rise tone** combines the falling tone's meaning of 'assertion, certainty' with the rising tone's meaning of 'dependence, incompleteness'. At the end of a sentence, it often conveys a feeling of reservation. It asserts something, and at the same time suggests that there is something else to be said. There is often an implied contrast:

   | That's not mỷ sígnature. | ('it must be somebody else's')

   [A] | Do you like póp-music? |

   [B] | Sǒmetimes, | ('but not in general')

   [A] | Are you búsy? |

   [B] | Not rěally. | ('Well, I am, but not so busy that I can't talk to you')

At the beginning or in the middle of a sentence, the fall-rise tone is a more forceful alternative to the rising tone, expressing the assertion of one point, together with the implication that another point is to follow:

   | Mòst of the tíme | we stayed on the bèach. |

   | Most yǒung people | take plenty of ěxercise. |

   | He's not a relǎxed lecturer | but he's a drǐving lecturer. |

A meaning which can be expressed by intonation may have to be expressed by a different grammatical construction in writing (*see* 496). Compare:

| You don't see a fox every dǎy. | <speech>

It is not every day that one sees a fox. <writing>

In both cases the implication is: 'it happens quite rarely'.

Conversation in transcription

42 After this brief survey of some basic features of spoken English and how intonation is represented in written transcription, it is time for an application of the system to a longer stretch of text than we have been able to offer in the isolated examples above. So, here again is the vivid account of the Sunday lunch (given in 19), but now with the intonation indicated as follows:

- **Tone units**: To highlight the chunking feature of speech, there is one tone unit per line, with | marking the end of each tone unit.
- **Tones**: There are three tone types: falling tone (dò), rising tone (dó), fall-rise tone (dǒ).
- **Pauses** are indicated by a dash (–).

| Well I had some people to lunch on Súnday |

and – they turned up half an hour èarly | – (laughs) –

I mean you know what [g] getting up Súnday's líke |

ànyway |

and – I'd – I was behind in any càse | –

and I'd said to them one o'clóck | –

and I ǎlmost phoned them up and said |

come a bit làter | –

and then I thought oh they've probably lèft by nów | –

so I dìdn't | –

and – twelve thìrty | –

nòw | –

that càn't be thém | –

and it wàs | –

and they'd they'd lèft |

plenty of tìme |

for all their conněctions |

and they got all their conněctions |

at ónce | –

and it was annŏying |

cos they came with this – chìld | –

you knów |

who was running all òver the place |

and they kept coming in and chàtting to mé |

and I couldn't get òn with things |

and | I get really erm – you know when when I'm trying to còok | –

and people come and chàt |

| I get terribly put òff | –

can't get on with things at àll |

erm – and yet you feel terribly anti-sŏcial |

if you you dò just stay in the kítchen |

ànyway |

If you read this extract aloud, giving emphasis to the pitch movements in the syllables with tone marks and making pauses where they are indicated, you will find this version less rambling and more coherent than the first version in 19. Yet the text is identical in the two versions.

This goes to show that intonation is an important part of spoken language. But, of course, we can never manage to give an adequate written representation of what real speech is like. What we can do to get a better idea of real speech – not only of **what** was said, but also **how** it was said – is at least to indicate, as here, the main features of spoken discourse – by far the most widely used form of English.

A note on phonetic symbols

43 Phonetic symbols are used only occasionally in this book, where they are needed to illustrate a grammatical point or rule. We have tried to use a system of transcription which is not biased towards a particular kind of speech, but this is not easy since British and American English (the two national varieties we are mainly dealing with) differ more in pronunciation than in any other respect. To make things simple, we consider only one accent from each national variety: **Received Pronunciation** (or **RP**), which is commonly used as a standard accent for the learning of British English pronunciation, and **General American pronunciation** (**GA**), which has a somewhat comparable status in the United States of America. However, considering the limited use we make of phonetic symbols, other standardized varieties of speech (e.g. for Australian English) are also reasonably well represented. Phonetic symbols, where they occur, will be enclosed in slant lines, for example: /θ/, /aʊ/, /mʌst/. We use the double bar (||) to separate RP and GA pronunciations, as in /klɑːk || klɜːrk/ for *clerk*.

Key to phonetic symbols

Vowels		Consonants	
iː	as in bead	p	as in pig
ɪ	as in bid	b	as in big
e	as in bed	t	as in two
æ	as in bad	d	as in do
ɑː	as in calm	k	as in come, king
ɒ	as in cot <RP>	g	as in gum
ɔː	as in caught <RP>	tʃ	as in cheap
ʊ	as in pull	dʒ	as in jeep, bridge
uː	as in pool	f	as in few
ʌ	as in cut	v	as in view
ɜː	as in bird <RP> (see Note)	θ	as in thing
ə	as in about	ð	as in then
		s	as in ice, say
Diphthongs		z	as in eyes, zoo
eɪ	as in fail	ʃ	as in pressure, show
oʊ	as in foal	ʒ	as in pleasure
aɪ	as in file	h	as in hot
aʊ	as in fowl	m	as in sum
ɔɪ	as in foil	n	as in sun
ɪə	as in peer <RP>	ŋ	as in sung
eə	as in pair <RP> (see Note)	l	as in lot
ʊə	as in pure <RP>	r	as in rot
		w	as in wet
		j	as in yet

Note

Corresponding to the <RP> diphthongs /ɪə/, /eə/, /ʊə/ are the <GA> r-coloured diphthongs which may be transcribed: /ɪr/, /ɛr/ and /ʊr/. Similarly, corresponding to the <RP> long vowel /ɜː/ is the r-coloured vowel which may be transcribed: /ɜːr/, e.g. /bɜːd ‖ bɜːrd/ for bird.

Geographical and national varieties: <AmE> and <BrE>

44 English is spoken as a first language by almost four hundred million people: in the United States of America, Great Britain, Canada, Australia, New Zealand, Ireland, the Caribbean, and other places. This means there is a great abundance of English dialectal variation throughout the world. But when we come to the study of grammar in standard varieties of English, the differences are small. Within each English-speaking country there are many differences of regional dialect, e.g. between the English spoken in the Southern States of the USA and in other parts of the same country. These differences rarely affect grammatical usage in written English or in standardized spoken English, and so we ignore them in this book.

Since the varieties of English used in the United States and in Britain are the most important in terms of population and use throughout the world, the only national varieties we shall distinguish in this book are American English <AmE> and British English <BrE>. The grammatical differences between these two varieties (in comparison with differences in pronunciation and vocabulary) are not very great, and are almost negligible in <formal, written> usage. However, some brief examples here will show the kinds of difference which exist between <AmE> and <BrE>, and which will be pointed out in Parts Two and Three.

● **Article usage:** <AmE>, but not <BrE>, tends to use the definite article with *university* and *hospital* (*see* 475):

> <AmE>: Our daughter is at **the university**.
>
> <BrE>: Our daughter is at **university**.
>
> <AmE>: I've got to go to **the hospital** for an operation.
>
> <BrE>: I've got to go to **hospital** for an operation.

● *got/gotten*: <AmE> has two past participle forms of *get*: *gotten* and *got*, whereas <BrE> has only one: *got* (*see* 559). The past tense is *got* in both varieties. For example:

> <AmE>: Have you **gotten/got** the theater tickets?
>
> <BrE>: Have you **got** the theatre tickets?

● **Simple past and present perfect:** There is also a tendency to use the simple past tense in <AmE> where the present perfect is used in <BrE>, for example, with *yet* or *already* (*see* 125, Note *a*):

> <AmE>: **Did** you **eat** breakfast already?
>
> <BrE or AmE>: **Have** you **eaten** breakfast already?

● **Subjunctive:** The use of the subjunctive is more common in <AmE> than in <BrE> after verbs like *demand*, *require*, *insist* and *suggest*, after adjectives like *important* and *necessary*, and after nouns like *demand* and *requirement*. In <BrE> *should* + infinitive is usually preferred (*see* 706):

> <typical of AmE>: The press suggested that Burt **be** dropped from the team.
>
> <typical of BrE>: The press suggested that Burt **should be** dropped from the team.

● *different from/than/to*: The adjective *different* can be used with *from* in both varieties, but *different than* is mostly <AmE> and *different to* uniquely <BrE>:

> <BrE & AmE>: He's just **different from** everybody else.
>
> <AmE>: He's just **different than** everybody else.
>
> <BrE>: He's just **different to** everybody else.

- *from . . . through, from . . . to*: There are some other differences in prepositional usage, such as the use of *from X through Y* in <AmE> to clarify that a period includes both *X* and *Y* (*see* 163):

  <AmE>: The tour lasted *from* July *through* August.

  <BrE>: The tour lasted *from* July *to* August (inclusive). [In <BrE> the word *inclusive* is sometimes added to make clear that the period includes the last-mentioned period, here August.]

On other differences *see* the listing in the index under <AmE> and <BrE>.

Levels of usage: formal and informal English <formal>, <informal>

45 We turn now to the way English varies not according to geographical differences, but according to differences in the relation between speaker (or writer) and hearer (or reader). We can refer to these as **levels of usage** (*see* 15–16).

Formal language is the type of language we use publicly for some serious purpose, for example in official reports, business letters, regulations, and academic writing. Formal English is nearly always <written>, but exceptionally it is used in <speech>, for example in formal public speeches or lectures. As an example of formal English, here is an extract from a book review:

> The approach is remarkably interdisciplinary. Behind its innovations is the author's fundamental proposal that the creativity of language derives from multiple parallel generative systems linked by interface components. This shift in basic architecture makes possible a radical reconception of mental grammar and how it is learned. As a consequence, the author is able to reintegrate linguistics with philosophy of mind, cognitive and developmental psychology, evolutionary biology, neuroscience, and computational linguistics.

Informal language (also called 'colloquial') is the language of ordinary conversation, of personal letters, and of private interaction in general. Here is another extract from an informal conversation <in AmE> (*see* further 19 and 42):

[A] So Larry did you manage to get any sleep beside Michelle's crying?

[B] I didn't hear a thing.

[A] Really.

[B] Yeah.

[A] God, I can't believe it.

[B] I didn't hear a thing.

[A] Well, it must have been around three o'clock this morning. Suddenly she couldn't sleep.

[B] Really?

[A] Yeah, I think she's getting a cold.

[B] What did she do?

[A] Every time I started to fall asleep she'd go Mommy, Mommy.

[B] Nope, I didn't hear a thing.

[A] Well, that's good.

[B] I can sleep through a hurricane, I guess.

Spoken language like this is typically informal, but informal English is now used more and more also in written communication of a popular kind, for example in newspapers, magazines, advertisements and popular fiction.

An example of the formality scale

46 The difference between <formal> and <informal> usage is best seen as a scale, rather than as a simple 'yes or no' distinction. Consider the following example:

> There are many friends to whom one would hesitate to entrust one's own children. <formal>　　　　　　　　　　　　　　　　[1]

This is towards the formal end of the scale for a number of reasons:

- Use of *there are*, which (unlike the less formal *there's*) maintains the plural concord with *many friends* as subject (*see* 547–9).
- Use of *many friends* itself, rather than the more informal *a lot of friends* or *lots of friends* (*see* 72–3).
- Use of the initial preposition to introduce a relative clause (*to whom*), rather than a construction with a final preposition *who(m)* . . . *to*. (Compare, for example, the formal *the firm for which she works* with the informal *the firm she works for* – *see* 686–94.)
- Related to the preceding feature is the use of *whom*, which is itself a rather formal pronoun (*see* 686–94) compared with *who* – for example, in *Whom did they meet?* compared with *Who did they meet?*
- Use of the generic personal pronoun *one* (*see* 98), rather than the more informal use of generic *you*.

47 If we replaced all these features of [1] by informal equivalents, the sentence would run as follows [1a]:

> There's lots of friends who you would hesitate to entrust your own children to. <informal>　　　　　　　　　　　　　　[1a]

31

However, it is significant that this sentence seems very unidiomatic. The reason is that a translation from one variety to another, like translation from one language to another, cannot be treated as a mechanical exercise. In practice, informal English prefers its own typical features, which include, for example, contracted forms of verbs (*there's* rather than *there is*, etc.), omission of the relative pronoun *who/whom/that*, and informal vocabulary rather than more formal vocabulary such as *entrust*. As an example of informal English, [1b] is a more natural-sounding sentence than [1a]:

> There's lots of friends you'd never trust with your own children.   [1b]

However, we could make more lexical changes to increase or decrease the formality of this sentence. For example, replacing *children* by *kids* would make the sentence even more informal:

> There's lots of friends you'd never trust with your own kids.   [1c]

On the other hand, the following, with its use of *there are* and *would*, is a more formal variant:

> There are lots of friends you would never trust with your own children.
>   [1d]

It is therefore possible to place the above sentences (leaving aside [1a]) on a scale from most to least formal in the following order:

> There are many friends to whom one would hesitate to entrust one's
> own children.   [1]
>
> There are lots of friends you would never trust with your own children.
>   [1d]
>
> There's lots of friends you'd never trust with your own children.   [1b]
>
> There's lots of friends you'd never trust with your own kids.   [1c]

However, it is difficult to be precise about degrees of formality and informality, so that we often have to be content with relative phrases such as <rather formal> or <rather informal>.

48 One reason for this vagueness is that formality, as a scale, can be applied on the one hand to aspects of the situation in which communication takes place, and on the other hand to features of language which correlate with those aspects. There is a two-way relation here: not only does situation influence the choice of language, but choice of language influences situation – or, more precisely, the nature of the situation as perceived by the speaker and hearer. Thus, someone answering the phone with the <very formal> question *To whom am I speaking?* would, by that very utterance, establish a more formal relationship with the other speaker than if the question had been *Who am I speaking to?*

Formality of vocabulary and grammar

49 In English there are many differences of vocabulary between formal and informal language. Much of the vocabulary of formal English is of French, Latin, or Greek origin. In contrast, informal language is characterized by vocabulary of Anglo-Saxon origin. Compare:

<formal>	<less formal>
aid	help
commence	begin
conceal	hide
continue	keep on
conclude	end

Many phrasal and prepositional verbs (*see* 630–4) belong to informal English. Compare:

<formal>	<informal>
delete	cross off
encounter	come across
enter	go in(to)
investigate	look into
surrender	give in
renovate	do up

These differences show how formal and informal English provide the speaker with substantially different resources for communication, and again illustrate the difficulty of translating a sentence in one variety into an equivalent sentence in the other. The choice of appropriate grammar is intimately connected to the choice of vocabulary.

Impersonal style <impersonal>

50 Formal written language often goes with an impersonal style, i.e. one in which the speaker avoids personal references to speaker and/or hearer, such as *I*, *you*, and *we*. Some of the common features of impersonal language are passives (*see* 613–18), sentences beginning with introductory *it* (*see* 542–6), and abstract nouns (*see* 67–9). All these features are illustrated in:

> *Announcement from the librarian*
> It has been noted with concern that the stock of books in the library has been declining alarmingly. Students are asked to remind themselves of the rules for borrowing and return of books, and to bear in mind the needs of other users. Penalties for overdue books will in the future be strictly enforced.

The author of the above could have written a more informal and less impersonal message as follows:

> *Bring those books back!*
> Books in the library have been disappearing. Please make sure you know the rules for borrowing, and don't forget that the library is for *everyone*'s convenience. From now on, we're going to enforce the rules strictly. *You have been warned!*

Polite and familiar language <polite>, <familiar>

51 Our language tends to be more <polite> when we are talking to a person we do not know well, or to a person more senior in age or social position. Context also plays a role: for example, if we are asking a big favour, such as the loan of a large sum of money, this will induce greater politeness than if we were asking a small favour, such as the loan of a pen.

English has no special familiar pronouns or polite pronouns, like some languages (e.g. French *tu*/*vous*, German *du*/*Sie* corresponding to English *you*). But familiarity can be shown in other ways. Thus, when we know someone well or intimately, we tend to drop polite forms of language. Instead of using a polite vocative such as *Mrs*, *Mr*, or *Ms* we tend to use first name (*Peter*) or a short name (*Pete*) or even a nickname or pet name (*Misty*, *Lilo*, *Boo-boo*, etc.). Interestingly, present-day English makes little use of the surname alone, except in third person reference (e.g. *Shakespeare*, *Bach*, *Bush*) to someone one does not know personally, but by repute, such as a famous author, composer or politician.

52 Polite language behaviour is most observable in such speech acts as requesting, advising, and offering (*see* 333–5, 347). Compare, for example, these requests:

> Shut the door, will you? <familiar>
>
> Would you please shut the door? <rather polite>
>
> I wonder if you would mind shutting the door. <more polite>

The word *please* has the sole function of indicating politeness when one is making a request. But it has little effect in itself: to give a really polite impression, *please* usually has to be combined with devices of indirectness such as using a question, the hypothetical *could* or *would*, etc. (*see* 248, 333–4).

At the other end of the scale, slang is language which is very familiar in style, and is usually restricted to members of a particular social group, for example 'teenage slang', 'army slang', 'theatre slang'. Slang is not easy to understand unless you are a member of a particular group or class of people. Because of its restricted use, and its short life, we will not be concerned with slang in this book.

Tactful and tentative language <tactful>, <tentative>

53 Politeness and indirectness are linked with tact. To be **tactful** is to avoid causing offence or distress to another person. Sometimes tact means disguising or covering up the truth. A request, suggestion or piece of advice can be made more tactful by making it more **tentative**. Compare:

> You'd better put off the meeting until tomorrow. <informal, familiar>
>
> Look – why don't you postpone the meeting until tomorrow? <informal>
>
> May I suggest you postpone the meeting until tomorrow? <tactful, tentative>
>
> Don't you think it might be a good idea to postpone the meeting until tomorrow? <more tactful, more tentative>

In other cases tentativeness is simply an indication of speakers' reluctance to commit themselves on given questions. For example, *might just* is a more tentative way of expressing possibility than *may*:

> Someone *may* have made a mistake.
>
> Someone *might just* have made a mistake. <more tentative)

Literary, elevated or rhetorical language <literary>, <elevated>, <rhetorical>

54 Some features of English of limited use have a 'literary' or 'elevated' tone: they belong mainly to the literary or religious language of the past, but can still be used today by someone who wants to move or impress us. An example of elevated language comes from a speech by President George W. Bush:

> Our nation – this generation – will lift a dark threat of violence from our people and our future. We will rally the world to this cause by our efforts, by our courage. We will not tire, we will not falter, and we will not fail.

We will not tire, we will not falter, and we will not fail echoes the rhetoric of Abraham Lincoln [1] and Winston Churchill [2]:

> But in a large sense we cannot dedicate – we cannot consecrate – we cannot hallow this ground. [1]
>
> We shall not flag or fail . . . We shall fight on the beaches, we shall fight on the landing grounds, . . . we shall never surrender. [2]

In addition to the variety labels <literary> and <elevated>, we occasionally use the similar label <rhetorical>. This signifies a stylized use of language, consciously chosen for an emphatic or emotive effect. A good example of this is the so-called 'rhetorical question' (*see* 305), which is meant to be interpreted as an emphatic statement:

> Is it any wonder that politicians are mistrusted? (= 'It is no wonder . . .')

Although we meet them in the literature of earlier periods, literary, elevated and rhetorical forms of language tend to be unusual in the English of today (and noticeable for that very reason). We will refer to them only very occasionally in this book.

Levels of usage: a map of variety labels

55 Apart from the national varieties <AmE> and <BrE>, the different types of English we have discussed are related to one another, and might go under the general title of **levels of usage**. We might attempt to place them on a scale running from 'elevated' English at one extreme to 'slang' at the other extreme. But it is probably better to think in terms of three pairs of contrasting values, as shown:

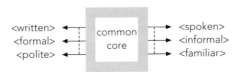

This diagram represents only the most important levels of usage, ignoring the more restricted variety labels, such as <impersonal> and <elevated>. The features on the left tend to go together – likewise the features on the right – and this is conveyed by the vertical broken lines. But the lines are broken because the connection does not always hold: for example, it is possible to express oneself politely in spoken English, and it is possible to express oneself informally in written English.

The horizontal arrows represent scales of contrast. The common core of 'unmarked' usage occupies a middle area between the extremes of each of the three scales.

56 In Parts Two and Three we make free use of the labels for varieties of English, because we feel it is important to give as full guidance as possible on the 'appropriate use' of English grammatical forms and structures. Some speakers of English may disagree with some of our judgements on the uses of these labels. This is because our knowledge of 'levels of usage' still remains, today, very much a subjective matter, depending on the perceptions of people who use the language. For example, an older English speaker might regard as <familiar> a form of language which might not seem so to a younger speaker. There are also differences of perception in different English-speaking countries. Thus, without considering these labels as descriptive of general standards of appropriateness, we would like you to use them for guidance in your own use of the language.

PART TWO

Grammar in use

Concepts

Referring to objects, substances and materials

57 Through nouns and noun phrases, grammar organizes the way we refer to objects. We begin with **concrete nouns**, or nouns referring to physical objects and substances. (We use the word 'object' to refer generally to things, animals, people, etc.) Our first topic will be **count** and **mass** concrete nouns, and the various ways in which they are linked by *of*.

Singular and plural: one and many

58 Count nouns refer in the singular to one object, and in the plural to more than one object. As the name implies, count nouns can be counted: *one star, two stars*, etc. (*see* 597–601):

Singular	*Plural*		
a star one star a single star	two stars	three stars	seven stars, etc.

Groups of objects

59 We may refer to objects as belonging to a group or set, as follows:

a $\begin{Bmatrix} \text{group} \\ \text{number} \end{Bmatrix}$ of stars   a small group of stars   a large group of stars

Group nouns: *a group (of stars)*

60 Nouns like *group, set,* and *class,* which refer to a set of objects, are called **group nouns**. Like other count nouns, group nouns may be singular or plural; e.g.

one *group* of stars	three *groups* of stars
a *set* of tools	two *sets* of tools
a *class* of insects	several *classes* of insects

Often a special group noun is used with certain kinds of objects:

an *army* [of soldiers]	a *crew* [of sailors]
a *crowd* of people	a *gang* of thieves, youths, etc.
a *herd* of cattle	a *pack* of cards
a *flock* of sheep	a *constellation* of stars
a *bunch* of flowers	a *series* of games

Many group nouns refer to a group of people having a special relationship with one another, or brought together for a particular reason: *tribe, family, committee, club, audience, government, administration, team, etc.* There is often a choice of whether to use a singular or plural verb (*see* 510), especially in <BrE>:

- **singular**: when we treat the group as a single thing
- **plural**: when we treat the group as a collection of individuals

> The audience is/are enjoying the show.

Notice also the difference between *its stated aims* (singular) and *their stated aims* (plural) in this example:

> The government *has* lost sight of *its* stated aims.
>
> The government *have* lost sight of *their* stated aims. <esp. BrE>

Part and whole: *part of the cake, a piece of cake*

61 Parts of objects can be referred to by

- **part nouns** like *part* (contrasted with *whole*), *half, a quarter, two thirds,* etc.
- **unit nouns** like *piece, slice*

the (whole) cake	a slice of the cake	half (of) the cake	(a) quarter of the cake

part of the cake

Mass nouns: *milk, sand*, etc.

62 Mass nouns (sometimes called 'non-count' or 'uncountable' nouns) are so called because they cannot be counted like count nouns (*see* 597). They typically refer to substances, whether

> solid, e.g. *butter, wood, rock, iron, glass*
>
> liquid, e.g. *oil, water, milk, blood, ink,* OR
>
> gas, e.g. *smoke, air, butane, steam, oxygen*

Mass nouns are always singular: it makes no sense to 'count' the quantity of a mass substance which cannot be divided into separate objects. You can say:

> There's no **milk** in the refrigerator.
>
> We had two **cartons of milk** to cook with.
>
> BUT NOT: *There are no milks in the refrigerator.
>
>   *We had two milks to cook with. (see 66)

Some mass nouns, we might argue, should 'really' be count, because the 'substance' consists of separate things: *furniture* consists of *pieces of furniture, grass* of separate *blades of grass, hair* of separate *strands of hair* (or *hairs*), *wheat* of separate *grains of wheat*. But **psychologically** we think of such things as indivisible when we use a mass noun.

Note
On mass nouns which can be 'converted' into count nouns (*two coffees, please*), see 66.

Division of objects and substances

Unit nouns: a piece of bread, a block of ice, *etc.*

63 As with single objects, masses can be subdivided by the use of nouns like *part*:

> Part of the butter has melted.

In addition, there are many countable **unit nouns**, as we call them, which can be used to subdivide notionally a mass into separate 'pieces'. *Piece* and *bit* <informal> are general purpose unit nouns, which can be combined with most mass nouns:

> a **piece** of bread   a **piece** of paper   a **piece** of land
>
> a **bit** of food   a **bit** of paint   a **bit** of air

There are also unit nouns which typically go with particular mass nouns:

a *blade* of grass	a *sheet* of paper
a *block* of ice	a *speck* of dust
a *pile* of rubbish	a *bar* of chocolate
two *lumps* of sugar	a *length* of new rope
several *cups* of coffee	a fresh *load* of hay

As with part nouns, unit nouns are linked to the other nouns by *of*. Sometimes, the word for a container (*cup*, *bottle*, etc.) is used as a unit noun, as in *a cup of tea, a bottle of wine*.

Nouns of measure: a kilo of flour, etc.

64 Another way to divide a mass into separate 'pieces' is to measure it off into length, weight, etc:

DEPTH: a *foot* of water   AREA: an *acre* of land

LENGTH: a *yard* of cloth   a *hectare* of rough ground

       20 *metres* of rope   12 *square miles* of woodland

WEIGHT: an *ounce* of low fat spread   VOLUME: a *pint* of beer

       a *kilo* of flour   a *litre* || *liter* of milk

Species nouns: a type of, etc.

65 Here is another type of division: nouns like *type, kind, sort, species, class, variety* can divide a mass or a set of objects into 'types' or 'species':

Teak is a *type* of wood.

A Ford is a *make* of car.

A tiger is a *species* of mammal. <rather formal>

We usually place adjectives and other modifiers before the species noun rather than the noun which follows *of*:

a Japanese make of car (NOT *a make of Japanese car)

a delicious kind of bread

Notice that the second noun, when count, usually has no indefinite article: *a strange kind of mammal* (NOT *a strange kind of a mammal*).

In <informal> English, there is a mixed construction in which the determiner (if any) and the verb are plural, although the species noun is singular:

These kind of dogs are easy to train. <informal>

The normal construction is:

This kind of dog is easy to train.

Nouns which can be both count and mass

66 Quite a number of nouns can be both count and mass (*see* 597). *Wood*, for instance, is count when it refers to a collection of trees (= a forest), and mass when it refers to the material of which trees are composed:

> We went for a walk in the **woods**. [count]
>
> In America a lot of the houses are made of **wood**. [mass]

Many food nouns are count when they refer to the article in its 'whole' state, but are mass when they refer to the food in the mass, e.g. as eaten at table:

	There was **a** huge **cake** in the dining room.
BUT:	'Let them eat **cake**', said the queen.
	She began peeling **potatoes**.
BUT:	She took a mouthful of **potato**.
	Do we have enough **food** for the weekend?
BUT:	Some of the tastiest **foods** are pretty indigestible.
	I'd like **a boiled egg** for my breakfast.
BUT:	I'd prefer **some scrambled egg** on toast, please.

In other cases English has a separate count noun and a separate mass noun referring to the same area of meaning:

Count	Mass
Do you have **a fresh loaf**?	Do you have **some fresh bread**?
Would you like **a meal**?	Would you like **some more food**?
She's looking for **a new job**.	She's looking for **some interesting work**.
There are too **many vehicles** on the road.	There is too **much traffic** on the road.

Sometimes words which are usually mass nouns are 'converted' into count unit nouns or count species nouns:

> Two more **coffees**, please. (= cups of coffee)
>
> Current London auctions deal with **teas** from 25 countries. (= kinds of tea)

Occasionally the opposite happens: count nouns are 'converted' into mass nouns after a noun of measure: *a few square metres||meters of floor; a mile of river.*

Concrete and abstract

67 Abstract nouns refer to qualities (*difficulty*), events (*arrival*), feelings (*love*), etc. Just like concrete nouns, abstract nouns combine with part nouns (*part of the time*), unit nouns (*a piece of information*), and species nouns (*a new kind of music*). Abstract nouns can be either count or mass, even though these notions cannot be understood in a physical sense.

In general, abstract nouns can more easily be both 'count' and 'mass' than concrete nouns. Nouns referring to events and occasions (*talk, knock, shot, meeting*, etc.) are usually count:

> There was **a loud knock** at the door.
>
> The committee has had **three meetings**.

But *talk* (together with other nouns like *sound, thought*) can also be a mass noun:

> I had **a long talk** with her. [count]
>
> In the country we now hear **talk** of famine. [mass]
>
> I couldn't hear a **sound**. [count]
>
> These modern planes can fly faster than **sound**. [mass]
>
> What are your **thoughts** on this problem? [count]
>
> He was deep in **thought**. [mass]

Other abstract nouns tend to be mass nouns only: *honesty, happiness, information, progress, applause, homework, research*, etc. (*see* 597):

> Her speech was followed by loud **applause**.
>
> I have some **homework** to finish.
>
> We offer **information** and **advice**.
>
> **Wealth** did not bring them **happiness**.

68 But again, many such nouns (e.g. *experience, difficulty, trouble*) can be either mass or count (with some difference of meaning):

> We had little **difficulty** convincing him. [mass]
>
> BUT: He is having financial **difficulties**. [count]
>
> He is a policeman of many years' **experience**. [mass]
>
> BUT: Tell me about your **experiences** abroad. [count]
>
> I have some **work** to do this evening. [mass noun **work** = labour, activity]
>
> BUT: They have played two **works** by an unknown French composer. [count noun **work** = artistic or musical works]

Some nouns are mass nouns in English, but not in some other languages. Examples are *advice, information, news, shopping*:

> Can you give me **some good advice** on what to buy here?
>
> Do you have **any information** about the airport buses?
>
> What's **the latest news** about the election?
>
> The department stores stay open for **evening shopping**.

Partition and division with abstract nouns: *a useful bit of advice*

69 *Part* with abstract nouns is illustrated by:

Part of his **education** was at the University of Cambridge.

Division is illustrated in these phrases:

Unit nouns:	We had *a (good) game of chess.*
	He suffered from *(terrible) fits of anger.*
	There was *a (sudden) burst of applause.*
	Let me give you *a (useful) bit of advice.*
	Here's *an (interesting) item of news.* (ALSO: *a news item*)
	This translation is one of *her best pieces of work.*

Time (period) nouns (the equivalent of measure nouns, for abstractions):

three months of hard work

(ALSO *three months' hard work*, 107)

Species nouns:	*a(n exciting) type of dance*
	a (strange) kind of behaviour || *behavior*

Amount or quantity

Amount words (or quantifiers) (see 675–80): *all, some,* etc.

70 Amount words like *all, some* and *none* can be used with both count and mass nouns.

(A) *Used with singular count nouns like cake, house* they are equivalent to part nouns:

all of the cake (= the whole of the cake)	some of the cake (= part of the cake)	none of the cake

(B) *Used with plural nouns like stars:*

all (of) the stars	some of the stars	none of the stars

(C) *Used with mass nouns like land:*

all of the land	some of the land	none of the land

Note these relations of meaning between *all, some* and *none*:

> **Some** of the stars were invisible.   = **Not all** (of) the stars were visible.
>
> **None** of the stars was visible.   = **All** (of) the stars were invisible.

Further examples:

> **Some of** the patients will have pain when they come to hospital.
> (i.e. Others will not)
>
> **None of** their attempts so far has been wholly successful.
> (i.e. All attempts have been unsuccessful.)

71 Amount words specify more precisely the meaning 'some':

A large quantity

> {They have lost **many** of their **friends**. [count]
> {They have lost **much** of their **support**. [mass]
>
> {**A lot of** our **friends** live in San Francisco. [count]
> {**A lot of** our **support** comes from city dwellers. [mass]
>
> {**A large number people** have recently joined the party. [count]
> {They've been making **a great deal of noise** recently. [mass]

A small quantity

> {We managed to speak to **a few of** the **guests**. [count]
> {Could you possibly spare **a little of** your **time**? [mass]
>
> {She invited just a **small number of** her **friends**. [count]
> {Im afraid we've run into **a bit of trouble**. [mass]

Not a large quantity

> {**Not many of us** would have been as brave as she was. [count]
> {I promise I'll take very **little of** your **time**. [mass]

Notice that *few* and *little* without *a* have a negative bias. Compare:

> **A few** (= a small number, some of) of the students pass the examination.
>
> **Few** (= not many) of the students pass the examination.

Other words of quantity or amount:

> **Two/three** (and other numerals, *see* 602) of our best players have been injured.
>
> **Half** (of) the money was stolen.
>
> **More** of your time should be spent in the office. (ALSO: **less** of your time)
>
> **Most** of our friends live locally.
>
> **Several** of the paintings (= 'slightly more than a few') are from private collections.

Note

With *a/the majority of* and *a minority of* (both <rather formal>) it is normal to use plural and group nouns (on concord with the verb in these and similar cases, *see* 510):

> *The majority of* the farmers *are* the sons and grandsons of farmers.
> (= Most of the farmers . . .)

> Only *a minority of* women *feel* able to report such attacks to the police.
> (= fewer than half . . .)

Many and *much*; *a lot of*, *lots of*

72 *Many* and *much* are often used in combinations with *as, too, so (as many/much as, too many/much, so many/much)* and in questions (*how many/much?*). Compare the count and mass words in the questions and answers below:

Count	*Mass*
[A] *How many* of the rolls have you eaten?	[A] *How much* of the bread have you eaten?
[B] { *All* of them *Most* of them *A lot* of them *Half* of them *Several* of them *A few* of them *None* of them	[B] { *All* of it *Most* of it *A lot* of it *Half* of it – *A little* of it *None* of it

Indefinite use of amount words

73 For the amount words above there is a definite 'total' (shown by the circles in the diagrams in 70) within which amounts are to be measured. Now we look at the general (indefinite) use of amount words, where no total is given. Here the amount word is used as a determiner e.g. *most people* (*see* 522), and *of* and *the* are generally omitted. (But *of* occurs with *a lot of, a great deal of, a number of, lots of*, etc., as in *a lot of fun, a number of people*, even where the following expression is indefinite.)

Count

All crimes are avoidable. (i.e. all of the crimes in the world)

We did**n't** buy *many* things.

Mass

All violence is avoidable.

We did**n't** buy *much* food.

Count

All pupils should learn to ski.

We saw *several snakes* down by the river.

Most men don't know how to dance.

Few new writers have their first story accepted.

I want to ask Mr Danby *a few questions*.

I think people catch *fewer colds* these days.

Mass

You'll do a lot better with *less food* in your stomach.

Plants in plastic pots usually need *less water* than those in clay pots.

The village can provide *no food* for the refugees.

It will take *a little time* to clear up the mess.

Put *a few pieces of butter* on top of the vegetables.

In <informal> style, *a lot of* (or *lots of*) is preferred to *many* or *much* in positive statements:

Many patients arrive on the surgical ward as planned admissions. <formal>

You find *a lot of* nurses have given up smoking. <informal>

There's *lots of* spare time if you need it.

But in questions and after negatives (*very*) *many* and *much* are not restricted to <formal> English:

Have you seen *much* of Julie recently?
I don't eat *much* in the mornings.

Do *many* people attend the meetings?
We don't get *many* visitors in the winter.

Words of general or inclusive meaning

74 *All, both, every, each,* and (sometimes) *any* are amount words of **general** or **inclusive** meaning. With count nouns, *all* is used for quantities of more than two, and *both* for quantities of two only:

The western is a popular kind of movie with *both* sexes and *all* ages.

Every, each

75 Words like *every* and *each* can be called **distributive**, because they pick out the members of a set or group singly, rather than look at them all together. Apart from this difference, *every* has the same meaning as *all*:

All good teachers study their subject(s) carefully. [1]

Every good teacher studies his or her subject carefully. [2]

The 'distributive' meaning of *every* shows in the use of singular forms *teacher, studies, his or her* in [2]. (However, *see* 96 on the use of *he or she, his or her, they, their* etc.)

76 *Each* is like *every* except that it can be used when the set has only two members. Thus *each* (unlike *all* and *every*) can sometimes replace *both* with little difference of meaning:

She kissed her mother tenderly on $\begin{cases} each\ cheek. \\ both\ cheeks. \end{cases}$

Note also the difference between:

She complimented *each*/*every* member of the winning team. [3]

She complimented *all* (the) members of the winning team. [4]

Whereas [3] suggests that she spoke to each member of the team separately, [4] suggests that she made one speech, addressing all members of the team at once. Like *every* in meaning are *everyone, everybody, everything*, and *everywhere*.

Any, either

77 The most familiar use of the determiners *any* and *either* is in negative sentences and questions (*see* 697–9), but here we consider them as inclusive words. *Any* can sometimes replace *all* and *every* in positive sentences:

These days *any* young man with brains can do very well.

Any new vehicle has to be registered immediately.

(Compare: $\begin{cases} \text{Every new vehicle } \textbf{has} \text{ to } \ldots \\ \text{All new vehicles } \textbf{have} \text{ to } \ldots) \end{cases}$

Here *any* has the same inclusive meaning as *all* and *every* in [1] and [2]. But *any* means something different in:

You can paint the wall *any* colour you like.

Any colour means 'red *or* green *or* blue *or* . . .', while *every colour* means 'red *and* green *and* blue *and*. . . .' *Any* means 'it doesn't matter who/which/what . . . one chooses'.

78 When there are only two objects or people, *either* is used instead of *any*:

You could ask *either of* my parents. (= either my father or my mother)

Compare the use of negative *neither* for two objects (*see* 379, 584):

Neither of my parents is keen on rock music.

79 *Any* can also be used with mass nouns and plural count nouns:

> Àny land is valuable thése days.
>
> You're lucky to find àny shops open on Súnday.

As shown here, *any* often takes nuclear stress (*see 36*). Like *any* are *anyone, anybody, anything, anywhere, anyhow, anyway* and <informal AmE> *anyplace*:

> **Anyone** will tell you the way. (= Whoever you ask, he or she will . . .)
>
> He will eat **anything**. (= He will eat whatever you give him.)

Scale of amount

80 We can order the most common amount words roughly on a scale, moving from the inclusive words at the top, to the negative words at the bottom:

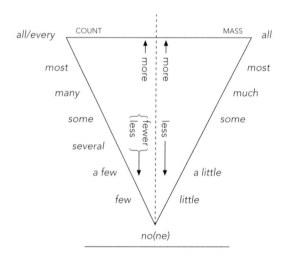

(*Any* we place separately, because its main use, in negative and interrogative contexts, does not fit into this scale.)

81 Positions on a scale of amount can be expressed not only through the words already discussed (which are determiners or pronouns) but by pronouns like *everybody, everything,* and by adverbs of frequency (*always*), degree (*entirely*), etc. We show some of the different areas of meaning in the table opposite.

Of the columns of the diagram, A–D represent noun phrases, and E–G represent adverbials (to be dealt with later in 449–63). The rows are in ascending order of amount, from the inclusive word *all* to the non-committal word *any*. Here are some examples labelled according to their position in the table opposite:

A1   *All* stress increases the body's need for nutrients.

B1   *All* faculty members were given bonuses.

B2   Are there *many* other names which come to mind?

B3   *Some* of these patients will be nursed in a surgical ward.

C6   *Nobody* was reported injured. / *No one* was hurt.

C7   *Anyone* would be astonished to see the amount of public money wasted.

D6   *Nothing* has yet been decided.

D7   He would do *anything* to please her.

E3   You ought to come over to Cambridge *sometimes*.

E4   Cook the vegetables slowly, stirring *occasionally*.

E5   Margotte *rarely* turned on the television set.

G5   He sounded terrified and I could *hardly* blame him.

A Mass	B Count	C Personal	D Non-Personal	E Frequency	F Duration	G Degree
(see 675–8)	(see 675–8)	(see 679)	(see 679)	(see 166)	(see 161–5)	(see 217–8)
1 all	all, every, each	everyone, everybody	everything	always	always, for ever	absolutely, entirely etc.
2 much, a lot (of)	many, a lot (of)	(many people)	(many things)	often, frequently	(for) a long time	very, (very) much
3 some	some	someone, somebody	something	sometimes	(for) sometime	rather, somewhat, quite
4 a little	a few	(a few people)	(a few things)	occasionally	(for) a while	a little, a bit
5 little	few	(few people)	(few things)	rarely, seldom	not . . . (for) long	scarcely, hardly
6 no(ne)	no(ne)	no one, nobody	nothing	never	—	not . . . at all
7 any	any	anyone, anybody	anything	ever	—	at all

Definite and indefinite meaning: *the, a/an*, zero

82 When we use the definite article *the* we presume that both we and the hearer or reader know what is being talked about: *the dog, the race.* Most of the words we have considered in 70–81 are indefinite; but if we want to express indefinite meaning without any added meaning of amount, etc, we use the indefinite article *a/an* (with singular count nouns), or the zero indefinite article with mass nouns or plural count nouns (*see* 597):

> Would you like *a drink*?   Do you like *chocolate*?

Uses of the definite article

To express definite meaning we use the definite article ***the***. There are four main cases.

Unique use of the

83 When the object or group of objects is the only one that exists (or has existed): *the stars, the earth, the world, the sea, the North Pole, the equator, the Renaissance, the human race*:

> The **North Pole** and **the South Pole** are equally distant from **the** equator.

This **unique** use of *the* also arises where what is referred to is 'understood' to be unique in the context: *the sun, the moon, the kitchen, the town-hall, the Queen, the last President,* etc. We could, if we wanted, make the definite meaning clear by modification after the noun (*the moon belonging to this earth, the kitchen of this house, the Queen of this country,* etc.), but this would normally be unnecessary.

Back-pointing use of the

84 When identity has been established by an earlier mention (often with an indefinite article):

> They have   *a son*   and two daughters, but
>
> FIRST MENTION

> *the son* is already grown up and has a family of his own.
>
> SECOND MENTION

Forward-pointing use of *the*

85 When identity is established by a modifier, such as a relative clause or an *of*-phrase (*see* 641) that follows the noun:

> *The* woman *who answered the door* helped Jack into the room.
>
> *The* wine *of France* is *the* best *in the world*.
>
> *The* discovery *of radium* marked *the* beginning *of a new era of medicine*.

Conventional use of *the* (*for institutions, etc.*): *the radio, the paper*

86 When reference is made to an institution shared by the community: *the radio, the television, the telephone, the newspaper, the paper, the train*:

> I read in *the paper* the next day that he'd been killed by burglars.
>
> We'll maybe go to Glasgow this week on *the train*.

Most cases of this institutional use are connected with communications and transport. Sometimes (*see* 475) the article may be omitted with this use:

> What's on (*the*) *television* tonight?

Note
After a preposition, *the* is used before parts of the body in constructions like these:

> She looked *him* in *the eye* and said 'No'.
>
> Lev smiled and shook *me* by *the hand*.

Usually, in such cases, the direct object refers to the person who 'owns' the body-part (*see* 624).

Generic use of articles

87 *The* also has a **generic** use, referring to what is general or typical for a whole class of objects. This is found with count nouns:

> *The tiger* is one of the big cats; it is rivalled only by *the lion* in strength and ferocity. *The tiger* has no mane, but in old males *the hair* on *the cheeks* is rather long and spreading.   [1]

Here *the tiger* indicates tigers in general, not one individual. Thus [1] expresses essentially the same meaning as [2] and [3]:

> *Tigers* have no mane.   [2]
>
> *A tiger* has no mane.   [3]

[2] is the generic use of the indefinite plural form; [3] is the generic use of the indefinite singular. When we are dealing with a whole class of objects

as here, the differences between definite and indefinite, singular and plural, tend to lose their importance. But there is a slight difference in the fact that *the tiger* (generic) refers to the species as a whole, while *a tiger* (generic) refers to any member of the species. We can say:

> The tiger is in danger of becoming extinct.

> Tigers are in danger of becoming extinct.

BUT NOT: *A tiger is in danger of becoming extinct.

Specific versus generic meaning

88 In contrast to the **generic** use of *the*, all the other uses (*see* 83–6) may be called **specific**. For mass nouns, there is only one generic form, which has a zero article:

> **Water** is oxidized by the removal of **hydrogen**, and **oxygen** is released.

The ways of expressing generic meaning with count and mass nouns are shown in the table:

	Count	Mass
generic meaning	*the tiger* *a tiger* *tigers*	*water*

As the table implies, *the* is always *specific* with mass nouns (*the water*) and also with plural nouns (*the tigers*) (with the exception of some nationality words, *see* 579). The following examples show generic meaning with three types of noun:

- *butter, gold, Venetian glass, Scandinavian furniture,* . . . [concrete mass nouns]

- *music, health, English literature, contemporary art,* . . . [abstract mass mouns]

- *dogs, friends, wooden buildings, classical languages,* . . . [plural nouns]

In specific use, these nouns take *the*.

Specific Use	Generic Use
Pass *the butter*, please.	*Butter* is expensive nowadays.
The acting was poor, but we enjoyed *the music.*	*Dancing* and *music* were her hobbies.
Before you visit Spain, you ought to learn *the language.*	The scientific study of *language* is called linguistics.
Come and look at *the horses*!	'I just love *horses*,' said Murphy.

89 Notice that English tends to treat mass nouns and plural nouns as generic when they have a modifier before them (*Chinese history*). But when they are followed by a modifier, especially by an *of*-phrase, *the* normally has to be present (*the history of China*). Compare:

Chinese history	*the* history of China
American social life	*the* social life of America
early mediaeval architecture	*the* architecture of the early middle ages
animal behaviour	*the* behaviour of animals

The tendency is strong with abstract mass nouns. It is less strong with concrete mass nouns and plural nouns. We can omit *the* in

eighteenth-century furniture	(the) furniture of the eighteenth century
tropical birds	(the) birds of the tropics

Compare:

She's one of the world's experts on { eighteenth-century furniture.
(the) furniture of the eighteenth century.

They are doing some interesting research on { Iron Age forts.
(the) forts of the Iron Age.

Generic *the* with adjectives, nationality nouns, and group nouns

90 Adjectives are used with generic *the*:

- To denote a class of people (*the poor, the unemployed, the young, the handicapped*) (*see* 448):

    They should see to it that there's work for **the unemployed**, food for **the hungry**, and hospitals for **the sick**.

- To denote an abstract quality (*the absurd, the beautiful, the sublime*) (*see* 448):

    His behaviour on the platform borders on **the ridiculous**.

- With nationality adjectives ending in a sibilant *-ch, -ese, -sh* or *-ss* used to refer to a people as a whole: *the Dutch, the English, the French, the Japanese, the Vietnamese* (*see* 579):

    The French say they must sell more wine to Germany.

Generic *the* is also commonly used:

- With nationality or ethnic nouns (except those ending in *-women* or *-men*), e.g. *the Indians, the Poles, the Zulus*:

    The plan has received warm support from **the Germans**.

- With group nouns like *the middle class, the public, the administration, the government* (*see* 60), or collective plural nouns such as *the clergy, the police*:

> He was a socialist and believed in the right of **the working class** to control their own destiny.
>
> **The public** can help by reporting anything suspicious to **the police**.

Other words of definite meaning

91 Apart from common nouns (i.e. count and mass nouns) with *the*, the following words have definite meanings:

> **Proper nouns** (see 667): *Susan, Chicago, Tuesday, Africa,* etc.
>
> **Personal pronouns** (see 619): *I, we, he, she, it, they, you,* etc.
>
> **Pointer words** or **demonstratives** (see 521): *this, that, these, those*

We will deal with these in turn, bearing in mind the types of definiteness already discussed (*see* 83–6).

Proper nouns

92 Proper nouns are understood to have unique reference: *Africa* refers to one particular continent, and *Susan* (in a given conversation) refers to one particular person. Here no *the* comes before the proper noun (*see* 667), because definite meaning is 'built into' the noun itself. This also normally applies when a proper noun is the first word in a two-word name, such as *Harvard University, Oxford Street*.

93 But when proper nouns change into common nouns, *the* can be used. This happens, for example, when we need to distinguish two or more things of the same name.

> **the Susan** next door (i.e. not the Susan who works in your office)　　[4]
>
> **the Venice** of story books (i.e. not the Venice of reality)　　[5]

In [5], we distinguish not two places of the same name, but two aspects of the same place. *The* is also sometimes used before modifiers + noun (*the young Catherine, the future President Kennedy*), but with place-names it is generally left out: *Ancient Greece, eighteenth century London, upstate New York*.
　　In a similar way proper nouns sometimes change to plural:

> I know several **Mr Wilsons**. (= 'people called **Mr Wilson**')
>
> He was a close friend of **the Kennedys**. (= 'the family named **Kennedy**')

A proper noun may also sometimes follow the indefinite article:

> A man called Wilson murdered **a Mrs Henrichson** because she refused to rent him a room.

This means 'a certain Mrs Henrichson' (a person you won't have heard of).

Third person pronouns

94 Third person pronouns (*he, she, it, they*) are usually definite because they point back to a previous mention. In a sense, they 'replace' an earlier noun phrase:

> I phoned *the police* and asked *them*   (*i.e.* the police) what to do.
>   FIRST   SECOND
>   MENTION   MENTION

Concrete nouns are replaced by *he, she, it,* or *they* as follows:

- *he* (*him, his, himself*) refers to a male person (or animal)
- *she* (*her, hers, herself*) refers to a female person (or animal)
- *it* (*its, itself*) refers to an inanimate thing (or an animal)
- *they* (*them, their, theirs, themselves*) is the plural pronoun, referring to either animate or inanimate.

95 *He* and *she* are used for animals when we think of them as having the personal qualities of human beings (e.g. family pets):

> Nemo, the killer whale, who'd grown too big for **his** pool on Clacton Pier, has arrived safely in **his** new home in Windsor safari park.

It is otherwise used for animals, and sometimes for babies and very young children, especially when their sex is unknown:

> In the farmyard a dog in **its** kennel was barking loudly.
>
> In her arms lay the delicate baby, with **its** deep blue eyes.

Mass nouns and singular abstract nouns are replaced by *it*:

> I've washed **my hair**, and **it** won't keep tidy.
>
> **Life** today is so busy that **its** true meaning often eludes us.

Note
She is sometimes used

- for inanimate objects (especially ships):

  > A ship had come in from Greece and was unloading **her** cargo.

- for countries seen as political units:

  > Last year **France** increased **her** exports by 10 per cent.

Referring to male and female

96 When a human noun is replaced by a pronoun and the sex is not known or specified, traditionally *he* is used rather than *she*:

> A martyr is someone who gives up **his** life for **his** beliefs.

However, nowadays this bias towards the male term is widely avoided, and *he or she* (or *him or her*, etc.) is often used instead:

A martyr is someone who gives up **his or her** life for **his or her** beliefs.

It's the duty of every athlete to know what **he or she** is taking to eat and drink.

As the first of these examples shows, however, *he or she* (etc.) can have an awkward effect, especially if repeated. Another method of avoiding sex bias, well established in <spoken English>, is the singular use of *they*:

A martyr is someone who gives up **their** life for **their** beliefs.

This 'ungrammatical' mixing of singular and plural is making its way into <informal> writing, although those with a strict sense of grammar avoid it. Since none of the above alternatives is entirely satisfactory, it is often possible to avoid the problem of sex-neutral third-person reference by changing from the singular to the plural:

Martyrs are people who give up **their** life/lives for **their** beliefs.

Here, of course, the use of *they* causes no problem in itself, although indirectly it may cause other problems, such as whether to use *life* or *lives* in the above example.

Note

Other solutions to the problem of how to avoid male bias include the use of the subjective pronoun form *s/he*, the use of *she or he*, and the use of *she* as a sex-neutral pronoun. The mixed form *s/he* is convenient in writing, but has the limitation of not having any oblique forms such as **s/him* or **s/his*. Another disadvantage is that its pronunciation is not distinguishable from that of *she*.

First and second person pronouns: *I, we, you*

97 The first and second person pronouns have reference to the situation as follows:

First person:

I (*me, my, mine, myself*)	'the speaker'
we (*us, our, ours, ourselves*)	'a group of people, including the speaker'

Second person:

you (*your, yourself, yourselves*)	a 'the hearer' (singular)
	b 'a group of people, including the hearer but excluding the speaker' (plural)

We sometimes **includes** the hearer (= 'you and I'), and sometimes **excludes** the hearer:

> Let's go back to the bar now, shall *we*? ['*inclusive we*': *let's* = *let us*] (see 498)

> *We*'ve enjoyed meeting you. ['*exclusive we*']

Inclusive *we* is often used by writers of books:

> In this section *we* shall consider a few examples . . .

> Let's look at this in further detail . . .

Generic use of pronouns: *one, you, they*

98 Three pronouns have a generic use, in reference to people in general.

- *One* (*one's, oneself* – singular) is rather <formal and impersonal> meaning 'people in general including you and me':

> *One* never knows what may happen. <rather formal>

> *One* has to help *one's* fellow human beings. <rather formal>

- *You* is its <informal> equivalent:

> *You* never know what may happen. <informal>

> All this exercise makes *you* hungry, doesn't it? <informal>

- *They* can also be used generically in <informal> English, but with a different meaning from *one* and *you*. It means roughly 'people (excluding you and me)':

> *They* say it's going to rain tomorrow. (= 'People say . . .')

Pointer words: *this, that*, etc.

99 We use the term **pointer words** for words like the demonstrative *this* and *that*, which refer by *pointing* to something in the context. They can have three different uses.

- Pointer words can be **situational**, i.e. they can point to something in the context outside language:

> Would you like to sit in *this* chair (= 'the one by me') or in *that* one? (= 'the one away from me, over there')

This identifies something near the speaker (either physically, in terms of space or time, or psychologically). *That* identifies something not so near the speaker.

- Pointer words can be **back-pointing**, i.e. they can point to something mentioned earlier:

  I then tried to force the door open, but *this/that* was a mistake.

- Pointer words can be **forward-pointing**, i.e. they can point to something to be mentioned later:

  This is what the graph shows. One line shows what has happened to personal wealth. The second line shows the fall in the savings ratio.

100 We may separate two classes of pointer words, those related to *this* (and having the 'near' meaning) and those related to *that* (and having the 'distant' meaning).

The *this*-type:	*this* (singular) *these* (plural)	*here* (= at this place) *now* (= at this time)
The *that*-type:	*that* (singular) *those* (plural)	*there* (= at that place) *then* (= at that time) (usually in the past)

This and *that* can replace each other with no difference of meaning in back-pointing, but *this* is commoner in <formal> English. For forward-pointing, only *this*, and the *this*-type words *these*, *here*, and *thus* can be used (but *see* 101):

This is what he wrote:
These are the latest results: } *(forward-pointing)*
Halliday and Hasan define cohesion *thus*:

This/That was what Charles had said.
These/those women knew what   } *(backward-pointing)*
  they wanted.

Notice the opening and close of a radio message or news bulletin:

Here is what the message said: Please leave this room as tidy as you found it. [*forward-pointing*]

And *that's* the end of the news. [*back-pointing*]

101 *Those* is forward-pointing when its meaning is defined by a following modifier: *those who are interested* (= 'people who are interested') (*see* 521).

In <informal> style, *this* can 'point forward' in the sense of setting up a new topic for discussion, whereas *that* can 'point back' to some vaguely shared experience:

Have you seen *this* report about smoking? (= 'a report I know about')

It gives you *that* great feeling of clean air and open spaces.
(= 'the feeling we all know about')

This can also be used <familiarly> to introduce something new in a narrative:

I was just coming out of the bank when *this* girl came up to me . . .
(= 'a girl I'm going to tell you about')

Relations between ideas expressed by nouns

Relations expressed by *of*

102 We have talked of *of* used in phrases of

- **partition**: *a part of the house* (*see* 61)
- **division**: *a kind of tree* (*see* 63)
- **amount**: *most of our problems* (*see* 70–81)

Of is also used more generally to indicate various relations between the meanings of two nouns:

the roof of the house (the house has a roof; the roof is part of the house)

a friend of my father's (my father has a friend, see 535)

the courage of the firefighters (the firefighters have courage; the firefighters are courageous)

the envy of the world (the world envies . . .)

the trial of the conspirators (someone tries the conspirators)

the causes of stress (stress is caused by . . .)

the virtue of thrift (thrift is a virtue)

a shortage of money (money is short, money is in short supply)

a glass of water (the glass has water in it; the glass contains water)

people of the Middle Ages (people who lived in the Middle Ages)

the house of my dreams (the house which I see in my dreams)

the College of Surgeons (the College to which surgeons belong)

The 'have' relation

103 Both *of* and *with* can indicate a relation of 'having'. From the sentence 'Noun1 has Noun2' we can focus either on **Noun2** or **Noun1**.

- **Noun2 of Noun1:**   *the roof of the house, the courage of the people*
- **Noun1 of Noun2:**   *people of (great) courage*
- **Noun1 with Noun2:**   *a house with a (flat) roof*

In the 'Noun1 + preposition + **Noun2**' construction, *of* is used where **Noun2** is abstract (*a performance of distinction, a country of enormous wealth*), and *with* is used where **Noun2** is concrete (*a woman with a large family, a man with a beard*).

The uses of the genitive

104 A genitive (ending *'s* or apostrophe only, *see* 530) can often be used with the same meaning as an *of*-phrase, especially where the genitive has human reference:

● **The 'have' relation** (*'Dr Brown has a son'*)

Dr Brown's son (definite)	$\begin{cases} a\ son\ of\ Dr\ Brown \\ or\ a\ son\ of\ Dr\ Brown's \\ (see\ 535)\ (indefinite) \end{cases}$
the earth's gravity	the gravity of the earth (more usual)

● **The subject-verb relation** (*'His parents consented'*)

his parents' consent	the consent of his parents
the train's departure	the departure of the train (more usual)

● **The verb-object relation** (*'They released the prisoner'*)

the prisoner's release	the release of the prisoner
a city's destruction	the destruction of a city (more usual)

● **The subject-complement relation** (*'Everyone is happy'*)

Marian's happiness	the happiness of Marian
the country's beauty	the beauty of the country

105 In the following cases, the *of*-phrase is NOT normally used:

● **The origin relation** (*'The girl told a story'*, etc.)

the girl's story (= a story that the girl told)

John's telegram (= a telegram from John OR a telegram that John sent)

● **Various classifying relations** (where the genitive behaves rather like a modifying noun or adjective)

a women's college (= a college for women)

a doctor's degree (= a doctoral degree)

Choice between an of-construction and the genitive

106 In general, the genitive is preferred for human nouns (*the girl's arrival*) and sometimes also for animal nouns (*horses' hooves*) and human group nouns (*the government's policy*). *Of* is usually preferred for inanimate nouns and abstract nouns (*the discovery of helium, the progress of science*). In general, the genitive is also preferred for the subject-verb relation:

> Livingstone's discovery (= 'Livingstone discovered something')

but *of* is preferred for the verb-object relation:

> the discovery of Livingstone (usually = 'Somebody discovered Livingstone')

The subject function can also be indicated by a *by*-phrase. Hence the idea 'The army defeated the rebels' might be expressed in three ways as a noun phrase:

> the army's defeat of the rebels
>
> the defeat of the rebels by the army
>
> the rebels' defeat by the army

(But *the rebels' defeat of the army* has to mean that the rebels defeated the army.)

The *of*-construction is also preferred, especially in <formal> English, to the genitive when the modifying noun phrase is long. We can easily say:

> the departure *of the 4.30 train for Edinburgh*
>
> BUT NOT:
>
> the 4.30 train for Edinburgh's departure (see 533)

107 Note two special cases of the genitive.

- Time nouns are frequently used in the genitive:

  > this year's crop of potatoes   two weeks' holiday
  >
  > a moment's thought   today's menu (OR the menu for today)

- Place nouns are also frequently used in the genitive, especially if followed by a superlative:

  > the town's oldest pub (OR the oldest pub in the town – NOT *the oldest pub of the town)
  >
  > Norway's greatest composer (OR the greatest composer in Norway)
  >
  > the world's best chocolate (OR the best chocolate in the world)

Relations between people: *with, for, against*

108 *With* often means 'together with' or 'in company with':

> I'm so glad you're coming *with us*.   [1]
>
> Sheila was at the theatre *with her friends*.   [2]

Sentence [2] is not very different in meaning from

Sheila *and her friends* were at the theatre.

Without is the negative of *with* in this sense:

Sheila was ill, so we went to the theatre *without her*.

With, in a situation of conflict or competition, means 'on the same side as':

Remember that every one of us is *with* you. (= 'on your side')

Are you *with* us or *against* us?

For conveys the idea of support (= 'in favour of') and, like *with*, contrasts with *against*:

Are you *for* or *against* the President?

Note
Also notice: *the fight against pollution, the campaign against inflation,* etc. In contrast to its meaning above, *with* can convey the idea of opposition between two people or groups in *fight with, argue with,* etc: *Stop arguing with me.*

Ingredient, material: *with, of, out of, from*

109 With verbs of 'making', use *with* for an ingredient, and *out of* or *of* for the material of the whole thing:

A fruit cake is made *with* fruit, but a glass jug is made (*out*) *of* glass.

Made from means that one is derived from another:

They lived in tents made *from blankets*.

Most paper is made *from wood-pulp*.

Of alone is used in postmodifying phrases: *a ring of solid gold* (i.e. . . . made out of solid gold), *a table of polished oak* (i.e. . . . consisting of polished oak). One noun in front of another can also refer to a material or ingredient: *a gold ring, an oak table, metal rods, banana cake.*

Restrictive and non-restrictive meaning

110 Modifiers before or after a noun usually help to specify its meaning exactly:

(A)	(B)
the children	the children *who live next door*
a king	a king *of Denmark*
buttered toast	*hot* buttered toast
these books	these *latest history* books

In each case, phrase (B) tells us more precisely than phrase (A) about what the noun refers to. It **narrows down** or **restricts** the meaning of the noun, by saying *what kind of* children, king, etc. the speaker is talking of. This type of modifier is called **restrictive**.

111 There is also a **non-restrictive** type of modifier which does not limit the noun in this way. Compare:

> She loved to talk about her sister who lived in Pàris. | (RESTRICTIVE) [1]
>
> She loved to talk about her sìster, | who lived in Pàris. | (NON-RESTRICTIVE)[2]

In [1], the relative clause is restrictive and tells us *which* sister she liked to talk about – we must assume she had two or more sisters. In [2], where the relative clause is non-restrictive, the speaker is talking about one sister – we assume she has only one – and gives us the extra information that she lived in Paris. This non-restrictive modification is typically signalled by a tone unit boundary (*see* 37) in <speech>, or a comma in <writing>, separating it from the preceding noun.

Non-restrictive adjectives

112 Adjectives, as well as relative clauses, can be non-restrictive. The clearest cases are adjectives before proper nouns: since a proper noun already has unique reference, it cannot be limited any further by the adjective (but *see* 93): *poor James, 73-year-old Mrs Cass, the beautiful Highlands of Scotland*.

Non-restrictive adjectives are not so clearly marked by punctuation or intonation, and so ambiguities can occur:

> The *patriotic* Americans have great respect for their country's constitution. [3]
>
> The *hungry* workers attacked the houses of their *rich* employers. [4]

We might ask: Does [3] mean that 'all Americans have great respect' (non-restrictive)? Or does it mean that 'only some Americans (those who are patriotic, as opposed to those who are not) have great respect'? Does [4] refer to *all* the workers and *all* the employers, or just to the hungry workers (as opposed to those with enough to eat), and to the rich employers (as opposed to the poor ones)? These sentences could have either meaning, but the non-restrictive meaning is more likely.

Note
The ordering of modifiers can make a difference to meaning:

> her last great novel [5]
>
> her great last novel [6]

In [5] *great* is restrictive, while in [6] *great* is non-restrictive. The meaning of [5] is therefore 'the last of her great novels', and the meaning of [6] is 'her last novel, which was great'.

Time, tense and aspect

113 We turn now to meanings expressed by the verb phrase. Tense and aspect (*see* 740–2) relate the happening described by the verb to time in the past, present, or future.

States and events

114 We must first give some attention to the different kinds of meaning a verb may have. Broadly, verbs may refer

- to an **event**, i.e. a happening thought of as a single occurrence, with a definite beginning and end e.g. *become, get, come, leave, hit, close, take.*

- to a **state**, i.e. a state of affairs which continues over a period, and does not need to have a well-defined beginning and end, e.g. *be, remain, contain, know, resemble, seem.*

> She *became* unconscious.   [event]
>
> She *remained* unconscious.   [state]

The difference between **event** and **state** verbs is similar to the difference between count and mass nouns. As we saw in 62 for count and mass, these categories are based not so much on the world itself, as on the way our minds look at the world. The same verb can change from one category to another, and the distinction is not always clear: *Did you remember his name?* could refer either to a state or to an event. To be more accurate, then, we should talk of 'state uses of verbs' and 'event uses of verbs'; but it is convenient sometimes to keep to the simpler terms 'state verb' and 'event verb'.

115 The distinction between 'state' and 'event' gives rise to the following three basic kinds of verb meaning (illustrated in the past tense):

————————	(1) STATE	Napoleon was a Corsican.
•	(2) SINGLE EVENT	Columbus discovered America.
• • • • • • • • •	(3) SET OF REPEATED EVENTS (HABIT)	Paganini played the violin brilliantly.

The 'habit' meaning combines 'event' meaning with 'state' meaning: a habit is a state consisting of a series of events. We often specify 'state' meaning by adding an adverbial of duration (161–5):

> Queen Victoria reigned *for sixty-four years*.

We specify 'habit' more precisely by adding an adverbial of frequency (166–9) or an adverbial of duration:

> He played the violin *every day from the age of five*.

(All three types of meaning can be clarified by an adverbial of time-when, *see* 151–60.)

To these three a further type of verbal meaning can be added:

~~~~~~ (4) THE TEMPORARY meaning expressed by the progressive aspect (*see* 132, 740–1):

> She *was cooking* the dinner.

Present time: *I adore your drawings!*

116 The following are the main ways of referring to something which occurs at the present time:

(A) PRESENT STATE (the Simple Present Tense)

> I'*m* hungry.
>
> *Do* you *like* my hat?

The state may stretch indefinitely into the past and future, and so this use of the simple present tense applies also to general truths such as *A cube has eight corners*.

117 (B) PRESENT EVENT (the Simple Present Tense)

> I *declare* the meeting closed.
>
> She *serves* – and it's an ace!

This use is rather specialized, being limited to formal declarations, sports commentaries, demonstrations, etc. In most contexts, one rarely has the occasion to refer to an event begun and ended at the very moment of speech.

118 (C) PRESENT HABIT (the Simple Present Tense)

> I *work* in two elementary schools.
>
> *Do* you *drink* beer?
>
> It *rains* a lot in this part of the world.

By 'habit' here, we mean a repetition of events.

119 (D) TEMPORARY PRESENT (the Present Progressive)

> Look! It'*s snowing*!   [1a]
>
> The children *are sleeping* soundly now.   [2a]
>
> They *are living* in a rented house (temporarily – for a short period)   [3a]

The meaning of the progressive aspect is 'limited duration'. Compare the meaning of the simple present in these examples:

It **snows** a lot in northern Japan. (habit) [1b]

The children usually **sleep** very soundly. (habit) [2b]

They **live** in a rented house. (permanently) [3b]

For single events, which in any case involve a limited time-span, the effect of the progressive is to emphasize the durational aspect of the event:

The champion **serves**. It's another double fault!

The champion **is serving** well. (The service is a continuing, repetitive activity)

With states, the effect of the progressive is to put emphasis on the **limited** duration of the state of affairs:

She **lives** with her mother. (permanently)

She**'s living** with her mother. (at the moment)

120 (E) TEMPORARY HABIT (the Present Progressive)

I'**m playing** golf regularly these days.

She**'s** not **working** at the moment.

He**'s walking** to work while his car is being repaired.

This use combines the 'temporary' meaning of the progressive with the repetitive meaning of the habitual present.

Other ways of referring to present time

121 Three rather less important ways of referring to the present are these:

● We can use the progressive aspect with *always* or a similar adverb, to emphasize that an action is continuous, or persistent:

Those children **are** always (= continually) **getting** into trouble.

This use carries with it some feeling of disapproval.

● Temporary and habitual meaning can be combined to indicate a repetition of temporary happenings:

He**'s chewing** gum whenever I see him.

● In special circumstances, the past tense can be used to refer to the present:

Did you **want** to speak to me? (= 'Do you want . . .')

I (just) **wondered** whether you would help me. (= 'I wonder . . .')

Here the past tense is an indirect and <more tactful> alternative to the simple present tense (*see* 136).

Past time: *I've read your book – and I loved it!*

122 Along with the present-time meanings in 116–21 above there are similar past-time meanings: we have already illustrated some of these (*see* 115). But there is a special problem of past-time reference in English: the question of how to choose between the use of the past tense and the use of the perfect aspect. The **past tense** is used when the past happening is related to a definite time, in the past, which we may call '**then**'. Hence the simple past tense means 'past-happening-related-to-past-time'.

> He *was* in prison for ten years. (this probably means 'Now he's out')

In contrast, the **perfect aspect** is used for a past happening which is seen in relation to a later event or time. Thus the present perfect means 'past-happening-related-to-present-time'. For example:

> He *has been* in prison for ten years. (this probably means 'He's still there.')

The past tense: *The parcel arrived last week*

123 The past tense refers to a **definite** time in the past, which may be identified by

> *a* a past-time adverbial in the same sentence,
>
> *b* the preceding language context, or
>
> *c* the context outside language.

(On these aspects of definite meaning, compare the use of *the* (*see* 83–5).) Examples of the three types are:

> *a* Chandra *came* to England in 1955.   The parcel *arrived* last week.
>
> *b* Joan *has become* engaged; it *took* us completely by surprise. (Here the past tense *took* can be used, because the event has already been identified in the first clause: *has become* . . .)
>
> *c* *Did* you *get* any letters? (Here we can use the past tense without language context, because it is understood that the mail arrives at a given time in the day.)

Note

[a] Because of its definite meaning, a proper noun can provide the conditions for the past tense: *Rome wasn't built in a day.* (a saying); *Caruso was a great singer.* (Here it is implied that Caruso is dead, or at least is no longer a practising singer.)

[b] The past tense can sometimes be used when no definite time 'then' is easily apparent: *Hello, how are you? They **told** me you were ill.* Perhaps this is like *c* above, in that the speaker is *thinking* of a definite time in the past.

124 The past tense also implies a gap between the time referred to and the present moment:

> His sister *suffered* from asthma all her life. (i.e. She's now dead)
>
> His sister *has suffered* from asthma all her life. (i.e. She's still alive)

Adverbials referring to a past point or period of time normally go with the past tense.

> Kites *were invented* in China *in the fifth century*. (see 129)

The present perfect: *I have written the letter*

125 Four related uses of the present perfect may be noted:

(A) PAST EVENT WITH RESULTS IN THE PRESENT TIME

> The taxi *has arrived*. (i.e. 'it's now here')
>
> All police leave *has been cancelled*. (i.e. 'the police remain on duty')
>
> Her doll *has been broken*. (i.e. 'it's still not mended')
>
> (Compare: Her doll was broken, but now it's mended.)

This is the most common use of the present perfect.

(B) INDEFINITE EVENT(S) IN A PERIOD LEADING UP TO THE PRESENT TIME

> *Have* you (ever) *been* to Florence?
>
> All the family *have suffered* from the same illness (in the last five years).

(C) HABIT IN A PERIOD LEADING UP TO THE PRESENT TIME

> She *has attended* lectures regularly (this term).
>
> He*'s played* regularly at Wimbledon since he was eighteen.

(D) STATE LEADING UP TO THE PRESENT TIME

> That supermarket – how long *has it been* open?
>
> She*'s* always *had* a vivid imagination.

In these instances (except for (B)) the states, habits, or events may be understood to continue at the present time; for example, the first sentence in (D) assumes '. . . it is still open'.

Note

[a] In sense (B), the present perfect often refers to the **recent** indefinite past: *Have you eaten (yet)? I've studied your report (already)*. In such cases, <AmE> often prefers the past tense: *Did you study John Grisham's novels yet? I didn't make any lunch yet.*

[b] There is an idiomatic use of the past tense with *always*, *ever* and *never* to refer to a state or habit leading up to the present:

> I *always said* (= have said) he would end up in jail.
>
> *Did* you *ever taste* that seaweed?

The perfect progressive: *I have been writing a letter*

126 The present perfect progressive (*have been writing*, etc.) has the same sort of meaning as the simple present perfect, except that the period leading up to the present typically has **limited duration**:

> I*'ve been studying* for the exams.
>
> What *have* you *been doing*, sleeping all day?
>
> She*'s been explaining* to me what you're doing.

The perfect progressive, like the simple perfect, can suggest that the results of the activity remain in the present: *You've been fighting!* (i.e. I can see that you have been fighting, because you have a black eye, torn clothes, etc.). In such cases the activity has continued up to the **recent past**, not up to the present. Unlike the present perfect, however, the present perfect progressive with event verbs usually suggests an action continuing into the present:

> I*'ve read* your book (= 'I've finished it').
>
> I*'ve been reading* your book (normally = 'I'm still reading it').

The past perfect: *I had written the letter*

127 The past perfect (simple or progressive) means 'past in the past'; that is, a time further in the past as seen from a definite time in the past:

> The house *had been* empty for several months (when we bought it).
>
> The goalkeeper *had injured* his leg, and couldn't play.
>
> It *had been* raining, and the streets were still wet.
>
> Their relationship *had been* ideal until Claire's announcement 'I'm leaving – there's someone else'.

The past perfect is neutral as regards the differences expressed by the past tense and present perfect. This means that if we put the events described in [2] and [3] further into the past, they both end up in the past perfect [2a, 3a].

They tell me that . . .	the parcel *arrived* on April 15th.	[2]
	the parcel *has* already *arrived*.	[3]
They told me that . . .	the parcel *had arrived* on April 15th.	[2a]
	the parcel *had* already *arrived*.	[3a]

When describing one event following another in the past, we can show their relation by using the past perfect for the earlier event, or else we can use the past tense for both, relying on a conjunction (e.g. *after*, *before*, *when*) to show which event took place earlier:

When the guests *had departed*, Sheila *lingered* a little while.

~ When the guests *departed*, Sheila *lingered* a little while.

After the French police *had* successfully *used* dogs, the German authorities too *thought* of using them.

~ After the French police successfully *used* dogs, the German authorities too *thought* of using them.

In these pairs of examples, both sentences have roughly the same meaning. Each sentence indicates that the first happening preceded the second.

Perfect aspect with infinitives and participles: *to have eaten, having eaten*

128 Infinitives and participles (*see* 738) have no tense, and so cannot express the difference between past tense and perfect aspect. Instead, the perfect expresses general past meaning:

He seems *to have missed* the point of your joke. [1]

More than 1,000 people are said *to have been arrested*. [2]

She is proud of *having achieved* stardom while still a child. [3]

Lawes was convicted of *having aided* the rebels by planting bombs. [4]

Sentence [1] could be alternatively expressed:

It seems that he *has missed* the point. OR

It seems that he *missed* the point.

Sentence [3] could be otherwise expressed:

She is proud that she *has achieved* stardom. OR

She is proud that she *achieved* stardom.

In [4], an alternative way of describing the happening would be to use the past perfect (see 127):

Lawes's crime was that he *had aided* the rebels by planting bombs.

There is no difference in the form of the *-ing* form, although the implied time and aspect may change. The same is true, for example, for the perfect infinitive following a modal auxiliary:

He *may have left* yesterday.   (i.e. Perhaps he *left* yesterday)

He *may have left* already.   (i.e. Perhaps he *has* left already)

Adverbials in relation to the past and the present perfect

129 Some adverbials go with the past and others with the present perfect, for example:

● **The past** (a point or period of time which finished in the past):

I *rang* her parents *yesterday* (*evening*).

My first wife *died some years ago*.

The fire *started* just *after ten o'clock*.

A funny thing *happened* to me *last Friday*.

I think someone *mentioned* it to her *the other day*.

In the evening he *attended* an executive meeting of the tennis club.

The conference *opened on Monday, October 30th*.

School *began in August*, the hottest part of the year.

In 2000 a new law *was introduced*.

● **The present perfect** (a period leading up to present, or recent past time)

Since January, life *has been* very busy.

I *haven't* *had* any luck *since I was a baby*.

Plenty of rain *has fallen* here *lately*.

Sixty-six courses *have been held so far*.

Up to now her life *hasn't been* altogether rosy.

● **Either the past or the present perfect**

The following pairs have almost the same meaning. However, in the first pair, the choice of the perfect suggests the speaker is speaking during the morning. The choice of the past, on the other hand, suggests that the morning is already past. But this is not a hard-and-fast rule.

{We *have seen* a lot of horses *this morning*.
{We *saw* a lot of horses *this morning*.

{I *have tried* to speak to you about this *today*.
{I *tried* to speak to you about this *today*.

{*Have* you *spoken* to him *recently*?
{*Did* you *speak* to him *recently*?

State or habit in the past: *used to* and *would*

130 *Used to* (*see* 485) expresses a state or habit in the past, as contrasted with the present:

My uncle *used to keep* horses. (i.e. 'He once kept horses.')

I *used to know* her well (when I was a student).

Would (*see* 291) can also express a past habit, with the particular sense of 'characteristic, predictable behaviour'. This use of *would* is typical of narrative style:

> He *would wait* for her outside the office (every day).

The simple present tense with past meaning

131 There are two special uses where the simple present tense is used with past meaning:

- **The 'historic present'** is sometimes used in past-time narrative, when we want to describe events vividly as if they are really happening now:

  > This lady yesterday, she *says* 'I can't believe this . . .'
  >
  > Then in *comes* the barman and *tries* to stop the fight.

- The present is used **with verbs of communication** (*hear*, *inform*, etc.), where more strictly the present perfect or past would be expected:

  > I *hear* you've finished the building project.
  >
  > The doctor *says* he thinks I had a mild concussion.

The progressive aspect

132 The progressive aspect (*see* 119, 739–42) refers to activity **in progress**, and therefore suggests

> (A) that the activity is *temporary* (i.e. of limited duration)
>
> (B) that it *does not have to be complete*

The second element of meaning (B) is most evident in the past tense or in the present perfect:

> { He *wrote* a novel several years ago. (i.e. he finished it)
>
> { He *was writing* a novel several years ago (but I don't know whether he finished it).
>
> { They*'ve mended* the car this morning. (i.e. the job's finished)
>
> { They*'ve been mending* the car this morning. (but the job may not be finished)

With verbs referring to a change of state, the progressive indicates movement towards the change, rather than completion of the change itself:

> The young man *was drowning* (but at the last moment I rescued him).

When linked to a non-progressive event verb, or to a point or period of time, the progressive verb normally shows that the activity or situation described by the verb is still in progress, i.e. has started but has not yet finished:

> When I went downstairs they **were** (already) **eating** breakfast.

Other examples:

> I knew the person who **was working** here last year.
>
> High winds and heavy seas **have been causing** further damage (today).
>
> As I came in, Agnes looked up from the book she **was reading**.
>
> I'm happy to say my arthritis **is getting** better.

Verbs which take, or do not take, the progressive

133 The verbs which most typically take the progressive are verbs denoting

- **activities** (*walk, read, drink, write, work*, etc.):

  > A small boy in a blue jacket **was walking** along the street.
  >
  > I'**m writing** a letter to my sister in England.

- or **processes** (*change, grow, widen, improve*, etc.):

  > Alec **was growing** more and more impatient.
  >
  > I believe the political situation **is improving**.

- Verbs denoting **momentary** events (*knock, jump, nod, kick*, etc.), if used in the progressive, suggest repetition:

  > He **nodded**. (one movement of the head)
  >
  > He **was nodding**. (repeated movements of the head)

134 State verbs often cannot be used with the progressive at all, because the notion of 'something in progress' cannot be easily applied to them. The verbs which normally do NOT take the progressive include the following classes.

Verbs of perceiving

135 *Feel, hear, see, smell, taste*. To express continuing perception, we often use these verbs with *can* or *could*:

> I **can see** someone through the window, but I **can't hear** what they're saying. (NOT *I am seeing ... *I'm not hearing ...)

Verbs which have as their subject the thing perceived, such as *sound* and *look*, can also be included here:

You *look* ridiculous, in that hat. (NOT *You are looking ridiculous . . .)

It *sounds* as if the concert's already started. (NOT *It is sounding . . .)

Verbs referring to a state of mind or feeling

136 *Believe, adore, desire, detest, dislike, doubt, forget, hate, hope, imagine, know, like, love, mean, prefer, remember, suppose, understand, want, wish,* etc.

I *suppose* I'd better buy them a Christmas present.
(NOT: *I am supposing . . .)

I *hope* I haven't kept you all waiting.

I *doubt* whether the standards of the schools are improving.

The verbs *seem* and *appear* may also be included here:

He *seems/appears* to be enjoying himself.

Verbs referring to a relationship or a state of being

137 *Be, belong to, concern, consist of, contain, cost, depend on, deserve, equal, fit, have, involve, matter, owe, own, possess, remain, require, resemble,* etc.

She *belongs* to the Transport and General Workers' Union.

Most mail these days *contains* nothing that could be truly called a letter.

Notice that all these verbs are used without the progressive even when they refer to a temporary state:

I'*m* hungry.

I *forget* his name for the moment.

Note
The verb *have,* when it is a state verb, does not go with the progressive: *He has a good job.* (NOT: *He is having a good job.*) But *have* often goes with the progressive when it denotes a process or activity: *They were having breakfast.*

Verbs referring to an internal sensation

138 There is a fourth group of verbs, referring to internal sensation (*hurt, feel, ache, itch,* etc.). These can be used either with the progressive or the non-progressive with little difference of effect:

My back $\begin{cases} \textit{hurts.} \\ \textit{is hurting.} \end{cases}$ I $\begin{cases} \textit{felt} \\ \textit{was feeling} \end{cases}$ ill.

Exceptions where the progressive is used

139 The types of verb in 134–7 above may be labelled 'non-progressive' but there are special cases in which you hear them used with the progressive. In many cases like these, it can be said that the state verb has changed into an 'activity verb' (referring to an active form of behaviour). Thus, in place of *see* and *hear*, we have the equivalent activity verbs *look* (*at*) and *listen* (*to*):

> Why *are* you *looking* at me like that?

> She *was listening* to the news when I phoned.

But for *smell*, *feel*, and *taste*, there is no special activity verb, so these verbs have the role of expressing activity as well as state meaning:

> She *was feeling* in her little pocket for a handkerchief. [activity]

> The water *felt* wonderful on her skin. [state]

> Similarly: The doctor *was listening to* her heartbeat. [activity] He says it *sounds* normal. [state]

> We've just *been tasting* the soup. [activity] It really *tastes* delicious. [state]

In the same way, *think*, *imagine*, *hope*, *expect* etc. are sometimes used as 'mental activity' verbs:

> I'*m thinking* about what you were saying.

> He'*s hoping* to finish his training before the end of the year.

The verb *be* can go with the progressive when the adjective or noun which follows it refers to a type of behaviour, or to the role a person is adopting:

> She's *being very brave*. (= 'acting very bravely')

> 'She is *being a hero* over all this,' thought Tom miserably. (= 'acting like a hero')

Note
Another exceptional case is the use of the progressive with *hope*, *want*, etc. to express greater <tentativeness> and <tact>:

> We *are hoping* you will support us.

> *Were* you *wanting* to see me?

Future time

140 There are five main ways of expressing future time in the English verb phrase. The most important future constructions are those which use *will* or *shall* and *be going to* (A and B below). Of these, *will* is by far the most common option, particularly in <writing>.

(A) Will or shall (*see* 483)

141 The neutral future of prediction is expressed by *will* (often reduced to *'ll*), or by *shall* (which is <rather formal and rare> and normally occurs only with a first-person subject):

> Temperatures tomorrow **will be** much the same as today.

> We **shall hear** the results of the election within a week.

Will is particularly common in the main clause of a conditional sentence (*see* 207–14):

> If the book has real merit, it **will sell**.

> Wherever you go, you **will find** the local people friendly.

> In that case, I guess I'**ll have** to change my plan.

But with personal subjects, *will/shall* usually suggests an element of intention:

> I'**ll see** you again on Tuesday.

> They'**ll make** a cup of coffee if you ask them.

(B) Be going to

142 *Be going to* + INFINITIVE tends to indicate the future as a fulfilment of the present. It may refer to a future resulting from a present intention:

> **Are**n't you **going to put** a coat on? It's cold out.

> She said that she'**s going to visit** Vic at two o'clock.

> She says she'**s going to be** a doctor when she grows up.

It may also refer to the future resulting from other causative factors in the present:

> I think I'**m going to faint**. (i.e. I already feel ill)

> It'**s going to rain**. (i.e. I can already see black clouds gathering)

> I'm afraid we'**re going to have to** stop the meeting now.

In sentences like these last three, *be going to* also carries the expectation that the event will happen **soon**.

(C) Progressive aspect

143 The present progressive is used for future events arising from a present plan, programme, or arrangement:

> We're *inviting* several people to a party.
>
> She's *going* back to Montreal in a couple of days.
>
> What *are* you *doing* for lunch?

Like *be going to*, this construction (especially when there is no time adverbial such as *in a couple of days*) often suggests the **near** future: *Charlotte's giving up her job* (= soon).

(D) Simple present tense

144 The simple present tense is used for the future in certain types of subordinate clause, especially adverbial time clauses (*when she comes in*) and conditional clauses (*if she comes in*) (160, 207):

> I'll get her to phone you *when/if/after* she *comes* in.

(Notice, though, that the verb in the **main** clause has *will*.) Some of the conjunctions which go with the present tense in this way are *after, as, before, once, until, when, as soon as, if, even if, unless, as long as. That*-clauses following *hope, assume, suppose*, etc. can also contain a verb in the present tense referring to the future:

> I hope the train *is* on time.   ~ I hope the train *will be* on time.
>
> Just suppose the network *fails*. It *will be* a total disaster.

Apart from these cases, the simple present is used (but not very often) for future events which are seen as absolutely certain, because they are determined in advance by calendar or timetable, or because they are part of an unalterable plan:

> Tomorrow *is* Wednesday.
>
> The term *finishes* at the beginning of July.
>
> Actually the match *begins* at three on Thursday.
>
> Miss Walpole *retires* at the end of the year.

In these sentences, the speaker treats the event as a fact, and puts aside the doubt one naturally feels about the future. Compare:

> When *do* we *get* there? (e.g. according to the flight schedule)
>
> When *will* we *get* there? (e.g. if we travel by car)

(E) Will/shall + progressive aspect (Shall is <rather rare and formal>)

145 *Will* (or *'ll* or *shall*) followed by the progressive can be used in a regular way to add the temporary meaning of the progressive to the future meaning of the *will* construction (*see* 141):

> Don't call her at seven o'clock – they'*ll* **be eating** dinner then.

But in addition, we can use the *will* + progressive construction in a special way to refer to a future event which will take place 'as a matter of course', especially in the near future:

> What do you think you'*ll* **be doing** at school today?
>
> We **will be taking part** in an international conference on global warming on January 30th.

This is particularly useful for avoiding the suggestion of intention in the simple *will*-construction. It can therefore be <more tentative and polite>:

> When **will** you **come** to see us again?   [4]
>
> When **will** you **be coming** to see us again? <more tentative>   [5]

Sentence [4] is most likely to be a question about the hearer's intentions, while sentence [5] simply asks the hearer to predict the time of the next visit.

Be to, be about to, be on the point of

146 Some less common ways of expressing future meaning are illustrated here:

> Jaguar *is to* launch a new saloon model, the XJ 4.0S. <rather formal>
>
> I'*m* **about to write** the director a nasty letter.
>
> She **was** just **on the point of moving** when the message arrived.

Be + *to*-infinitive signifies a plan for the future (especially an official arrangement), while both *be about to* and *be on the point of* both emphasize the nearness of a future event.

The future in the past

147 We can put the future constructions already mentioned (except the simple present) into the past tense. We then arrive at a 'future in the past' meaning (i.e. future seen from a viewpoint in the past). But such a meaning, e.g. with *was going to* and *was about to*, usually conveys the idea that the anticipated happening did not take place:

They *were* just *going to arrest* him, when he escaped from the building.

The priceless tapestry *was about to catch* fire, but was fortunately saved through the prompt action of the fire service.

Was/were to and *would* can refer to the fulfilled future in the past, but in this sense they are rather rare and <literary> in style:

After defeating Pompey's supporters, Caesar *returned* to Italy and proclaimed himself the permanent 'dictator' of Rome. He *was to pay* dearly for his ambition in due course: a year later one of his best friends, Marcus Brutus, *would lead* a successful plot to assassinate him.

For a series of events like this, the ordinary past tense can also be used throughout: *returned, . . . paid, . . . led*, etc.

Note

The future in the past is often expressed by *would, was going to*, etc. in **reported speech** (*see* 264–8).

The past in the future

148 The past in the future is expressed by *will* + perfect infinitive:

I am hoping that by the end of the month you **will have finished** your report.

In three months' time, the plant **will have taken** root.

In subordinate clauses which allow the simple present for future time (*see* 144), the present perfect can express past in the future:

Phone me later, when you **have finished** your dinner.

Summary

149 In conclusion, here is a table summarising some of the commonest meanings expressed through tense and aspect. The symbols used are explained first.

single event	•
state	——————
habit or series of events	• • • • • • • •
temporary state or event	〰〰〰
temporary habit	ᰜᰜᰜ

The time dimension is expressed by a left-to-right arrow chain:
(→ → → → → →).
A definite point of time ('NOW' or 'THEN') is expressed by a dotted vertical line (⋮). The broken arrow (·········▶) indicates anticipation of something happening at a later time.

'THEN'   'NOW'   'THEN'
Past time   Present time   Future time

A PRESENT TIME

1 State (see 116)   I like Mary.
2 Single event (see 117)   I resign.
3 Habitual (see 118)   She gets up early.
4 Temporary (see 119)   He's drinking Scotch.
5 Temporary habit (see 120)   She's getting up early (nowadays).

THE PRESENT PROGRESSIVE

B PAST TIME

1 State up to present time (see 125)   I've known her for years.
2 Indefinite event(s) (see 125)   I've seen better plays.
3 Habit up to present time (see 125)   He's conducted that orchestra for 15 years.
4 With present result (see 125)   You've ruined my dress!
5 Temporary state up to present time (see 126)   I've been waiting for an hour.
6 Temporary habit up to present time   He's been walking since he was 8 months old.
7 Temporary, with present result (see 126)   You've been smoking!

THE PRESENT PERFECT

THE PRESENT PERFECT PROGRESSIVE

THE PRESENT PERFECT

THE PRESENT TENSE

	1 Definite state (see 115)	I lived in Africa when I was young.
	2 Definite event (see 115)	I saw him yesterday.
	3 Definite habit (see 115)	I {got / used to get} up early in those days.
THE PAST PROGRESSIVE	4 Definite temporary (see 132)	We were watching TV.
THE PAST PERFECT	5 Past before past time (event) (see 127)	I had visited the island before.
	6 State up to past time (see 127)	I had known him since birth.
THE PAST PERFECT PROGRESSIVE	7 Temporary state up to past time (see 127)	They had been lying in wait for him.

THE PAST TENSE

C FUTURE TIME

	1 Future time (neutral) (see 141)	The letter will arrive tomorrow.
Will/shall		
Be going to	2 Future time (arising from present time) (see 142)	Prices are going to rise.
THE PRESENT PROGRESSIVE	3 Future time (plan or arrangement) (see 143)	We're moving next week.
THE SIMPLE PRESENT	4 Future time (as fact) (see 144)	The match starts at 2.00 p.m.
Will/shall + THE PROGRESSIVE	5 Future time (as matter of course) (see 145)	I'll be seeing you soon.
Will/shall + THE PROGRESSIVE	6 Future time (temporary) (see 145)	The astronauts will be sleeping at 4.00 a.m.
Will/shall + THE PERFECT	7 Past in Future time (see 148)	The plane will have landed by then.

Time-when

151 Notions of time-when are expressed either by tense, aspect, and auxiliaries in the verb phrase, or by adverbials. The adverbial can be of a number of types:

They fixed the radiator **yesterday**.	(ADVERB)
She phoned **on Thursday**.	(PREPOSITIONAL PHRASE)
Jennifer's coming to lunch **next week**.	(NOUN PHRASE)
Twelve months ago he found himself without a job.	(NOUN PHRASE + **ago**, **back**, etc.)
We met several years ago **while I was working in China**.	(ADVERBIAL CLAUSE)

Such time expressions normally have an adverbial function in the sentence (*see* 451), but they can also act as the modifier in a noun phrase (*the meeting yesterday; yesterday's meeting*), and occasionally as subject or complement: *The day after tomorrow will be Friday.*

Time-when adverbials answer the question 'When?' Thus all the adverbials listed above could answer the questions *When did they fix it? When did she phone?*, etc. It is most useful to begin the study of time-when with prepositional phrases.

At, on, in and during

152 *At* is used for points of time, and *on* and *in* for periods of time. In general, *on* is used for days, and *in* (or *during*) for periods longer or shorter than a day:

Clock time:	at 10 o'clock, at 6.30 p.m., at noon
Days:	on Sunday, (on) the following day
Other periods:	in/during the morning/April/the nineteenth century during (the) spring/2002/the Stone Age

Some examples:

Her father arrived home **at six o'clock**.

A meeting will be held **at 12.45 p.m.** in the Committee Room.

We're going to the cottage **on Sunday**.

In the summer, roses climb the walls of the courtyard and **in autumn ‖ the fall** the country smell of burning leaves hangs in the air.

Many varieties of shrubs blossom **during April and May**.

For periods identified by their beginning and ending points, *between* is used:

Between 1918 and 1939 many people in the West lost their faith in democracy.

In and *during*

153 *In* and *during* are more or less equivalent:

> He had been an airman *in/during the Second World War*.
>
> You can come back tomorrow *in/during visiting hours*.

Only *during* can be used to mean 'in the course of' before nouns like *stay, visit, meal, conversation*, etc. referring to an event lasting some time:

> We went to the zoo *during our stay in Washington*.
>
> *During the peace talks*, there was a complete news blackout.
>
> The Mayor always falls asleep *during the after-dinner speeches*.

Note
The preposition *in* (or *within* <more formal>) can have the meaning 'before the end of' a specified length of time:

> Phileas Fogg travelled round the world *in eighty days*.
>
> Phone me again *within a week*. (OR: Phone me again *in a week's time*.)

Exceptions: *at, on,* and *by*

154 ● *At* can be used for periods identified vaguely, as in *at that time, at breakfast time, at night*; also for short holiday periods (*at Christmas, at Easter*). In <BrE>, *at the weekend* is used, but in <AmE> *on the weekend*.

> Cars belonging to visitors at a local beauty spot were broken into *at || on* the weekend.

● *On* is used before *morning, afternoon, evening,* and *night* when these periods are identified by the day they belong to: *on Monday night, on the following evening,* but *in the evening/night*. (On omitting the definite article in such time expressions, *see* 475.)

> A Yamaha motorbike was stolen from the Kwik Save car park *on Saturday morning*.

● *By day* and *by night* are idioms which can replace *during the day/ night* with some activities such as travelling:

> We travelled *by night* and rested *by day*.

Omitting the preposition

155 We almost always leave out the preposition before phrases beginning *last, next, this, that;* also before *today, yesterday, tomorrow*:

He enjoyed coming out with us *last Saturday*.

Next time you're in town, phone me at this number.

We can't afford to go abroad *this year*.

That day I had nothing important to do.

See you *tomorrow*!

The phrases *at this/that time, on this/that occasion* are however exceptions:

On that occasion the government was saved by the intervention of the Liberal Democrats. <rather formal>

In <informal> English, we also usually leave out the preposition in phrases pointing to a time related indirectly to the present moment, or to a time before or after a definite time in the past or future:

I met her (*on*) *the day after her birthday*.

She got married (*in*) *the year after her graduation*.

(*During*) *the week before last*, I was at a conference in Warsaw.

The festival will be held (*in*) *the following spring*.

The preposition is also sometimes omitted directly before days of the week:

I'll see you (*on*) *Wednesday*, then.

Well, Iris is there (*on*) *Wednesdays and Fridays*. (see 167 Note)

This omission is especially common in <informal AmE>.

Time relationships: *before, after, by, etc.*

156 ● *Before* and *after* (as prepositions, adverbs, and conjunctions) indicate a relation of one time or event to another, as in:

The service was so much better *before the war*. (*before* = preposition)

We'd never met her *before*. (*before* = adverb = 'before that time')

Before she had gone very far, she heard a noise. (*before* = conjunction)

The secretary had left immediately *after the meeting*. (*after* = preposition)

After they had gone, there was an awkward little silence. (*after* = conjunction)

Before and *after* have opposite meanings, so the following are equivalent:

She arrived *after* the play started.

~ The play started *before* she arrived.

● *By* identifies a time when the result of an event is in existence ('not later than'):

By Friday I was exhausted. (i.e. I became exhausted in the period that ended on Friday)

Please send me the tickets **by next week**. (i.e. I want to have the tickets not later than next week)

● *Already*, *still*, *yet*, and *any more* are related in meaning to *by*-phrases.

Already and *yet* require the perfect aspect (or the Simple Past in <AmE>) when referring to a single event: *They have already left; Have you eaten yet?* With state verbs and with the progressive aspect, they can occur with the present tense: *I know that already; He's not yet working*. Note the negative relation of *already* and *yet* to *still* and *any more*:

He **still** works at the City Hall. (= He hasn't stopped working there **yet**.)

He's **already** stopped working there. (= He isn't working there **any more**.)

● We use **by now** often when we are not certain that the event has happened:

The wound should have healed **by now**. (. . . but I'm not sure)

Otherwise we prefer to use *already*:

We've **already** done everything we can.

Comparing prepositions of time

157 Here, for comparison, are some examples of time phrases with a particular noun, *night*:

What are you doing, throwing stones into our yard **in the middle of the night**?

It often rains quite heavily **in the night**. (*see* 153)

During the night the rain stopped. (*see* 153)

At night I relax. (*see* 154)

By night, Dartmouth was a dazzling city. (*see* 154)

I shall have to work **nights**. (*see* 167 Note)

I'll be there **by Friday night**. (*see* 156)

For several nights he slept badly. (*see* 161)

They walked **all night**. (*see* 162)

We're staying on the island **over night**. (*see* 163)

Measuring time: *ago, from now*, etc.

158 *Ago* following a noun phrase of length-of-time measure means '. . . before now': *We met a year ago*. For a similar measurement into the future, we use *from now*, or *in* + measure phrase, or *in* + genitive measure phrase + *time*:

$$\text{I'll see you} \begin{cases} \textit{in three months.} \\ \textit{(in) three months from now.} \\ \textit{in three months' time.} \end{cases}$$

In measuring forwards from a point of time in the past, only the first alternative is available:

They finished the job **in three months**. (i.e. from when they started it)

Before and *after*, and the adverbs *beforehand* and *afterwards*, *earlier* and *later*, can also follow a length-of-time measure phrase:

I had met them **three months before**(hand).

Ten years after his death, he suddenly became famous.

Time-when adverbs

159 There are two main groups of time-when adverbs (*see* 456):

[A] *again, just* (= 'at this very moment'), *now, nowadays, then* (= 'at that time'), *today*, etc.

[B] *afterwards, before*(hand), *first, formerly, just* (= 'a very short time ago/before'), *late*(r), *lately, next, previously, recently, since, soon, subsequently* <formal>, *then* (= 'after that'), *ultimately* <formal>, etc.

Group [A] identifies a point or period of time directly; Group [B] identifies a time indirectly, by reference to another point of time understood in the context.

Examples:

[A] Prices in the UK are **now** the second lowest in Europe.

She's not in town much **nowadays**.

Is the show **just** starting?

[B] We'll see the movie first, and discuss it **afterwards**.

Lucy has/had **just** made the tea.

Mr Brooking was **previously** general sales manager at the company.

Anna was **recently** offered a job as top fashion designer for Harrods.

At the next election he lost his seat, and has not turned to politics **since**. (= 'since that time')

Time-when conjunctions

160 The main time-when conjunctions are *when, as, before, after* (*see* 156), *while* (*see* 164), *as soon as, once, now* (*that*):

It was almost totally dark **when they arrived**.

We'll let you know **as soon as we've made up our minds**.

Once you have taken the examination, you'll be able to relax.

Duration: *for, over, from . . . to,* etc.

161 Phrases of duration answer the question 'How long?' Compare:

[A] *When* did you stay there? [B] *In the summer.* (TIME-WHEN)

[A] *How long* did you stay there? [B] *For the summer.* (DURATION)

The phrase *in the summer* here indicates that the stay was **included** in the summer period. The phrase *for the summer* indicates that the stay lasted **as long as** the summer period. *For* with this meaning can also precede phrases of length-of-time, e.g. *for a month, for several days, for two years.*

Omitting *for*: *I'll be at home all day*

162 The preposition *for* is often left out:

I went to Oxford in the autumn of 1989, and was there (*for*) *four years*.

The snowy weather lasted (*for*) *the whole winter*.

For must be omitted before *all*:

Except for about half an hour, I'll be at home *all day* today.

For is generally not omitted when it comes first in the sentence:

For several years they lived in poverty.

or when it follows a negative

I haven't seen him *for eight years*.

Note
With the verbs *spend, take* and *waste, for* is never used:

We spent *two weeks* at the seaside.

It took me *a couple of hours* to finish the job. [Here the phrase of duration is a direct object, rather than an adverbial.]

Other uses of prepositions meaning duration

163 ● *Over* can be used instead of *for* for short periods such as holidays:

We stayed with my parents *over the holiday/weekend*.

She had such an unhappy time *over Christmas*.

What have you been doing with yourself *over the New Year*?

 ● *From . . . to* identify a period by its beginning and end: *from nine to five; from June to December:*

Hayes worked for the CIA *from 1949 to 1970*.

- *From . . . through*, in <AmE>, are used to make clear that the whole period includes the second period named. Thus *from June through December* means '. . . up to and including December'.

- *Up to* often specifies that the longer period does NOT include the period named:

    He worked *up to Christmas*. (i.e. but not over Christmas)

- *Until* (or *till*) (*see* 164) can replace *to* in the construction *from . . . to . . .*: *from Monday until Friday*. But, with *from* absent, *to* cannot be used:

    We stayed *until five*. (NOT: *We stayed *to five*.)

While, since *and* until

164 ● *While* is a conjunction meaning either (*a*) 'duration' or (*b*) 'time-when', depending on the kind of verb meaning (*see* 114–15).

    a   I stayed *while the meeting lasted* (i.e. for the duration of the meeting). [*stay* is a STATE VERB]

    b   I arrived *while the meeting was in progress* (i.e. in the course of the meeting). [*arrive* is an EVENT VERB]

- *Since* as a conjunction or preposition also has these two functions:

    a   He's lived here (*ever*) *since he was born* (i.e. for his whole life, from his birth up to now). [*live* is a STATE VERB]

    b   They've changed their car twice *since 1999* (i.e. between 1999 and now). [*change* is an EVENT VERB]

It is important to notice that *since* normally requires the perfect aspect in the verb of the main clause:

    I*'ve been* here in the laboratory *since four o'clock*. (NOT: *I am here in the laboratory . . .)

- *Until* (or *till*) as preposition and conjunction has a meaning comparable to example *a* of *since* (the STATE VERB sense). But it names the end-point (rather than the beginning point) of a period:

    I think you'd better stay in bed *until next Monday*. (i.e. from now to next Monday)

In the negative, *until* can occur with event verbs, and is similar in meaning to *before*:

    He didn't learn to read *until he was ten*.

    ~ He didn't learn to read *before he was ten*.

Adverbs and idioms of duration: *always, recently, etc.*

165 The following adverbs and idiomatic phrases indicate duration:

> *always, for ever* (both meaning 'for all time') (but *see also* 166)
>
> *since* ('since then'), also *recently, lately* (both meaning 'since a short time ago')
>
> *temporarily, for the moment, for a while* (all meaning 'for a short time')
>
> *for ages* <informal> ('for a long time')

Examples:

> There's something I'(ve) *always* wanted to ask you.
>
> They thought their city would last *for ever*.
>
> I've been suffering from sleepless nights just *lately*.
>
> *For the moment* there was no woman in his life.
>
> I waited *for ages* but your phone was apparently disconnected.

Since, lately, and *recently* indicate either time-when or duration according to the type of verb meaning:

> They got married only *recently*. (= 'a short time ago')
>
> He's *recently* been working nights. <informal> (= 'since a short time ago')

Frequency

166 Expressions of FREQUENCY answer the question 'How many times?' or 'How often?' The upper and lower limits of frequency are expressed by *always* ('on every occasion') and *never* ('on no occasion'). Between these extremes, a rough indication of frequency (INDEFINITE FREQUENCY) can be given by:

most frequent	*nearly always, almost always*
	usually, normally, generally, regularly (= 'on most occasions')
	often, frequently (= 'on many occasions')
	sometimes (= 'on some occasions')
	occasionally, now and then <informal> (= 'on a few occasions')
least frequent	*rarely, seldom* (= 'on few occasions')
	hardly ever, scarcely ever (= 'almost never')

(Compare 80–1.)

Being more precise about frequency

167 A more exact measurement of frequency (**definite frequency**) can be expressed in one of the following three ways:

- **once a day**, *three times an hour, several times a week* (sometimes *per* <formal, official> is used instead of *a(n)* here: *once per day*):

> They ate only *once a day*.
>
> I go to the office *five times a week*.

- **every day** (= 'once a day'), *every morning, every two years*:

> We went for long walks *every day*.
>
> The board meets *every week* in Chicago.

- **daily** (= 'once a day'), *hourly, weekly, monthly, yearly. Daily, weekly*, etc. can act as adjectives as well as adverbs:

> I read *The Times daily*.   A *daily* newspaper.
>
> She is paid *monthly* in arrears.   A *monthly* magazine.

Notice the equivalence of:

$$
\text{He visits me} \left\{ \begin{array}{l} \textit{once a week} \\ \textit{every week} \\ \textit{weekly} \end{array} \right\} = \text{He pays me a } \textit{weekly} \text{ visit.}
$$

We can also say *once every day, twice weekly*, etc. *Every other day/week* etc. means '*every two days/weeks*'.

- A further type of frequency expression involves the use of quantifiers like *some, any, most, many* (*see* 80, 676):

> *Some days* I feel like giving up the job altogether.
>
> Come and see me *any time you like*.
>
> We play tennis *most weekends*.
>
> He's been to Russia *many times* as a reporter.

Note

There is an <informal> usage in which a plural time noun appears without any determiner: *mornings, nights, weekends, Saturdays*:

> I always worked *Friday nights*.

This can be classified either as a frequency or as a time-when phrase (*see* 155).

On . . . occasions

168 Frequency phrases generally have no preposition: we say *every week*, NOT **in every week*. One exception is when we use the word *occasion(s)*, which is <rather formal>:

> *On several occasions* the President has refused to bow to the will of Congress.
>
> It has been my privilege to work with Roy Mason *on numerous occasions*.

Abstract frequency

169 Frequency phrases sometimes lose much of their time meaning, and get a more abstract meaning, referring to **instances** rather than **times**. *Always* and *sometimes* (for example) can be interpreted 'in every case', 'in some cases', rather than 'on every occasion', 'on some occasions':

> Medical books *always* seem to cost the earth.
>
> The young animals are *sometimes* abandoned by their parents.
>
> Children *often* ('in many cases') dislike tomatoes. (roughly = 'Many children dislike tomatoes')
>
> Students *rarely* ('in few cases') used to fail this course. (roughly = 'Few students used to fail this course.')

Place, direction and distance

170 Expressions of place and direction are mainly adverbials and postmodifiers. They answer the question *Where?*, so that all of the following could be answers to the question *Where did you leave the bicycle?*:

I left it
- *(over) there.* (ADVERB – *see* 454, 469)
- *in the park.* (PREPOSITIONAL PHRASE – *see* 645–6)
- *two miles away.* (NOUN PHRASE + *away*, *back*, etc. – *see* 595–6)
- *where I found it.* (ADVERBIAL CLAUSE – *see* 495)

Place expressions occasionally also act as subject or complement of a sentence:

> *Over here* is *where I put the books*. <informal>

You will see that the range of grammatical structures and functions for expressing place is similar to that for expressing time (*see* 151). Also notice that many words (e.g. the prepositions *at*, *from*, and *between*) have related meanings in the two fields.

Prepositions of place

171 Apart from general adverbs like *here*, *there*, and *everywhere*, the most important words for indicating place are prepositions. The choice of preposition is often governed by the way we see an object, i.e. whether we see it:

(A)	as a point in space	×	(*see* 172)
(B)	as a line	⎯⎯	(*see* 173–4)
(C)	as a surface		
(D)	as an area		(*see* 175–6)
(E)	as a volume		

The difference between 'surface' and 'area' will be explained below (*see* 174–5, 183). We distinguish

- **'*at*-type' prepositions**, which indicate a point (A)
- **'*on*-type' prepositions**, which indicate a line or a surface (B or C)
- **'*in*-type' prepositions**, which indicate an area or a volume (D or E)

Some prepositions (such as *across*) belong to more than one of these types.

At-type prepositions

172 (A) **The place is seen as a POINT** (i.e. a location which is identified quite generally, without being thought of in terms of length, width, or height).

	to	*at*	*(away) from*	*away from*
	→×	●×	×→	×　　●
	1	2	3	4

1 We went ⎰ to Stratford. / to the hotel. / to the door. ⎱

3 We came (away) ⎰ from the theatre. / from the house. / from the bus-stop. ⎱

2 We stayed ⎰ at home. / at an inn. / at the entrance. ⎱

4 We stayed ⎰ away from home. / away from England. / away from the village. ⎱

On-type prepositions: *line*

173 (B) **The place is seen as a LINE**, i.e. is a place thought of in terms of length, but not breadth or height (depth):

	on (to)	*on*	*off*	*off*	*across, over*	*along*
	1	2	3	4	5	6

1. The wagon rolled back **on to the road**. (ALSO written **onto**)
2. The company headquarters was at a town **on the Mississippi River**.
3. We turned **off Greenville Avenue** onto Cherry Hill Road.
4. They were a hundred miles **off the coast of Sri Lanka**.
5. Another man tried to swim **across the river**.
6. The power was off in houses **along Smith Street**.

On-type prepositions: *surface*

174 (C) **The place is seen as a SURFACE,** i.e. is thought of in terms of length and width, but not height (or depth). (The surface need not be flat or horizontal.)

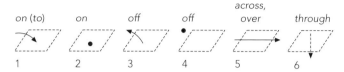

The surface is often the *top* of some object (*on* = *on top of*): *He was lying on the bed; The book fell off the table.*

1. fall **on** (to) the floor	4. a place **off** the map
2. the label **on** the bottle	5. a walk **across** the fields
3. take the picture **off** the wall	6. looking **through** the window

Note

[a] *On* etc. is also used for public transport:

There were only a few passengers **on the bus/train/plane.**

We can also say: *He travelled by bus/train/plane*, etc. (see 197, 475)

[b] Notice also *an apple* **on** *a tree, the ring* **on** *her finger* (where *on* = 'attached to' or 'adhering to')

In-type prepositions: *area*

175 (D) **The place is seen as an AREA** (usually an area of ground or territory enclosed by boundaries):

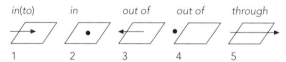

1. Crowds pour *into the city* from the neighbouring villages.
2. They had found suitable lodgings for her *in the town*.
3. The manuscript was smuggled *out of the country*.
4. He stayed *out of the district*.
5. We went for a walk *through the park*.

In-type prepositions: *volume*

176 (E) **The place is seen as a VOLUME,** i.e. is thought of in terms of length, width, height (or depth):

1. The girl stepped *into the hall*.
2. The food is *in the cupboard*.
3. He climbed *out of the water*.
4. He *was out of the room*.
5. The wind blew *through the trees*.

Note

<BrE> has *out of* but <AmE> usually just *out* in expressions like this:

She looked *out of* || *out* the window.

Inside, outside, within

177 *Inside* and *outside* are sometimes used instead of *in*(to) and *out of*:

Were you *inside the house* when the fire started?

She was sitting just *outside the surgery*.

Within is a slightly more <formal> word than *in*, and often indicates a location bounded by limits, or by a given distance (*within 3 miles*, etc.):

Many prisoners died *within the walls of the castle*. (= inside)

He lives *within a stone's throw of the office*. (= not beyond)

Put in, put on, etc.

178 Some common transitive verbs such as *put, place, lay, stand* are followed by *on* and *in* rather than *on to* and *into*:

Jane *put* each object back *in* its allotted place.

She *placed* her hand *on* Kate's hair.

Also, *arrive* goes with *at, on,* or *in*: *The train arrives at/in Brussels at 7.15.* (*see* 171, 180)

Overlap between types of preposition

179 We can often use different prepositions with the same noun. But in such cases, the meaning will be slightly different:

My car is *at the cottage*. (POINT, i.e. the cottage as a general location)

They are putting a new roof *on the cottage*. (SURFACE)

There are only two beds *in the cottage*. (VOLUME)

Overlap between *at*-type and *in*-type prepositions

180 For towns and villages, either *at* or *in* is used, depending on point of view. *At Stratford* means we are seeing Stratford simply as a place on the map; *in Stratford* means we have a 'close up' view of the place as a town covering an area, and containing streets, houses, etc. A very large town or city is generally treated as an area: *in New York*. *At New York* would be used only in a context of worldwide travel:

> We stopped to refuel **at New York** on our way to Tokyo.

Parts of cities also require *in*:

> **in Chelsea** (part of London), **in Brooklyn** (part of New York)

For continents, countries, states, and other large areas we use *in*:

> **in Asia, in China, in Virginia**

However, the directional words *to* and *from* are preferred to *into*, etc. even for large territories, except where those territories border one another:

> He sailed **from** Europe **to** Canada.
> We crossed the Rhine **into** Germany.

At/in the post office, etc.

181 For buildings or groups of buildings, you can use either *at* or *in*, but it is better to use *at* when thinking of the building as an institution – a place with a special function – rather than simply as a place. (Many such nouns with *at* take no definite article: *at school*, etc. – *see* 475.)

> You can buy stamps **at the post office**.
> BUT: I left my purse **at/in the post office**.

> The princess, aged 24, is now studying history **at Cambridge** (= the university).
> BUT: She is staying with a friend **at/in Cambridge** (= the city).

Shout to, shout at, etc.

182 *At* is used instead of *to* when the following noun indicates a target:

> He threw the ball **at me**. (i.e. 'He tried to hit me')
> Eddie threw the ball **to Phil**. (i.e. 'for him to catch')

Note also a similar contrast between:

> 'Hey, you', the man shouted **at her**. (suggests that he was angry with her)
> Peter shouted **to me**. (suggests that Peter was trying to communicate with me at a distance)

Other contrasts of the same general kind are seen in:

He pointed his pistol **at Jess**. 'Don't shoot!' cried the old man.

She passed/handed a note **to the next speaker**.

Similar cases are: *aim* [*a gun*] *at, hand* [*a ball*] *to.*

Overlap between *on*-type and *in*-type prepositions: *sit on/in the grass*, etc.

183 There is a difference between 'surface' and 'volume' in:

We sat **on the grass**. (SURFACE: i.e. the grass is short)

We sat **in the grass**. (VOLUME: i.e. the grass is long)

Another difference (between 'surface' and 'area') is seen in:

Robinson Crusoe was marooned **on a desert island**. (SURFACE: i.e. the island is small)

It's the most influential newspaper **in Cuba**. (AREA: i.e. Cuba is a large island, and a political unit with boundaries)

Position: *over, under, in front of, behind*, etc.

184 Position is a relation between two objects, and can best be explained by a picture. Imagine a car standing on a bridge:

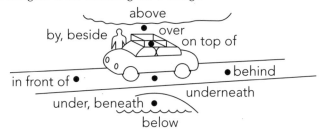

- *Over* and *under* tend to indicate a direct vertical relationship, or nearness:

The injured girl had a bad cut **over the left eye**.

The doctor was leaning **over her**.

On the other hand, *above* and *below* may mean simply that one object is on a higher or lower level than the other. *Under* and *underneath* often mean that one object is actually touching the other. In this respect they are the opposite of *on top of*:

The children evaded capture by hiding **under(neath) a pile of rugs**.

- *By* and *beside* mean 'at the side of', but can also be used more generally to indicate the nearness of one object to another:

Uncle Harry chose a big chair **by** (= 'near') **the fireplace**.

Prepositional adverbs of place: *overhead*, *in front*, etc.

185 The following prepositional adverbs (*see* 660) or fixed phrases correspond to the prepositions of position we have just dealt with:

overhead	(over)	*above*	(above)
underneath	(under)	*below*	(below)
in front	(in front of)	*behind*	(behind)
on top	(on top of)	*beneath*	(beneath)

Examples:

Florentines are delicious, with bumpy nuts and cherries **on top**, and silky chocolate **underneath**.

The sky **overhead** was a mass of stars.

Huge waves are crashing on the rocks **below**.

Mr Smart drove to church with a guard of mounted police **in front** and **behind**.

Some other positions: *between*, *among*, *opposite*, etc.

186 ● *Between*, *among* and *amid* are related. *Between* normally relates an object to two other objects, and *among* to more than two:

The house stands **between two trees**.

The house stands **among trees**.

But *between* can relate to more than two objects, if we have a definite set in mind:

Manila lies on the shore of Manila Bay, **between the sea, the mountains, and a large lake called Laguna de Bay**.

● *Amid* <formal> means 'in the midst of', and like *among*, can apply to an indefinite number of objects:

The house stands **amid trees**.

Unlike *among*, it can also be followed by a mass noun:

Amid the wreckage of the plane they found a child's doll.

● *Opposite* means 'facing':

His house is **opposite mine**. (i.e. 'facing mine, on the other side of the street') [1]

● *Around* (preferred in <AmE>) or *round* (preferred in <BrE>) refers to surrounding position or motion:

The police were standing on guard *around the building*.

About and *around* in <informal> English often have a vaguer meaning of 'in the area of' or 'in various positions in':

The guests were standing *about/around the room*, looking bored.   [2]

There's quite a lot of woodland *about/around here*.   [3]

Note
Some of these prepositions also have corresponding prepositional adverbs (see 185). Compare [1], [2] and [3] above with:

His house is (right) *opposite*.

The guests were standing *around*, looking bored.

There's quite a lot of woodland *about*.

Motion from one place to another

187 In 173–6, those meanings illustrated by diagrams 1, 3, 5, and 6 involve **motion**. The prepositions in the other diagrams (2 and 4) indicate **state**. Some different aspects of motion can be pictured as follows:

But the prepositions used to indicate position in 184–6 can also signify **motion** to the position concerned:

1   The bush was a good hiding-place, so I dashed *behind it*.

2   When it started to rain, we all ran *underneath the trees*.

Passage: We drove past the town hall

188 The same prepositions can also be used, like *through* and *across*, to indicate motion towards, then away from a place (i.e. **passage**):

1   The photographers ran *behind the goal-posts*.

2   I crawled *underneath the fence*.

Other prepositions can be used similarly:

1   We drove *by/past the town hall*.

2   We passed *over/across the bridge*.

3   We turned *(a)round the corner*.

Around and *round* can also refer more generally to circular motion: (*round* is more common in <BrE>, and *around* in (AmE>):

The earth moves (a)*round the sun.*

Direction: *up, down, along, across,* etc.

189 *Up, down, along,* and *across/over* represent motion with reference to a direction or axis:

I crept silently *along the passage*.
He ran *across the lawn* to the gate.
She flung open the french windows and ran *over the sodden grass*.
They were rolling *down the hill* without brakes.
The royal couple went *up the steps* together.
She walked very quickly *up/down the street*.

The last sentence here does not necessarily mean that the street was on a hill: <informally>, we use *up* and *down* with practically the same meaning as *along*. (*Downtown* <AmE> means simply the central or business part of a town.)

Note
We can express **repeated motion** by joining two prepositions with *and*:

He walked *up and down the room*. (in one direction and then in another, repeatedly)

The oars splashed *in and out of the water*.

They danced *round and round the room*.

In such cases we can omit the noun phrase after the prepositions: *They danced round and round.*

Combining space and motion

190 ● Viewpoint: The preposition *beyond* makes reference not only to two objects, but to a third factor, the 'viewpoint', or place where the speaker is standing (in reality or in imagination):

I could see the town *beyond the lake*. (i.e. 'on the other side of the lake [from me]')

We can also express 'viewpoint' by using *across, over, through, past*, etc. in a sense similar to their 'passage' or 'direction' sense (*see* 188–9):

the people (who live) **over the road**	a café **round the corner**
an office **along the corridor**	the garage **past the supermarket**
friends **across the sea**	the hotel **down the road**
the house **through the trees**	a man **up a ladder**

We can, if we like, specify the viewpoint by using a *from*-phrase:

He lives up/down/along/across the road **from me**.

● **Resulting place meaning**

Prepositions which have the meaning of 'motion' can also have a 'state' meaning, indicating the state of having reached a particular destination:

David Stoddart gathered the ball and was **over the line** in a flash.
(i.e. he had run over the line – in a game of rugby)

They were **out of the snow** now, but it was still very cold.

● **Pervasive meaning**

Over and *through* can have 'pervasive' meaning, especially when preceded by *all*:

There was blood (**all**) **over the sheets**. (i.e. 'the sheets were covered with blood').

Soccer-mad males can be seen (**all**) **over the city**. (i.e. 'the city is full of them')

Through is restricted to areas and volumes (*see* 175–6). *Throughout* can be used instead of *all through*:

His views were widely echoed **throughout Germany**.

Abstract place meaning

191 Place prepositions are often used in more abstract senses, which relate to their basic sense by metaphor.

In, out of (condition or inclusion): *in danger, out of danger; in practice, out of practice; in a race, in plays, in a group*

People never behave **in real life** as they do **in plays**.

Above, below, beneath (high or levels on a scale):

His grades are **above/below the average**.

He rejects such activity as **beneath** (= not worthy of) **him**.

Over, **under** (power, surveillance, scale): *over* (= 'more than') *ten miles*; *under orders, under suspicion*:

> Ezinma wielded a strong influence **over her half-sister**.

Up, **down** (movement on a scale): *up the scale, down the social ladder*

From, **to** (giving and receiving):

> Did you get a letter **from Leslie** about this?
> He gave a lot of money **to his family**.

Between, **among** (involving two or more people):

> My sister and I share the place **between us**.
> They agree **among themselves**.

Past, **beyond** (going too far):

> Modern times have changed the world **beyond recognition**.
> I'm **past** (= too old for) **falling in love**.

Place adverbs and their relation to prepositions

192 Most place prepositions (except the *at*-type prepositions) correspond in form to prepositional adverbs (*see* 660), and in general their meanings correspond as well. Here are some examples:

> We stopped the bus and got **off**. (i.e. '**off** the bus')
> Have you put the cat **out**? (i.e. 'out of the house')
> The child ran **across** in front of the car. (i.e. 'across the road')
> When they reached the bridge, they crossed **over**, looking **down** at the water **beneath**.

But some prepositional adverbs have special uses:

> They travelled **on**. (i.e. 'they continued their journey')
> The thieves snatched her handbag and ran **off** (= 'away').
> A man came **up** (i.e. 'approached') and introduced himself.
> You don't see many parrots **about** nowadays (i.e. 'about the place').
>   <informal BrE, AmE prefers **around**>

[In this last example, *about* is so vague as to be almost meaningless.]

Note
In addition to *up* and *down*, the following are adverbs of direction: *upward*(*s*), *downward*(*s*); *forward*(*s*), *backward*(*s*); *inward*(*s*), *outward*(*s*); *homeward*(*s*).

Distance

193 Distance can be expressed by noun phrases of measure such as *a foot, a few metres || meters, ten miles, a kilometre || kilometer, a long way,* etc. These phrases can modify a verb of motion:

He ran *several miles*.   [1]

They can also precede and modify an adverbial of place:

They live *a long way away*.   [2]

The valley lay *two thousand feet below them*.

Here the meaning is one of static location. Notice the question forms corresponding to [1] and [2]:

How far did he run?   [1a]

BUT: *How far away* do they live?   [2a]

Manner, means and instrument

Answering the question *'how'*

194 If you want to specify **how** an action is performed or **how** an event takes place, you can use an adverbial of **manner, means,** or **instrument**:

[A]   *How* did you write the letter?

[B]   I wrote it
$\begin{cases} \textbf{\textit{(very) hurriedly.}} & \text{(MANNER)} \\ \textbf{\textit{by hand.}} & \text{(MEANS)} \\ \textbf{\textit{with a red ball-point pen.}} & \text{(INSTRUMENT)} \end{cases}$

You can ask a more specific question about the instrument with which an action is performed as follows:

What did you write it *with*? <rather informal>

What tools did the artist use to create this remarkable effect?

Manner

195 The three chief ways of expressing manner are:

[A]   *adverb* (usually ending in *-ly*) or *adverb phrase*

[B]   *in a . . . manner (or way)*

[C]   *with + abstract noun phrase*

Most adjectives have matching *-ly* adverbs, and many adjectives have matching abstract nouns. Thus there may be three ways of expressing the same idea:

He spoke
- [A] *confidently*. (most common)
- [B] *in a confident manner*. <more formal>
- [C] *with confidence*. <formal>

Examples of manner adverbs and manner phrases are:

She stirred her coffee *thoughtfully* before answering.

The task was done *in a workmanlike manner/way*.

His father stopped and looked *in a startled manner* at his mother.

Joanna stubbed out her cigarette *with unnecessary fierceness*.

I answered *without hesitation*. (i.e. 'unhesitatingly')

'Next year', she replied *gently, with a smile*.

Like this, like that (or *this way, that way*) are phrases with the meaning 'in this/that manner':

I'm sorry you had to hurt yourself *like this*.

Please, Ralph, don't talk *like that*.

Notice that *in* can be omitted before *way* in certain <informal> constructions:

Monica and her sister do their hair (*in*) *the same way*.

She prepared the dish (*in*) *the way he liked*, with slices of oil-bean and fish.

You can cook turkey (*in*) *a number of different ways*.

Combining manner with comparison

196 A manner phrase sometimes expresses a comparison:

She sings *like a professional*. (i.e. 'in the manner of a professional, as well as a professional')

Sarah Morgan came into the room *like a ghost*.

Manner clauses introduced by *as* can be used in a similar way. Compare:

Pat cooks turkey
- *as my mother did*.
- *in the way that my mother did*. <formal>
- *the way my mother did*. <informal>

They hunted him *as a tiger stalks its prey*. <formal>

In these examples, *as* can be replaced by *like*. However, *like* is <informal>, and is less acceptable in <BrE>.

Comparisons with unreal situations can be expressed by a clause beginning *as if* or *as though*:

She treats me { *as if* / *as though* } *I were one of the family*.

(On the verb form *were* here, *see* 277.)

Means and instrument: *by* and *with*

197 ● **Means** is expressed by a phrase introduced by *by*:

> You're going to France **by car** are you? (*see* Note [b] below)
>
> She slipped into the house **by the back gate**.
>
> We managed to sell the house **by advertising it in the paper**.

● **Instrument** is expressed by a phrase introduced by *with*:

> She reached down and touched the lace **with her fingers**.
>
> The young man had been attacked **with an iron bar**.

The verb *use* and its object also convey the idea of instrument:

> She always opens her letters **with a knife**.
>
> ~ She always **uses a knife** to open her letters.

The non-use of an instrument can be expressed by *without*:

> You can draw the lines **without (using) a ruler**.

Notes

[a] We sometimes prefer to replace a *by*-phrase of means by a different type of prepositional phrase, e.g. one of place:

> [A] How did he get in?　　　　[B] He came in **through the window**.
> 　　　　　　　　　　　　　　　　　(more usual than **by the window**)
>
> [A] How did you hear the news?　[B] I heard it **on the radio**.

[b] The article is omitted in *by*-phrases denoting communication: *by car, by train, by letter, by fax, by post/mail, by e-mail, by radio* (*see* 475).

Cause, reason and purpose

Direct cause: actors and causative verbs

198 There are many different answers to the question 'What causes such-and-such an event?' The means and instrument, just discussed, may be said to be kinds of cause. More important, though, is the *person* who causes an event to take place, i.e. the **actor**. The actor is usually specified by the subject of a clause ([B] below), or by the agent in the passive ([C]) (*see* 613–15):

> [A] *How* did the fire start?
>
> [B] *Some children* started it. (i.e. 'caused it to start')
>
> [C] It was started by *some children*.

Start in [B] may be called a **causative verb**, and *some children* names the actor.

Many adjectives and intransitive verbs in English have a corresponding causative verb. The causative verb may match them in form:

The dam *blew up*.	The terrorists *blew up* the dam.
The road became *wider*.	They *widened* the road.
The tree has *fallen*.	Someone has *felled* the tree.
The supplies *came in* yesterday.	They *brought* the supplies *in* yesterday.

Other examples:

	not causative	causative verb
adjective	*narrow, open, strong, clear*	*narrow, open, strengthen, clarify*
verbs	*narrow, open, begin, rise, learn*	*narrow, open, begin, raise, teach*

Is the front door *open*? (adjective)

The shop *opens* at nine o'clock. (non-causative verb)

You want me to *open* your mail? (causative verb)

She wanted to *learn* how to use a computer. (non-causative verb)

She *taught* me how to sing. (causative verb)

199 Sometimes, when the actor is not mentioned, the instrument or means takes the position of subject, i.e. the role of the 'causer' of the action:

They killed him *with his own gun*.	*His own gun* killed him.
They brought the supplies *by train*.	*The train* brought the supplies.

In the passive, the actor can be expressed by a *by*-phrase (*see* 613–15):

The dam was blown up *by terrorists*.

The same is true of instrument:

He was killed *by his own gun*.

Cause and result: *because,* etc. (see also 365)

200 In answer to the question 'why?', you can indicate cause or reason by an adverbial *because*-clause, or by a prepositional phrase beginning *because of, on account of* <formal>, *from, out of*:

***Because*:**

The accident occurred *because the machine had been poorly maintained*.

[1]

Because of:

> She can't go to work *because of the baby*. [2]

On account of <formal>:

> Many fatal accidents occurred *on account of icy road conditions*. [3]

From, out of (mainly to express motive, i.e. psychological cause):

> He did accept the award, not *from/out of pride*, but *from/out of a sense of duty*. [4]

Other prepositions that sometimes express cause are *for* (mainly with nouns of feeling) and *through*:

> He jumped *for joy*.

> Hussein has missed five matches *through injury*.

Indirect cause as subject

201 We can often make the 'cause' the subject of the sentence, using a general causative verb like *cause* or *make*:

> The driver's carelessness *caused the crash*. [active]

> ~ *The crash was caused by* the driver's carelessness. [passive]

Other verbal constructions expressing cause are these:

> Such slipshod security is bound to *lead to* trouble.

> Many of these prosecutions *result in* acquittals.

> We are trying *to bring about* equal rights for all people.

> He argues that higher wages inevitably *give rise to* higher prices.

We can also express cause with a noun like *effect*:

> The *effect* of higher wages is to raise prices.

Result

202 Result is the opposite of cause (compare [3] in 200):

> Icy conditions *cause* many accidents. [cause]

> ~ Many accidents *result from* icy conditions. [result]

Notice also that *result in* and *result from* are opposites:

> The celebrations *resulted in* a serious riot.

> ~ A serious riot *resulted from* the celebrations.

Result can be expressed by a clause beginning with *so that*, or just *so* [*so* is more <informal> than *so that*]:

> The cleaner has gone on holiday ǁ vacation *so (that)* everything is so dirty.

This is another way of saying:

Everything is so dirty **because** the cleaner has gone on holiday || vacation.

Purpose

203 The intended result (*see* 323) or PURPOSE of an action is described by an adverbial of purpose, usually a *to*-infinitive clause:

He left early **to catch the last train**.

Penelope leaned forward **to examine the letter more closely**.

To improve the railway service, they are electrifying all the main lines.

An adverbial of purpose may also be a finite verb clause beginning *so that*:

They advertised the concert **so that everyone should know about it**. (The **so that**-clause often contains **would** or **should**, see 280.)

In order that is a <more formal> alternative for *so that*:

They advertised the concert **in order that everyone should know about it**.

In <informal BrE>, *in case* can introduce the idea of negative purpose (compare 208):

He left early **in case he should miss the last train**. (i.e. '. . . so that he should not miss it')

Reason and consequence: *because (of), as, since, etc.*

204 *Because, because of,* and *on account of* can express **reason** as well as cause. Cause and reason are overlapping notions (both answering the question *Why?*), but the difference between them is that cause concerns the events themselves, while reason concerns the way a person interprets the events, and acts upon this interpretation:

We have lunch early on Saturday **because the girls are always in a hurry to go out**.

We decided to stay and watch the procession – but Amy, **because of her height**, could see nothing.

The contest was abandoned **on account of bad weather conditions**. <formal>

Reason can also be expressed by *as*-clauses and *since*-clauses:

As Jane was the eldest, she had to look after her brothers and sisters.

The report is out of date – which is hardly surprising, **since it was published in 1989**.

The main clause indicates the **consequence** of the reason clause.

Now that *and* seeing that, *etc.*

205 *Now that* and *seeing that* are conjunctions which have a meaning very close to *as* and *since*, except that *now that* also has an element of time meaning:

> We hope to see much more of you **now that you're living in Vicksburg**.
>
> **Seeing that he could not persuade the other members of the committee**, he gave in to their demands.

Another <more formal> way to express the same idea is a participle clause (*see* 493):

> **The weather having improved**, the game was enjoyed by players and spectators alike. <formal>
>
> **Being a man of fixed views**, he refused to listen to our arguments. <rather formal>

Yet another construction expressing reason is a *for*-phrase, following certain adjectives and verbs of emotion and attitude:

> She laughed at herself **for being so silly and self-pitying**.
>
> They were praised **for their outspoken defence of free speech**. ('because of their . . .')

The following prepositions also express cause or reason: *due to, owing to*.

Linking adverbials: therefore, hence, *etc.*

206 Also important are linking adverbials of cause or reason (*see* 360, 365) meaning 'because of that' or 'for that reason': *therefore, thus, accordingly, hence*, and *consequently* are <formal>, whereas *so* is <informal>:

> Very shortly afterwards, however, he began to suffer from attacks of angina pectoris. **Accordingly**, he was excused all serious exertion. <formal, written>
>
> After all, Glasgow was where she really belonged. **So** this year she had decided to spend her annual holiday in the city. <informal>

A linking adverbial corresponding to *seeing that* (205) is *in that case*:

> [A] The weather has improved.
>
> [B] **In that case**, we can go out and enjoy our game.

Condition and contrast

Open and hypothetical conditions: *if, etc.*

207 Conditional clauses are related to reason clauses, but they discuss the consequence of something which may or may not be a real event. Notice the difference between:

I'll lend Peter the money *because he needs it*. [1]

I'll lend Peter the money *if he needs it*. [2]

The speaker of sentence [1] knows that Peter needs the money, while the speaker of [2] does not know whether he does. A sentence like [2] expresses what we call an **open condition**, because the truth or falsehood of what the sentence describes is 'open', i.e. unknown. The conditional clause often precedes the main clause:

If you feel seasick, take one of these pills.

There is another type of conditional sentence, which expresses an unreal or **hypothetical condition**. For this type of sentence the speaker assumes the falsehood or unlikelihood of what is described:

I would lend Peter the money *if he needed it*. [3]

I would have lent Peter the money *if he had needed it*. [4]

You'd be bored *if you had no children*. [5]

The speaker's assumptions are [3] 'he doesn't need the money', [4] 'he didn't need the money' (on some past occasion) and [5] 'you do have children'. As these examples show, the hypothetical meaning is signalled by the use of the hypothetical past tense (*see* 275), and past hypothetical meaning, in [4], is signalled by the past perfect.

In case (of), on condition that, provided that

208 Condition can also be expressed by the conjunctions *in case*, *on condition that*, *provided that*, and the preposition *in case of* <formal>:

● *In case* names a future condition which may or may not arise:

Take these pills, *in case you feel ill on the boat*.

I had to watch where I put my feet *in case I fell*.

● *On condition that* specifies a condition to which a person must agree:

I'll lend you the money *on condition that you return it within six months*.

● *Provided that* and *as/so long as* are like *on condition that* in expressing a strong condition 'if and only if . . .':

Provided that ⎱ they had plenty to eat and drink, the crew seemed
So long as ⎰ to be happy.

● *In case of* is a preposition expressing condition:

In case of emergency, the simplest thing is to flick off the switch.

Negative condition: *unless*

209 *Unless* expresses a negative condition. Thus we could change the emphasis of

> I'll lend Peter the money if he needs it. (*see* 207 sentence [2])

by saying:

> I won't lend Peter the money *unless he needs it*.

Note the equivalence of:

> *Unless* Paul *improves* his work, he'll fail the exam.
> ~ If Paul *doesn't improve* his work, he'll fail the exam.
> You can take a book out of the library and keep it for a whole year *unless it's recalled*.

Negative hypothetical conditions can be expressed by *but for* + noun phrase or *if it hadn't been for* + noun phrase (*unless* CANNOT be used in this type of context):

> *But for Jenny*, we would have lost the match (i.e. 'If Jenny hadn't played well', etc.).
> Adam would have faced almost certain death, *if it hadn't been for his quick thinking*.

Otherwise is a sentence adverb expressing negative condition (*see* 367):

> I'm sorry I had a previous engagement: *otherwise*, I'd have been here much earlier.

Use of *any, ever,* etc.

210 Because they imply uncertainty, conditional clauses often contain *any*-words like *any, anyone, ever*, etc. (rather than *some*-words like *some, someone, sometimes – see* 697–9):

> If you *ever* have *any* problems, let me know.
> Unless *anyone* has *any* questions, the meeting is adjourned.

But to express special positive bias (*see* 243), conditional clauses can contain *some*-words:

> Help yourself if you want *something* to eat.

Clauses of contrast: *although,* etc. (*see also* 361)

211 A further type of adverbial meaning overlapping with conditional meaning is that of **contrast**, also called **concession**. If two circumstances are in contrast, it means that the one (*b*) is **surprising** or **unexpected** in view of the other (*a*):

{
a The weather is bad.
b We are enjoying ourselves.

{
a He hadn't eaten for days.
b He looked strong and healthy.

We can link the contrasting ideas *a* and *b* by using the coordinating conjunction *but*:

> The weather is bad, **but** we're enjoying ourselves.

> He hadn't eaten for days, **but** he looked strong and healthy.

We can also put *a* and *b* together by making one of them into a subclause beginning *although* or *though* <informal>:

> We are enjoying ourselves, **although/though the weather is bad**.

> (**Even**) **though he hadn't eaten for days**, he looked strong and healthy.

(*Even though* is slightly more emphatic than *although*.)

The conjunctions *while* and *whereas* can express contrast between two equivalent ideas:

> **While we welcome his support**, we disagree with a lot of his views.

> Elizabeth was lively and talkative, **whereas her sister was quiet and reserved**.

Note

There are special constructions for expressing the meaning of 'even though':

> **Much as I would like to help**, I have other work I must do. ('Even though I would like to help very much . . .')

> **Absurd as it may seem**, she grew tired of being a success. ('Even though it may seem absurd . . .')

In sentences like these, the conjunction *as* occurs in the middle of the subclause, after an emphatic adjective (*absurd*) or an adverbial (*much*). Sometimes *though* is used instead of *as*: *Absurd though it may seem . . .* These constructions can sound rather <elevated> and <rhetorical>:

> **Unarmed as/though he was**, he bravely went forward to meet his enemies.

Phrases and adverbs of contrast: *in spite of*, etc.

212 *In spite of, despite* <formal>, *notwithstanding* <very formal>, *for all* are prepositions of contrast:

> We are enjoying ourselves *in spite of the weather*.

> *Despite her fabulous wealth*, Sara's only property is a humble house in the oldest part of Seville.

Notwithstanding state aid, the local governments are continuing to seek extra revenue. <formal>

For all his skill, he has accomplished very little. (= 'Despite his great skill . . .')

There are also a number of sentence adverbials (*see* 361, 462) expressing the meaning 'in spite of this/that': *yet, however, nevertheless* <formal>, *all the same* <informal>, *still, even so*:

The weather was absolutely dreadful; **however**, the children enjoyed themselves.

Britain was mopping up yesterday after one month's rain fell overnight; **yet** we're still in the middle of a drought.

He has, presumably, the main weight of local opinion behind him, not to mention the considerable resources of the French government. **Nevertheless**, the omens are not good. <rather formal, written>

Yet can be used in the main clause to reinforce the contrast made by the subclause:

Although he hadn't eaten for days, **yet** he looked strong and healthy.

Note

The adverb *even* is used to imply a contrast with what we might usually expect:

Well, you know, even in Alaska the summers get pretty devastating.

The implied message here is that in such a northerly place as Alaska it is surprising to have hot summers, whereas (say) in Texas they would be expected.

Condition + contrast

213 The ideas of condition (*if*) and implied contrast (*even*) come together in the conjunction *even if*:

I always enjoy sailing, **even if the weather is rough**. ('You wouldn't expect me to enjoy sailing in rough weather, but I do.')

We will take appropriate action, **even if we have to go it alone**.

The meaning of *even if* is sometimes conveyed by *if* alone, or *if . . . (at least)*:

If nothing else, (**at least**) two good things came out of the project. ('Even if nothing else came out of the project . . .')

Even if expresses the same contrastive meaning in hypothetical conditions:

She wouldn't give me the money, **even if I begged her for it**.

Alternative conditions: *whether . . . or, whatever,* etc.

214 Condition is combined with the meaning of *either . . . or* in the parallel conjunctions *whether . . . or,* which specify two contrasting conditions:

> **Whether we win or lose**, the match will be enjoyable. ('If we win or even if we lose . . .')

> They were guaranteed 40 hours' pay per week **whether they worked or not**. ('If they worked or even if they didn't.')

The meaning of 'contrary to expectation' is also present here, as the examples show.

A similar meaning is present in the *wh*-words *whatever, whoever, wherever,* etc.:

> These shoes are ideal: I'll buy them, **whatever the cost**. [1]

> I intend to support the nominee of the party at St Louis, **whoever that may be**. [2]

> **Wherever he goes**, he makes friends. [3]

The meaning is that the statement in the main clause is true on **any of the conditions** covered by the subclause. Again, contrasting meaning is present, in that [1] implies, for example, 'I'll buy them, *even if* they cost a fortune'. The same meaning can be expressed by an adverbial clause beginning *no matter wh-*:

> I'll buy them, **no matter what they cost**. [1a]

Two general adverbials with this type of meaning are *anyway* and *in any case* (= 'whatever the circumstances'):

> I don't know how much they cost, but I'll buy those shoes **anyway/in any case**. [1b]

Degree

215 Expressions of **degree** usually modify the meaning of a particular word in the clause. Degree is largely expressed by adverbs, which either act as **modifiers** of adjectives, adverbs, etc. (*see* 464–9), or else act as **adverbials** in clause structure.

- **modifying degree adverbs** (*see* 465)

  [A] *How* hungry are you?   [B] (Actually I'm) **very** hungry.

  [A] *How* soon are they leaving?   [B] (They're leaving) **quite** soon.

- **degree adverbs as adverbials** (*see* 459). Here the degree adverbs usually modify the meaning of the verb (here *agree*):

  [A] *How far* do they agree?   [B] (They agree) **completely**.

Applied to nouns, degree is expressed by quantifiers like *much* (*see* 220, 232):

[A] *How much* of a dancer is he?   [B] (He's) *not much* of one.
<rather informal>

Degree expressions can answer the questions *How?* (for adjectives and adverbs); *How much?* (for verbs); and *How much of?* (for nouns). More <formal> questions of degree are *To what degree?* and *To what extent?* Applied to verbs, degree adverbials sometimes answer the question *How far?* and sometimes *How much?*:

[A] *How far* do you disagree   [B] (I disagree with you)
with me?   *absolutely*.

[A] *How much* did she enjoy   [B] (She enjoyed it) *immensely*.
the ballet?

Gradable words and degree

216 Not all verbs, adjectives, etc. can be modified by a degree expression. Degree applies only to **gradable words**, i.e. words whose meaning can be thought of in terms of a **scale**. Most pairs of words of opposite meaning, like *old* and *young*, are gradable:

[A] *How old* is your dog?   [B] He's *very old/quite young*.

If you want to make the degree more exact, you can use a measure phrase (*five years*, *six foot*, etc.) as a degree expression: *She's five years old. He's six foot tall.* There are two main kinds of gradable words:

- SCALE words indicate a relative position on a scale (e.g. *large, small*)
- LIMIT words indicate the end-point of a scale (e.g. *black, white*)

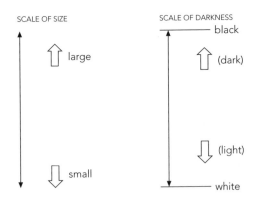

(For the idea of darkness, we also have the scale words *dark* and *light*.)

Degree with scale words

217 The same degree expression can sometimes act either as a modifier or as an adverbial:

> She was *absolutely* crazy about him. <informal> [MODIFIER]
>
> I must say I agree with you *absolutely*. [ADVERBIAL]

In other cases a different adverb has to be used in the different functions: for example, *very* and *too* are limited to the modifying function. The most important differences concern scale words and are given in this table, which also shows the differences between types of adverbs modifying scale words:

Degree expressions with adjectives and verbs as scale words

WITH ADJECTIVE SCALE WORDS	WITH VERB SCALE WORDS
(A) Indicating extreme position on the scale	
very (see 220): He's very friendly. It's a very tall building.	*(very) much* (see 220) *a lot* <informal>, *a great deal*: I like her very much.
(B) Intensifying the meaning slightly	
quite, rather, fairly; *pretty* <informal>: She's still quite young. It's rather expensive. It's a fairly modern motel. She was pretty annoyed.	*considerably, rather*; *quite, a lot* <informal>: I quite enjoy the job. Prices have increased considerably. We talked a lot about old times. I rather like her.
(C) Toning down or decreasing the effect of the scale word	
a bit <informal>, *a little, slightly*: She's a bit upset. The journey was slightly uncomfortable. It's a little surprising.	*a bit* <informal>, *a little, slightly*: I've read a bit about it. Prices have fallen slightly. I know him a little.

Degree with limit words

218 With limit words (*see* 216) the same adverbs can function as modifiers and as adverbials. The two main classes of such adverbs are:

● Adverbs indicating that the limit word's meaning is used to its fullest extent: *absolutely, altogether, completely, entirely, quite, totally, utterly*:

> I'm *absolutely* positive it's the truth.
>
> I *completely* disagree with you.
>
> I don't *entirely* agree with what Mr Turner says.
>
> We were *utterly* powerless to defend ourselves.

- Adverbs indicating a position near the limit of the scale: *almost, nearly, practically* <informal>, *virtually*:

> Mr Player was **almost** in tears.
>
> I've **nearly** finished my work.
>
> At the beginning of this term, she **virtually** had a nervous breakdown.
>
> Johnny Mercer **practically** grew up with the sound of jazz and the blues in his ears.

Note

Notice that *quite* has two uses: *quite* (= 'considerably') goes with scale words (e.g. *quite young*), while *quite* (= 'absolutely') goes with limit words (e.g. *quite impossible*).

Degree with comparatives and superlatives

219 The same degree words which modify adjectives can also modify adverbs. But comparative adjectives and adverbs are modified by the degree words which function elsewhere as adverbials (*see* 217):

$$
\text{I am feeling} \begin{cases} much \\ a\ great\ deal \\ a\ lot\ \text{<informal>} \end{cases} \text{more healthy than I was.}
$$

Superlatives can be intensified by degree adverbs like *altogether* and *absolutely* which apply to limit words:

> It is **altogether/absolutely** the best show in town.

But *very* can also have an intensifying effect if placed directly before the superlative word (but not before *most*):

> We want to pick the **very** best person for the job.

Very and much

220 We have seen (*see* 217) that *very* acts as a modifier, whereas *much* acts as an adverbial. However, the adverb *much* on its own is of limited occurrence. It normally has to be preceded by another degree word such as *very* or *so*. Compare:

> The novel has some **very** enjoyable characters in it. (MODIFIER)
>
> I **very much** hope that you will accept. (MID-POSITION ADVERBIAL)
>
> I enjoyed the party **very much**. (END-POSITION ADVERBIAL)

Many verbs cannot go with *much* alone: we can say (for example) *I much prefer . . .* , but not **I much like. . . . I very much like . . .* , on the other hand, is acceptable:

[A] I **very much like** her latest recording.

[B] I (**very**) **much preferred** her earlier ones.

Positive and negative attitude

221 Some degree adverbs, although they have the same meaning with respect to 'scale' and 'limit', tend to be distinguished in terms of positive and negative **attitude**:

POSITIVE ATTITUDE	NEGATIVE ATTITUDE
It's **quite** warm today.	It's **rather** cold today.
She's **entirely** satisfied.	That is **completely** wrong.
The project looks **fairly** promising.	He felt **utterly** exhausted.

Fairly (= 'considerably'), *quite* (= 'considerably') and *entirely* sometimes suggest a positive or 'good' meaning, whereas *rather*, *completely*, and *utterly* sometimes suggest a negative or 'bad' meaning. Thus *fairly warm* implies that warmth is a good thing; but someone who said *It's rather warm today*, on the other hand, would probably be thinking that the weather was a little **too** warm. The expressions *a bit, a little* and *a little bit* also tend to go with negative meanings: *These boxes are a bit/a little heavy.*

Other aspects of degree adverbs

222 ●Some words can be used both as scale words and as limit words, e.g. the adjectives *new, full,* and *empty*:

The furniture looked {**very** new. / **absolutely** new.}   The glass is {**very** full. / **absolutely** full.}

● We can have a **scale word and a different limit word dealing with the same area of meaning**:

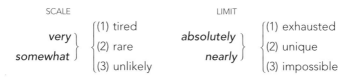

SCALE   LIMIT

very ⎱ (1) tired   **absolutely** ⎱ (1) exhausted
somewhat ⎰ (2) rare   **nearly** ⎰ (2) unique
         (3) unlikely   (3) impossible

● A scale word often corresponds to one or more limit words, which intensify its meaning, and add emotive emphasis: for example, *terrible* intensifies the meaning of *bad*:

	ORDINARY			INTENSIFIED
very	(1) good	absolutely	(1) perfect/marvellous
	(2) bad		(2) terrible/awful
	(3) large		(3) massive/colossal
	(4) annoyed		(4) infuriated

Note

[a] You can also intensify meaning by repeating the word *very*, or by adding *very . . . indeed*:

> He was a **very**, **very** special man.   That is **very** strange **indeed**.

[b] Scale words and limit words are sometimes difficult to separate, because there is a tendency to 'convert' limit words to scale words in everyday language. Hence we sometimes hear expressions like *too perfect* and *very unique*. Some speakers, however, regard such expressions as illogical and 'bad English'.

223 ● In addition there are **negative** degree adverbs (*barely*, *hardly*, and *scarcely* – *see* 584), and the **any**-word (*see* 697–8) degree adverbial *at all* (= 'to any degree'):

> I **scarcely** noticed him. (= 'I almost didn't notice him')
>
> I didn't notice him **at all**. (= 'I totally failed to notice him')
>
> Was it **at all** enjoyable?   The text wasn't **at all** difficult.

● Apart from the degree adverbs listed so far, **there are many degree adverbs which are more restricted in their use**. These tend to intensify a particular set of gradable words, e.g. *badly* goes with the verbs *need* and *want*; *thoroughly* goes with the verbs *enjoy*, *disapprove*, *dislike*, etc.; *hard* goes with the verbs *work*, *try*, etc.:

> They were both **thoroughly enjoying** their first tour of Greece.
>
> I welcome this scheme, which is **badly needed**. (= 'needed very much')

Role, standard and point of view

224 A gradable word can also have its meaning qualified in terms of **role** or **standard**. Using *at* or *as* you can specify the **role** which the gradable word implies; using *for* you can specify the **standard** by which the speaker is judging its use (gradable words in **bold type**):

> Anna is **clever**. ⎫
> Anna is **very clever**. ⎭   (DEGREE)

Anna is *clever at swimming*.

As a swimmer, she's *outstanding*. } (ROLE)

Anna is a *good* swimmer *for a youngster*.

For a learner, she swims *well*. } (STANDARD)

Further, you can specify the **point of view** from which a word or phrase is understood:

Morally, it was not an easy problem. (i.e. 'From a moral point of view . . .')

In a way, I was very resentful about leaving. (i.e. 'In one respect/from one point of view . . .')

He is a good swimmer *in a technical sense*. (i.e. 'from a technical point of view')

These trials were termed 'political cases' *in that the trial itself was a political act*. <formal>

You can also name the person(s) whose point of view it is:

To his parents, his behaviour was astonishing.

Comparison

225 To compare two things with respect to their position on a scale of degree or amount, use comparative words *taller*, *happier*, etc. or comparative phrases *more careful*, *less careful*, etc. (*see* 500). A following phrase or clause introduced by *than* can indicate the 'standard' against which the comparison is made.

Jack is *taller than* Jill (is).   [1]

Jill is *shorter than* Jack (is).   [2]

Jill is *less tall than* Jack (is).   [3]

Jack is *less short than* Jill (is).   [4]

Sentences [1]–[4] have the same meaning, but are listed in order of their likelihood. A sentence like [4] is very unusual, and would only be said if we were comparing Jack and Jill in terms of their shortness.

Equal comparisons

226 For an equal comparison, e.g. when Jack and Jill are the same height, we use *as . . . as* instead of *more . . . than*:

Jack is *as* tall *as* Jill (is).

~ Jill is *as* tall *as* Jack (is).

To negate equal comparison, we say *not as . . . as*, or *not so . . . as*:

Jill is **not as** tall **as** Jack (is). [5]

~ Jack is **not so** short **as** Jill (is). [6]

Again, sentences [5] and [6] have the same basic meaning as [1]–[4] in 225.

Comparative and superlative

227 When comparing only two things, we use the comparative forms:

Jill is **the shorter** of the two children.

Jack is **the taller** of the two children.

When comparing more than two objects we use superlative forms *tallest, most useful, least tall*, etc.:

Susan is the **tallest** of the three.

Jill is the **shortest** of the three.

Tourism is our **most important** industry.

Things were being done in the **least efficient** way.

To define the set of things being compared, you use *of*, as above, followed by a noun phrase:

Miller scored **the best goal of the game**. (i.e. 'best . . . of the goals scored in the game')

Luxembourg is the **smallest** of the **countries** of the European Union.

The *of*-phrase is sometimes placed for emphasis at the beginning of the clause:

Of all the capital cities in the world, Bangkok is the one I would **most** like to visit.

To name the sphere or range of comparison use *in* with a singular noun phrase:

He was the ablest man **in** the civil service.

It was the worst moment **in my life**. (ALSO: **of my life**)

Other constructions which can specify the range of comparison with superlatives are (a) possessive determiners, (b) genitives, (c) adjectives and (d) relative clauses:

(a) **my** best friend, **her** greatest success

(b) **the world's** highest mountain

(c) the greatest **living** composer

(d) the most boring speech **I ever heard**

Comparison with a definite norm

228 Sometimes a comparison is made between an object and a definite standard or 'norm' understood in context (often through back-pointing). In such cases, you can use *than that* or *as that*:

[A] Jack must be six foot tall. [B] $\Big\{$ No, he's taller (*than that*). [7]
Is he really as tall *as that*? [8]

In [7] you can omit the comparative part *than that* altogether. For [8], you can also say: *Is he* THÁT *tall?* <informal>. The *than*-phrase is usually omitted when we are comparing not two different things, but the same thing at an earlier and at a later time:

All over the world the crime rate is growing **worse** (i.e. 'worse than it was'), but in many cases the criminal is becoming **more difficult** to catch (i.e. 'more difficult than before').

229 To express continuing change, repeat the comparative word with *and*:

Germany's position as our principal ally grows **stronger and stronger**.

Many painters feel **more and more** out of tune with modern society.

Fewer and fewer families are working on the land these days.

Enough and *too*

230 *Enough* and *too* are words indicating 'as much as' and 'more than' some (usually desirable) norm. The norm these words relate to can be indicated by a *to*-infinitive clause (*see* 493):

This new boat is **big enough to cross the Atlantic**.

This just sounds **too good to be true**.

Some of the new laws are **too complex for the ordinary citizen to understand**. <rather formal>

The viewpoint or standard for judging what is 'enough' or 'too much' can be expressed by a *for*-phrase:

Is the room **warm enough for you**?

The portrait was **too big for the room**.

Where the meaning is obvious, reference to norm and viewpoint can be omitted:

Are you **warm enough**? (i.e. 'warm enough to be comfortable')

We have been looking at all kinds of new properties, but they're all **too expensive**.

So . . . (that) and such . . . (that)

231 Degree or amount constructions with *so . . . (that)* and *such . . . (that)* (*see* 716) express a meaning similar to *enough* and *too*, except that it is more emphatic:

> It moved **so** quickly **that we didn't see anything**. (meaning roughly 'too quickly for us to see anything')
>
> The bed was **so** comfortable **that visitors always overslept**.
>
> He's **such** a miser **that he doesn't even stick stamps on his letters**.

The *so . . . (that)* and *such . . . (that)* constructions also add a meaning of result (*see* 202), expressed by a *that*-clause:

> Mrs Lewis was beaten up – kicked **so** hard **that three ribs were broken**.
>
> The interview was **such** a nightmare **that I prefer to forget all about it**.

So and *such* in these sentences add emotive emphasis, and this emphasis can also be expressed without the *that*-clause:

> The delay was 'such a nuisance!
>
> I'm 'so hungry! (*see* 300)

Comparison with nouns: *more of a success, etc.*

232 The various types of comparison just illustrated can be applied to gradable countable nouns (like *success, fool, coward*) by the use of *more of a, as much of a, less of a*, etc.:

> I'm **more of a socialist** now than before.
>
> It was **as much of a** success as I hoped (it would be).
>
> You're **less of a** fool than I thought (you were).
>
> He's **too much of a** coward to tell the full story.

Proportion

233 To compare equivalent tendencies, you can use an adverbial clause of **proportion** introduced by *as*:

> Things got worse and worse **as time went on**.
>
> **As children get older** women are more likely to work outside the home.

There is a more <formal> construction in which *so* is added to a following main clause:

> **As** the slope of the table increased, **so** everything on it began to slide downwards, nearer to its edge.

Yet another construction expressing proportion consists of two clauses beginning with *the* + a comparative word:

Kids! **The** older they get, **the** more trouble they become.

Sandra couldn't deny that, **the more** she thought about the question **the more** curious it became.

Notice that *the* here is not the definite article, but a kind of degree adverb (as in *It was all **the** more surprising that she lost the third set*). The comparative element of the clause has to come first after *the*, and so often requires a change from normal word order. Compare (for clause elements S, V, O, A, *see* 487):

$\Big\{$ **He takes little notice** at the best of times. [SVO]

BUT: **The more** you argue with him, **the less notice** he takes. [ASVA], [OSV]

The subject and verb of the second clause, or of both clauses, can be omitted if their meaning is obvious:

The more tickets you can sell, **the better**. (i.e. . . . the better it will be)

The more the merrier. (proverb)

We'll have to begin our journey early tomorrow; in fact, **the earlier**, **the better**.

Addition, exception and restriction

Addition

234 To express **addition** we can use the prepositions *in addition to*, *as well as*, and *besides*:

They stole three valuable paintings, **in addition to** the money. [1]

As well as $\Big\}$ eating a four-course meal, they drank three
Besides $\Big\}$ bottles of wine. [2]

In a coordinate construction, the idea of addition can be simply conveyed by *and*, or (with more emphasis) by *not only . . . but (also)* (*see* 520). Thus [1] is equivalent to:

~ The money (was stolen) and three valuable paintings were stolen. [1a]

~ **Not only** the money, **but (also)** three valuable paintings were stolen. [1b]

The adverbials *also*, *too* <informal>, *as well* <informal>, and *in addition* <rather formal> all have the meaning 'in addition to that' (where *that* points back to something mentioned earlier):

They ate a four-course meal: they **also** drank three bottles of wine.
(i.e. 'in addition to eating a four-course meal')

~ they drank three bottles of wine, **too/as well**.

~ **in addition**, they drank three bottles of wine.

The preferred positions of these adverbials are different: *also* prefers mid-position (*see* 451), *too* and *as well* end-position, and *in addition* front-position (but *see* 238).

So am I, etc.

235 *So* can be placed first in the sentence and followed by inversion (*see* 415) of subject and operator. It then combines the meaning of *also* or *too* with the function of a substitute form (*see* 418):

I live close to the office. **So does my secretary**. (= 'and my secretary does too')

If the fascists had gained time to prepare for war, **so had their enemies**.

While *so* and *too* have a positive meaning, *neither* and *nor* have the corresponding negative meaning. For negative clauses, there is also the corresponding *any*-word (*see* 697) and adverb *either* <informal>, which occurs at the end of a clause. Note that *so*, *neither*, and *nor* cause inversion (*see* 417–18):

| [A] I'm hungry. | [B] I am, **too** | POSITIVE |
| | [B] **So** am I. | |

[A] I'm not hungry.	[B] **Neither** am I.	NEGATIVE
	[B] **Nor** am I.	
	[B] I'm not, **either**.	

Exception: *except (for)*, *apart from*, etc.

236 **Exception** is the opposite of addition: it indicates 'subtraction' from a general truth. This meaning can be expressed by a number of prepositions: *except*, *except for*, *apart from*, *bar*, *but* (*but* occurs only as part of a modifier):

None of us had any money **except** **(for)** **James**.

Apart from herself and the MacGregors, the house appeared to be empty.

In everything **but title**, he is deputy Premier.

All the heavy guns **bar one** were lost in the river crossing. (less common)

We can also use an adverbial clause beginning with the conjunction *except (that)*:

The expedition was working well, **except that** no one could figure out who was the leader.

Otherwise and *else* are adverbs of exception:

> You have a good tan, but *otherwise* (= 'apart from that') you don't look like a man fresh back from sunny Italy.

> I noticed that the attic door had been forced open but everything *else* (= 'apart from that') seemed to be intact.

In this sense, *otherwise* occurs as a sentence adverb, whereas *else* occurs as a modifier following a pronoun.

The adverb *even* expresses the negation of exception ('not excepting') normally with an effect of surprise and emphasis (*see* 213):

> They stole everything – *even* the clothes in the cupboard. ('not excepting the clothes in the cupboard')

Even is also closely related to the notion of addition:

> He knows several languages; he even claims to speak Chinese. ('that in addition to all the others')

Restriction: *only*, etc.

237 The word *only* is **restrictive**: it combines negative meaning with the idea of exception:

> He was wearing *only* his shorts. (= 'he was wearing *nothing but* his shorts')

> *Only* James had any money. (= 'no one except James . . .')

With expressions of amount (*see* 70–80) and degree (*see* 215–22) etc., *only* means 'no more than . . .':

> *Only a few* banks have published their balance sheets. (= 'no more than a few . . .')

> I know her *only slightly*. (= '. . . no more than slightly')

Other words with a meaning similar to *only* are *merely, simply, just*:

> She did not reply, but *merely* smiled, admitting nothing.

> I don't mind who wins the contest: for me it's *simply* a matter of curiosity.

> This offer is more to me than *just* a job.

The restrictive meaning of *only* and *just* can be applied, in a slightly different way, to time:

> I saw her *only/just last week*. (= 'no earlier than', 'as recently as')

Notice the contrast between *only* and *even*:

> *Only my coat* was wet. ('that and nothing else')

> *Even my underclothes* were soaked. ('those as well as everything else')

Ambiguity with *also, only*, etc.

238 Adverbs of addition, exception and restriction (like *also, even, only*) often 'focus' their meaning on a particular part of the sentence, such as a noun phrase or a verb or the whole of the sentence following the subject. A sentence can be ambiguous, depending on the element that is 'focused': *I only lent her the books.* But contrastive intonation (*see* 400) can help to clarify the meaning:

> (I didn't gǐve her anything –) I only lènt her the books.   [1]
>
> (I didn't lend her the compǔter –) I only lent her the bòoks.   [2]

An example with *also* is:

> (He's not only a gòod ́actor –) He's also a succèssful actor.
>
> (He's not only a successful mǎnager –) He's also a successful àctor.
>
> (He's not only a wrǐter –) He's also a successful àctor.

(The parts underlined are those which are 'focused'.) In writing, it is best to put the focusing adverb as near to the focused element as possible. Put *only* and *even* before it, and *also* and *too* after it. Thus you could pick out the meaning of [2] by writing *I lent her only the books*, instead of *I only lent her the books.*

Only and *even* in front-position focus on the next element of the sentence – usually the subject:

> Only **one of us** had a sleeping bag.
>
> Even **the BBC̀** makes mistakes sómetimes.

Compare:

> **His wife** àlso has a degree in medicine. ('His wife, as well as he himself')
>
> I tòo thought he looked ill. ('I thought so, as well as you.')

Subject matter: *about* and *on*

239 *About* and *on* can both indicate the subject of a communication or discussion:

> She **told** me **about** her adventures.
>
> She gave us **an excellent lecture on/about** European social history.
>
> Have you **any books on/about** stamp-collecting?

Some verbs and nouns go with *about* or *on*, others go with *about* only:

speak about/on	teach (someone) about
lecture about/on	learn about
argue about/on	read about

write about/on	a quarrel about
a book about/on	a story about
a discussion about/on	ignorance about

On, unlike *about*, tends to be limited to deliberate, formal acts of speaking and writing, and also suggests a more definite focusing on the subject matter or topic. *About* can also be used of mental states: *think about, know about, be sorry about*, etc.

Note
Of is sometimes used instead of *about*: *I wouldn't dream of asking him; All you think of is money*. But notice the difference between *He thought about the problem* (= 'He considered the problem') and *He thought of the problem* (= 'He brought the problem to his mind').

Information, reality and belief

Statements, questions and responses

240 Why do we need to use language? Probably the most important reason (but not the only one) is that we wish to give some piece of information to someone who may not know about it already. **Statements** (*see* 696) are typically sentences which give information. **Questions** (*see* 681–4, 696) are typically sentences by which someone asks the hearer to give information. In this section, we discuss the ways in which information is given and received and we also consider people's attitudes to information, and the reality it deals with. This means considering such notions as truth, belief, probability, and indirect speech.

Questions and answers

241 In conversation, both statements and questions often evoke a **response**. For questions, the most natural response is an answer to the question, giving the speaker the information needed:

Yes-no questions (*see* 682)

> [A] Is the dinner nearly réady?
>
> ⎧[B] Yes, it's already còoked. (POSITIVE ANSWER)   [1]
> ⎩[B] No, it's not còoked yet. (NEGATIVE ANSWER)   [2]

You can generally shorten the answer by omitting some or all of the information already contained in the statement. Thus a shorter version of [1] is: *Yes, it ìs* or simply *Yès*. Shorter versions of [2] are:

> No, it ìsn't.
> No, not y˅et.
> Not y˅et.
> Nò.

Wh-questions (see 683)

[A] Where are you going?   [B] (I'm going) to the òffice.

[A] What's this thing called?   [B] (It's) a wire whìsk.

Here again, part of the answer (the part in brackets) can be omitted.

Questions about alternatives

242 *Yes-no* questions are **limited**: only one of two answers (positive or negative) is possible. *Wh*-questions are **unlimited**, because any number of answers can be given, so long as they give information required by the *wh*-word (*who, what, when, where, how,* etc.; *see* 536–41). Another type of limited question is one which expects as an answer one of two or more alternatives mentioned in the question:

[A] Shall we go by tráin or by bùs?   [B] By bùs.

[A] Would you like cóffee, téa, or còcoa?   [B] Còffee, pléase.

Notice that the intonation rises on each alternative except the last, on which it falls.

There is a type of alternative question which is like a *yes-no* question in expecting a positive or negative answer:

yes-no   Are you cóming?

alternative   { Are you cóming or nòt?

                    Are you cóming or àren't you (coming)?

Such alternative questions have a rather impatient tone. Another type of alternative question is more like a *wh*-question in form:

What would you like to drìnk? Cóffee, téa, or còcoa?

Questions with positive or negative bias

Questions with some, always, already, *etc.*

243 *Yes-no* questions are mostly neutral as between positive and negative replies, e.g. when they have *any*-words like *any, ever, yet,* etc. (*see* 697–9). You can, however, use forms like *some, sometimes, already,* etc., to indicate that you expect a positive answer to your question:

Did **someone** cáll last night? ('Is it true that someone called last night? I have reason to believe that they did.')
(Compare: Did **anyone** call last night? (neutral))

Has she gone to bed **alréady**? ('Am I right in thinking that she's gone to bed already?')
(Compare: Has she gone to bed **yet**? (neutral))

Do you *sometimes* regret giving up your jób?
(Compare: Do you *ever* regret giving up your job?)

For <politeness>, use *some*-forms in making an offer:

Would you like *something* to éat? ('I expect you would!')

Do you need *some* money for the párking meter?

The response here is assumed to be positive, and so the speaker politely encourages acceptance rather than refusal.

Questions in statement form

244 You can strengthen the positive bias of a question by putting it in the form of a statement (using, however, the rising tone of a question):

You got home sáfely then?

I take it the guests have had something to éat?

These questions are rather casual in tone, as if you are assuming in advance that the answer is 'Yes'. With a negative, such questions assume the answer 'No': *The shops weren't ópen?* (You might say this on seeing someone come home with an empty shopping bag.)

Tag questions: requests for confirmation

245 Tag questions (*see* 684) added to the end of a statement ask for confirmation of the truth of the statement. The answer expected is

● 'Yes' if the statement is positive.

● 'No' if the statement is negative.

If the statement is positive, the tag question is negative, and vice versa:

He likes his jòb, dóesn't he? ('I assume he likes his job. Am I right?')

Nobody was wàtching me, wére they? ('I assume nobody was watching me. Am I right?')

If the tag question has a falling tone, the positive or negative bias is stronger, and the tag question merely asks the hearer to confirm what the speaker is already sure of. The sentence is more like a statement than a question:

It's beautiful wèather, ìsn't it?

You've mèt my wife Ánne, hàven't you? (said by a man introducing his wife to another person)

(*See* 246 Note on how negative questions are answered in English.)

Note

There is a less common type of tag question where both statement and question are positive: *You've managed to telephone, have you?* Here the statement expresses a conclusion which the speaker has arrived at from the situation. We can call them 'just checking' questions. The tone is sometimes ironic: *So you call that hard work, do you?*

Negative questions

246 One might suppose that *yes-no* questions with a negative form assume a negative answer. In fact, such questions have a mixture of positive and negative bias:

> Haven't you had breakfast yet? ('Is it really true that you haven't had breakfast? I thought you would have had it by now!') [1]
>
> Can't you drive straight? ('I thought you could, but apparently you can't!') [2]
>
> Won't anyone help us to clear up? [3]

As the examples suggest, this construction usually expresses some degree of surprise (or even annoyance). The speaker, it implies, would normally assume the positive, but now expects the negative. Thus a situation in which you would say [1] might be: you visit Mary at 10.30 a.m. and find that she is still preparing breakfast. Your earlier (and normal) assumption is that she has had breakfast; your later assumption (when you see her preparing breakfast) is that she hasn't.

Note

Some languages answer questions in a different way from English. To the question *Isn't she here yet?*, the English answer *No* means 'She is *not* here', while *Yes* means 'She is here': the answer is given to the underlying statement 'She is here', ignoring the negative grammatical form of the question.

Questions with more than one *wh*-word

247 It is possible (though unusual) to have more than one *wh*-word in the same *wh*-question. In this case, only one of the *wh*-elements is moved to the front of the sentence (unless the two *wh*-elements are coordinated):

> [A] *Who*'s bringing *what*?
>
> [B] I'm bringing the drinks, and Gary's bringing the sandwiches.
>
> [A] *How* and *when* did you arrive?
>
> [B] I arrived by train, on Friday.
>
> [A] *Who* did you send those books to, and *why*? <informal, impolite>
>
> [B] I sent them to Tanya, because she asked me for them.

Polite questions

248 You can make a question more <polite> (e.g. when addressing a stranger) by adding *please,* or by using an introductory formula like *Could you tell me.* These four questions are listed in order of politeness, from least to most polite:

> What's your nàme, pléase?
>
> Would you mind telling me your nàme?
>
> Please can I have your address and télephone number?
>
> Could I àsk you if you are driving to the stàtion?

(On *can* and *could* here, *see* 325.)

Responses to statements: backchannels

249 Unlike a question, a statement does not demand a response. But in conversation, we often make a response to a statement in order to express interest, surprise, pleasure, regret, etc., or simply to show the speaker that we are still attending:

> [A] I've just had a phone call from the travel agent . . . [B] Yés? [A] . . . you know those plane tickets to Sydney that you ordered for next Tuesday. [B] Mm? [A] well, he says they are now ready to be collected . . . [B] Oh, that's níce. [A] . . . but unfortunately, he says there's been a mistake . . . [B] Oh dèar. [A] Yes, apparently the plane doesn't arrive in Australia until 9.00 a.m. on Wednesday. [B] I sèe.

Mm /m/, *Mhm* /mhm/, *Uh-huh* /əhə/ and *Yeah* /jeə/ are casual alternatives to *Yes.* These 'backchannels' are particularly important in telephone conversations. Other signals of this kind are *Oh?* and *Really?,* to express surprise and interest:

> [A] I hear Paul's getting married.   [B] Réally?

Other backchannels are: *ah, sure, quite, right, good heavens, oh God, that's right* (*see* 23).

Short questions

250 Questions can be used as responses to statements, when the hearer wants more information. Like other responses, these questions are often shortened by omitting repeated matter. They can be shortened to the question word alone – for example, when we want to clarify the meaning of the previous utterance:

> [A] The old lady's buying a house.
>
> [B] Whèn? / Whère? / Why? / Whìch house? / Whàt old lady?

There are also two-word questions with an end-placed preposition:

[A] I'm going to write an adventure story.

[B] What fòr? / Who fòr? / What abòut?

Similar questions are: *Who with?*, *Where to?*, etc. (These questions with end-placed prepositions are <informal> in style: in <formal> English we would say *With whom?*, etc. (*see* 537). All these shortened questions are rather <familiar> and abrupt. For greater <politeness>, use a fuller question: *When is she going to buy it?*, etc. Questions like these can also be asked when what the speaker says isn't clear in some respect, e.g. where the meaning of a definite word like *this* or *the* is not specified:

[A] Were you there when they erected **the new** sígns?

[B] **Whìch** new signs?

Note
Answering a negative statement, use *Why not?* rather than *Why?*

[A] Joan is very upsèt.   [B] Whý?

[A] She hasn't been invìted.   [B] Why nòt?

Echo questions: requests for repetition

251 Another type of response question is an **echo question**. Here we ask the speaker to repeat some information (usually because we failed to hear it, but sometimes also because we can't believe our ears):

[A] I didn't enjoy that meal.

[B] Did you say you didn't enjóy it?

Here the request is explicit, but we can leave out *Did you say*, and simply 'echo' part or all of what has been said, using a (sharply rising) question intonation: *You didn't enjóy it?* In these examples, brackets show how some repeated elements may be omitted:

[A] The Browns are emigrating.   [B] (They're) émigrating?

[A] Switch the light off, please.   [B] (Switch) the líght (off)?

You can also use a **wh-echo question**, indicating by the *wh*-word which part of the sentence that you didn't hear:

[A] It cost five dollars.   [B] Hów much did (you say) it cost?   [1]

[A] He's a dermatologist.   [B] Whát is he?   [2]

Note that the nucleus occurs on the *wh*-word in these questions.

Note

The *wh*-word can also be placed later in the sentence, in its statement position. Thus instead of [1] and [2], you could say:

It cost hów much?   He's (a) whát?

But such questions, again, are <familiar> and often <impolite>, unless preceded by an apology or mark of politeness:

Sorry, whát was his job?

I'm sorry, I didn't quite hear: whát does he do?

General requests for repetition

252 General requests for repetition are very commonly used:

[A] I'll make some coffee.
- [B] ((I) beg your) párdon?
- [B] Excúse me? <AmE>
- [B] Sórry? <BrE>
- [B] Whát? <familiar, often impolite>

A more explicit general request for repetition (e.g. where you have heard most, but not all, of what was said) can take one of the following forms:

I'm sorry, I didn't quite hear/follow what you sàid.

Sorry, I didn't quite gèt that. <informal>

Sorry, would you mind repéating that?

I'm very sorry, would you mind saying that agáin?

Omission of information

253 The last section has already illustrated the general rule that we omit information which is already obvious from the preceding context. The rule is further illustrated by the following statement and six possible replies:

[A] This country must economize if it's going to increase its prosperity.

[B]
- I agrèe.
- Absolùtely.
- Certainly nòt.
- Nònsense.
- True enŏugh, but the problem is hŏw to economize.
- And the only way to do it is by greater taxàtion.

All these responses in some way lack the structure of a 'complete sentence' (*see* 695–6), but are acceptable because the structure omitted contains information already understood.

'Incomplete' sentences and formulae

254 Elsewhere, it is the situation outside language which makes certain information unnecessary. Examples are the brief 'incomplete' or formulaic utterances you may hear in various situations:

> *Commands:* Càreful! Òut with ìt! Fàster! Not so fàst!
>
> *Questions:* More cóffee? How about jòining us? Any gráduate students here?
>
> *Slogans:* Republicans òut. Republicans for èver.
>
> *Exclamations:* Goal! Good! Excellent! You lucky boy! What a pity! Shame! Oh God, what an experience! Poor you! Oh for a drink! Now for some fun!
>
> *Alarm calls:* Hèlp! Fìre!

Sometimes, in casual <familiar> speech, you will notice that words are omitted from the beginning of a sentence. These are usually words which carry little information, such as a pronoun subject and/or an auxiliary verb. They are bracketed in the following examples:

Beg your párdon. (I . . .)	Want a drínk? (Do you . . .)
Serves you rìght. (It . . .)	Sorry I mìssed you. (I am . . .)
No wònder he's late. (It is . . .)	See you làter. (I will . . .)

255 In public notices, headings etc., a noun phrase, nominal clause, or adjective phrase often stands on its own:

Exit	Where to eat in London
College Officers – Private	Fresh Today
Members' Handbook	Setting the new agenda

Prohibition notices are often put in the form of a noun phrase: No Smoking, No Entry, No Parking, etc.

Also in some broadcasting situations, such as sports commentaries, a great deal of grammatical structure is omitted. This extract could be from a television football commentary:

> Jagtman to Jaeger: a brilliant pass, that. And the score still: Holland 1, Germany 0. The ball in-field to – oh, but beautifully cut off, and . . .

Reported statements and questions

Reported statements

256 To report what somebody has stated, you can use either quotation marks (**direct speech**) or a *that*-clause (**indirect speech**) (*see* 589):

> Marie said: 'I need more money'. (DIRECT SPEECH)
>
> Marie said that she needed more money. (INDIRECT SPEECH)

Marie said (in this example) can be called the **reporting clause**, and the rest of the sentence can be called the **reported clause**. In direct speech, the reporting clause can also be placed after the reported clause or in the middle of it:

	Marie exclaimed.	[1]
'I need more money',	exclaimed Marie.	[2]
	she exclaimed.	[3]
'That child', she said, 'is a monster.'		[4]

The subject can be placed after the verb of saying, as in [2], unless the subject is a pronoun. In present-day English, *exclaimed she* is NOT an option.

Indirect speech

257 In narrative, the reporting verb is usually in the past tense. In this case, certain changes are normally made in converting from direct speech to indirect speech:

1. Change present tense verbs into the past tense (to match the reporting verb).
2. Change 1st and 2nd person pronouns into the 3rd person.
3. (Sometimes) change pointer words (*see* 99–100): e.g. change *this* into *that*, *now* into *then*, *here* into *there*, *tomorrow* into *the next day*, and *ago* into *before*.

Direct speech (i.e. what the speaker actually said)	Indirect speech (i.e. reporting it from the narrator's viewpoint)	
'I *moved* here two years ago.'	~ He explained that **he had moved** there two years before.	[1]
'Our team **has won**.'	~ They claimed that their team **had won**.	[2]
'I **will** see you tomorrow.'	~ She promised that she **would see** him the next day.	[3]
'They **can sleep** in this room.'	~ She suggested that they **could sleep** in that/this room.	[4]

Notice that the change to the past tense applies not only to ordinary present tense verbs, but to the present perfect (*has won/had won*) (*see* 127), and to modal auxiliaries (*will/would*, *can/could*, etc.) (*see* 483). The shifting of a verb to an earlier time reference generally applies also to past tense verbs, which are shifted to the past perfect (the pluperfect) in indirect speech. Thus:

'I **saw** them yesterday.'

~ He told me that he **had seen** them the day before.

But sometimes the shift does not take place (*see* 258 (3)).

Special cases

258 There are four special cases to bear in mind in the shifting of tense in indirect speech.

(1) **Past perfect verbs** in direct speech are not changed in indirect speech: these verbs cannot be shifted 'further into the past':

'I *had seen* Mac an hour before the meeting.'

~ She said (that) she *had seen* Mac an hour before the meeting.

(2) **Modal auxiliaries** like *must*, *should*, and *ought to* do not change since they have no past tense. But *must* can also be reported as *had to*:

'You *must go*.'　　　　　　　　　 ~ She said that they $\begin{cases} must\ go. \\ had\ to\ go. \end{cases}$

'You *should be* more careful.'　 ~ He said that they *should be* more careful.

(3) **When the idea expressed in the reported statement can also be applied to the time of reporting**, there is no need to change the tense or other forms:

'The world *is* flat.'　　　　　　 ~ Ancient philosophers argued that the world *is/was* flat.

This is because the question of whether the world is flat or round can apply as much to the present time as to the ancient world.

(4) **Some verbs of saying** used in direct speech narrative cannot be so easily used in indirect speech. For example:

'The game is up,' growled Trent.

is normal in mystery and crime fiction, but not:

Trent growled that the game was up.

These verbs include verbs which emphasize vocal effect (like *gasp*, *grunt*, *laugh*, *shout*):

'Give the poor girl a chance to get a word in!', Jean *laughed*.

'I'm done', he **gasped**.

'See for yourself', **shouted** Derieux.

Other verbs like *answer*, *declare*, *reply*, *say* can be readily used for both direct and indirect speech, while verbs like *assert*, *confirm*, *state* occur mainly with indirect speech:

Stacey *replied* that it would bankrupt Forbes.

The club **confirmed** that Irons was one of its leading members.

Indirect questions

259 The rules for indirect speech apply not only to indirect statements but also to indirect questions. The only difference is that for indirect questions, a *wh*-clause (*see* 590–1) is used instead of a *that*-clause:

Direct speech	Indirect speech	
'*Do you **live** here?*'	~ She asked him if (OR whether) he **lived** there.	[5]
'*Did our team **win**?*'	~ They asked if (OR whether) their team **had won**.	[6]
'Why **won't** you come with **us**?	~ He asked her why she **wouldn't come** with them.	[7]
'Which chair **shall I sit** in?'	~ He wondered which chair he **should sit** in.	[8]

Indirect *yes-no* questions ([5], [6]) are introduced by *if* or *whether* (*see* 591). Indirect *wh*-questions are introduced by the *wh*-word which begins the question in direct speech.

260 Questions about alternatives (*see* 242) behave in the same way. The *yes-no* type of alternative question is generally introduced by *whether* in indirect speech:

'Is it **your** turn or **Susan's**?'

~ She asked him whether it was **his** turn or **Susan's**.

There is also a type of indirect question in which the reported clause is a *to*-infinitive clause beginning with a *wh*-word (compare commands, *see* 336):

I asked him what to **do**. (= 'I asked him what I should do.')

He wondered whether to **leave**. (= 'He wondered whether he ought to leave.')

Denial and affirmation

Negative sentences

261 When speakers want to deny the truth of something, they use a **negative sentence** containing one of the negative items *not* (or *n't*), *no*, *nothing*, *nowhere*, etc. (*see* 581–4). The part of a sentence or clause which follows the negative word is called the **scope of negation**, and it is this part of the sentence that is negated. The scope of negation is here signalled by **bold type**:

He definitely has**n't taken the job**. ('It's definite that he hasn't')	[1]
He has**n't definitely taken the job**. ('It's not definite that he has')	[2]

In these examples, the meaning is different because in [1] *definitely* is outside the scope of negation, while in [2] *definitely* is within the scope of negation. A final adverbial may or may not be in the scope of negation:

They were**n't** at h**o**me | for the whole d**a**y. ('For the whole day, they weren't at home.')

They were**n't** *at home for the whole* d**a**y. ('It's not true that they were at home for the whole day.')

(On the intonation here, *see* 33–41, 397–8.) Notice the difference in meaning between the first and second sentence in the following pairs:

Crime necessarily does**n't** *pay*.   (= 'Crime never pays.')

Crime does**n't** *necessary pay*.   (= 'It doesn't always pay.')

I really do**n't** *mind waiting*.   (= 'I don't mind at all.')

I do**n't** *really mind waiting*.   (= 'I DO mind, but not too much.')

262 Inside the scope of negation, *any*-words like *any, yet, ever* (*see* 697–9) are used:

I did**n't** *attend* **a**ny *of the lectures*. ('I attended none of the lectures.')   [3]

We have**n't** *had* d**i**nner *yet*.   [4]

But we can also use *some*-words like *some, already, sometimes* after the negative word, and these words lie outside the scope of negation. Therefore the meaning of [3] is different from that of [5]:

I did**n't** *attend* s**o**me *of the* l**e**ctures. ('There were some lectures that I didn't attend.')   [5]

263 Occasionally a negative word does not have scope in a clause or sentence at all. Instead, it applies its meaning only to a phrase or part of a phrase in the sentence:

No food at all is better than unwholesome food. (i.e. '*Eating nothing at all* is better than . . .').

We *not infrequently* go abroad. (i.e. 'We *quite often* go abroad.')

They stayed at a *not very* attractive hotel. (i.e. '. . . at a *rather un*attractive hotel')

Affirmation

264 To place emphasis on the positive meaning of a sentence, we put the intonation nucleus on the operator (or first auxiliary of the verb phrase, *see* 609–12). This is done especially for contrast, when someone has suggested or assumed the negative:

[A] So you two haven't met before?   [B] Well, we h\`ave m\´et – but it was
                                           \`ages ago.

[A] What a pity Mary isn't here!   [B] (But) she \`is here.

If the response is not a straightforward denial, but contains new positive information, the new information is stressed by a fall-rise tone (*see* 43):

[A] Surely they wouldn't have   [B] N\`o, but they c\`ould have taken
    stolen it?   it by mist\ˇake.

If there is no other operator, use *do* as dummy operator (*see* 611):

Oh, so you d\`id stay after \`all. I thought you were leaving \`early.

I'm afraid I don't know much about cooking. But I d\`o bake my own br\ˇead.

Denial

265 To DENY what someone has suggested or supposed, you can again place the nucleus on the operator, but this time on a negative one (*can't*, *didn't*, etc.):

So you h\`aven't lost your keys! ('I thought you had.')

[A] When did he pass his ex\ˇam?   [B] Well, actually, he d\`idn't pass it.

When the negative is not contracted, the nucleus falls on *not*:

Well, actually, he did n\`ot pass it.

Short affirmations

266 There is a shortened type of affirmation in which everything in a clause is omitted after the operator. This is usual when you are simply affirming a question or statement, and do not need to repeat what has already been said:

[A] This book is interesting.   [B] Yes, it \`is. (i.e. 'It \`is interesting')

[A] I assume I will be invited   [B] Yes, you w\`ill.
    to the meeting.

[A] Can you speak German?   [B] Well, I c\`an, but not very w\ˇell.

[A] Have I missed the bus?   [B] Yes, I'm afraid you h\`ave.

To agree with a negative statement, use a negative operator:

[A] Your mother doesn't look w\`ell.    [B] No, she d\`oesn't, I'm afr\´aid.

Short denials

267 Shortened statements (in the negative) are also used to deny a statement:

[A] You worry too much.	[B] No, I dón't. [6]
[A] I'll probably fail my driving test.	[B] No, you wǒn't. [7]

Notice that when we deny or contradict a statement, as in [6] and [7], we use a rise or fall-rise tone. Similar shortened statements are used to answer a question:

[A] Can you speak German?	[B] No, I'm afraid I càn't.
[A] The line's busy. Will you hold?	[B] No, I wòn't, thanks.

More <formal> or emphatic sentences contain operator + *not*. In these cases the nucleus is on *not*:

[A] Did she fail the test?	[B] No, she did nòt.

To deny a negative statement, you can use the positive operator with a rising or fall-rise tone:

[A] I understand most people didn't agree with me.	[B] Yes, they díd.
[A] I won't pass the exam.	[B] I bet you wǐll.

268 A denial can seem blunt and <impolite> unless we tone it down in some way. We can make a denial more <tactful> by only <tentatively> expressing the contrary view:

[A] He's married, isn't he?	[B] Actually, I don't think he ìs.
	[B] Ís he? I thought he was divǒrced.
	[B] Are you súre? I had the impression that he was still sìngle.

Denial combined with affirmation

269 The construction *not* (or *n't*) . . . *but* is used to deny one idea and to affirm another, contrasting, idea:

He did**n't** look at Captain Mosira, ***but*** stared at the ceiling.

The land does**n't** belong to me, ***but*** to the government.

We can also say:

The land belongs ***not*** to me, ***but*** to the government.

The land belongs to the government, ***not*** to me.

Notice a nucleus can be on the operator in both the positive and negative clause:

I dòn't like mathemǎtics, but dò enjoy biòlogy.

Agreement and disagreement

Agreement

270 It is all the more necessary to be <polite> when the other person's **judgement** or **opinion** is in question. In agreeing with an unfavourable opinion, you may wish to qualify your agreement with an expression of regret, etc:

[A] His speech was so boring.
- [B] Yes, I'm afraid it wàs.
- [B] Yes, I have to agree with you it wàs.
- [B] I have to admit I found it só.

In other cases, you can be as enthusiastic as you like in expressing your agreement:

[A] It was an interesting exhibition, wasn't it?

[B] (Yes,) it was supèrb/absolutely splèndid, etc.

[A] A referendum will satisfy everybody.

[B] (Yes,)
- dèfinitely.
- exăctly.
- absolùtely.

[A] A referendum won't satisfy everybody.

[B]
- Definitely nòt.
- It certainly wòn't.
- You're absolutely rĭght, it wòn't.
- I agrèe. It wòn't.

Tactful disagreement

271 When you deny or contradict what someone else has stated, the effect is often <impolite>, unless the denial is softened in some way. You can soften it by an apology or by adjusting to the speaker's point of view:

[A] English is a difficult language to learn.
- [B] I'm afraid I disagrèe with you: some languages are even mòre difficult, I thínk.
- [B] Trŭe, but the gràmmar is quite éasy.
- [B] Yĕs, but it's not so difficult as Rŭssian.
- [B] Do you thĭnk so? Àctually, I find it quite èasy.

[A] The book is tremendously well wrĭtten.

[B] Yès, (well written) as a whŏle – but there are some pretty boring pătches, àren't there?

Partial or qualified agreement

272 In discussion and argument, there is often a need to agree with one part of a speaker's view, and to disagree with another. Here are some of the methods you might use to express this sort of qualified agreement (X and Y here stand for statements, and x and y for noun phrases).

> Certainly it's true that [X] *drugs are a menace*, but on the other hand [Y] *we have to take a pragmatic stance*.

> I realize that [X] *every form of taxation has its critics*, but surely [Y] *this is the most unfair and unpopular tax that was ever invented*.

> I'm in total agreement with you/Joan, etc. about [x] *the need for international action*, but we also have to consider [y] *the right of nations to take charge of their own internal affairs*.

> Agreed, but if we accept [X] *that narcotics have to be illegal*, then it must (also) be accepted that [Y] *tobacco has to be banned*.

Strengthened agreement

273 We can also agree, and add a further point to strengthen the argument:

> [A] The government will have to take steps to limit the number of cars on the road.

> [B] Yes, in fact *I believe public opinion is now in favour of banning cars in the central areas of major cities*.

Other ways of strengthening agreement (following utterance [A] above) are:

> [B] Yes, and what is more, *it will have to curb the transportation of heavy goods by road*.

> [B] I agree, and in fact one might go so far as to say *that this is the greatest challenge facing the government today*.

> [B] Absolutely. Actually, I would go further, and say *most people would favour a totally new look at all aspects of transport policy*.

Fact, hypothesis and neutrality

274 We have considered the truth and falsehood of statements in terms of affirmation, denial, negation, etc. but there are many cases where truth or falsehood is ASSUMED rather than directly stated.

Compare:

> I'm glad that the minister has agreed. (FACT)   [1]

> I wish that the minister had agreed. (HYPOTHESIS)   [2]

In [1], the speaker assumes the truth of the statement *the minister has agreed*, while in [2], the speaker assumes its falsehood. We will call something assumed to be false **hypothetical**.

Hypothetical meaning

275 ● A **fact** (or factual meaning) is usually expressed by a finite verb clause, as in [1] in 274, or by an *-ing* clause (*see* 493) or a noun phrase with an abstract noun:

> I'm surprised *that he made that mistake.*
>
> ~ I'm surprised *at his making that mistake.*
>
> ~ I was surprised *at his mistake.*

● A **hypothesis** (or hypothetical meaning) is usually expressed by the past tense in dependent clauses, as in [2] in 274, and by *would* (or *'d*) + infinitive in main clauses. These two constructions can be seen in the conditional subclause and in the main clause of hypothetical conditions (*see* 207):

> SUBCLAUSE
>
> If we *saw* anything strange, we *would let* you know.
>
> MAIN CLAUSE

Notice that the past tense (*saw, would*) here has nothing to do with past time: its reference is to PRESENT or FUTURE time.

Past time, when combined with hypothesis, is expressed by the perfective construction *had* + *-ed* participle:

> If we*'d seen* anything strange, we *would have let* you know.

Would in the verb of the main clause can be replaced by another past tense modal auxiliary:

> If Monty *hadn't been* there, you *could have told* ('would have been able to tell') the whole story.

Other constructions containing hypothetical clauses

276 Apart from conditional clauses, hypothetical meaning occurs in a few other special constructions. The main ones are illustrated here (with the negative statements they imply in brackets):

> *It's time* you were in bed. ('but you're not in bed')
>
> He behaves *as if* he owned the place. ('but he doesn't own the place')
>
> It's not *as if* you were all that fond of Alice. ('You're not fond of Alice')

Suppose (that) the United Nations had the power to impose a peaceful solution. ('It does not have the power . . .')

If only she had kept her eyes open. ('She didn't keep them open')

In your place, I'd have taken the taxi. ('I didn't take the taxi')

Very often *would* is used where there is no *if*-clause, but where a conditional 'if' is implied:

I can't let anyone see the letters – it **wouldn't** be right, **would** it? ('. . . if I let them see them')

(There are special hypothetical uses of modal auxiliaries for tentative meaning – *see* 286, 322, 325.)

Other ways of expressing hypothetical meaning

Were, were to, should

277 In addition to the past tense, there are three less common ways of expressing hypothetical meaning in subclauses:

● The *were*-subjunctive (*see* 708).

I'd play football with you if I **were** younger.

If I **were** Home Secretary, I would impose no restriction whatsoever in such matters.

In <informal> style the ordinary past tense *was* can replace *were* with a singular subject.

● *Were to* + infinitive:

If it **were to rain** tomorrow, the match would be postponed. <rather formal>

This construction expresses hypothetical future. Again, *was to* is an <informal> equivalent.

● *Should* + infinitive

If a serious crisis **should arise**, the government would have to take immediate action. <rather formal>

The constructions with *were to* + infinitive and *should* + infinitive are slightly <formal or literary>, and suggest <tentative> conditions. They are in general limited to conditional clauses (and constructions related to conditions, like *Suppose he should see us!*).

Conditionals with inversion

278 Another type of hypothetical conditional clause has no *if*, but instead begins with an operator (609) placed before the subject (inversion – *see* 416).

The three operators which occur in this construction are *had*, subjunctive *were*, and putative *should* (*see* 280 below):

> **Had they known**, they would have been more frightened. <formal>
> ('If they had known . . .')
>
> **Were a serious crisis to arise**, the government would have to act swiftly.
> <formal> ('If a serious crisis were . . .')
>
> **Should you change your mind**, no one would blame you. ('If you
> should . . .')

These clauses with *were* and *should* are rather <literary> in tone, and can always be replaced by an *if*-clause: *If they had known*, etc.

Note
In the negative of clauses beginning with *had*, *were* and *should*, there is no contracted form: instead of **Hadn't I known*, etc. we have to say *Had I not known*, etc.

Neutrality

279 In addition to fact and hypothesis, there is a third type of situation, in which the speaker assumes neither truth nor falsehood. We will call this situation **neutrality**. For example:

> It's best **for Sarah to be patient**.   [1]
>
> I want **all of us to agree**.   [2]

In sentence [1], we do not know whether Sarah will be patient or not; in sentence [2], we do not know whether all of us will agree or not. In this sense, the assumptions are **neutral**. Infinitive clauses usually express neutrality.

Open conditions with *if* or *unless* are another case of a construction which is **neutral** with regard to truth and falsehood:

> It's best **if Sarah is patient**.   [3]
>
> **Unless we all agree**, the whole project will collapse.   [4]

Sentences [1] and [3] have the same effect. Also neutral are *wh*-clauses, which in this respect sometimes contrast with *that*-clauses:

> Did you know **that** the minister has agreed? ('I'm telling you – the
> minister has agreed.')
>
> Do you know **whether** the minister has agreed? ('Please tell me')

There is a similar contrast between:

> Yesterday, he told me **that** he had passed the exam. ('So I know, already')
>
> Tomorrow, he will tell me **whether** he has passed the exam. ('I don't
> know yet')

Doubt is another verb that can be followed by either a *that*-clause or a *wh*-clause. *Not + doubt*, on the other hand, expresses certainty, and so takes a *that*-clause:

I doubt whether ⎫
                ⎬ James will cooperate with us.
I don't doubt that ⎭

Putative *should*

280 We have already said that *should* expresses a tentative condition in *if*-clauses. This is true not only for hypothetical conditions, but for OPEN conditions (*see* 207):

⎧*hear*   ⎫
If you ⎨   ⎬ the news, Jane, please let me know.
⎩*should hear* <tentative> ⎭

(We do not know from this whether or not Jane will hear the news.)

In other dependent clauses, too, *should* is used neutrally, to represent something as a neutral 'idea' rather than as a 'fact'. We call this use of *should* **putative**. Contrast these two sentences:

FACT: The fact is that the referendum will be held next month.

We know that the referendum will be held next month.

IDEA: The idea is that the referendum **should** be held next month.

Someone is suggesting that the referendum **should** be held next month.

281 Putative *should* occurs quite widely in *that*-clauses (*see* 589), especially in <BrE>:

It's a pity that you **should have** to leave.   [4]

I'm surprised that there **should be** any objection.   [5]

It's unthinkable that he **should resign**.   [6]

What gets me is that men **should be able** to threaten ordinary
    peaceful citizens with bombs and bullets.   [7]

In some of these sentences, there is no neutrality: for example, the speaker of [5] assumes that 'somebody objects'. Even so, there is a difference between [5] and the factual sentence *I'm surprised that there is an objection*, because in [5] it is the 'very idea' of the objection that surprises me, not the objection as a fact. Putative *should* in [4]–[7] has a more emotional tone.

Note

[a] Putative *should* is also found in some questions and exclamations:

How should I know?

Why should she have to resign?

[*b*] In some sentences, putative *should* is difficult to distinguish from *should* in the sense of 'ought to' (292, 328): *He has urged that private firearms should be banned.*

The subjunctive

282 The subjunctive (*see* 706–8) also has neutral meaning. It can be used:

● **In some *that*-clauses**, where the clause expresses an intention (this is especially common in <AmE>):

> Congress has **voted**/**decided**/**decreed**/**insisted** that the present law **continue** to operate.

Here putative *should* + infinitive can also be used: . . . *should continue to operate.*

● **In some conditional, contrast and purpose clauses** (*see* 207–14):

> Whatever **be** the reasons for it, we cannot tolerate disloyalty.
> <formal, elevated>
>
> (= 'Whatever the reasons for it may be . . .')

● **In certain idioms**, in main clauses:

> **God save** the Queen!   **God Bless** America.
>
> If you want to throw your life away, **so be it**. It's your life, not mine.
>
> **Heaven forbid**! (about something unfortunate that might happen)
>
> **Bless you** for coming, all of you.

These idioms tend to be rather <elevated or archaic>. In general, this formulaic subjunctive is an infrequent construction in present-day English.

Degrees of likelihood

283 Instead of thinking of truth and falsehood in black-and-white terms, we can think in terms of a **scale of likelihood**. The extremes of the scale are **impossibility** and **certainty** (or **logical necessity**). Other intermediate concepts to be considered are **possibility**, **probability**, **improbability**, etc. These notions are expressed in various ways:

● most importantly, by modal auxiliaries (*can, may, must*, etc., *see* 501):

> I **may** be wrong.
>
> Somebody's car **must** have been leaking oil.

● more <formally>, by a sentence with introductory *it* and a *that*-clause:

> **It's possible** that you're right. (*see* 542)

● by an adverbial such as *probably, perhaps, necessarily* (*see* 461–3):

> **Perhaps** there was some mistake.

We show these various constructions in 284–92. We will give special attention to the use of auxiliaries in negative sentences, in questions, in reference to past time, and in hypothetical clauses.

Auxiliaries such as *can, may,* and *must* can refer to the future as well as to the present:

> You **may feel** better tomorrow. (= 'It's possible that you will feel better')

Possibility

Can, may, could, might

284 ● **Possibility of the fact** (*factual*)

The railways **may** be improved.	[1]
It is possible that the railways will be improved.	[2]
Perhaps/possibly/maybe the railways will be improved.	[3]

● **Possibility of the idea** (*theoretical*)

The railways **can** be improved.	[4]
It is possible for the railways to be improved.	[5]

Theoretical possibility (*can*) is 'weaker' than factual possibility (*may*). Sentence [4], for example, says merely that **in theory** the railways are 'improvable', i.e. that they are not perfect. Sentence [1], on the other hand, could suggest that there are definite plans for improvement.

Note
In general or habitual statements of possibility, *can* has roughly the same meaning as *sometimes*: *A good leather bag can last* (= 'sometimes lasts') *a lifetime; She's very helpful, but she can be short-tempered; Lightning can be dangerous.*

285 ● **Negation**: For impossibility, use *cannot* or *can't* (but not *may not*):

> He **can't** be working at this time! ('It is impossible that he is working . . .')

He may not be working, on the other hand, means 'It is possible that he is not working'.

● **Questions**: Use *can* (not *may*): *Can he be working?* (= 'Is it possible that he is working?')

- **Past time**: For something which was possible in the past, use *could*:

  In those days, you **could** be sentenced to death for a small crime.

  For the (present) possibility of a past happening, use *may* + the perfect:

  Krasnikov **may** have made an important discovery. ('It is possible that he (has) made a . . .')

- **Hypothetical**: For hypothetical possibility, use *could* or *might*:

  If someone were to come to the wrong conclusion, the whole plan **could/might** be ruined.

Tentative possibility (could, might)

286 *Could* and *might* in their hypothetical sense often express <tentative> possibility, i.e. they refer to something which is possible, but unlikely:

He **could/might** have been telling lies. ('It is just possible that he was/has been telling lies.')

I wonder if there **could be** a simpler solution to the problem.

Ability (can, be able to, be capable of, etc.)

287 The notion of 'ability', also expressed by *can, be able to*, and *be capable of*, is closely related to 'theoretical possibility':

She **can** speak English fluently.

Will you **be able to** meet us in London tomorrow?

She **is capable of** keeping a secret when she wants to.

It's nice to **know how to** swim.

- **Negation**: Use *cannot, can't* (or *be unable to*, or *be incapable of*):

  I **can't speak** a word of German, and I doubt if Count Zeppelin will be able to speak English.

  I **cannot** explain what happened.

  Maria **was unable to** speak and **incapable of** moving.

- **Questions**:

  Can you drive a car?

  Do you **know** how to unlock this door?

- **Past time**: *Could* sometimes means 'knew how to'. It refers to a permanent or habitual ability:

Marcus knew that I *could* play the piano a little.

Was/were able to often combines the ideas of 'ability' and 'achievement':

By acting quickly, we *were able to* save him from drowning. ('We could, and did save him.')

● **Hypothetical**:

I'm so hungry, I *could* eat two dinners!

Deane *could* no more play Falstaff than Britt *could* play Cleopatra.

Certainty or logical necessity (*must, have to*, etc.)

288 *Must* + infinitive and *have* + *to*-infinitive (or *have got to*) can express certainty or logical necessity:

There *must* have been some misunderstanding.

You *have to* be joking! ALSO: You*'ve got to* be joking!

The bombing*'s got to* stop sometime.

It is (almost) *certain that* the hostages will be released.

Many people will *certainly/necessarily/inevitably* lose their jobs.

~ Many people are *certain/sure/bound* to lose their jobs.

Inevitably, some changes will take place.

The contrasting relation between possibility and certainty can be seen in:

She's over ninety, so

    her father *must* be *dead*.

    ~ her father *can't* still be *alive*.

    ~ *it is impossible* that her father is still *alive*.

    ~ *it is certain* that her father is *dead*.

All four sentences have in effect the same meaning.

289 ● **Questions**:

Does there *have to* be a motive for the crime?

~ Is there *necessarily* a motive for the crime?

● **Negation**:

Strikes *don't have to* be caused by bad pay (they can also be caused by bad conditions, etc.).

Strikes are *not necessarily* caused by bad pay.

There's *no need* to be upset. You *don't need* to worry about it.

Note

The modal auxiliary *need* (484) is used <*esp* in BrE> in place of *must* in questions and negatives:

> You **needn't** wait for me. ('It is unnecessary . . .')

However, this use of *need* is not common, and *need to* + infinitive or *have to* + infinitive can be used instead: *You don't need/have to wait for me. Must* is rare in questions. The following example is ironic:

> **Must** we have slurping noises?

290 ● **Past time:** We have to distinguish a past certainty (*had to*) from a certainty about the past (usually expressed by *must* + the perfect):

> Don't worry. Someone **had to** lose the game. ('It was necessary, by the rules of the game, for someone to lose.')
>
> John **must** have missed his train. ('It appears certain that John missed his train.')

● **Hypothetical:** You can use *have to* in the past tense or with *would*:

> If I **had to** choose, I'd prefer this job to any other.
>
> You **would have to** be brilliant, to win a prize.

Prediction and predictability (*will, must*)

291 As already seen (*see* 288), *must* often expresses a feeling of certainty when we draw a conclusion from evidence. On hearing the phone ring, someone might say

> That **must** be my daughter. (= 'I **know** that she is due to phone at about this time, and I therefore **conclude** that she is phoning now')

In a similar way, you can use *will* to express a '**prediction**' about the present (just as you can use *will* to make a prediction about the future – *see* 141):

> That **will** be my daughter.

There is little difference here between *must* and *will*:

> They **will** have arrived by now. (ALSO: They **will** have arrived by tomorrow.)
>
> They **must** have arrived by now. (BUT NOT: *They **must** have arrived by tomorrow.)

This sort of prediction with *will* often occurs with conditional sentences:

> If you are full, you **won't** need any pudding.
>
> If you pour boiling water on ordinary glass it **will** probably crack.

Will can also be used in a habitual sense, to express the idea of 'predictability' or 'characteristic behaviour':

> Accidents *will* happen. (a saying)

> A lion *will* attack a human being only when it is hungry.

We have noted (*see* 130) the equivalent use of *would* to express habitual or characteristic ('predictable') behaviour in the past:

> She *would* often go all day without eating.

Probability (*should, ought to,* etc.)

292 The auxiliaries *should* and *ought to* (*see* 483) can express 'probability'; they are weaker equivalents of *must* (= 'certainty'). Compare:

> Our guests *must* be home by now. ('I am certain')

> Our guests $\begin{cases} should \\ ought\ to \end{cases}$ be home by now. ('They probably are but I'm not certain.')

Should is more frequent than *ought to*. Other ways of expressing probability are:

> It is quite *probable/likely* that they didn't receive the letter.

> He is *probably* the best chess player in the country.

> They have *very likely* lost the way home. (Here *likely* is an adverb.)

> The concert is *likely* to finish late. (Here *likely* is an adjective.)

● **Negation**: Improbability can be expressed by *shouldn't, oughtn't to,* or *it is improbable/unlikely that*:

> There $\begin{cases} shouldn't \\ oughtn't\ to \end{cases}$ be any difficulties.

> ~ It *is unlikely that* there will be any difficulties.

● **Questions** (not common):

> *Is* there *likely* to be any difficulty in getting tickets?

Note
Must and *will* (*see* 291), as well as adjectives like *sure*, are sometimes used in a weakened sense that one feels is nearer to 'probability' than to 'certainty'. This is because people have a natural tendency to overstate their convictions:

> You'*ll* be feeling hungry after all that work.

> They *must* have spent years and years building this cathedral.

> I'*m sure that* they can all be trusted.

Attitudes to truth

293 We now consider the ways in which people may be committed or uncommitted to the truth or reality of something. The people concerned may be the speaker ('I') or another person, or a group of people. To express such attitudes, we often use:

- a ***that*-clause**: I know *that his answer will be 'No'*.

- a **wh-clause**: I know *what his answer will be*.

- Sometimes **adverbials**, e.g. *obviously, without doubt*:

    Without doubt, she is one of the best teachers in the school.

- **Other constructions**, such as the type of parenthetical clauses we call **comment clauses** (*see* 499), e.g. They can all be trusted, *I hope*.

Note
In <impersonal> style, people prefer to use the methods of expressing certainty, probability, etc. discussed in 288–92, rather than those which involve a 1st person pronoun. Thus *It is certain . . .* and *It is unlikely . . .* can be impersonal alternatives to *I am certain . . .* or *I doubt . . .*

Certainty

294   Polly *knew* (that) she was being watched.

You *know* what I'm like: I hate a big fuss.

I'm *certain/sure* (that) the party will be a success.

~ The party will be a success, I feel *sure*.

They were (absolutely) *convinced* $\begin{cases} \text{(that) they would succeed.} \\ \text{of their success.} \end{cases}$

It is *obvious/clear/plain* (to us all) that he has suffered a great deal.

~ He has *clearly/obviously/plainly* suffered a great deal.

We *don't doubt* that he is honest.

~ We *have no doubt* of his honesty.

Doubtless it doesn't always rain at Barnard Castle: that's just the way it seems.

Doubt or uncertainty

295 Doubt is the opposite of certainty:

I am *not certain/sure/convinced* that he deserves promotion.

~ I am *not certain/sure* whether he deserves promotion.

They were *uncertain/unsure* (*of*) who was to blame.

I *doubt* if many people will come to the meeting.

~ I *don't think* many people will come to the meeting (*see* 587).

There were some *doubts about* your pricing policy.

We have *doubts about* the risks everyone is taking.

They were *uncertain of/about* the best course to take.

Belief, opinion, and similar meanings

296 ● **Belief, opinion**

I *believe* (that) the lecture was well attended.

~ The lecture was well attended, I *believe*.

She *thinks* (that) she can dictate to everybody.

It was everybody's *opinion* that the conference was a success.

It's my *belief* that global warning will lead to widespread shifts of population.

In my opinion, he was driving the car too fast.

You may *consider* yourselves *lucky*. The hurricane could have wrecked your house. (On the use of an object complement here, *see* 508, 733.)

She was *thought/believed/considered* to be the richest woman in Europe.

Tag questions (*see* 684), especially with a falling tone, can be used to express an opinion:

He was driving too f`ast, w`asn't he?

Note

There is a slight difference between 'opinion' and 'belief': an opinion is usually something that someone arrives at on the basis of observation and judgement:

It's my belief that he drinks too much. ('I don't know how much he drinks, but . . .')

It's my opinion that he drinks too much. ('I know how much he drinks, and in my judgement, it's too much.')

● **Assumption**

We *assume/suppose* that you have received the package.

All the passengers, I *presume*, have been warned about the delay.

~ All the passengers have *presumably* been warned about the delay.

I *guess* I'm a kid at heart. <informal, AmE>

Will in the sense of 'present prediction' (*see* 291) can be used here:

I *assume you will* all have heard the news.

● **Appearance**

It *seems/appears* (to me) that no one noticed his escape.

~ No one *seems/appears* to have noticed his escape.

~ *Apparently*, no one noticed his escape.

It *looks as if* he's ill. <rather informal> (Here *looks* may refer to visual appearance only.)

Note
Like can replace *as if* in the last example in <informal AmE>. In <BrE> this use of *like* as a conjunction is less acceptable.

297 In *that*-clauses of the types shown in 296 above, transferred negation (*see* 587) is common. Thus instead of *I think he hasn't arrived*, we prefer to say *I don't think he has arrived.*

Notice that in shortened reply statements of these three categories, the clause which is the object of belief, etc. can usually be replaced by *so* (*see* 386):

	⌈I think **so**.
	⎢I suppose **so**.
[A] Has the race been postponed?	[B] ⎨It seems **so**.
	⎢Apparently **so**.
	⌊I don't think **so**.

(Here *so* replaces '(that) the race has been postponed'.)

Mood, emotion and attitude

298 In Section B, we looked at the English language as a means of giving and receiving information. But language is more than this: it is communication *between people*. It often expresses the emotions and attitudes of the speaker, and the speaker often uses it to influence the attitudes and behaviour of the hearer. These are the aspects of English we consider in this section.

Emotive emphasis in speech

Interjections

299 In this part of Section C, we shall be dealing mainly with <familiar> forms of English. Interjections are words whose main or only function is to express emotion. Common English interjections are:

Oh /oʊ/ (surprise):

> *Oh*, what a beautiful present.

Ah /ɑː/ (satisfaction, recognition, etc.):

> *Ah*, that's just what I wanted.

Aha /əˈhɑː/ (jubilant satisfaction, recognition):

> *Aha*, these books are exactly what I was looking for.

Wow /waʊ/ (great surprise):

> *Wow*, what a fantastic goal!

Yippee /ˈjɪpiː/ (excitement, delight):

> *Yippee*, this is fun!

Ouch /aʊtʃ/: (pain)

> *Ouch*, my foot!

Ow /aʊ/ (pain):

> *Ow*, that hurt!

Ugh /ʌx/ (disgust):

> *Ugh*, what a mess.

Ooh /uː/ (pleasure, pain):

> *Ooh*, this cream cake's delicious.

Other ways of giving emotion emphasis

300 ● **Exclamations** (*see* 528)

> What a wonderful time we've had!
>
> How good of you to come! <rather formal>

Exclamations are often shortened to a noun phrase or an adjectival phrase: *What a girl!* ('What a girl she is!'); *How funny!* ('How funny it is!').

● **Emphatic *so* and *such*** (*see* 528)

> The whole place was 'such a mess!
>
> I'm 'so afraid they'll get lost.
>
> I didn't know he was 'such a nice man.

These have an emotive emphasis similar to that of exclamations, but their tone can be rather 'gushy'. The words *so* and *such* are stressed, and for extra emphasis, may receive nuclear stress.

● **Repetition** (which also denotes degree = *extremely*)

> This house is 'far, 'far too expensive.
>
> I agree with *every* word you've said – 'every 'single 'word.
>
> I think that the lecturers are 'very 'very boring.
>
> You 'bad, 'bad boy! (spoken to a naughty child)

Note the use of stress (') to emphasize the repetition.

● **Stress on the operator** (*see* 609–12)

> That will be nice!
>
> What are you doing?
>
> We have enjoyed ourselves!

The operator often has nuclear stress. *Do* can be used as a dummy auxiliary to express emphasis (*see* 611–12):

> You do look pretty.
>
> You 'did give me a fright.

There is a similar use of *do* to give persuasive emphasis to a command:

'Do be qu**i**et! <impolite>

D**o** come **e**arly.

● **Nuclear stress on other words**

I w**i**sh you'd s**ee** to it.

I'm t**e**rribly s**o**rry!

Intensifying adverbs and modifiers

301 As we noted in 217–18, many degree adverbs and other degree expressions intensify the meaning of the word they modify:

Well, that's **very** nice **indeed**.

We are **utterly** powerless.

It's this sort of thing that makes me look an **absolute** fool.

In <familiar> speech, some adjectives and adverbs (such as *terrific, tremendous, awfully, terribly*) have little meaning apart from their emotive force. Thus *terrific, great, grand, fantastic* are simply emphatic equivalents of *good* or *nice*: *The weather was terrific*; *It was a great show*; etc. Notice that *awfully* and *terribly* can be used in a 'good' sense, as well as in a 'bad' sense:

She's **terribly** kind to us.

In addition to degree adverbs, certain adverbs like *really* and *definitely* have an emphatic effect:

We **really** have enjoyed ourselves.

He **definitely** impressed us.

It was **truly** a memorable occasion.

She **literally** collapsed with laughter. <familiar>

Emphasis

302 You can intensify the emotive force of a *wh*-question by adding *ever, on earth*, etc. to the *wh*-word:

How **ever** did they escape? ('I just can't imagine')

Why **on earth** didn't you tell me? ('How silly of you!')

What **the hell** does he think he's doing? ('The idiot!')

These forms are typical of <informal or familiar speech>. (*What the hell, why the hell*, etc. are mildly taboo expressions.) In <writing>, *ever* is sometimes spelled as part of the *wh*-word: *whoever, wherever*, etc., but so spelled, these words have other uses apart from intensifying (*see* 214, 592). *Why ever* is always spelled as two words.

Emphatic negation

303 ● **You can intensify a negative sentence** by adding *at all* either directly after the negative word, or in a later position in the sentence.

> The doctors found nothing *at all* the matter with him.
>
> She didn't speak to us *at all*.

Other negative intensifiers are *a bit* <informal> and *by any means* (both adverbials of degree); and *whatever* (modifier after a negative noun phrase):

> They weren't *a bit* apologetic.
>
> You have no excuse *whatever*.

Further examples of negative intensifiers are:

> I didn't sleep *a wink*. <informal> (used only with the verb *sleep*)
>
> He didn't give me *a thing*. <informal> (= 'anything at all')

● **A negative noun phrase beginning *not a*** can be used for emphasis:

> We arrived *not a* moment too soon. (= We didn't arrive one moment too soon.)

● **Fronted negation**

The negative element can be placed at the beginning of the clause. This rather <rhetorical> form of negative emphasis is often combined with the forms already mentioned:

> *Not* a penny of the money did he spend.
>
> *Never* have I seen such a crowd of people. <rather formal>

As the examples show, the operator (*did, have*, etc.) is placed before the subject (unless the negative element is itself the subject: *Not a single word passed her lips*) (*see* 417).

Exclamatory and rhetorical questions

304 An **exclamatory question** is a *yes-no* question spoken with an emphatic falling tone, instead of the usual rising tone. The most common type has a negative form:

> Hasn't she gròwn! ('She's grown very very much!')   [1]
>
> Wasn't it a marvellous còncert!   [2]
>
> [A] The picture's faded.   [B] Yes, isn't it a pìty.   [3]

Here the speaker vigorously invites the hearer's agreement; the effect of [2] is similar to:

> It was a marvellous còncert, wàsn't it? (*see* 245)

Another type of exclamatory question is positive in form, with stress on the operator and subject:

'Am 'I hùngry! ('I'm very very hungry.')

'Did 'he look annòyed! ('He certainly looked very annoyed.')

'Has 'she gròwn! ('She's grown such a lot!')

305 A **rhetorical question** is more like a forceful statement than an exclamation.

● **Positive**

A *positive* rhetorical question is like a strong *negative* statement:

Is this a reason for saving nó one? ('Surely that is not a reason . . .')

● **Negative**

A *negative* rhetorical question is like a strong *positive* statement:

Didn't I tèll you he would forgét? ('You know I told you . . .')

There are also rhetorical *wh*-questions:

What dìfference does it make? ('It makes no difference.')

How many employees would refuse a rise in pày? ('Very few or none.')

As the name suggests, rhetorical questions are often rather <rhetorical> in tone. They challenge the hearer to deny what appears obvious.

Describing emotions

306 We come now to the description or reporting of emotive behaviour. An emotive reaction to something can be expressed by the preposition *at*:

I was *alarmed at* his behaviour.	[1]
An audience will always *laugh at* a good joke.	[2]
She was very *surprised at* your resignation from the club.	[3]

In <BrE>, *with* is often used instead of *at* when what causes the reaction is a person or object rather than an event:

I was *furious with* him for missing that penalty.

Is she *pleased with* her present?

Other prepositions used are *about* and *of*: *worried about*, *annoyed about*, *resentful of*, etc. (*see* 239).

As a former champion, he was *annoyed about* his own failures, and *resentful of* the successes of others.

What causes the emotion is often expressed by a *to*-infinitive clause or a *that*-clause (with or without *should*, *see* 280), and in these cases the preposition is omitted (*see* 655):

> They were alarmed **to find the house empty**.
>
> I'm sorry **to have kept you waiting**.
>
> He was delighted **to see them so happy**.
>
> We're anxious **that everything should go smoothly**.

307 The cause of emotion may also be expressed by the subject (or, in the passive, by *by* + the agent). Compare [3] in 306 above with:

> Your resignation from the club surprised her very much.
>
> ~ She was very surprised **by** your resignation from the club.

Other constructions for describing emotions do not specify the person affected, and are therefore more <impersonal>:

> The accommodation was **satisfactory/delightful**, etc. [4]
>
> The news from the front is **very disturbing**. [5]
>
> **It's amazing** that so many passengers were unhurt. (*see* 438, 542) [6]
>
> **It is a pity** that the government should ever have been led to abandon its principles. [7]
>
> **It's a pity** to leave the party before the fun starts. [8]

In most of these cases, the person affected is likely to be 'me' (the speaker). The person affected can sometimes be made clear by a phrase introduced by *to* or *for*: *satisfactory for most people, disturbing to me*, etc. Thus [6] can be expanded:

> **To me**, it's amazing that so many passengers were unhurt.

Sentence adverbials expressing emotion

308 Some sentence adverbials (including comment clauses, *see* 499) can express an emotional reaction or judgement:

> **To my regret**, he did not accept our offer. (i.e. 'I regretted that he did not accept the offer.')
>
> **Surprisingly**, no one has objected to the plan. (i.e. 'It is surprising that . . .')
>
> She is **wisely** staying at home today. (i.e. 'She is wise to stay . . .')
>
> The children were rather noisy, **I'm afraid**. (i.e. 'I'm afraid the children were . . .')

Other sentence adverbs similar to *surprisingly* and *wisely* are *amazingly, strangely, regrettably, fortunately, luckily, happily, hopefully, preferably, foolishly, sensibly*. For example:

Amazingly, the dog survived.

Fortunately we were outside the building when the fire started.

Hopefully all my problems are now behind me.

Liking and disliking

309 Verbs such as *like, love, hate,* and *prefer* can be followed either by a noun phrase object [9], by a *to*-infinitive clause [10] or by an *-ing* clause [11] (*see* 721–3):

	parties.	[9]
She likes/loves/hates	*to give parties*.	[10]
	giving parties.	[11]

Some English speakers see a slight difference between last two sentences: the infinitive clause in [10] expresses an 'idea' ('She likes/loves/hates the idea of it'), while the *-ing* clause in [11] expresses a 'fact' ('She likes/loves/hates it when she does it') (*see* 274). Thus in some contexts (but not in [10]), the infinitive clause may have **neutral** meaning (*see* 279):

He likes me **to work** late.
'. . . and that's why I do it.'
OR
'. . . but I never do it.'

He likes me **working** late. ('. . . and that's why I do it.')

When the main verb is hypothetical, usually only the infinitive clause can be used:

[A] Would you like **to have** dinner now?

[B] No, I'd prefer **to eat** later.

Note
Enjoy, dislike, and *loathe* take only *-ing* clauses: *He enjoys/dislikes/loathes cleaning the car.*

Preference

310 *Prefer* means 'like more' or 'like better'. The rejected alternative is expressed by a *to*-phrase, or by a clause introduced by *rather than*, which may be followed by an infinitive (with or without *to*) or by an *-ing* participle:

Most people prefer trains **to** buses.

They prefer renting a car **to** having one of their own.

~ They prefer to rent a car **rather than** to have one of their own.

~ **Rather than** buy a car of their own, they prefer to rent one.

She has always preferred making her own clothes,

$\begin{cases} \textit{rather than} \\ \textit{instead of} \end{cases}$ buying them in the shops.

Would prefer + *to*-infinitive (hypothetical preference) can be replaced by *would rather* + bare infinitive, which may be followed by a *than*-construction (*see* 715):

I**'d prefer to stay** in a house **rather than** in a hotel.

~ I**'d rather stay** in a house **than** in a hotel.

Some other emotions

311 Here are some of the ways of expressing other emotions. Many of them have already been discussed and exemplified. Notice that adverbs of degree (*see* 217–26) can be used to indicate the 'strength' of the emotion. Many of the sentences are <informal and familiar>.

Hope

312   I (very much) *hope* (that) he $\begin{cases} \text{will arrive} \\ \text{arrives} \end{cases}$ on time.

I *am hoping* that they get that letter tomorrow. <tentative> (*see* 139)

I *was hoping* we would get a bit more time. <more tentative> (*see* 121, 139)

I *hope to see* you soon.

Hopefully, next spring will bring an improvement in the economic situation.

Anticipation of pleasure

313   I am *looking forward to* receiving your reply.

I know we*'ll enjoy* meeting you again.

Disappointment or regret

314   I'm (rather/very) disappointed that the match has been cancelled.

It is (somewhat) disappointing that over half the tickets are unsold.

It's a (great) shame/pity that this is the last party.

I'm (very) sorry to hear that you have to leave.

I had hoped that she would change her mind. (unfulfilled hope) (*see* 275)

I wish (that) someone had let me know. (unfulfilled wish) (*see* 321–2)

If only I had known! (*see* 322)

Unfortunately we're having trouble with the builder.

Approval

315   I (very much) approve of $\begin{cases} \text{the plan.} \\ \text{your asking for his opinion. <formal>} \end{cases}$

It wasn't a bad movie, was it? <familiar> (mild) (*see* 684)

I (quite) like the new boss.

I $\begin{cases} \text{love} \\ \text{do like} \end{cases}$ your dress. (enthusiastic)

What a great/terrific/marvellous/ . . . movie! (enthusiastic) (528)

Disapproval

316   I don't like the way she dresses (very much).

I don't (much) care for iced tea, actually.

I didn't think $\begin{cases} \text{much of the orchestra.} \\ \text{the orchestra was much/very good.} \end{cases}$

I thought the novel was poor/dreadful/appalling, didn't you.

It would have been better, I think, if you hadn't mentioned it.

You shouldn't have bought such an expensive present. (*see* 328)

You could have been more careful.

I don't think you should have told the children.

I had hoped you would have done more than this.

Disapproval can often be expressed more indirectly by means of a question:

Did you have/need to work so late?

Why did you do a thing like that?

Was it really necessary to be so rude to the waiter?

Don't you think it would have been better if you had told me in advance?

Surprise

317 It's (rather) surprising/amazing/astonishing that so many people come to these meetings.

I am/was (very) surprised that so many turned up.

What a surprise!　　　How amazing!

How strange/odd/astonishing/amazing that you both went to the same school!

Wasn't it extraordinary that the child was totally unhurt? (*see* 304)

Surprisingly/strangely/incredibly, James slept soundly through the whole affair.

Concern, worry

318 I am (a bit) concerned/worried that our money will be used unnecessarily.

I am (rather) worried/concerned about what will happen to the union.

It's (very) disturbing/worrying that no one noticed the break-in.

I find his behaviour very disturbing/worrying.

Her health gives (some) cause for anxiety/concern. <formal, impersonal>

Volition

319 We distinguish four types of volition: **willingness, wish, intention, insistence**. These are listed in order of increasing 'strength'.

Willingness

320 Willingness can be expressed by the auxiliary *will* (or *'ll* <informal>):

[A] *Will* you lend me those scissors for a minute or two?

[B] OK, I *will*, but only if you promise to return them.

The porter *will* help if you ask him.

Here the future meaning of *will* is mixed with that of volition (*see* 129). For past or hypothetical willingness, use *would*:

● **Past time:**　　We tried to warn them about the dangers, but no one *would* listen.

● **Hypothetical**: My boss is so greedy, he *would* do anything for money.

Won't and *wouldn't* express the negative of willingness, i.e. **refusal**:

> My father's rich, but he **won't** give me any money. (= 'He refuses/ declines to give any money.')

> The guards just **wouldn't** take any notice. They **wouldn't** listen to me. (= 'They refused . . .')

Wish

321 For neutral volition, **want** is a less <formal> verb than **wish**:

> I **want** (you) to read this newspaper report.

> Do you **want** me to sign this letter?

> The manager **wishes** (me) to thank you for your cooperation. <rather formal>

For a hypothetical circumstance, use only *wish*:

> I **wish** you would listen to me! ('. . . but you won't')

322 The exclamatory construction *If only . . .* can also be used for hypothetical meaning:

> **If only** I could remember his name!

> ~ I 'do **wish** I could remember his name!

When expressing your own wishes, or inviting the wishes of others, you can make the wish more <tentative> and <tactful> by using *would like, would prefer,* or *would rather* (*see* 309–10):

> **Would you like** me to open these letters?

> I **would prefer** to stay in a less expensive hotel.

Another way to consult someone's wishes is to use a question with *shall* <mainly BrE>, or more <tentatively>, with *should*:

> **Shall** I make you a cup of coffee? ('Do you want me to . . . ?')

> What **shall** we do this evening?

> **Shall** we cancel the order if it's not needed?

> **Should** we tell him that he's not wanted?

Note
1st and 3rd person commands with *let* (*see* 498) also express a kind of wish:

> **Let's** listen to some music (, shall we?)

> **Let** everyone do what they can.

Intention

323 The verbs *intend, mean, plan* and *aim* (+ infinitive clause) express intention:

> He *intends/plans/aims* to arrest them as they leave the building.   [1]
>
> That remark was *meant/intended* to hurt her.   [2]

Intention can also be expressed by *be going to* (*see* 142) or, in the 1st person, by *will/shall* (*see* 141) or the contraction *'ll*:

> *Are* you *going to* catch the last train?
>
> We *won't* stay longer than two hours.

These forms also have an element of prediction, and so are more definite about the fulfilment of the intention than [1] and [2]. (On clauses and phrases of purpose, or 'intended result', *see* 203.)

Insistence

324 He *insists* on doing everything himself.

> We *are determined* to overcome the problem.

Insistence is occasionally expressed by *will/shall* with strong stress:

> He 'will try to mend it him<u>self</u>. ('He insists on trying . . .')
>
> I w<u>on't</u> give in! ('I am determined not to give in.')

Permission and obligation

Permission: *can, may,* etc.

325 *Can* we sit down in here? Yes, you *can*.

> *May* I speak to you for a minute? <more formal, polite>
>
> *Are we allowed to* use the swimming pool?
>
> *Is it all right if* we smoke in here? <informal>
>
> They have *allowed/permitted her to* take the examination late.
>
>   (*permit* is <more formal> than *allow*)
>
> They *let* him do what he wants.

Nowadays *may* is rarely used for permission: *can* is used instead.

- **Past**: *could*

> The detainees *could* leave the camp only by permission of the governor. ('. . . were allowed to . . .')

● **Hypothetical**

> If you were a student, you *could* travel at half-price. ('. . . would be
> allowed to . . .')

You can also use hypothetical *could* (and rarely *might*) in <tactful> requests
for permission:

> *Could* we ask you what your opinion is?
> I wonder if I *could* borrow your pen?

Another construction for asking and giving permission involves the verb *mind*:

[A] *Would you mind* { if I opened a window?
opening a window for me? }

[B] No. { *I don't mind* at all.
not at all. (= 'certainly you can') }

Again, the hypothetical form is more <tactful>.

Obligation or compulsion: *must, have to*, etc.

326 You *must*
You'll *have to* } be back by 2 o'clock – (I want you to do
some cleaning). [1]

You *have to* sign your name here (otherwise the document isn't valid). [2]

I've *got to* finish this essay by tomorrow. <informal> [3]

The university *requires* all students to submit their work by a date.
<formal, written> [4]

Must and *have (got) to* + infinitive (*see* 288, 483) both express obligation, but
some English speakers feel a difference between them. For such speakers,
must involves the speaker's authority (*see* [1]), while *have (got) to* may
involve some other authority than the speaker – e.g. official regulations
(*see* [2]). With a first person subject, *must* expresses my authority over
myself, e.g. my sense of duty:

> I *must* phone my parents tonight. ('They'll be worrying about me.') [5]
> We *must* invite the Stewarts to dinner. ('It's months since we last saw them.')

● **Past**: *had to*

> Beckham *had to* withdraw from the match because of injury.
> ('was obliged to . . .')

● **Hypothetical**:

> If you went abroad, you *would have to* earn your own living.
> ('. . . would be obliged to . . .')

327 ● Questions: *have got to, have to, need to,* etc.

> Why *have* you *got to* work so hard?
>
> Do we *have to* fill out all these forms?
>
> Does anyone *need to* leave early?

● **Negation:**

> We don't *have to* pay for the digital equipment – it comes for nothing.
>
> You don't *need to* pay that fine.
>
> There's no *need to* buy the tickets yet.

Note

[a] *Must* sometimes occurs in questions expecting a negative answer:

> *Must* you leave already? ('Surely you don't have to!')

[b] Especially in <BrE>, *need* as an operator can be used instead of *must* in questions and negatives. However, this is now <rare>:

> *Need* you work so hard?; We *needn't* hurry.

Other ways of expressing obligation: *should, ought to,* etc.

328 ● *Should* and *ought to* (*see* 292) express an obligation which may not be fulfilled. Compare [4] and [5] in 326 above with:

> All students *should* submit their work by a given date ('. . . but some of them don't!').
>
> I *ought to* phone my parents tonight ('but I probably won't have time').

● *Need to* + **infinitive** (where *need* is a main verb, not an auxiliary, *see* 484) indicates 'internal obligation' caused by the state of the person referred to:

> He *needs to* practise more if he is to improve his game of golf.
>
> I really *need to* clear this place up.

We can also use *need* with a direct object:

> This country *needs* a strong prime minister.

● *Had better* (or *'d better*) <informal> + **infinitive** (without *to*) means that the speaker strongly recommends or advises an action:

> You*'d better* be quick { or you'll miss the train.
> if you want to catch the train.

He'**d better not** make another mistake.

I suppose I'**d better** lock the door.

● **Shall** in the sense of 'obligation' is normally limited to official regulations and other <formal> documents:

The Society's nominating committee **shall** nominate one person for the office of President. <very formal>

Prohibition (and negative advice)

329 Prohibition is the negation of permission ('he/she is not allowed to do something'). *Can* and *may* (= 'permission') and *must* (= 'obligation') can all have the meaning of 'prohibition' with a negative:

[A] **Can** the children play here?

[B] No, I'm afraid they **can't** ('they're not allowed to') – it's against the rules.

Children **may not** use the swimming pool ('They're not allowed to . . .') unless they are accompanied by an adult. <formal, rather rare>

You **must not** tell anyone about this letter: it's confidential. ('You're obliged not to . . .')

A weakened prohibition (more like negative advice) can be expressed by *shouldn't, oughtn't to* <esp BrE>, and *had better not*:

She **shouldn't** be so impatient.

You **oughtn't to** waste all that money on smoking.

We'**d better not** wake the children up.

Note
Recently *must* in its 'obligation' sense has become less common, especially in <AmE>, perhaps because it tends to imply that the speaker is claiming authority over the addressee. *Have to, need to,* or *should* can be used instead.

Influencing people

Commands

330 ● With the aim of getting someone to do something, a **direct command** can be used: *Shut the door. Follow me. Just look at this mess.* etc. (*see* 497). A negative command has the effect of forbidding an action: *Don't be a fool. Don't worry about me.* However, an imperative is often less 'forbidding' than it seems. It can have a friendly effect, if the action is in the hearer's interest: *Help yourself.* Or it can be used jokingly: *Don't overdo it!*

● In addition, with a 2nd person subject, the **verb forms expressing obligation and prohibition** (*see* 326, 329) can have almost the same effect as a command: *You must be careful; You must not smoke here.*

● The construction *be to* + **infinitive** can convey a command given either by the speaker, or (more usually) by some official authority:

> He *is to* return to Germany tomorrow. ('He has been given orders to return to Germany.')

> You *are to* stay here until I return. ('These are my instructions to you.')

Note
[a] Some verbless sentences have the effect of brusque commands: *Out with it! This way! Here!* (= 'Bring/put it here'). Another type is especially used in addressing children and pets: *Off you go! Down you get! Up you come!* <familiar>
[b] *Will* in its future sense can sometimes be used (e.g. in military contexts) with the force of a severe command:

> Officers *will* report for duty at 0600 ('six hundred') hours.

> You *will* do exactly as I say.

Commands with grammatical subjects, etc.

331 You can specify the people who have to perform the action by putting a 2nd or 3rd person subject in front of the imperative verb (*see* 497), or else by using a vocative:

> 'You take this tray, and 'you take that one. (pointing to the people concerned; note that *you* is stressed)

> Jack and Susan stand over there.

> Somebody open this door, please.

> Come here, Michael.

Elsewhere, a command with *you* has a tone of impatience:

> 'You mind your own business!

Another form of impatient command begins with *will*:

> 'Will you be quiet!

Although this has the grammatical form of a question, its falling intonation gives it the force of a command. In many circumstances, commands are <impolite>, and therefore we shall consider in 332–5 various ways of toning down the effect of a command.

Note

However, it is <not impolite> to use a command when you are telling someone to do something for his or her own good:

> Have another chocolate.   Make yourself at home.
>
> Just leave everything to me.   Do come in.

These are in effect offers or invitations rather than commands.

Weakened commands

332 One way to tone down or weaken the imperative force of a command is to use a rising or fall-rise tone, instead of the usual falling tone:

> Be cǎreful.
>
> Don't forget your wállet.

Another way is to add *please*, or the tag question *won't you*:

> Plèase hurry úp.
>
> Look after the chìldren, wón't you.
>
> Thìs way, pléase.

However, if you are asking a favour, none of these alternatives is <polite>.

Note

Two other tags, *why don't you* and *will you* (after a negative command), can tone down a command:

> Have a drìnk, why don't you.
>
> Don't be lǎte, wìll you.

But after a positive command, *will you* has rising intonation, and usually expresses impatience (*see* 331).

> Sit dòwn, wíll you.

Requests

333 It is often more <tactful> to use a request rather than a command: i.e. to ask your hearer whether he or she is willing or able to do something. The auxiliaries *will/would* (= willingness) and *can/could* (= ability) are very often used:

> [A] *Will* you make sure the water's hót?   [B] Yès, okáy. <familiar>
>
> [A] *Would* you please tell me your   [B] Yès, cèrtainly, it's . . .
>   phóne number?
>
> [A] *Can* anyone tell us what the tíme is?   [B] Yèah, half past four.
>
> [A] *Could you* lend me a pén.   [B] Okáy. <familiar> Hére it ìs.

(These examples also show some typical replies.) *Would* and *could* are more <tactful> than *will* and *can*. You can also use a negative question, which expects a positive answer (*see* 246), and is to that extent <less tentative> and more persuasive:

> Won't you come in and sit down?
>
> Couldn't you possibly come another day?

Other <polite> forms of request

334 There are many other indirect ways of making a <polite> request; e.g. you can make a statement about your own wishes. The following are listed roughly in order of least to most <polite>:

> I wouldn't mind a drink, if you have one.
>
> Would you mind starting over again?
>
> I wonder if you could put me on your mailing list, please.
>
> Would you be good/kind enough to let me know? <more formal>
>
> I would be (extremely) grateful if you would telephone me this afternoon.
>
> I wonder if you'd mind writing a reference for me.

These sentences are typical of <polite, spoken> English. In formal letters, useful formulae are:

> I would be very grateful if you would . . .
>
> I would appreciate it if you could . . .
>
> Would you kindly . . .

Advice and suggestions

335 As ways of influencing other people, **advice** and **suggestions** are milder than commands. Strictly, these leave the decision about what to do in the hands of the hearer. But in practice, as the examples show, they are often <tactful> ways of giving commands or instructions.

● **Advice**

> You *should* stay in bed until you start to recover.
>
> You *ought to* keep your money in a bank account.
>
> There's a new book you *ought to* read.
>
> You'*d better* take your medicine.
>
> I'*d advise* you to see a doctor.
>
> *If I were you, I'd* wear proper running shoes.

● **Suggestions**

> I *suggest* they take the night train.
>
> You *can* read these two chapters before tomorrow (if you like).
>
> You *could* lose six to eight pounds, Missy.
>
> You *might* have a look at this book.
>
> *Why don't you* call on me tomorrow?
>
> *Perhaps you could* call again tomorrow?

Could and *might* indicate more <tentative> suggestions.

● **Suggestions involving the speaker**

> I *suggest* we go to bed early, and make an early start tomorrow.
>
> *Shall we* listen to some music?
>
> *Let's not* waste time.
>
> *Why don't we* have a party?
>
> *How about* a game of cards?
>
> *What about* having a drink?

Reported commands, requests, etc.

336 Commands, like statements and questions (*see* 264–8), can be reported either in direct speech or in indirect speech:

| *Direct speech:* | 'Put on your space-suits,' he said. |
| *Indirect speech:* | He told/ordered/instructed them to put on their space-suits. |

In indirect speech, put the command in the form of a *to*-infinitive clause. The hearer can be identified by an indirect object (*see* 608, 730) – *them* in the above examples. Note the passive construction:

> They *were told/ordered/instructed* to put on their space-suits.

The same construction can be used for advice, requests, permission, obligation, persuasion, invitations, etc.:

She *advised* me to telephone for a doctor.	[1]
Liam *asked/begged* me to help him with his homework	[2]
Jane *allowed* Patrick to borrow her car.	[3]
They *compelled* him to answer their questions.	[4]
Mary has *persuaded* me to resign.	[5]
We were *invited* to attend the performance.	[6]
The priest *recommended* him to try for the job.	[7]

Notice also direct object constructions:

> The doctor *advised* a rest.
>
> He *begged* our forgiveness.
>
> I (can) *recommend* the local cuisine.

337 Not all verbs for 'influencing people' take an infinitive. *Suggest* takes a *that*-clause (often with putative *should* or with the subjunctive, *see* 280–2):

> He *suggested* that they (should) play cards.

This construction may also follow other verbs, such as *recommend*:

> The doctor *recommends* that you (should) take plenty of rest.

Requests, acts of permission, etc. can also be put in the form of indirect statements and questions. Thus instead of [2] and [3] (in 336) you could say:

> He *asked* me if I would help him with his homework.   [2a]
> (Compare DIRECT SPEECH: 'Will you help me with my homework?')
>
> Jane *said* Patrick could borrow her car.   [3a]
> (Compare DIRECT SPEECH: 'You can borrow my car.')

The rules for changing into the past tense, etc. (*see* 256–7) for indirect statements and questions apply also to indirect commands, requests, etc. – except that there is no tense-change in infinitive clauses. After a past-tense reporting verb, *will, shall, can, may* and *have to* change to their past tense forms *would, should, could, might,* and *had to* (*see* [2a], [3a]) but *must, ought to, should,* and *had better* do not change:

> 'You *must* be careful.'   I told them they *must* be careful.
>
> 'You *should* stay in bed.'   I told him he *should* stay in bed.

Reported prohibitions, refusals, etc.

338 The verbs *forbid* <formal>, *prohibit* <formal>, *dissuade, refuse, decline* and *deny* already contain a negative meaning, so the clauses which follow them are normally positive:

> They were *forbidden* to smoke. }
> They were *prohibited* from smoking. } ('They were ordered not to smoke')
>
> His wife *dissuaded* him from leaving the country. ('She persuaded him not to . . .')
>
> The minister *refused/declined* to comment on the press report.
>
> He *denied* that any promises had been broken.

Warnings, promises and threats

339 Finally, we turn to three types of utterance involving future time:

- **Warnings**

  Mind (your head)!

  Look out!

  Be careful (of your clothes).

  I warn you it's going to be foggy.

  If you're not careful, that pan will catch fire.

Short warnings are often spoken with a fall-rise intonation: Mǐnd!

- **Promises**

  I'll let you know tomorrow.

  I (can) promise (you) it won't hurt.

  Can I borrow your road atlas? I promise to bring it back.

  You won't lose money, I promise (you).

  Assuming that the order reaches our office by tomorrow, our firm will undertake to supply the goods by the weekend. <formal, written>

- **Threats**

  I'll report you if you do that again.

  Don't you dàre talk to me like that.

  You dàre come near me with that silly spray!

  Touch me, and I'll tell your mother. (see 366)

  Stop eating those sweets, or I'll take them away. (see 367)

Warnings, promises and threats in reported speech

340 ● Reported warnings

  Jim Moore *warned* parents to keep their children away from the area.

  They *warned* us of/about the strike.

  We were *warned* that the journey might be dangerous.

- **Reported promises**

  He *promised/undertook* to let me know.

  Olly has *promised* Billy to take him fishing next Sunday.

  He *promised* that he wouldn't bet on horses.

  They *promised* him that he would not lose his job.

Her boss <familiar> has **promised** her a rise.

She has been **promised** a rise.

● **Threats**

She **threatened** to report me to the police.

The manager has **threatened** that they will lose their jobs.

He has **threatened** them with dismissal.

Friendly communications

341 Let us now look at some of the simple acts of communication whereby people establish and maintain friendly relations with one another. Common intonations are given where they are important (*see* 33–42).

Beginning and ending conversation

342 ● **Greetings**

Hì. <informal, esp. AmE>   Helló. <informal, esp. BrE>

Good mòrning. Good afternòon.   Good èvening. <formal>

It is common to omit *Good*: e.g. *Morning.* It is also common to use a rising tone, e.g.:

(Good) morning.

Helló (with a rising tone) is also used in answering the phone.

● **Farewells** (temporary)

Goodbýe.

(Bye)-býe. <familiar>

Sèe yóu. <familiar>

See you at six o'clòck. <familiar>

See you làter. <familiar>   See you tomòrrow. <familiar>

Cheerió. <familiar BrE>   Chèers. <very familiar, BrE>

Good-níght. (final word before parting for the night or before going to bed)

● **Farewells** (more permanent):

Goodbýe.

Other remarks may be added for politeness:

It's been nice knòwing you.

(I hope you) have a good jŏurney.

● **Introductions** (when we meet for the first time)

> May I introduce (you to) Miss Brown? <formal>
>
> This is (a friend of mine,) Gordon McKeag.
>
> I don't think you've met our neighbour, Mr Quirk.

● **Greetings on introduction**

> How do you do? <formal> How are you?
>
> Glad to meet you. Hello. <informal>
>
> Hi. <familiar, especially AmE>

'Small talk'

343 After a greeting, a conversation may continue with a polite inquiry about health, etc:

> How are you?
>
> How are you getting on? <familiar>
>
> How's things? <very familiar>
>
> How are you doing? <familiar, esp. AmE>

Common replies to such questions are:

> (I'm) fine. How are you?
>
> Very well, thank you. And you?

If someone is liable to poor health, you might begin: *How are you feeling today/these days?* OR *I hope you're well.*

Especially in Britain, opening remarks about the weather are common:

> [A] (It's a) lovely day, isn't it? (*see* 245)
>
> [B] Yes, isn't it beautiful. (*see* 304)
>
> [A] What miserable weather! (*see* 528)
>
> [B] Dreadful!

Beginning and ending letters

344 ● **Example of a <formal> official letter**

> Dear Sir,/Dear Madam,
> With reference to your letter of...
> ....
> Yours faithfully,
> A R Smith
> (Manager)

● **Example of a <less formal> letter**

> Dear Dr Smith,/Miss Brown,/George,
> Thank you for your letter of...
> ....
> (With best wishes)
> ⎰Yours sincerely, <BrE>
> ⎱Sincerely (yours), <AmE>
> James Robertson

● **Example of an <informal> letter between acquaintances**

> Dear George,
> ....
> ....
> (Best wishes)
> Yours (ever),
> Janet

More intimate letters may begin and end with endearments:

> *My dear George,/Dearest George,* . . . *Love from Janet*, etc.

Thanks, apologies, regrets

345 ● **Thanks**

> Thank you (very much). Thanks very much.
>
> (Many) thanks.   Ta. <BrE slang>

● **Responses to thanks**

> Not at all.   You're welcome.
>
> That's all right.

Note that in English such responses are not so common (esp. in <BrE>) as in some other languages. Often the 'giver' makes no reply. In shops, etc. the customer will say *Thank you* for the article bought, and the shopkeeper will often likewise say *Thank you* in return, on receiving the money.

● **Apologies**

> (I'm) sorry. (I beg your) pardon. Excuse me.

Excuse me can be a proper apology in <AmE>, but in <BrE> is limited to mild apologies for routine 'impolite' behaviour; e.g. for interrupting, for sneezing, for pushing in front of somebody, for starting up a conversation with a stranger. One could say *I beg your pardon* for mishaps such as treading on someone's toe. More lengthy apologies are:

I'm extremely sorry
- (about that letter).
- (I forgot to phone you).
- (for being late again).

Will you forgive/excuse me if I have to leave early?

I hope you will forgive/excuse me if I have to leave early.

● **Responses to apologies**

That's all right.   Please don't worry.

● **Regrets**

I'm sorry I couldn't come in to congratulate you. <informal>

I regret that we were unable to provide the assistance you required. <formal, written>

Good wishes, congratulations, condolences

346 These are normally spoken with a falling tone.

● **Good wishes**

Good luck!

Best wishes for your holiday || vacation.

Have a nice day. <esp. AmE>

Have a good time at the theatre.

I wish you every success in your new career. <more formal>

● **Good wishes sent to a third person**

Please give my best wishes to Sally.

Please remember me to your father.

Please give my kindest regards to your wife. <formal>

Give my love to the children. <informal>

Say hello to Joe. <informal, esp. AmE>

● **Seasonal greetings**

Merry Christmas.   Happy New Year.

Happy birthday (to you).   Many happy returns (of your birthday).

● **Toasts**

Good health. <formal>   Your health. <formal>

Cheers! <familiar>   Here's to your new job. <familiar>

Here's to the future. <familiar>

● **Congratulations**

Well done! <familiar> (for a success or achievement).

Congratulations on your engagement.

I was delighted to hear about your success/that you won the competition.

I congratulate **The Times** on the high quality of its reporting.

May we congratulate you on your recent appointment. <formal>

● **Condolences, sympathy**

Please accept my deepest sympathy on the death of your father. <formal>

I was extremely sorry to hear about your father/that your father has been so ill. <informal>

Offers

347 In making an offer, you can make use of questions about the wishes of the hearer (*see* 319–24):

Would you like another couple of slices of túrkey?   [1]

Would you like me to mail these létters?   [2]

Shall I get you a cháir? <esp. BrE>   [3]

Can I carry your bágs upstairs?   [4]

Do you want us to drive you hóme?   [5]

Want some sóup? <casual>   [6]

In answering an offer in the form of a question, we say

either   Yès, pléase. (acceptance)

or   Nò, thánk you. (refusal)

More <polite> acceptances:

Yès, pléase. That's very kìnd of you.

Yès, thànk you, I'd lòve some more. (answer to [1] above)

Note that *thank you* can be used in accepting, as well as refusing. More <polite> refusals include an explanation of the refusal:

That's very kĭnd of you, but I couldn't pòssibly manage any móre. (answer to [1] above)

Nò, thank you very múch. I'm just lèaving. (answer to [3])

In <familiar> English, commands are often used in making offers:

Have some more coffee.

Sit down and make yourself at home.

Let me get a chair for you. (*see* 498)

After the offer has been accepted, the other person need not say anything when he/she performs the service. Especially in <BrE>, quite often people just smile, or say *Here you are* (e.g. on bringing some food), or *There you are* (e.g. on opening a window, bringing a chair, etc.).

Invitations

348   Come in and sit down. <familiar>

Would you like to come with me?

How would you like to come and spend a week with us next year?

May we invite you to dinner next Saturday? <formal, polite>

Here is a typical sequence:

[A] Are you doing anything tomorrow evening?

[B] No.

[A] Then perhaps you'd be interested in joining us for a meal at a restaurant in town.

[B] Thank you very much. That's very kind of you. I'd love to.

In <politely> refusing the invitation, [B] might say:

Well, that's very kind of you – but I'm afraid I have already arranged/ promised to . . . What a pity, I would have so much enjoyed it.

Vocatives

349 To get someone's attention or to select your addressee, you can use a vocative such as *John, Mrs Johnson, Dr Smith*:

John, I want you.

Please, Jenny, stop.

Now just a moment, Mr Williams.

Thank you, Dr Gomez.

Vocatives can also be used more generally to mark the speaker's relation to the hearer. Nowadays by far the most common forms of address are given names (*Susan, Peter,* etc.), including short forms or pet forms (*Sue, Pete, Suzy,* etc.). These are no longer felt to be 'familiar', but can be used for acquaintances as well as friends. The following are some of the many examples of the <familiar> use of vocatives: *dad(dy)*; *mum(my)*; (*you*) *guys* <familiar AmE>; (*my*) *dear*; (*my*) *darling*; *honey* <AmE>.

In contrast, *sir* and *madam* are vocatives which mark respect to a stranger (typically used by service personnel such as hotel staff in addressing a customer):

> Did you order a t̀axi, mádam? <formal>

In special situations, other titles of respect can be used as vocatives: *Ladies and gentlemen!* (<formal> opening of a speech); *My Lord* (to a peer, a bishop, a British judge, etc.); *Your honor* (to an American judge); *Your Excellency* (to an ambassador); *Mr President*; *Prime Minister*. These are mostly <infrequent and formal>. Somewhat more common are respectful professional forms of address, e.g. *Father* (to a priest); *Doctor* (to a medical doctor).

350 English is restricted in forms of address to strangers. *Sir* and (especially) *madam* are too <formal> to be used in most situations. *Miss* as a vocative is by many considered <impolite>. Many people even feel that occupational vocatives like *waiter* or *driver* are <rather impolite>, although others, like *nurse* (= 'nursing sister') or *operator* (telephone operator) are acceptable:

> Would you help me, please, **operator**? I'm trying to get through to a number in Copenhagen.

Thus to get the attention of a stranger, you have to rely on *Excuse me!* or in <AmE> *Pardon me!*: *Excuse me, is this the way to the post office?*

Meanings in connected discourse

351 In Sections A, B and C we have considered aspects of meaning in isolation, but in this final section we will think about how meanings may be put together and presented in a spoken or written discourse. That is, we shall be discussing style and presentation of ideas. We start with the organization of connections within and between sentences.

Linking signals

352 Whether in speech or in writing, you help people to understand your message by signalling how one idea leads on from another. The words and phrases which have this connecting function are like 'signposts' on a journey. Most of them in English are sentence adverbials, and they generally come at the beginning of a sentence. Their most important functions are as follows.

Making a new start or a transition

353 *Well* and *now*, placed at the front of an utterance in <speech>, signal a new start in the train of thought:

> [A] You remember that puppy we found?
>
> [B] Yes.
>
> [A] Wěll, we adopted it, and now it has some puppies of its own.

Well here means roughly 'I am now going to tell you something new'. But elsewhere, *well* often signals an in-between response, for example, where a speaker cannot give a definite 'yes' or 'no' answer:

[A] He's selling you those for two hundred and fifty bucks?

[B] *Well*, seventy-five.

Well is particularly common when the speaker is asked for an opinion:

[A] What did you think of that play?

[B] *Well*, I wasn't really happy about the translation into the television medium.

Now often signals a return to an earlier train of thought:

Well, that finishes tha̍t. *Now* what was the o̍ther thing I wanted to ask you?

Changing the subject

354 *Incidentally* or *by the way* <informal> can be used to change the subject:

I think I've been a bit absent-minded over that letter. *Incidentally,/By the way*, this fax machine doesn't seem to be working properly.

Listing and adding

355 In <writing> and <formal speech>:

● You can list a series of points by such adverbs as *firstly* (or *first*), *second(ly)*, *next*, *last(ly)* (or *finally*).

● Phrases such as *to begin with*, *in the second place*, and *to conclude* can also be used.

● Similar to these adverbials are *also, moreover, furthermore, what is more,* etc. which indicate that an additional point is being made (*see* 238):

Several reasons were given for the change in the attitude of many students in the 1960s. *To begin with*, they feared the outbreak of nuclear war. *Secondly*, they were concerned over the continuing pollution of the environment. Not enough progress, *moreover*, had been made in reducing poverty or racial discrimination . . . And *to conclude*, they felt frustrated in their attempts to influence political decisions. <formal, written>

Expressions like *And another thing* . . . and *I might add* . . . are useful, particularly in spoken debate or discussion.

Reinforcement

356 *Besides, in any case* <informal>, *in fact* and *anyway* <informal> are other sentence adverbials indicating an additional point in an argument. They are used to reinforce an argument in a situation where a preceding argument might not seem sufficient:

Ray won't have any proof of my guilt. *Besides*, he doesn't suspect me of having any connection with the recent robberies.

Further(more) <more formal> and *what is more* can be used in a similar way.

Summary and generalization

357 To lead into a brief summary of points already made, you can write *in a word, in short,* or *to sum up*:

> The Foundation could be custodian of a central fund of charities. It could plan and finance a stock of books, tapes and films. **In a word**, it could do plenty.

Here is another example, from a book review:

> The techniques discussed are valuable. Sensible stress is laid on preparatory and follow-up work. Each chapter is supported by a well-selected bibliography. *In short*, this is a clearly written textbook that should prove extremely valuable to teachers.

Other linking phrases serve to indicate a generalization from points already made: *in all, all in all, altogether, more generally*, etc. These are used in a similar way to the summary signals. Thus *in all* could replace *in short* in the quotation above.

Explanation

358 A point already made can be explained in three ways:

- by **expanding** and **clarifying** its meanings: *that is, that is to say, i.e.*
- by giving a more **precise description**: *namely, viz.*
- by giving an **illustration**: *for example, for instance*

These expressions are typical of <written> English:

> It is important that young children should see things, and not merely read about them. **That is**, the best education is through direct experience and discovery.

> Role-playing can be done for quite a different purpose: to evaluate procedures, regardless of individuals. **For example**, a sales presentation can be evaluated through role-playing.

In the middle of a sentence, these forms can also link two structures in apposition (*see* 470–2):

> A good example is a plant, proverbial for its bitter taste, *namely* wormwood.

Note
The Latin abbreviations *i.e., viz.* and *e.g.* are mainly found in <formal written> texts. They are normally read aloud as 'that is', 'namely', and 'for example', respectively.

Reformulation

359 Sometimes, to make our ideas clearer, we explain or modify them by putting them in other words. Such **reformulation** can be introduced by an adverbial like *in other words, rather, better*:

> Be natural. *In other words*, be yourself.
>
> We decided, or *rather* it was decided, to pull the place down.

The following can also be used in spoken discussion: *What I mean is . . . ,* *What I'm saying is . . .*

Linking clauses and sentences

360 We can think of a clause – the unit which may express a statement – as the basic unit of meaning in a discourse. Grammar provides three main ways of putting clauses together:

> [A] COORDINATION: You can coordinate them by the conjunctions *and, or, but, both . . . and*, etc. (see 515–20).
>
> [B] SUBORDINATION: You can subordinate one clause to another (i.e. make it into a subclause, *see* 709–17), using such conjunctions as *when, if,* and *because.*
>
> [C] ADVERBIAL LINK: You can connect the two ideas by using a linking sentence adverbial (*see* 479), such as *yet, moreover,* and *meanwhile.*

Contrast

361 The three methods (coordination, subordination, and adverbial link) are illustrated here for the relation of **contrast** (*see* 211):

> [A] The conversation went on *but* Rebecca stopped listening.
>
> [B] *Although* Quebec did not break its ties with the rest of Canada, it did not feel itself part of the Confederation.
>
> The country around Cambridge is flat and not particularly spectacular, *though* it offers easy going to the foot traveller.
>
> [C] In theory, most companies would like to double their profits in a year. *However*, few could really handle it, and most companies wouldn't even try.

Note

For a stronger and more emphatic link, occasionally we find a combination of a sentence adverbial with coordination or subordination:

[A] + [C] He was extremely tired, *but* he was *nevertheless* unable to sleep until after midnight.

[B] + [C] *Although* he was suffering from fatigue as a result of the long journey, *yet* because of the noise, he lay awake in his bed, thinking over the events of the day until the early hours of the morning. <formal, rather rhetorical>

Choice between coordination, subordination and linking adverbial

362 [1] **Coordination** is often a 'looser' connection than the others, because it is more vague (*see* 371) and less emphatic. Clause coordination is more characteristic of <informal> than of <formal> style.

[2] **Subordination** tends to give a clause a less important part in the information conveyed by a sentence. Thus an adverbial subordinate clause is often used when the information in that clause is already wholly or partly known or expected by the hearer (*see* 405–7):

They gave her something warm to wear, and she went to change in the bathroom. *When she came back*, the dinner was already on the table.

[3] **Adverbial links** are often used to connect longer stretches of language, perhaps whole sentences which themselves contain coordinate or subordinate clauses (*see* example [C] in 361).

Other meaning-links

363 Here are some other examples of meaning-links to show how English offers a choice between coordination [Co], subordination [Sub], and adverbial links [Ad]. In the case of coordination (and sometimes of subordination), we place an adverbial in brackets where it can be added to make the link more specific. (Cross-references show where these meaning-links are discussed in Section A.)

Time-when (see 151–60)

364   [Co] Penelope stopped the car *and* (*then*) rolled down the windows.

[Sub] *After* chatting to Davidson for a few minutes longer, he went back to his office.

[Ad] She studied the letter for a long time. *Then* she turned back to Wilson and smiled.

Cause, reason, result (see 197–207)

365 [Co] She ran out of money, and (*therefore*) had to look for a job.

[Sub] *Since* a customer had arrived in the shop, Samantha said no more.

The prisoners had a secret radio, so (*that*) they could receive messages from the outside world.

[Ad] When children reach the age of 11 or 12, they start growing fast. They *therefore* need more protein.

Positive condition (see 207–8)

366 The conjunction *and* can express a condition, but only in some contexts such as commanding, advising, etc.:

[Co] Take this medicine, and (*then*) you'll feel better. <informal>

[Sub] *If* you take this medicine, you'll feel better.

[Ad] You ought to take your medicine regularly, as the doctor ordered. You'd feel better, *then*. <informal>

Negative condition (see 209)

367 *Or* can be used to express a negative condition in the same contexts as in 366[Co].

[Co] You'd better put your overcoat on, or (*else*) you'll catch a cold. <informal>

[Sub] *Unless* you put on your overcoat, you'll catch a cold.

[Ad] I should wear an overcoat if I were you; *otherwise*, you'll catch a cold.

Condition + contrast (see 213–14)

368 [Sub] *However* much advice we give him, he (*still*) does exactly what he wants.

[Ad] It doesn't matter how much advice we give him: he *still* does exactly what he wants.

(Coordination alone cannot indicate condition + contrast.)

Addition (see 238–42, 355–6)

369 [Co] She's (*both*) a professional artist *and* a first-rate teacher (*see* 520).

~ She's *not only* a professional artist, *but* (*also*) a first-rate teacher.

[Sub] *As well as* (being) a professional artist, she's (*also*) a first-rate teacher.

[Ad] She's well known all over the country as a professional artist. *What's more*, she's a first-rate teacher.

Alternatives (compare 242)

370 [Co] We can (*either*) meet this afternoon, *or* (*else*) we can discuss the matter at dinner (*see* 520).

[Ad] Would you like us to have a meeting about the matter this afternoon? *Otherwise* we could discuss it at dinner.

[Ad] I may be able to cross the mountains into Switzerland. *Alternatively*, I may get a boat at Marseilles.

(Alternatives cannot be expressed by subordination.)

'General purpose' links

371 As you can see from 364–6, 369, *and* is a 'general purpose' linking word, which can adapt its meaning according to context. Any positive link between two ideas can be expressed by *and*. English has three other methods of vague or 'general purpose' connection of this kind. They are:

[A] **Relative clauses** (*see* 686–94)

[B] **Participle and verbless clauses** (*see* 493–4)

[C] Grammatically **unlinked** clauses

Relative clauses

372 Notice the equivalence between a coordinate clause with *and*, and a **non-restrictive** relative clause (*see* 110–11, 693):

We have arrived at the hotel, and find it very comfortable.

~ We have arrived at the hotel, *which we find very comfortable*.

The same equivalence is seen in **sentence relative** clauses (*see* 694). Here the relative pronoun points back to a whole clause or sentence:

He's spending too much time on sport, and that's not good for his school work.

~ He's spending too much time on sport, *which is not good for his school work*.

Restrictive clauses also have a flexible connecting function. In the sentences [1–3], the implied links are reason, time-when, and condition:

- **Reason:**

    I don't like people *who drive fast cars*.   [1]

    ('Because they drive fast cars, I don't like them')

- **Time-when:**

    The man *I saw* was wearing a hat.   [2]

    ('When I saw him, he was wearing a hat')

- **Condition:**

    Anyone *who bets on horses* deserves to lose money.   [3]

    ('If anyone bets on horses, he or she deserves to lose money')

Participle and verbless clauses

373 These clauses (*see* 493–4), more characteristic of <formal written> English, also have a varied 'general purpose' linking function, as these examples show:

- **Reason:**

    Being an only child, she had never seen a baby without its outer wrappings.

    ('As she was an only child...')

- **Time-when:**

    Cleared, the site will be very valuable. <rather formal>

    ('When it is cleared...')

- **Condition:**

    Cleared, the site would be very valuable. <rather formal>

    ('If it were cleared...')

- **Means:**

    Using a sharp axe, they broke down the door. <rather formal>

    ('By using a sharp axe...')

- **Reason:**

    She stared silently at the floor, *too nervous to reply*. <rather formal>

    ('...because she was too nervous...')

Unlinked clauses

374 Two neighbouring clauses may be grammatically unlinked. For example, they may be separated in writing by a period (.) or a semi-colon (;) a colon (:) or a dash (–). But this does not mean there is no connection of meaning between them; it means, rather, that the connection is implicit, and has to be inferred by the hearer or reader.

In <informal speech>, a speaker frequently relies on such implied connections, whereas in <writing>, the writer would often make the connection clear by sentence adverbial or coordination. These examples can be compared with the [Ad] sentences of 364–70 (the 'missing link' is indicated in small type in [square brackets]):

> He loaded the pistol carefully; [then] he took aim . . . a shot rang out. (TIME)
>
> She had to look for a job – [because] she had run out of money. (REASON)
>
> Take this medicine: [if you do] it'll make you feel better. (CONDITION)

Cross-reference and omission

375 Clauses are often connected not only because of a meaning-link of the kinds we have considered, but because they SHARE some content, e.g. they may be talking about the same person:

> *My brother* was wearing a raincoat. *So my brother* didn't get wet.

We can, if we like, link these two sentences into one sentence, linking them with an adverb like *so*, without changing them: *My brother was wearing a raincoat, so my brother didn't get wet*. But generally, we avoid repeating the shared words and content, either

- by **cross-reference** (using a pronoun such as *he*); or
- by **omitting** the repeated element(s):

> *My brother* was wearing a raincoat, and so (*he*) didn't get wet.

Cross-reference and omission are very useful and important: (A) they shorten the message, and (B) they can make the connections of meaning more easy to grasp. We may say that they make the structure of the sentence 'tighter'. The general rule is: CROSS-REFER AND OMIT WHEREVER YOU CAN, EXCEPT WHERE THIS LEADS TO AMBIGUITY. We now consider some of the ways in which the English language allows these things. We consider cross-reference and omission together, and see how repetition can be avoided by these methods. Sometimes one method is available, sometimes the other, and sometimes both. Similar to cross-reference in shortening and 'tightening' the message is **substitution** – where a pronoun or other 'pro-form' replaces another expression (*see* 379–389).

Cross-reference to noun phrases

3rd person pronouns

376 The personal pronouns *he, she, it, they*, etc. (*see* 619–22) cross-refer to noun phrases, and agree with them in number and/or gender (*see* 529, 597–601). In these examples, the noun phrase and the pronoun are in *italics*:

> *Henrietta* looked down at *her left hand*. *It* was covered with blood.
>
> *The new psychology professor* kept *her* distance. *She* did not call *students* by *their* first names.
>
> *Bill* gave an inward groan. *He* felt that the situation was getting beyond *him*.
>
> *Millions of flies* were on *their* way towards us.

Notice that the plural pronouns *they, them*, etc. substitute not only for plural noun phrases, but for coordinated singular noun phrases such as *Red* and *Handley*:

> I know *Red and Handley* well. *They* are both painters.
>
> In the morning, *Power and Ross* rose at dawn and began *their* day's work.

Note

[a] On the choice between *he, she* and *they* when sex is unspecified, *see* 96.

[b] Reflexive pronouns (*himself, themselves*, etc.) (*see* 626–8) and relative pronouns (*see* 686–94) behave in a similar way to personal pronouns in signalling cross-reference:

> *He* hurt *himself*. ~ *She* hurt *herself*. ~ *They* hurt *themselves*.
>
> *The man who* was injured . . . ~ *The house which* was destroyed . . .

1st and 2nd person pronouns

377 Occasionally, 1st and 2nd person pronouns substitute for coordinate noun phrases. If a 1st person pronoun is present in the noun phrase, agreement is with the 1st person:

> *You and I* should get together sometime and share *our* ideas.
>
> *My wife and I* are going to Argentina. *We* hope to stay with some friends.

If a 2nd person pronoun is present without a 1st person pronoun, agreement is with the 2nd person pronoun:

> *You and John* can stop work now. *You* can both eat your lunch in the kitchen.
>
> Do *you and your husband* have a car? I may have to beg a lift from *you*.

Special cases

378 ● **Quantifiers** (*see* 675–80). Sometimes a plural pronoun cross-refers to quantifier pronouns like *everybody, somebody, no one,* and *anyone*:

> Everybody looked after **themselves**.

This compares with the more <formal> use of singular pronouns such as *he or she* (*see* 96):

> One of the most important things anyone can do in business is consider **his or her** future connections.

● **Group nouns.** For cross-reference a singular noun referring to a group of people can be treated as a singular inanimate noun (when we are thinking of the group as a unit):

> It is a family **which** traces **its** history from the Norman Conquest. (*see* 510)

A group noun can also be treated as a plural human noun (when we are thinking of the members of the group):

> They are a family **who** quarrel among **themselves**.

Quantifier pronouns as substitutes for noun phrases

379 Other pronouns such as *one, some, each, none* (*see* 676) can act as **substitutes** for a noun phrase.

● **Substitution for singular count noun phrases**

> [A] Would you like *a cup of tea*?
>
> [B] No, thanks – I've just had **one**. (**one** = 'a cup of tea')

● **Substitution for plural count noun phrases**

> Can you give me *a few stamps*? I need **some** for these postcards. (**some** = 'some stamps')
>
> The museum has **twenty rooms**, **each** portraying a period in the country's history. (**each** = 'each room')
>
> We lost **most of the games**, but not quite **all**. ('all of them')
>
> *Proust and James* are great novelists, but I like Tolstoy better than **either**. ('either of them')
>
> *Two members of the panel* later told the Court about receiving anonymous telephone calls. **Neither** was seated on the jury. ('Neither of the two members')
>
> *These books* are heavy. You carry one **half**, and I'll carry the **other**. ('You carry half of them, and I'll carry the other half of them')

She had learned from her *mistakes* of the past – only *a few* but *enough*. ('only a few mistakes, but enough mistakes')

[A] You've only got one *CD*, haven't you?

[B] I've got *several*. ('several CDs')

● **Substitution for mass noun phrases**

Some of the equipment has been damaged, but *none* has been lost.

I'd like *some paper*, if you have *any*.

380 ● **Substitutes for nouns and parts of noun phrases**

The pronoun *one* (680) can substitute for a noun, as well as for a whole noun phrase:

Have you seen any *knives*? I need a sharp *one*. ('a sharp knife')

She moved down the row of freight cars, checking for the *serial number* which corresponded to the *one* ('serial number') Teufel had written down for her.

The plural of *one* in this sense is *ones*:

Plastic *pots* are usually more expensive than clay *ones*.

Notice that *one* cannot replace mass nouns; instead, the noun is omitted: *Which wine would you like? The red or the white?* ('The red wine or the white wine?')

381 Sometimes there is a choice (with count nouns) between *one* and omission:

This house is bigger than my last (one).

Navneet had a shop in Hong Kong and another (one) in Bombay.

His bus broke down, and he had to wait for over two hours for the next (one).

I know her two older children, but I don't know the youngest (one).

382 With following modifiers, the pronouns *that* and *those* can act as substitutes with definite meaning (= 'the one', 'the ones'). *That* as a substitute pronoun always has non-personal reference:

The hole was about as big as *that* ('the hole') made by a rocket. <rather formal>

The paintings of Gaugin's Tahiti period are more famous than *those* (= 'the ones') he painted in France. <rather formal>

That can also be used as a substitute with a mass noun:

The plumage of the male pheasant is far more colourful than *that* (= 'the plumage') of the female. <rather formal>

These uses of *that* and *those* are rather <formal>, and are virtually restricted to <written> English.

Substitutes for structures containing a verb

The auxiliary verb *do*

383 The dummy auxiliary verb *do* (479) can act as a substitute for the whole of a clause apart from the subject:

She doesn't work any harder than Bùrt dóes. ('than Burt works')

[A] Did you read that book in the end?　　　[B] Yes I dìd.

[A] Who wants to play tennis this afternoon? $\begin{cases} \text{[B] İ do.} \\ \text{[B] İ dón't.} \end{cases}$

You can also omit the whole clause following the subject:

He can **cook** as well as $\begin{cases} \text{Helen.} & \text{[1a]} \\ \text{she. <formal, rather rare>} & \text{[1b]} \\ \text{her. <informal, normal in speech>} & \text{[1c]} \end{cases}$

[A] Who wants to play tennis?　　　[B] $\begin{cases} \text{Mè. <informal>} \\ \text{Not mĕ. <informal>} \end{cases}$

Notice that in <informal> English, speakers change the pronoun subject from *I* (etc.) to its objective form (*me*, etc.) when the rest of the sentence is omitted. But in place of [1b] and [1c] above, the choice that is most generally acceptable is *He can cook better than **she can*** (*see* 384 below).

Do can also substitute for the part of a clause excluding subject and adverbial:

[A] *Have you written to your father yet*?

[B] Yes, I *did* last week. ('I wrote to my father . . .')

Occasionally *do* acts as a substitute for a verb phrase alone:

She likes Ryan's Steak House better than she **does** Old Country Buffet. (**does** = 'likes')

Omission following an operator

384 In cases like those in 383, you can use other auxiliaries in a parallel position to *do*. That is, you can omit the whole or part of the sentence following an auxiliary:

I'll *open a bank account* if you will. (= '. . . if you will do so')

He *can cook* as well as she can. (= 'can cook')

[A] He *is working* late this week.   [B] Yes, he *was* last week, too.

(= '. . . was working late last week, too')

You *can play* in the garden, but you *mustn't* in the garage.

(= '. . . mustn't play in the garage')

Do and the other auxiliaries are unstressed, except in cases of affirmation and denial (*see* 264–5), or where they have some sort of contrastive meaning:

[A] Are you going to clean the car?

[B] I could, and should, but I don't think I will.

The omission also occurs after two or three auxiliaries:

[A] Is the kettle boiling?   [B] It may be. ('. . . be boiling')

[A] Did you lock the door?   [B] No, I should have, but I forgot.

Note

[a] *Be* as a main verb (*see* 482) cannot be omitted after an auxiliary:

If they're not asleep, they should be. (= '. . . be asleep')

[b] In <BrE>, *do* or *done* is sometimes added after another auxiliary:

He can't promise to come tonight, but he may *do*. (= '. . . come
    tonight')

[A] Would you please unlock the door?   [B] I have *done*.

The main verb do: do it, do that, do so

385 The main verb *do* (*see* 479) acts as a substitute for a main verb, normally a verb denoting some action or activity. *Do* requires an object, which may be *it, that*, or *so*:

If we want to preserve our power, this is the way to *do it*. ('to preserve
    our power')

They have promised to increase pensions by 10 per cent. If they *do so*,
    it will make a big difference to old people. ('If they do increase
    pensions . . .')

Do that is generally more emphatic and <informal>:

They say he sleeps in his shoes and socks. Why ever does he *do that*?

It's easy for you to talk – you travel around the world. We would love to
    do that too.

Substitutes for *that*-clauses

So after a verb, and omission after a verb

386 *So* is a substitute for *that*-clauses representing reported statements, beliefs, assumptions, emotions, etc.:

> The government won't provide the money – I have heard the minister **say so**. ('. . . say that the government won't . . .')

> It's silly, childish, running after them like that. I **told Ben so**. ('. . . told him that it's silly . . .')

> [A] Has Ivan gone home?

> [B] I think so. / I guess so. <AmE> / I suppose so. / I hope so. / I'm afraid so.

Not replaces *so* in negative clauses: I *hope not, I'm afraid not,* etc. But, with verbs taking transferred negation (*see* 587), it is more natural to say: *I don't think so; I don't suppose so;* etc.:

> [A] Are there any questions you want to ask us, Ms Blake?

> [B] No, **I don't think so**.

In sentences expressing certainty and doubt (*see* 294–5) we cannot use *so*, but have to say: *I'm sure they are; I'm sure of it; I doubt if they are; I doubt it;* etc.

In comparative clauses (505), the whole of a *than*-clause can be omitted:

> He's older than I thought ('. . . than I thought he was').

> The journey took longer than we had hoped.

Also, after the verbs *know, ask,* and *tell,* a whole *that*-clause is frequently omitted in conversation:

> [A] She's having a baby.   [B] I **know**.

> [A] { How did you **hear**?   [B] She **told** me (so) herself.
>   { How did you **hear that**?   Why do you **ask**?

So cannot be used after *know* and *ask*.

Substitutes for *wh*-clauses

387 The whole of a *wh*-clause following the *wh*-word can be omitted:

> **Someone has hidden my notebook**, but I don't know **who/where/why**.

> (= 'I don't know who has hidden my notebook', etc.)

This cannot be done with *whether* and *if*.

Substitutes for *to*-infinitive clause

388 With infinitive clauses, you can omit the whole of the clause following *to*:

> [A] Why don't you come and stay with us?
>
> [B] I'd lòve to (do so).
>
> You can **borrow** my **pèn**, if you wánt to (do so).
>
> If this pain gets much worse, I shan't be able to **move around** much. The doctor has told me nòt to (do so), anyway.
>
> Somebody ought to **help you**. Shall I ask Pěter to (do so)?

As we see, there is a choice between including *do so* (which is <more formal>) and omitting it. With some verbs, such as *want, like* and *ask*, the whole of the infinitive clause, including *to*, can be omitted, especially in <informal> English:

> You can borrow my pen, if you want/like. <informal>
>
> Shall I ask Peter? <informal>

It, that, this as clause substitutes

389 The definite pronouns *it, that,* and *this* are widely used as substitutes for clauses as well as for noun phrases (*see* 94, 99, 376):

> **If you make a sound**, you'll regret *it*. ('regret making a sound')
>
> [A] **She's having a baby**.
>
> [B] How did you know **thàt**? (i.e. '. . . know that she's having a baby')
>
> After many weeks of rain, **the dam burst**. **This** resulted in widespread flooding and much loss of livestock and property. ('The bursting of the dam resulted in . . .')

Other strategies of omission

390 Other structures which allow us to shorten a sentence by omission are coordinated structures, non-finite clauses, and verbless clauses. All these structures will be further discussed in Part Three (515–20, 493–4), so here we merely give a few examples of the varied types of omission that occur in them, showing how these provide briefer alternatives to substitution and repetition.

Omission through coordination

391 (The elements which are or can be omitted in coordination are in *italics*.)

> George Best travelled fearing the worst, **but** was pleasantly surprised.
>
> ('. . . but **he** was pleasantly surprised.')

Particular attention was given to the nuclear tests conference and to the question of disarmament.

('Particular attention was given to the nuclear tests conference and **particular attention was given** to the question of disarmament.')

Peter cut himself a slice of bread and some cheese.

('Peter cut himself a slice of bread; **he** (also) **cut himself** some cheese.')

She is not only a trained mathematician, but a good singer.

('She is not only a trained mathematician, but **she is** a good singer.')

Either Germany or Brazil will win the World Cup.

('Germany will win the World Cup; or (else) Brazil **will do so**.')

Tom washes and irons his own shirts.

('Tom washes his own shirts; he irons **them** (too).')

In general, the same omissions cannot be made when one of the clauses is subordinate to the others. We can say:

She was exhausted and went to sleep.

BUT NOT:

*She was so exhausted that went to sleep.

In the subclause we have to repeat the subject:

She was so exhausted (that) **she** went to sleep.

But there are a few cases where subclauses follow the coordinate clause pattern:

The rain stopped, **though** not the wind.

Omission in non-finite clauses

392 Non-finite clauses (*see* 493) have no operator (*see* 609–12), and most of them have no conjunction or subject. Thus in comparison with finite subclauses they are more economical and avoid repetition. Probably for this reason, adverbial *-ing* clauses and *-ed* clauses are particularly favoured in <formal or written> styles of English. We now illustrate these points with equivalent finite clauses:

● *to*-INFINITIVE CLAUSE: I hope *to get in touch with you soon.*

(= 'I hope **that I will get in touch with you soon**.')

● *-ing* CLAUSE: *Coming home late one evening,* I heard something which made my blood freeze in horror.

(= '**When I was coming home** . . .')

● *-ed* CLAUSE: The man *injured by the bullet* was taken to hospital.

(= 'The man **who was** injured by the bullet . . .')

393 The same applies to adverbial non-finite clauses introduced by a subordinator:

- *-ing* CLAUSE: It's a trick I learned *while recovering from an illness*.

    (= '... *while I was recovering*...')

- *-ed* CLAUSE: *Though defeated*, she remained a popular leader of the party. <rather formal>

    (= 'Though *she had been* defeated...')

Omission in verbless clauses

394 Verbless clauses (*see* 494) have no verb and usually no subject:

Whether right or wrong, he usually wins the argument.

   (= 'Whether *he is* right or wrong...')

A man of few words, Uncle George declined to express an opinion. <formal>

   (= '*Being* a man of few words/*As he was* a man of few words...')

Verbless clauses, like participial clauses, often belong to a more <formal> style, and belong mainly to <written> English.

Note
Not all subordinators can introduce participial and verbless clauses. For example, *although, if, once* and *when* can do so, but *because, as,* and *since* (as conjunctions of reason) cannot. Compare:

Since she left school, she's had several different jobs. [1]

Since you knew the answer, why didn't you speak up? [2]

In [1], the clause of time can be replaced by *Since leaving school*, but in [2], the clause of reason cannot be replaced by **Since knowing the answer*.

Presenting and focusing information

395 We now deal with the ways in which meanings can be presented and arranged for effective communication. For a message to be properly understood,

- the message has to be cut up into individual pieces of information (*see* 396–8)
- the ideas have to be given the right emphasis (*see* 399–409)
- the ideas have to be put in the right order (*see* 410–32).

Pieces of information

396 In <written> English, a **piece of information** can be defined as a piece of language which is separated from what goes before and from what follows by punctuation marks (.,;:–?!), and which does not itself contain any punctuation marks. In <spoken> English, a piece of information can be defined as a **tone unit** (*see* 37), i.e. a unit of intonation containing a **nucleus** (*see* 36). Notice the difference, in <written> English, between:

> Mr Average has a wife and two children. [1]

> Mr Average has a wife; he also has two children. [2]

In a sense (*see* 369, 374) [1] and [2] 'mean the same', but [1] presents the message as ONE piece of information, while [2] presents it as TWO pieces of information, separated by a punctuation mark (;). In <speech>, the same contrast is seen in:

> He has a wife and two chìldren | ONE TONE UNIT   [1a]
> He has a wífe | he also has two chìldren | TWO TONE UNITS   [2a]

Dividing the message into tone units

397 There is no exact match between punctuation in <writing> and tone units in <speech>. Speech is more variable in its structuring of information than writing. Cutting up speech into tone units depends on:

- the speed at which you are speaking,
- what emphasis you want to give to parts of the message,
- the length of grammatical units.

A single sentence may have just one tone unit, like [1a]; but when the length of a sentence goes beyond a few words, it is difficult not to divide it into two or more separate pieces of information.

> | The man tòld us | we could park hère. |
> | The man tòld us | we could pàrk | at the ràilway station. |
> | The man tòld us | we could pàrk | in that strèet | over thère. |

398 For guidance, the following general rules are useful in knowing when to start a new tone unit:

- If a sentence begins with a **clause or adverbial phrase**, give the clause or adverbial element a separate tone unit:

  > | *Last yéar* | the IT bubble bùrst. |

- If a sentence contains a **non-restrictive modifier** (*see* 99–102), such as a non-restrictive relative clause (*see* 693), give the modifier a separate tone unit:

| The emergency services were hampered by thick smoke, | *which spread quickly* | *through the station.* |

- Similarly, give any **medial phrase or clause** a separate tone unit:

| The government, | *in Mr Howell's view,* | must ensure | that we have enough energy. |

- A **vocative** or **linking adverb** usually has its own tone unit (or at least ends a tone unit):

| Mary | are you coming? |

| The police | *however* | thought she was guilty. |

- Give a separate tone unit to **a clause or long noun phrase acting as a subject**:

| *What we need* | is plenty of time. |

- If **two or more clauses are coordinated**, give them each a separate tone unit:

| He opened the door | and walked straight in. |

But the overriding rule is: give a separate tone unit to each separate piece of information, even if none of the above conditions apply. For example:

| The college employs | a number of staff | without qualified teacher status. |

End-focus and contrastive focus

399 The nucleus is the most important part of a tone unit: it marks the **focus of information**, or the part of the unit to which the speaker especially draws the hearer's attention. Normally, the nucleus is at the end of the tone unit; or, to be more precise, on the last major-class word (noun, main verb, adjective, or adverb – *see* 744), in the tone unit. Which syllable of the word is stressed, if it has more than one syllable, is determined by ordinary conventions of word stress: to'day, 'working, 'photograph, conver'sation, etc. This neutral position of the nucleus, which we see in nearly all the examples in 398, is called **end-focus**.

Note
Two or more nouns together (*see* 651) often behave, for stress purposes, like a single word (i.e. like a noun compound), with the main stress on the first noun: 'export records; 'building plan; 'traffic problem. (But this is not an invariable rule: contrast town 'hall, country 'house, lawn 'tennis, etc.)

400 But in other cases speakers shift the nucleus to an earlier part of the tone unit. They do this when you want to draw attention to an earlier part of the tone unit, usually to contrast it with something already mentioned, or understood in the context. For this reason, we call earlier placing of the nucleus **contrastive focus**. Here are some examples:

[A] | It must have been last Mŏnday. | [B] | Nŏ. | It's nèxt Monday. | [1]

[A] | Have you ever driven a sports car? | [B] | Yés, | I've ŏften driven one. | [2]

In cases like the following examples, contrastive meaning is signalled by a fall-rise tone (see 41), with a fall on the nucleus and a rise on the last stressed syllable in the tone unit:

Those pàrcels – ŏne of them has arríved. | (But the other one hàsn't arrived) [3]

| Àfter you get márried, | people stŏp giving you things. | (In a discussion of wedding presents.) [4]

In other sentences, there can be a double contrast, each contrast indicated by its own nucleus:

| Her fàther | is Áustrian, | but her mŏther | is Frènch. | [5]

401 Sometimes contrastive focus draws attention to a whole phrase (e.g. *her mother* in [5]); at other times, it is a single word that receives the focus (e.g. *often* in [2]). Even words like personal pronouns, conjunctions, prepositions, and auxiliaries, which are not normally stressed at all, can receive nuclear stress for special contrastive purposes:

(I've never been to Paris) | but I wìll go thére | sŏme dáy. | [6]

[A] (What did she say to Kath?)

[B] | She was speaking to mè | (not to Kath). [7]

I know he works in an office, | but who does he work fòr? | [8]

(I don't know if you mean to see Peter.) | But ìf you sée him |, please give him my good wishes. [9]

In some cases, e.g. [7] and [8], contrastive focus comes later rather than earlier than normal end-focus. Thus the normal way to say *Who does he work for?* [8] would be with focus on the verb, not the preposition:

Who does he wòrk for?

Note
In exceptional cases, contrastive stress in a word of more than one syllable may shift to a syllable which does not normally have word stress. For example, if you want to make a contrast between the two words normally pronounced *bu'reaucracy* and *au'tocracy* you may do so as follows:

| I'm afraid that bŭreaucracy | can be worse than àutocracy. |

Given and new information

402 We can roughly divide the information in a message into

- **Given information** (something which the speaker assumes the hearer knows about already) and

- **New information** (something which the speaker does not assume the hearer knows about already).

In [7] above, 'She was speaking' is given information: it is already given by the preceding clause; in [9], 'you see him' is given information for the same reason:

As new information is obviously what is most important in a message, it receives the information focus (i.e. nucleus), whereas old information does not. Naturally, personal pronouns and other substitute words, because they refer to something already mentioned or understood, normally count as given information.

Note

Notice that given information and new information are what the speaker *presents* as given and new respectively. What *in fact* the hearer knows or assumes may be a different thing. For example, consider this dialogue:

[A] Do you like Picasso?

[B] No, I hate modern painting.

The position of the nucleus here means that speaker [B] takes it as 'given' that Picasso is a modern painter.

Information given by situation

403 'Given information' is not just information which has already been mentioned or suggested. We may extend this notion to include information which is 'given' by the situation outside language. In this respect 'given' information is like definite meaning (*see* 82–99), and there is indeed a strong connection between given information and definiteness. In the following examples, for which we give the most natural intonation, the definite items *today*, *here*, and *mine* in [10], [11], [12] do not have a nuclear stress because their meaning is given by the situation. In contrast, the items *Saturday*, *factory*, and *sister's* in [10a], [11a], and [12a] are most likely to be new information, and therefore to receive nuclear stress:

| What are you doing today? | [10]
| What are you doing on Saturday? | [10a]

$$\left\{\begin{array}{l}\text{| I wòrk here. |}\\ \text{| I work in a fàctory. |}\end{array}\right.$$ [11]
[11a]

$$\left\{\begin{array}{l}\text{| Carol is a frìend of mine. |}\\ \text{| Carol is a friend of my sìster's. |}\end{array}\right.$$ [12]
[12a]

But the definite items *today, here,* etc., could have nuclear stress if some contrast were implied:

(I know what you did yesterday,) | but what are you doing todày? | [10b]

(I used to work in a factory,) | but now I work hère. | [11b]

404 In other examples, the information given by the situation outside language is more a matter of what is expected in a given context:

| The kèttle's boiling. | | The màil's come. |

| Is your fàther at home? | | Dìnner's rèady. |

In a natural situation, the final part of each of these sentences conveys little information, and therefore does not receive the nucleus. In a home, the one thing to announce about kettles is that they are 'boiling'; and the one thing you expect the mail to do is to 'come' etc. Therefore the nucleus occurs, contrary to end-focus, on the earlier and more informative part of the sentence.

Main and subsidiary information

405 Information is also relevant to the choice of **tone** (*see* 38–41) on the nucleus. We tend to use a falling tone to give emphasis to the main information in a sentence, and a rising tone (or, with more emphasis, a fall-rise tone) to give subsidiary or less important information, i.e. information which is more predictable from the context. Subordinate clauses and adverbials often give information which is subsidiary to the idea in the rest of the main clause:

Subsidiary information may either precede or follow the main information. Speaker [B] could also say here:

Adverbials as main and subsidiary information

406 Adverbials following the main clause often have a rising tone to indicate subsidiary information added as an afterthought:

| It was snòwing | when we arríved. |

| I will get excèedingly drunk | if I drink shérry. |

But a final adverbial clause can also occasionally contain the main new information:

| She had only just finished dréssing | when her gùests arrived. |

Shorter final adverbials are often included in the same tone unit as the rest of the clause, and may bear the main focus:

| She plays the piano bèautifully. |

Main and subsidiary information in writing

407 In <writing>, you cannot point to important information by using intonation, so you have to rely on ordering and subordination of clauses instead. The general rule is that the most important new information is saved up to the end, comparable to the **end focus** principle in <speech>. Thus the sentence finishes with a sort of climax (here indicated by *italics*):

> Arguments in favour of a new building plan, said the mayor, included suggestions that if a new shopping centre were not built, the city's traffic problems *would soon become unmanageable.*

In reading this sentence aloud, it is natural to put a rising or fall-rise tone on all points of information except the last, which receives a falling tone.

| . . . bǔilding plan | . . . máyor | . . . suggéstions | . . . bǔilt | . . . traffic próblems | . . . unmǎnageable. |

End-focus and end-weight

408 When deciding in which order to place the ideas in a sentence, there are two principles to remember:

- **End-focus** (*see* 399): The new or most important idea or message in a piece of information should be placed towards the end, where in speech the nucleus of the tone unit normally falls. In <writing> and prepared <speech>, as we saw in 407, this principle can be applied not just to a single piece of information, but to a whole sentence containing many pieces of information. A sentence is generally more effective (especially in <writing>) if the main point is saved up to the end.

- **End-weight**: The more 'weighty' part(s) of a sentence should be placed towards the end (*see* 409, 416, 424–7, 429). Otherwise the sentence may sound awkward and unbalanced. The 'weight' of an element can be defined in terms of its length (i.e. the number of its syllables or words).

409 Both end-focus and end-weight are useful guiding principles, not invariable rules. As we have said, although end-focus is normal, you are allowed in speech to shift the nucleus to an earlier position in the tone unit, for **contrastive** focus. Similarly, there are exceptions to end-weight:

My home was that wasteland of derelict buildings behind the
morgue.   [1]

That wasteland of derelict buildings behind the morgue was my
home.   [2]

In [1], a long complement phrase (*that wasteland of derelict buildings behind the morgue*) follows a short subject (*my home*) and a short verb (*was*). This sentence keeps to the principle of end-weight. But in [2], the long noun phrase comes first. This sentence breaks the end-weight principle, but it could easily be said by someone wanting to place the main focus of information on *my home*. In such a case the two principles of end-weight and end-focus conflict. Generally, however, the two principles work together: it is usual for a short element in a sentence (e.g. a pronoun) to have less information than a longer element. For example, in

I've been reading *a fascinating biography of Catherine the Great*.

the subject (*I*) carries far less information than the long object noun phrase (in italics).

Order and emphasis

Topic

410 In the rest of this section, we will show that English grammar has quite a number of ways to arrange the message for the right order and the right emphasis. Because of the principles of end-focus and end-weight, the **final** position in a sentence or clause is, usually, the most important for communication. But the **first** position is the second most important, because it is usually the part of the sentence which is familiar territory from which we begin the sentence as a mental 'journey into the unknown'. This is why we call the first element in a clause (leaving aside conjunctions and many adverbials, *see* 414, Note) the **topic**. In most statements, the topic is the subject of the sentence. If the statement has only one tone unit, usually the topic does not receive focus, because it often contains old (given) information, and links the statement in meaning to what was said before:

(Have you seen Bill?) | He   owes me   five dòllars. |

TOPIC	INFORMATION FOCUS

But sometimes topic and information focus coincide, and in this case, the topic is especially prominent:

(Who gave you that magazine?) | Ò | ga gave it to me. |

TOPIC
AND
FOCUS

Fronted topic

411 Instead of the subject, you can make another element the topic, by moving it to the front of the clause or sentence. This shift, called **fronting**, gives that element a kind of psychological prominence, and has three different effects, represented by the following terms:

- emphatic topic (*see* 412)
- contrastive topic (*see* 413)
- semi-given topic (*see* 414)

Emphatic topic

412 In <informal> conversation, it is quite common for a speaker to front an element (particularly a complement) and to give it nuclear stress, thus giving it double emphasis:

| *Very strange* | his eyes lóoked. | (~ His eyes looked very strange) [1]
| *An utter fòol* I felt | tòo. | (TOPIC = COMPLEMENT)   [2]
| *Relaxàtion* you call it. | [3]

| *Excellent fòod* they serve here. | (~ They serve excellent food here) [4]
(TOPIC = OBJECT)

It is as if the speaker says the most important thing in his or her mind first, adding the rest of the sentence as an afterthought. The ordering of the elements here is CSV (in [1] and [2]), CSVO (in [3]), and OSVA (in [4]), instead of the normal order SVC, SVOC, SVO (*see* 487–490).

Contrastive topic

413 Here the fronting helps to point dramatically to a contrast between two things mentioned in neighbouring sentences or clauses, which often have parallel structure:

| *Some things* | we'll tĕll you | (~ We'll tell you some things)

(TOPIC = OBJECT)

| but *some* | you'll have to find out about yoursĕlf. |

(TOPIC = PREPOSITIONAL COMPLEMENT)

| *Bloggs* | my náme is | (TOPIC = COMPLEMENT)
so *Bloggs* | you might as well càll me. |

| *Willingly* | he'll nĕver do it. | (TOPIC = ADVERBIAL)
(he'll have to be fŏrced.)

| *Rĭch* | I mày be | (TOPIC = COMPLEMENT)
(but that doesn't mean I'm happy.)

This construction is not very common, and is associated with <rhetorical> speech.

Semi-given topic

414 Another type of fronting is found in more <formal>, especially <written> English:

Most of these problems a computer could solve easily.

(TOPIC = OBJECT)   [1]

(~ A computer could easily solve most of these problems.)

(A thousand delegates are too many for corporate thinking,) but *corporate thinking* there must be if all members are to have a voice.   (TOPIC = SUBJECT/COMPLEMENT)   [2]

Everything that can be done the administration has attended to already.   (TOPIC = PREPOSITIONAL OBJECT)   [3]

The fronting here is more negative: a less important idea is shifted to the front so that end-focus can fall on another, more important idea (*easily* [1], *voice* [2], *already* [3]). The word *this* or *these* (as in *most of these problems*) is often present in the fronted topic, showing that it contains given information. Yet the topic receives a kind of secondary emphasis as the starting-point of the sentence.

Note
We do not normally consider an initial adverbial to be a 'fronted topic', because many adverbials can occur fairly freely in front of the subject (*see* 451):

Yesterday she was trying on her new school uniform.

But some adverbials which are closely connected with the verb, such as those of manner and direction, do not usually occur in front position.

These may be said to be 'fronted' for special prominence in clauses like

Willingly he'll never do it.

The moment had come. *Upon the ensuing interview* the future would depend. <formal, rhetorical>

Inversion

415 Fronting is often accompanied by **inversion**; that is, not only the topic element, but the verb phrase, or part of it, is moved before the subject. There are two types of inversion:

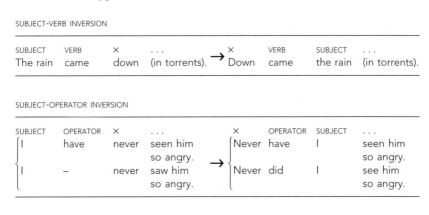

SUBJECT-VERB INVERSION

SUBJECT	VERB	×	...		×	VERB	SUBJECT	...
The rain	came	down	(in torrents).	→	Down	came	the rain	(in torrents).

SUBJECT-OPERATOR INVERSION

SUBJECT	OPERATOR	×	...		×	OPERATOR	SUBJECT	...
I	have	never	seen him so angry.	→	Never	have	I	seen him so angry.
I	—	never	saw him so angry.		Never	did	I	see him so angry.

Subject-verb inversion

416 Subject-verb inversion is normally limited as follows:

- The verb phrase consists of a single verb word, in the past or present tense.
- The verb is an intransitive verb of position (*be*, *stand*, *lie*, etc.) or verb of motion (*come*, *go*, *fall*, etc.).
- The topic element (X in the diagram above) is an adverbial of place or direction (e.g. *down*, *here*, *to the right*, *away*):

Here's *a pen*, Brenda.
Here *comes McKenzie*.   } <informal speech>
Look, there *are your friends*.

There, at the summit, *stood the castle* in its mediaeval splendour.
To the right *lay the pillars* of the Hall entrance.   } <more formal, literary>
Away *went the car* like a whirlwind.
Slowly out of its hangar *rolled the gigantic aircraft*.

The examples from <informal speech> give end-focus to the subject. In <literary> style, the fronted topic is more useful in giving end-weight to a long subject.

Subject-verb inversion does not take place with a fronted topic when the subject is a personal pronoun:

Here it is. (NOT *Here is it)   Away they go! (NOT *Away go they)

Note

The adverb *there* is stressed in the example above: *There, at the summit, stood the castle.* . . . This distinguishes it from the introductory subject *there* (*see* 547), which has no stress. Contrast:

'There are your fri̇ends. [*there* = adverb of place]

There are 'too many pėople here. [*there* = introductory]

Subject-operator inversion in statements

417 The inversion of subject and operator (*did, can,* etc.) is of course obligatory in most questions: e.g. *Can you swim?* (*see* 681–4). But here we are concerned with the obligatory subject-operator inversion when a negative element is fronted for emphasis (especially in <formal> and rather <rhetorical> style) (*see* 303):

NOT A WORD *did he* say. (= 'He didn't say a word')

UNDER NO CIRCUMSTANCES *should the door* be left unlocked. <formal>

The negative element is in small capitals above. Inversion is also obligatory after the fronting of words of negative meaning such as *never, hardly, scarcely, few, little, seldom, rarely, nor, (not) only* (*see* 584–5):

HARDLY *had I* left before the trouble started. (= 'I had hardly left before . . .')

Well, she would go and see what it was all about, for ONLY IF SHE KNEW THE WHOLE STORY *could she* decide.

LITTLE *did he* realize how much suffering he had caused. (= 'He little realized . . .')

Notice that the dummy operator *do* is used for the inversion where there is no other operator in the normal-order sentence:

He little realized . . . ~ Little *did* he realize . . .

Note

In <written, literary> English, subject-operator inversion with *be* sometimes serves the purpose of end-weight, where the subject is long and complex:

OPPOSING HIM **was the French Admiral**, Jean de Vienne – a great sailor and an able strategist.

NEATLY RANGED AGAINST THE ROCK WALLS **were all manner of chests and trunks**.

Here the sentence begins with a participle construction (in capitals), which is then followed by the operator and finally by the subject.

Fronting with *so*

418 Notice the following constructions in which *so* is placed first:

- *So* **as a substitute form with subject-operator inversion** (for end-focus) has the meaning of 'addition' (*see* 234) in sentences like:

    [A] (I've seen the play.)

    [B] | So have Ì. | (= 'and I have, too') <especially in speech>
    (I enjoyed the play) | and so did my frìend. |

- *So* **as a substitute form WITHOUT inversion** is fronted to express emphatic affirmation:

    [A] (You've spilled coffee on your dress.)

    [B] | Oh dèar, | so I hàve. | <speech>

    [A] (It's raining hard outside.)

    [B] | So it ìs. |

The *so*-construction here expresses the hearer's surprise at discovering that what the speaker says is true. As with emphatic affirmation in general (*see* 264), the nucleus comes on the operator, not on the subject.

- *So* **introducing a clause of degree or amount** (*see* 231) can be fronted for emphasis, with subject-operator inversion:

    So well did he play that he was named man of the match. (= 'He played so well that . . .') <rather literary>

Other constructions affecting the topic

Cleft sentence (*it*-type)

419 The cleft sentence construction with introductory *it* (*see* 496) is useful for fronting an element as topic, and also for putting focus (usually for contrast) on the topic element. It does this by splitting the sentence into two halves, highlighting the topic by making it the complement of *it* + *be*:

    [A] (Would you like to borrow this book on dinosaurs?)

    [B] | Nò, | it's **the òther book** | that I want to réad. | [1]
    (TOPIC = OBJECT; **compare:** I want to read the òther book.)

(For centuries London had been growing as a commercial port of world importance.) But it was **in the north of England** that industrial power brought new prosperity to the country. (TOPIC = ADVERBIAL)   [2]

The contrastive meaning of the topic can be seen if we make clear the implied negative in [1] and [2]:

It's the other book, [**not that book**,] that I want to read.

But it was in the north of England, [**not in London**,] that . . .

The cleft sentence with *it* is particularly useful in <written> English, where we cannot mark contrastive emphasis by intonation.

The verb *be* in *it*-cleft sentences can be negated:

It's **not** low pay (that) we object to, it's the extra responsibilities.

As this example shows, there is often a contrast between the negative cleft sentence and a following positive clause.

Cleft sentence (*wh*-type)

420 A nominal relative clause (*see* 592), like an *it*-cleft sentence, can be used to highlight one element for contrast. It can be either subject or complement of the verb *be* (the subject position is more common):

NORMAL PATTERN	CLEFT SENTENCE
	| It's more tìme | that we nèed. | (*it*-type)
We need more time ~	| What we nĕed | is more tìme. | (*wh*-type)
	| More tìme | is what we nèed. | (*wh*-type)

The *wh*-type cleft sentence, like the *it*-type, usually implies a contrast; e.g.:

We don't need more money – what we need is more time.

Comparison of *it*-type and *wh*-type cleft sentences

421 The *it*-type and the *wh*-type cleft sentences cannot always be used in the same circumstances. For example, the *it*-type is more flexible in certain ways:

● The focus of the *wh*-type sentence normally has to be in the form of a noun phrase or nominal clause. An adverbial phrase or prepositional phrase, for example, sounds less natural in this construction than in the *it*-type sentence:

It was **only recently** that I noticed the leak in the roof.

It was **in 1896** that he went to Europe on his first mission.

It was **on this very spot** that I first met my wife.
(BETTER THAN: Where I first met my wife was **on this very spot**.)

If the *wh*-word is an adverb such as *where* and *when*, the *wh*-type sentence sounds somewhat better when the *wh*-clause comes last:

> **On this very spot** is where I first met my wife.

● But if an adverbial can be put in the form of a noun phrase, it can be the focus of a *wh*-type sentence with a final *when*- or *where*-clause:

> { It is **in the autumn** that the countryside is most beautiful.
> { ~ Autumn is (the time) when the countryside is most beautiful.

> { It was **at Culloden** that the rebellion was finally defeated.
> { ~ Culloden was (the place) where the rebellion was finally defeated.

Note

A *wh*-type sentence using one of the *wh*-words *who*, *whom*, or *whose* is usually awkward or impossible:

> It was the ambassador that met us. BUT NOT: *Who met us was the ambassador.

We can, however, say:

> The one/person who met us was the ambassador.

422 The *wh*-type cleft sentence is more flexible than the *it*-type in the following ways:

● The *wh*-type can focus on the complement of a clause, whereas the *it*-type normally cannot:

> She is a brilliant reporter ~ What she is is a brilliant reporter.
>
> BUT NOT: *It's a brilliant reporter that she is.

● The *wh*-type can focus on the verb, by using the substitute verb *do*:

> He's spoilt the whole thing. ~ { What he's done is spoil the whole thing.
> { BUT NOT: *It's spoil the whole thing that he's done.

Notice that the complement of the *wh*-type sentence takes the form of a non-finite clause, most commonly a bare infinitive (*spoil the whole thing*).

Note

The non-finite verb may be a bare infinitive, a *to*-infinitive, an *-ed* participle, or an *-ing* participle (*see* 493):

What he'll do is	**spoil the whole thing**.	[bare infinitive]
	{ **spoil the whole thing**.	[bare infinitive]
What he's done is	{ **to spoil the whole thing**.	[*to*-infinitive]
	{ **spoilt the whole thing**.	[*-ed* participle]
What he's doing is	**spoiling the whole thing**.	[*-ing* participle]

The bare infinitive is the most usual construction, except after *done* (where the *-ed* participle is just as acceptable), and after *doing* where the *-ing* participle has to be used.

Sentences with *wh*-clauses and demonstratives

423 A common type of sentence in <informal> English is one in which a *wh*-clause is linked by the verb *be* to a demonstrative pronoun (*this* or *that*). These sentences are similar to *wh*-cleft sentences both in their structure and in their focusing effect:

> **This is where** I first met my wìfe.
>
> **This is how** you start the èngine.
>
> Are you trying to wreck my career? Because **that's what** you're doing.
>
> I had difficulty starting the car today. **That's what** always happens when I leave it out in cold weather.

Postponement

Introductory-*it* construction

424 The introductory-*it* construction (*see* 542–6) (not to be confused with the *it*-type cleft sentence in 420) is a means of postponing a subject clause to a later position in the sentence, either for end-weight or for end-focus:

> *That income tax will be reduced* is unlikely.
>
> ~ *It* is unlikely *that income tax will be reduced*.

Here the subject is a *that*-clause: *that income tax will be reduced*. The *it*-construction is, in fact, more usual than the same construction without postponement. If you keep the *that*-clause in front position, this is exceptional, and suggests (a) that the *that*-clause is somehow given information, and (b) that you want to put special contrastive emphasis (*see* 413) on the rest of the main clause:

> | That income tax will be redŭced | is unlìkely; | that it will be abŏlished | is out of the quèstion. |

In some instances, such as the passive construction (*see* 543, 613–18), it is impossible to keep the clause in subject position:

> It is said that fear in human beings produces a smell that provokes animals to attack.
>
> BUT NOT: *That fear in human beings produces a smell that provokes animals to attack is said.

For other examples of *it* replacing a postponed clause as subject, *see* 542. Main focus often occurs in the postponed clause:

It is unlikely that they will hold a referèndum.

But when an *-ing* clause is the postponed subject, the main focus normally falls on the rest of the main clause, and the *-ing* clause is treated as an afterthought:

| It's hard wòrk | being a fáshion model. |

Postponing an object clause

425 Occasionally introductory *it* displaces a clause in object position. Just as in the case of subject clauses (424), the clause (here *working here*) is postponed:

{ You must find *it* enjoyable **working here**.
{ ~ You must find **working here** enjoyable.

(Compare: *It* is enjoyable **working here**.)

I owe *it* to you **that the jury acquitted me**.

(Compare: *It* is thanks to you **that the jury acquitted me**.)

Something put *it* into his head **that she was a spy**.

(Compare: *It* came into his head that **she was a spy**.)

This displacement MUST occur when the object clause is a *that*-clause or an infinitive clause. Thus we can have:

I'll leave *it* to you **to lock the door**.

(BUT NOT: *I'll leave to lock the door to you.)

Postponing parts of sentence elements

426 The *it*-construction postpones a whole sentence element, whether a subject or object. You may also wish to postpone a 'heavy' PART of a sentence element. For example you may wish to postpone part of a complement, splitting an adjective from its modifier or modifiers:

How ready are they **to make peace with their enemies?**

This can avoid the awkwardness of a long or emphatic element coming in non-final position, as in *How ready to make peace with their enemies are they?* The most important cases of such postponement are discussed in 427–9.

Postponing the modifier following a noun

427   *The time* had arrived **to leave our homes for ever**.   [1]

(BETTER THAN: The time to leave our homes for ever had arrived.)

> *The problem* arose *of what to do with the money.* [2]
>
> (BETTER THAN: The problem of what to do with the money arose.)
>
> *What business* is it *of yòurs?* [3]
>
> (MORE IDIOMATIC THAN: What business of yòurs is it?)
>
> We heard *the story* from her own lips *of how she was stranded for days without food.* [4]

This postponement avoids awkwardness particularly when the rest of the sentence is short in comparison with the subject. However, in contrast to [2], the word order is normal and fully acceptable in the following sentence with a long agent phrase, where the sentence has a more balanced structure:

> *The problem of what to do with the money* was discussed by all members of the family.

Postponing the emphatic reflexive pronoun

428 When the reflexive pronouns *myself, himself, themselves,* etc. are used for emphasis, they normally have nuclear stress. If a reflexive pronoun is in apposition as part of the subject, it is common to postpone it for end-focus:

> The president himsèlf gave the order.
>
> ~ The president gave the order himsèlf.
>
> ('It was the president, and no one else, who gave the order.')

Postponing comparative clauses, etc.

429 A comparative clause or phrase can be separated, by postponement, from the preceding word it modifies. In some cases, the same sentence without postponement would be extremely awkward:

> *More people* own houses these days *than used to years ago.*
>
> (NOT: **More people than used to years ago* own houses these days.)
>
> He showed *less pity* to his victims *than any other tyrant in history.*
>
> (NOT: **He showed *less pity* than any other tyrant in history* to his victims.)

Other modifiers, like comparative clauses, are sometimes postponed for end-weight. These include phrases of exception (*see* 236):

> *All of them* were arrested *except the gang leader himself.*

Also clauses of amount or degree following *too, enough,* and *so:*

> *Too many people* were there *for the thief to escape unseen.*
>
> I've had *enough trouble* from those children *to last me a lifetime.*
>
> I was *so excited* by the present *that I forgot to thank you.*

Other choices of position

The passive

430 Passive sentences provide an important example of a grammatical process which changes the positions of elements in the sentence (*see 613–18*).

> [A] (Where did these chairs come from?)
>
> [B] They were bought by my ùncle. [5]
>
> The President was mistrusted by most of the radical and left wing politicians in the country. [6]

In [5], the passive gives the sentence end-focus, where the active (*My uncle bought them*) would not. In [6], the passive gives end-weight, where the active sentence (*Most of the radical . . . mistrusted the President*) would be awkward because of a 'heavy' subject. You can readily use the passive for end-weight where the subject of the sentence is a clause:

> I was surprised that so much had changed so quickly.
>
> (BETTER THAN: That so much had changed so quickly surprised me.)

(The preposition *by* is omitted with the passive here, because a *that*-clause cannot be complement of a preposition – *see 655*.)

Position of direct object

431 In normal order, a direct object precedes an object complement or a final position adverbial (*see 488*). But if the object is long, it can be postponed to the end for end-weight:

> NORMAL ORDER: We have proved **them** wrong.
>
> FINAL OBJECT: We have proved wrong **the forecasts made by the country's leading economic experts**.
>
> NORMAL ORDER: He condemned **them** to death.
>
> FINAL OBJECT: He condemned to death **most of the peasants who had taken part in the rebellion**.

The same choice can be made when a noun phrase object comes before a particle (e.g. the second part of a phrasal verb such as *make up, give away, let down*):

> ⎰He gave all his books awày.　　⎰She made the story ùp.
> ⎱He gave away all his bòoks.　　⎱She made up the stòry.

The choice may be made either for end-weight, or, as in these examples, for end-focus which falls either on the phrasal verb (*gave . . . away, made . . . up*) or on the object. Notice that personal pronoun objects cannot be moved to the end in this way: *He gave them away* (BUT NOT **He gave away them*) (*see 631*).

Position of indirect object

432 In a similar way, an indirect object can in effect be postponed, by converting it into a prepositional phrase (*see* 608, 730):

> The twins told their mother all their sècrets.   [7]
>
> The twins told all their secrets to their mòther.   [8]

This change, like the others, can be used for a different end-focus. For example, [7] answers the implied question 'What did the twins tell their mother?' but [8] answers the implied question 'Who did they tell their secrets to?'

Avoiding intransitive verbs

433 Connected with the principle of end-weight in English is the feeling that the predicate of a clause should be longer or grammatically more complex than the subject. This helps to explain why we tend to avoid predicates consisting of just a single intransitive verb. Instead of saying *Mary sang*, many would probably prefer to say *Mary sang a song*, filling the object position with a noun phrase which adds little information but helps to give more weight to the predicate.

434 For such a purpose English often uses a general verb (such as *have*, *take*, *give*, and *do*) followed by an abstract noun phrase:

She's having a swim.	Compare: She's swimming.
He's taking a bath.	Compare: He's bathing.
They took a rest (after lunch).	Compare: They rested (after lunch).
The driver gave a (hoarse) shout.	Compare: The driver shouted (hoarsely).
She does (very) little work.	Compare: She works (very) little.

The sentences on the left are more idiomatic and natural than those on the right.

In a similar way a transitive verb can be replaced by an indirect object construction with the verb *give*, etc.:

I gave the door a kick.	(= 'I kicked the door')
I paid her a visit.	(= 'I visited her')

A–Z in English grammar

435 Part Three of this book, called 'A–Z in English grammar', covers all the important areas of English grammatical form and structure, and is arranged alphabetically under topic headings. The arrangement is alphabetical because this part of the grammar is primarily meant to be used for reference, especially as an explanation of grammatical terms and categories referred to in Part Two.

Each entry in 'A–Z in English Grammar' has a reference to the most relevant sections of *A Comprehensive Grammar of the English Language* (abbreviated *CGEL, see* preliminary page xi), so that, if required, a more detailed treatment of the topic can be consulted in that book.

Adjective patterns

(*see CGEL* 16.68–83)

436 Adjectives can have different types of complement, such as

- a prepositional phrase: I feel very sorry *for Ann.*
- a *that*-clause: Everybody's pleased *that she is making such good progress.*
- a *to*-infinitive: I'm glad *to hear she is recovering.*

Adjectives with a prepositional phrase: *Ready for lunch?*

437 Adjectives are followed by different prepositions. As a dictionary will tell you, a particular adjective usually requires a particular preposition: *curious about, good at, ready for, interested in, afraid of, keen on, close to, content with,* etc. Adjectives with prepositions are often *-ed* adjectives, i.e. participial adjectives like *worried* (*about*), *interested* (*in*). Here are some examples:

Planners are **worried about** the noise and dirt in our environment.

I may have sounded a bit **annoyed at** her for turning up late.

Would you be **interested in** writing an article for our magazine?

The reader must be **convinced of** what is happening at one time, and not **surprised at** sudden changes of character and place.

I was increasingly **conscious of** being watched.

Anna was **uncertain of** what the words meant.

Industry is **independent of** natural conditions, while agriculture is continually **dependent on** the fluctuations of nature.

This film is **based on** a best-selling novel.

Adjectives with a *that*-clause: *I'm not sure (that) I understand.*

438 Adjectives which take a *that*-clause as complement may have personal subjects or introductory *it* as subject.

Adjectives with personal subjects

That is often omitted (called 'zero *that*'). Here are two sets of adjectives which have *that*-clauses as complement:

● 'Certainty adjectives' such as *certain, confident, convinced, positive, sure*

We are **confident** (that) Fran will have a brilliant career.

Everybody's **sure** (that) she can do it.

● 'Affective adjectives' such as *afraid, alarmed, annoyed, astonished, disappointed, glad, hopeful, pleased, shocked, surprised*

Bill was **disappointed** (that) Betty hadn't phoned.

I'm **glad** (that) you were able to cheer them up a bit.

Such adjectives can also have a prepositional phrase as complement (*see* 437): *confident about, sure of, disappointed with, glad of*, etc. But note that, in English, a preposition cannot introduce a *that*-clause. Compare:

They were **pleased at** the good news.

BUT: They were **pleased that** the news was good. (NOT *pleased at that the news . . .)

When the *that*-clause expresses something as an 'idea' rather than as a 'fact' (expressing joy, surprise, etc.), it contains *should* (*see* 'putative *should*' 280–1):

We were **amazed** that the cost should be so high.

Adjectives with introductory *it* as subject or object

Adjectives with *that*-clauses frequently have introductory *it* as subject or object (*see* 542):

It's *possible* that we'll all be a bit late.

Is it *true* that Liz never turned up?

We find it *odd* that this city has no university.

Other adjectives with *it*-constructions and *that*-clauses are, for example *certain, curious, evident, extraordinary, fortunate, important, likely, obvious, probable, sad*. Many are *-ing* adjectives, i.e. they have the form of an *-ing* participle: *disconcerting, embarrassing, fitting, frightening, irritating, shocking, surprising*.

When the *that*-clause expresses something as an 'idea' rather than as a 'fact' (expressing joy, surprise, etc.) the *that*-clause often contains 'putative *should*' (*see* 280–1):

The school board considered it *essential* that the opinions of teachers *should be* ascertained.

Instead of *should* + verb the *that*-clause can have the alternative constructions with the verb in the subjunctive, i.e. just the base form. This is more common in <AmE> than in <BrE> (*see* 706):

The school board considered it *essential* that the opinions of teachers *be* ascertained.

Adjectives with a *to*-infinitive: *It's **good** to have you back.*

439 There are different types of adjectives which have a construction with *to*-infinitive, for example:

Sue is *wrong* to say a thing like that. [1]

Such people are *hard* to find nowadays. [2]

'I'm *delighted* to be here', the speaker said. [3]

Many dealers were *quick* to purchase the new shares. [4]

The meanings of the four constructions are different, as can be seen from these paraphrases:

It's *wrong* of Sue to say a thing like that. [1a]

It's *hard* to find such people nowadays. [2a]

'It makes me *delighted* to be here', the speaker said. [3a]

Many dealers *quickly* purchased the new shares. [4a]

Type **[1]** Other adjectives like *wrong* in [1] are *clever, cruel, good, kind, naughty, nice, rude, silly, splendid, stupid*:

He was *silly* to go ahead with the plan.

Note the position of *not* and *never* before the *to*-infinitive:

He was *silly not to follow* your advice.

They were *stupid never to take* the opportunity offered.

Type [2] Other examples of adjectives like *hard* in [2] are:

The extent of this tendency is **difficult** to assess.

All this is very **easy** to arrange.

Your question is of course **impossible** to answer.

Similarly: *convenient, enjoyable, fun* <informal>, *good, pleasant.* The construction with introductory *it* [2a] is the more common and sometimes the only possible alternative:

It's **difficult** to assess the extent of this tendency.

It was really **good** to see you before Christmas.

It is **important** to create a new image of the Church.

It's almost **impossible** to say this in English.

It would be **nice** to have a portable TV at the end of one's bed.

It is now **possible** to make considerable progress in the negotiations.

It is **necessary** to distinguish between English and Scots law.

The infinitive clause can have a subject introduced by *for*:

It is **necessary for you** to distinguish between English and Scots law.

Type [3] Here are more examples of adjectives like *delighted* in [3]:

She'll be **furious** to see him behave that way.

I'm **glad** to see you looking so well.

If interviewed I should be **pleased** to provide further references.

I'm very **sorry** to learn that Hattie has been ill.

I'm rather **surprised** to learn that you have sold your stocks.

Other adjectives with this construction, all of which express some kind of emotion, are *amazed, angry, annoyed, disappointed, worried.*

Type [4] Other examples of adjectives like *quick* in [4]:

Nick is **willing** to do the hard work. ('Nick does it willingly')

The management was **careful** to avoid all mention of the problem. ('carefully avoided')

The police were **prompt** to act. ('acted promptly')

The entertainment industry has been **slow** to catch on. ('has caught on slowly')

There are also other adjectives which take an infinitive-construction but do not fit into the four types described:

We might be **able** to afford a new car.

I've been **unable** to contact him during the past week or so.

Ann is now very *anxious* to return to her university.

There are *bound* to be economic differences between distant parts of the country.

Our boss is always *ready* to listen to the views of others.

Adjectives

(*see CGEL* 7.1–22, 31–44)

440 Here are four features of adjectives:

- Most adjectives can have two uses: attributive and predicative. An attributive adjective occurs before the noun it modifies:

  This is a *difficult* problem.

  A predicative adjective occurs as the complement of a linking verb. Linking verbs (also called copular verbs, *see* 719) are *be, seem*, etc.:

  This problem is *difficult*.

- Most adjectives can be modified by degree adverbs like *very, quite, rather*, etc. (*see* 217):

  I'm on *quite* good terms with him.

- Most adjectives can have comparative and superlative forms (*see* 500):

  We have a *bigger* problem than inflation – our *biggest* problem now is high unemployment.

  This must be one of the *most beautiful* buildings in Europe.

- Many adjectives are derived from nouns and can be recognized by their endings, e.g. *-ous (fame ~ famous), -ic (base ~ basic), -y (sleep ~ sleepy), -ful (beauty ~ beautiful)*.

Attributive-only adjectives: *She's our **chief** financial adviser.*

441 Most adjectives can be both attributive and predicative, but some adjectives can only be used in attributive position, for example:

She was the *former* prime minister.

The adjective *former* can be related to the adverb *formerly*:

She was *formerly* the prime minister.

Here are some more such adjectives, where each example with an attributive-only meaning is followed by an example of its corresponding adverb:

Many changes occurred in Asia in the *late* 1990s.

~ I've not heard much from her *lately*.

They went to an *occasional* play.

~ *Occasionally* they went to see a play.

He was a popular colleague and a *hard* worker.

~ He worked *hard*. [NB same form of the adjective and adverb *hard*]

Some attributive-only adjectives are derived from nouns, for example:

A new *criminal* justice bill will soon come before Parliament. (*crime* ~ *criminal*: 'a bill concerned with the punishment of crimes')

He thought *atomic* weapons had deadened the finest feeling that had sustained mankind for ages. (*atom* ~ *atomic*)

There will be no need for a *medical* examination. (*medicine* ~ *medical*)

The predicative use of adjectives: *I feel sick.*

442 ● Adjectives can be used predicatively as subject complement after linking verbs like *be, seem, look, feel* (*see* 491, 719):

[A]: I feel *sick*.   [B]: Yes, you do look *awful*.

● Adjectives can also be used predicatively as object complement after verbs like *consider, believe, find* (*see* 733):

It makes me *sick* to see how people spoil the environment.

● Adjectives can be complement to a subject which is a finite clause (*see* 492):

Whether the minister will resign is still *uncertain*.

But the construction with introductory *it* gives end-weight (*see* 408) and is the more common:

It is still *uncertain* whether the minister will resign.

● Adjectives can also be complement to a non-finite clause (*see* 493):

Driving a bus isn't so *easy* as you may think.

● Although most adjectives can be used both attributively and predicatively (*see* 440), some groups of adjectives are predicative-only. One such group is 'health adjectives' like *faint, ill*, and *well*:

Oh doctor, I feel *faint*.

Several people are critically *ill* after the accident.

He doesn't look *well*, does he Anna?

When *faint* is not a health adjective but means 'slight' it can be attributive:

Katie bears a **faint** resemblance to my sister.

● Some predicative-only adjectives, including *afraid, fond, present, ready*, are often followed by clauses:

I'm **afraid** I don't really agree with that, Bill.

or prepositional phrases (*see* 437):

I'm very **fond** of Hemingway.

I hope you are **ready** for some hard work. ('I hope you are prepared for some hard work.')

All the persons **who were present** at the meeting were in favour of the proposal. ('All the persons who attended the meeting . . .')

Some such adjectives can also precede a noun, but with different meanings: *fond memories* are 'sweet memories', *a ready answer* is 'an answer which was given readily', *the present situation* means 'the situation at the present time'.

Adjectives after the head: *all the problems* **involved**

443 ● An adjective which modifies a noun is usually placed before its head (*see* 596). This is the attributive position: *the difficult problems*. But some adjectives, especially predicative-only adjectives (*see* 442), are placed immediately after the head they modify: *the problems involved*:

This is one of the problems **involved** in the scheme.

~ This is one of the problems **that are involved** in the scheme.

Such adjectives can usually regarded as reduced relative clauses (*see* 686):

All the persons **present** at the meeting were in favour of the proposal.

~ All the persons **who were present** at the meeting were in favour of the proposal.

The two adjectives *involved* and *present* cannot be attributive with the same meaning: we cannot say *the present persons* or *the involved problems* in these sentences.

● Quantifiers (amount words) ending in *-body, -one, -thing, -where* can only have modifying adjectives placed after them:

How long does it take to train **somebody new** on the job? ('How long does it take to train **somebody** who is **new** on the job?')

The chairman's remark astonished **everyone present**.

Is there **anything interesting** in the papers today?

Think of **somewhere nice** to go for the next weekend!

- There are adjective phrases consisting of an adjective plus an infinitive, as in

> These dogs are *easy to teach*.

Such phrases cannot come before a noun as head. We can NOT say

> *The easiest to teach dogs are Labrador retrievers.

But the adjective + infinitive phrase can be placed after its noun head:

> The dogs *easiest to teach* are Labrador retrievers.

The corresponding construction with a relative clause is more common in <informal> English:

> ~ The dogs *that are easiest to teach* are Labrador retrievers.

The construction with the adjective placed after its head is also used for other types of complement, such as *than*-clauses:

> Our neighbours have a house *much larger than ours*.

But it is more usual to separate the adjective and its complement:

> The *easiest* dogs *to teach* are Labrador retrievers.
> Our neighbours have a *much larger* house *than ours*.

Adjectives and participles: *Emma's attitude is rather* **surprising**.

444 There are many adjectives that have the same form as *-ing* or *-ed* participles (*see* 574):

> Emma's attitude is rather *surprising*.
> The professor had been *retired* for several years.

These adjectives can also be attributive:

> We were struck by Emma's rather *surprising* attitude.
> The *retired* professor seemed to spend most of his time on his yacht.

A verb corresponding to the adjective may have a different meaning. Compare these two uses:

Relieved used as an adjective:

> We are very *relieved* to know that you are all right. ('glad, pleased')

Relieved used as the past participle of the verb *relieve*:

> Our anxiety was *relieved* by the good news. ('eased, lessened')

The different functions of a form used as adjective and as participle are not always obvious.

- It is clear that an *-ing* form is a present participle (and not an adjective) when a direct object is present:

  The teacher was *entertaining* students at her home together with other friends.

But *entertaining* is an adjective in:

The teacher was brilliantly *entertaining* in her lecture.

- For both *-ed* and *-ing* forms, modification by the adverb *very* indicates that the forms are adjectives:

  The poor attendance at the meeting is not *very encouraging*.

  His remarks made me *very annoyed.*

When used as a verb, *annoyed* is modified by *very much*:

His remarks *annoyed* me *very much.*

Adjective or adverb?

(*see CGEL* 7.6–11, 7.71–3)

445 Most adverbs in English are derived from adjectives by the addition of *-ly*: *quick ~ quickly, careful ~ carefully*, etc. (*see* 464). But there are some adverbs which do not end in *-ly*, for example *direct, fast, hard, high, late, long, straight, wrong*. These words can be used both as adjectives and adverbs. In the following pairs, the first is an example of the word used as an adjective, and the second is an example of the word used as an adverb:

I think she has a *direct* line.

~ Why don't you call her *direct*?

Bill is a *fast* driver.

~ Don't drive too *fast*.

Alice is a *hard* worker.

~ Alice works *hard* at preparing new teaching materials.

That wall is too *high* to climb.

~ Don't aim too *high*.

We met in *late* August.

~ The modern industrial city developed relatively *late*.

What I really need now is a *long* rest.

~ You mustn't stay too *long*.

It was a long *straight* road.

~ The best thing would be to go *straight* back to Stockholm.

I may have said the *wrong* thing once too often.

~ There's always the chance of something going *wrong*.

These adverbs are mostly connected with time, position and direction. In some cases, there is also an adverb in *-ly* (*directly*, *hardly*, *lately*, *shortly*), but with a different meaning:

> Don't hesitate to get in touch with us **directly** ('immediately').
>
> We've had **hardly** any replies to our advertisement. (**hardly any** = 'almost no')
>
> I haven't seen him **lately** ('recently').
>
> We'll be in touch with you again **shortly**. ('soon')

There is a meaning difference between *strong* as an adjective and *strongly* as an adverb in:

> Ben felt **strong** enough to win the contest. (**strong** = 'fit, powerful')
>
> Ben felt **strongly** enough about the suggestion to object. (**strongly** = 'firmly')

Early can be used both as adjective and adverb:

> The **early** bird catches the worm.
>
> ~ I hate having to get up too **early**.
>
> The population explosion occurred in the **early** part of the nineteenth century.
>
> ~ I'll see you after you return **early** in February.

Some words ending in *-ly* can be used only as adjectives:

> That's a **lovely** present!
>
> That was an **ugly** incident.

Adjectives as complements: *It tastes good*.

446 An adjective is used after verbs like *taste* and *smell*. Here we consider the adjective to be a complement (*see* 508), not an adverbial:

> The food tasted **good**. ('The food was good to taste.')
>
> I thought the dish smelled absolutely **revolting**.

Well is the adverb corresponding to the adjective *good*:

> Grace is a **good** writer. ~ Grace writes **well**.

But *well* can also be used as an adjective. In these examples both *good* and *well* are adjectives (but with different meanings):

> Those cakes look **good**. ('Those cakes look as if they taste good.')
>
> Your mother looks **well**. ('Your mother seems to be in good health.')

Do you drive slow or slowly?

447 Compare these expressions:

a *rapid* car ~ drive *rapidly* [BUT NOT *drive *rapid*]   [1]

a *slow* car ~ drive *slowly* OR drive *slow*   [2]

[1] represents the normal case where there is regular variation between form and function of the adjective (*rapid*) and adverb (*rapidly*). In [2] *slow* can function both as adjective and adverb. Here is another example:

You can buy these things very *cheap*/*cheaply* now when the sale is on.

There is no difference in meaning between *drive slow* and *drive slowly* or *buy cheap* and *buy cheaply*, but the adjective form tends to be more <informal>:

Why do you have to drive so *slow* when there's no speed limit here?

The days passed and *slowly* the spring came. <rather elevated>

The form without *-ly* is especially common in comparative and superlative constructions. Again, the adverb form is the more <formal>:

We have to look *closer*/*more closely* at these problems.

Let's see who can run *quickest*/*most quickly*.

In their base form (i.e. when they are not comparative or superlative) these words would normally end in *-ly*: *look closely, run quickly*.

In <AmE conversation> *real* and *good* are commonly used as adverbs in expressions like *Ann's playing real good today*, corresponding to usual <BrE> *Ann's playing really well today*.

Adjectives as heads

(*see CGEL 7.23–26*)

448 The typical function of adjectives is to modify the head of a noun phrase: *the rich people, a supernatural phenomenon*. But some adjectives can themselves be heads of noun phrases: *the rich, the supernatural*. There are two kinds of such adjectives, both with generic reference (*see 90*):

● Adjectives denoting a class of people (plural), for example *the rich* = 'those who are rich':

We must care for *the elderly, the unemployed, the homeless, the sick* and *the poor, the weak* and *the vulnerable*.

Many people prefer the term *the physically challenged* to *the disabled* or *the handicapped*.

The young and *the old* don't always understand each other.

- Adjectives denoting an abstract quality (singular), for example *the supernatural* = 'that which is supernatural':

  Do you believe in **the supernatural**?

Adverbials

(*see* CGEL Chapter 8)

449 Adverbials often tell us something extra about an action, happening or state as described by the rest of the sentence, for example:

- the time when it happened (time adverbial):

  We got together *late in the evening*.

- the place where it happened (place adverbial):

  Will you be staying *in a hotel*?

- the manner in which it happened (manner adverbial):

  We have to study this plan **very carefully**.

There are of course many other meanings of adverbials. The meanings of adverbials are dealt with in Part Two (*see* 151–206). Here we will discuss the different forms and positions that adverbials can have in sentences.

The forms of adverbials

450 The position that adverbials can occupy depends very much on their form, and they have a number of different forms. Adverbials can be

- adverbs or adverb phrases (*see* 464):

  A friend of mine has **very kindly** offered to baby-sit.

- prepositional phrases (*see* 654):

  I found several people waiting **outside the doctor's door**.

- noun phrases (*see* 595):

  What are you doing **this afternoon**?

- clauses with a finite verb (*see* 492):

  We have to preserve these buildings **before it's too late**.

- infinitive clauses (*see* 493):

  As usual, Sarah was playing **to win**.

- *-ing* participle clauses (*see* 493):

  Mrs Cole filled her teacup, *adding a touch of skimmed milk*.

- *-ed* participle clauses (*see* 493):

  Two people were found dead, *presumably killed by cars*.

- verbless clauses (*see* 494):

  The actor admitted to driving *while under the influence of drink*.

The positions of adverbials: front, mid or end?

451 Most adverbials are mobile, so that they can occur in different places in the sentence. We distinguish three main positions:

- Front-position is before the subject:

  Fortunately I had plenty of food with me.

- Mid-position is immediately before the main verb, if no auxiliaries are present (the verb phrase printed in **bold**):

  His wife *never protests* and she *always agrees* with him.

If there is an auxiliary verb present, the adverbial is placed after the auxiliary:

You*'ll never be* lonely because we *will often come* along and pay visits.

If there is more than one auxiliary verb present, the adverbial is placed after the first auxiliary (called the operator, *see* 609):

This is an idea which *has never been tried*.

This is an idea which *may never have been tried*.

Occasionally a mid-position adverbial comes before the operator (*see* 261, 610). This may, for example, happen when the operator (including the linking verb *be*) is stressed for the purpose of contrast:

It *never was* my intention to make things difficult for you.

- End-position is after the verb, if there is no object or complement present:

  I'd like to *leave as soon as possible*.

An adverbial in end-position comes after an object or complement:

Please don't *call* me *before nine o'clock*.

The place of an adverbial depends partly on its form (whether it is an adverb, a prepositional phrase, a clause, etc.), partly on its meaning (whether it denotes time, place, manner, degree, etc.). End-focus and end-weight also play a part (*see* 408).

Long and short adverbials

452 Long adverbials normally occur in end-position.

> Clair's going **to Chicago on Monday next week**.

> There will be delegations from several countries **at the opening meeting of the conference in Rio de Janeiro later this year**.

> He was a complete failure **as far as mathematics is concerned**.

Long adverbials rarely occur in mid-position. Mid-position is usually restricted to short adverbs like *almost, hardly, just, never*:

> Our chairman **just** resigned.

Front-position gives contrast, or provides the background or setting for the clause which follows:

> **As far as mathematics is concerned**, he was a complete failure.

> **Outside the window** a low and cold bank of cloud hung over the streets of our little town.

> **Last year** there were riots. **Now** we have strikes and demonstrations.

Adverbials denoting manner, means, and instrument: *Did you come by bus?*

453 Adverbials which denote manner, means, and instrument (*see further* 194–7) usually have end-position:

> Will you be coming **by car**?

> He threatened the shop owner **with a big knife**.

> The conference opened **formally** today.

In the passive, however, mid-position is common:

> The conference was **formally** opened by the Secretary-General.

In an active sentence like this one, *well* can only have end-position:

> The Secretary-General put the point **well**.

But in the corresponding passive sentence we can have either end- or mid-position:

> ~ The point was put **well**.

> ~ The point was **well** put.

Place adverbials: *See you at the gym.*

454 Place adverbials (*see further* 170–92) usually have end-position:

Today's meeting will be *in room 205*.

He showered, shaved, dressed and went down *to the breakfast room*.

Hans Christian Andersen, the master of the fairy tale, was born *in Denmark in the town of Odense*.

Two place adverbials can occur together in end-position, usually with the smaller location before the larger one:

Many people eat [*in Japanese restaurants*] [*in the United States*].

Only the larger locational unit can be moved to front-position:

In the United States many people eat *in Japanese restaurants*.

Time adverbials: *I haven't seen Anna for a long time.*

455 There are three types of time adverbials (for a more detailed dicsussion *see* 151–69):

- adverbials denoting time-when (*see* 456, 151–9):

  I'll send you an e-mail *when I get the results*.

- adverbials denoting duration (*see* 457, 161–5):

  I haven't seen Anna *for a long time*.

- adverbials denoting frequency (*see* 458, 166–9):

  This week I'll be in the office *every day*.

Time-when adverbials: *See you tomorrow.*

456 Adverbials which denote a point of time or a period of time normally have end-position:

I hope to see you *tomorrow*.

My father retired *last year*.

The rail strike lasted *for a whole week*.

Adverbials such as *once* and *recently*, which denote a point of time, but also imply the point from which that time is measured, occur either in front-, mid- or end-position:

Once you said you'd like to be a vet.

You *once* said you'd like to be a vet.

You said *once* you'd like to be a vet.

In end-position these adverbs often have a rising-tone nucleus (*see* 406):

| We owned an Alsatian do̗g | o̗nce. |

Time duration adverbials: *Don't stay too long!*

457 Time duration adverbials normally have end-position:

> I'll be in California *for the summer*.
>
> The security guards were on duty *all night long*.
>
> I've been staying here *since last Saturday*.

But single-word adverbs usually take mid-position:

> Jessica Smith has *temporarily* taken over the art column of the newspaper.

Time frequency adverbials: *I jog every morning.*

458 Time frequency adverbials denoting definite frequency usually have end-position:

> Your salary will be paid *monthly*.
>
> Our office gets about a hundred requests *every day*.
>
> About this question we have to think *twice*.

Time frequency adverbs denoting indefinite frequency typically have mid-position (but *see* 610 on contrastive function). Such adverbs are, for example, *always, nearly always, ever, frequently, generally, never, normally, occasionally, often, rarely, regularly, seldom, sometimes, usually*:

> You are *always* assured of a warm and friendly welcome here.
>
> Daniel *generally* leaves home at seven in the morning.
>
> We don't *normally* go to bed before midnight.
>
> Mr Lake was *occasionally* carried away by his own enthusiasm.
>
> Important decisions can *rarely* be based on complete unanimity.
>
> At night the temperature *regularly* drops to minus five degrees Celsius.
>
> Women *usually* live longer than men.

But prepositional phrases denoting indefinite frequency have front- or end-position:

> *As a rule* it's very quiet here during the day.
>
> ~ It's very quiet here during the day, *as a rule*.
>
> *On several occasions* we've had reason to complain.
>
> ~ We've had reason to complain *on several occasions*.

Degree adverbials: *I fully agree with you.*

459 Degree adverbials like *definitely, entirely, really, thoroughly, very much* have a heightening effect on some part of the sentence (*see further* 215–23). Degree adverbs often occur in mid-position:

Abigail and I are **definitely** going to join the salsa club next year.

I **entirely** agree with your diagnosis.

I don't think this **really** affects the situation at all.

Your frustration is **thoroughly** justified.

We'd **very much** appreciate some further information.

There are also degree adverbs like *hardly, nearly, rather* and *scarcely* which have a lowering effect. They also have mid-position:

We can **hardly** expect people to take this election seriously.

Your friends **nearly** missed you at the airport.

I **rather** doubt I'll be back before nine tonight.

Jim felt Zoe was **scarcely** listening to what he was saying.

For emphasis, degree adverbs can occur before the operator:

I **really** don't know where we would be without you.

I **simply** can't speak too highly of our English teacher.

For some degree adverbials end-position is also possible:

Fortunately, our relationship did not cease **entirely**.

Two or more adverbials: *See you in class tomorrow.*

460 Time adverbials in end-position tend to occur in the order **duration + frequency + time-when**. In the following examples the different adverbials are indicated by square brackets:

Our electricity was cut off [*briefly*] [*today*].

I'm paying my rent [*monthly*] [*this year*].

I used to swim [*for an hour or so*] [*every day*] [*when I was younger*].

When more than one of the main classes of adverbials occur in end-position, the normal order is **manner/means/instrument + place + time**:

We go [*to bed*] [*very early*].

I have to rush to get [*into the supermarket*] [*before they close*].

Place adverbials tend to follow verbs of movement immediately and can therefore come before manner adverbials:

Anna put the crystal vase [*on the table*] [*with the utmost care*].

An adverbial clause normally comes after other adverbial structures (adverbs, prepositional phrases, etc.):

We plan to stop [*for a few days*] [*wherever we can find reasonable accommodation*].

A sentence like this one with a string of end-placed prepositional phrases is 'heavy':

The mayor was working [*on her speech*] [*in the office*] [*the whole morning*].

Some adverbials which normally have end-position can be put in front-position to avoid having too many adverbials at the end of a sentence:

[*The whole morning*], the mayor was working [*on her speech*] [*in the office*].

It is not usual for more than one adverbial to be in front-position or mid-position, but there are exceptions. For example, to introduce a new topic in a conversation we might find sentences like this one:

| Ányway | the next mórning | sòmehow or òther | I hadn't got any business to do. |

Sentence adverbials: *Frankly, this isn't good enough.*

461 The adverbials we have discussed so far are integrated to some extent in the structure of the sentence. For example, they can modify the verb:

Alex *always* drives *carefully*.

and they can be affected by negation:

Alex doesn't *always* drive *carefully*.

Here both *always* and *carefully* are in the scope of the negative (*see* 261).

462 There is also another type of adverbials, **sentence adverbials**, which are not integrated but are peripheral to the sentence structure. The difference between the integrated and peripheral types becomes clear with adverbs that can have both functions:

| It all happened quite náturally. | [*naturally* is a manner adverbial = 'in a natural manner']

| Nǎturally | the population is rìsing. | [*naturally* is a sentence adverbial = 'of course']

Haven't you eaten your breakfast *yet*? [*yet* is a time adverbial = 'so far']

Yet the police have failed to produce any evidence. [*yet* is a sentence adverbial = 'nevertheless']

463 Sentence adverbials have a wide range of possible structures (*see further* 308, 352–9). For example, instead of the adverb *frankly* in this sentence

Frankly, this isn't good enough.

we could use infinitive clauses like *to be frank, to put it frankly*, -*ing* participle clauses like *frankly speaking*, or finite verb clauses like *if I may be frank*.

Sentence adverbials often convey speakers' comments on the content of what they are saying:

> *Certainly* Nicole's German is very fluent.
>
> The document should be signed, *hopefully* by December.
>
> *Of course*, nobody imagines that Mr Brown will ever repay the loan.
>
> *Strangely enough*, Harry's face reminds me vividly of Eleanor Peters.
>
> *To be sure*, we've heard many such promises before.
>
> *Surely* no other novelist can give such a vivid description.
>
> *Unfortunately* that is an oversimplification of the problem.

Other sentence adverbials with this function are, for example, *actually, admittedly, definitely, fortunately, in fact, indeed, luckily, obviously, officially, possibly, preferably, really, superficially, surprisingly, technically, theoretically.*

Sentence adverbials like *however, therefore, moreover,* have a connective role:

> The hockey team didn't like the food. *However*, they have not complained.

The usual place for most sentence adverbials is front-position. They are often separated from what follows by a tone unit boundary in speech, or a comma in writing:

> <Spoken> | Ŏbviously | they expect us to be on tìme. |
>
> <Written> Obviously, they expect us to be on time.

Adverbs

(see CGEL 7.46–70)

464 Most adverbs are formed from adjectives with the suffix *-ly*: *frank/frankly, happy/happily*, etc. (For the change in spelling from *y* to *i* in *happy/happily*, etc., *see* 701.)

Adverbs have two typical functions: as adverbial in sentences and as modifier of adjectives, adverbs and other phrases.

- Adverb as adverbial (*see* 449):

  > The conference was *carefully* planned.

- Adverb as modifier of adjectives (*see* 465):

  > Louise is an *extremely* talented young woman.

- Adverb as modifier of other adverbs (*see* 465):

  > One has to read this document *very* closely between the lines.

- Adverb as modifier of prepositions, etc. (*see* 466):

  > We live *just* outside of Chicago.

Adverbs as modifiers of adjectives and other adverbs:
That's a **very** good idea!

465 Most modifying adverbs are degree adverbs like *absolutely, extremely, rather* (*see* 215, 459).

- When an adverb modifies an adjective, the adverb regularly precedes the adjective:

    I thought it was an **absolutely** awful show myself. <familiar>

    George said everybody was **deeply** affected.

    It's **extremely** good of you to do this for me.

    Rachel's **rather** tall for her age, isn't she?

But *enough* is placed after its adjective:

    No, this just isn't good **enough**!

    We were naive **enough** to be taken in.

When *too* and *how* modify an adjective in a noun phrase, the indefinite article is placed after the adjective. Compare these two sentences:

    Charlotte's a good accountant and never makes any mistakes.

    BUT: Charlotte's **too** good **an** accountant to make any mistakes.

    How strange **a** feeling it was, seeing my old school again! <elevated>

- An adverb which modifies another adverb is placed before the adverb:

    Melissa did **rather** well in her exams.

However, *enough* is an exception, and is placed after the adverb:

    Oddly **enough**, nothing valuable was stolen.

Adverbs as modifiers of prepositions, etc.: I'm **dead** against it.

466 An adverb can also modify

- **a preposition:** Emily's parents are *dead* against her hitch-hiking. <familiar>

- **a determiner** (*see* 522): The Johnsons seem to have *hardly* any books at home.

- **a numeral** (*see* 602): *Over* two hundred deaths were reported after the disaster.

- **a pronoun** (*see* 661): *Nearly* everybody seemed to be at the party.

The modifier *else*: *What* **else** *can we do?*

467 *Else* can modify

- the quantifiers *much* and *little* and is placed after these headwords:

  The Nelsons seem to do **little else** but watch TV in the evening.

- the adverbs ending in *-where*:

  Hey Bill, let's go **somewhere else**!

- the interrogatives *who*, *what*, *how* and *where*:

  What else can we do?

- the pronouns ending in *-body*, *-one*, *-thing*:

  Why don't you ask **somebody else**?

However, with determiners like *some*, *other* is used instead of *else*. These two sentences have the same meaning:

Someone else will have to take my place.

~ **Some other person** will have to take my place.

Adverbs as modifiers of nouns or noun phrases: *What* a fool he is!

468 The degree words *quite, rather, such,* and *what* (in exclamations) can modify noun phrases:

My grandmother used to tell me **such** funny stories.

The noun phrase is normally indefinite, and the degree word precedes the indefinite article (*see* 524):

She told me **such** a funny story.

The place was in **rather** a mess. <informal>

What a fool he is!

Some adverbs of place (e.g. *home*) or time (e.g. *before, ahead*) can modify nouns. The adverb is placed after the noun (see 648):

Our journey **home** was pretty awful.

The weather was fine the day **before**.

We always try to plan several years **ahead**.

In some phrases the adverb can stand both before and after the noun:

an **upstairs** window ~ a window **upstairs**

the **above** table ~ the table **above** (BUT ONLY: the table **below**, NOT *the **below** table)

Adverbs as complements of prepositions:
*I don't know anybody around **here**.*

469 Some adverbs of place (such as *here, home, downstairs*) and time (such as *today, later, yesterday*) act as complements of prepositions (printed in **bold**):

> I don't know anybody ***around here***. <informal>
>
> Are we far ***from home***?
>
> Ben shouted at me ***from downstairs***.
>
> ***After today***, there will be no more concerts until October.
>
> I'm saving the chocolates you gave me ***for later***.
>
> I haven't eaten ***since yesterday***.

Here are more examples of the preposition *from* + adverb combinations: *from above, from abroad, from below, from inside, from outside*. Several prepositions can form combinations with the place adverbs *here* and *there*, for example:

from here, from there	*in here, in there*
near here, near there	*over here, over there*
through here, through there	*up here, up there*

Apposition

(*see CGEL* 17.65–93)

470 Two or more noun phrases which occur next to each other and refer to the same person or thing are said to be **in apposition**:

> *A famous author, Ted Johnson,* is coming here next week.

The noun phrases in apposition can also occur in a different order:

> *Ted Johnson, a famous author,* is coming here next week.

In the last sentence we can regard the second noun phrase as a reduced non-restrictive relative clause (*see* 693):

> *Ted Johnson,* (who is) *a famous author,* is coming here next week.

The meaning relation expressed by apposition is the same as that expressed by a subject and its complement:

> *Ted Johnson* is *a famous author.*

Restrictive and non-restrictive apposition: *spokeswoman Ann Guthrie*

471 Just like relative clauses (*see* 692) apposition can be restrictive or non-restrictive.

● Non-restrictive apposition:

> I want to speak to Mr Smith, the electrician.
>
> | I want to speak to Mr <u>Smith</u> | the elec<u>tri</u>cian |

Here *the electrician* does not restrict or limit the meaning of *Mr Smith*. The noun phrases in non-restrictive apposition are here separated by a comma <in writing>, or by separate tone units <in speech>, as in non-restrictive relative clauses (*see* 398).

● Restrictive apposition:

> Which Mr Smith do you mean? | Mr Smith the <u>ar</u>chitect | or Mr Smith the elec<u>tri</u>cian? |

Here *the architect* and *the electrician* restrict and narrow down the meaning of *Mr Smith*.

Restrictive apposition is common, especially when the first element defines the meaning of the second element:

> the famous writer Ted Johnson
>
> the novel *Moby Dick*
>
> my good friend Barbara

Sometimes the determiner is omitted <*esp.* written AmE>:

> writer Ted Johnson
>
> hospital spokeswoman Ann Guthrie

Here, the first noun phrase is almost like a title (as in *President Lincoln, Professor Crystal, see* 668).

Explicit apposition: *some poets, **chiefly** Shelley and Wordsworth*

472 Sometimes the appositional relation of the noun phrases is made explicit by an adverbial such as *especially* and *chiefly*:

> Alice and Oliver had travelled in **many countries, especially those in South-East Asia**.
>
> Natalie Evans has written about **the English romantics, chiefly Shelley and Wordsworth**.

Other expressions of explicit apposition are *for example, for instance, particularly, in particular, notably, mainly* (for appositive clauses, *see* 646).

Articles

(*see CGEL* 5.10–11. 5.26–72)

473 There are two articles in English, the definite article *the* (*the book*) and the indefinite article *a* (*a book*) or *an* (*an eye*). Sometimes nouns require no article at all. This is called the 'zero article' (*books, eyes*). The articles are a subclass of the determiners (*see* 522).

It is the initial sound of the word following the article that determines how the indefinite article is spelled, and also how the definite and indefinite articles are pronounced.

● The unstressed definite article is always written *the*, but is pronounced /ðə/ before consonants and /ðɪ/ before vowels: /ðə/ *the car, the pilot* BUT /ðɪ/ *the egg, the idea*.

● The indefinite article is *a* /ə/ before consonants and *an* /ən/ before vowels: *a* /ə/ *a car, a pilot* BUT /ən/ *an egg, an idea*.

It is the pronunciation, not the spelling, of the following word that determines the choice of the indefinite article:

a UN /ə ˈjuː ˈen/ spokesperson [BUT *an EU* /ən ˈiː ˈjuː/ spokesperson]

an X-ray /ən ˈeksreɪ/

an hour, an heir [both nouns beginning with silent *h*]

The articles are normally unstressed, but may be stressed for special emphasis. The stressed forms of the indefinite article are *a* /eɪ/ and *an* /æn/. The stressed form of the definite article is *the* /ðiː/. It is often used to denote excellence or superiority:

The president's press conference will be *the* /ðiː/ event this week.

Article usage: *a book, the books, milk*

474 The general rules for the use of the articles are as follows:

● The definite article is used to express definiteness for all kinds of nouns (except proper nouns, such as *Susan, Asia* or *San Francisco*, which do not take an article; *see* 92).

Singular count nouns:
the book   *the child*   *the exam*

Plural count nouns:
the books   *the children*   *the exams*

Mass nouns:
the gold   *the knowledge*   *the milk*

● The indefinite article is used to express indefinite meaning of singular count nouns: *a book, a child, an exam*.

● Zero article (i.e. no article at all) or unstressed *some* /səm/ is used to express indefinite meaning of plural count nouns and of mass nouns.

Plural count nouns: (*some*) *books*, (*some*) *children*, (*some*) *exams*
Mass nouns: (*some*) *gold*, (*some*) *knowledge*, (*some*) *milk*

The general rules of meaning for the use of articles with common nouns are discussed in Part Two (*see* 83). Here we give some information about article usage with common nouns that occur without an article and the use of count nouns as complements. (For proper nouns, *see* 667.)

Common nouns without article: *I felt sleepy after **dinner**.*

475 Here we list some exceptional groups of common nouns that occur without article. This usage chiefly occurs in idiomatic expressions and certain fixed combinations of words (*at night*, etc.). For contrast, examples of regular uses of the article are also given (*during the night*, etc.).

● Means of transport (in expressions with *by*)

Did you get here **by train** or **by car**? [BUT: We slept **in the car**.]

Also: *by bus, by boat, by bike* etc.

● Times of the day and night

These birds are mostly active **at dawn** and **at dusk**.

We arrived rather late **at night**.

Also: *after daybreak, by sunrise, before sunset, at midnight, at twilight, at noon* [BUT article after *in* and *during*: *in the afternoon, in the night, during the night*, etc.]

● Meals

We were given scrambled eggs for **breakfast**.

Natasha is having **lunch** with her publisher.

I felt sleepy after **dinner**.

● <BrE>, but not <AmE>, usually omits the definite article with *university* and *hospital*:

Mrs Anderson has to **go to hospital** || **the hospital** for an operation. [BUT ALWAYS: Where is the hospital?]

We were **at university** || **the university** together.

● Other expressions:

Do you **go to church** regularly? [BUT: We walked towards the church.]

Young people should not be **sent to prison**. [BUT: We drove past the prison.]

Let's have lunch **in town** tomorrow. [BUT: She knows the town well.]

We met **at school** and began courting **in college**.

I like **going to bed** late.

Also: *stay in bed, get out of bed, put the children to bed, be ill in bed.* [BUT: *sit on the bed, lie down on the bed*]

● Parallel phrases

They walked *arm in arm*.	BUT: He took her by the arm.
We walked *hand in hand*.	BUT: What have you got in your hand?
They are *husband and wife*.	BUT: She's the wife of a famous artist.
We met *face to face*.	BUT: He punched me right in the face.

Count nouns as complement: *She wants to be a doctor.*

476 Unlike many other languages, English requires an article with singular count nouns as complement (e.g. after *be* and other linking verbs, *see* 508, 719). With indefinite reference, the indefinite article is used:

Mary always wanted to be *a scientist*.

With certain verbs, e.g. *consider*, the complement follows the object or the passive:

Everybody considered Mr Heyman (to be) *an excellent music teacher*.

Mr Heyman was considered (to be) *an excellent music teacher*.

With other verbs, e.g. *regard*, the complement follows *as*:

Many people regarded her *as a goddess*.

With definite reference, the definite article is normally used:

Phil Moore was regarded as *the best disc jockey* in town.

However, the definite article can be omitted when the noun designates a unique role, office or task:

Who's (*the*) *captain of the team*?

We've elected Mr Cook (*the*) *chairman of the committee*.

In these examples the definite article can be left out because there is only one captain of a team and one chairman of a committee. The definite article can also be omitted with a noun phrase in apposition (*see* 470):

Mrs Peterson, (*the*) *wife of a leading local businessman*, was fined for reckless driving.

Auxiliary verbs

(*see CGEL* 3.21–51)

477 Auxiliary verbs are, as their name suggests, 'helping verbs'. They are a small class of words including primary auxiliaries like *be* and modal auxiliaries like *can* and *will*. Auxiliaries do not make up a verb phrase on their own but help to make up a verb phrase in combination with a main verb (such as *work*) (*see* 735):

> I'm *working* all day today.
>
> I *can* even *work* at weekends if you need me.

An auxiliary verb can also occur without a main verb, but only where the main verb is omitted because it is supplied by the earlier context (*see* 384):

> I can speak French as well as she *can*.

In English, auxiliary verbs are required in certain constructions, especially questions and negative clauses (*see* the *do*-construction in 611):

> [A] *Do* you *want* a cup of coffee? [B] No, I *don't think* so, thank you.

● Auxiliary verbs can be placed before *not*, but main verbs require the *do*-construction:

> I'm not working today. [BUT: I don't *work* every day.]

● Auxiliary verbs can be placed before the subject in questions, but main verbs require the *do*-construction:

> *Can* I help you? [BUT: Do you *want* me to help you?]

478 Some auxiliary verbs have short (contracted) forms, for example: *I'm* (contracted form) instead of *I am* (uncontracted form). Contracted forms are common in <spoken> and <informal> English. Contracted forms can be used

● after pronouns:

> *I'll* see you tomorrow.

● after short nouns:

> The *dog's* getting ready for his walk.
>
> The *soup'll* get cold.

● after short adverbs such as *here*, *there*, *how*, and *now*:

> *Here's* your key.
>
> *How's* everything with you?
>
> *Now's* the time to act.

● after introductory *there* (*see* 547):

> I think *there's* going to be trouble.

In addition to verb contraction, as discussed above, English also has *not*-contraction: *isn't, can't,* etc. (*see* 582):

> The dog*'s not* here. ~ The dog *isn't* here.

The auxiliary verb *do*: *What **do** you say to that?*

479 The auxiliary *do* has the following forms:

	Positive	Uncontracted negative	Contracted negative
present: 3rd person singular	*does*	*does not*	*doesn't*
present: not 3rd person singular	*do*	*do not*	*don't*
past	*did*	*did not*	*didn't*

Do is also a main verb ('perform', etc.):

> What have you been **doing** today?

In addition, *do* is a substitute verb (*see* 383), as in:

> [A] You said you would finish the job today.

> [B] I have **done**. OR: I have **done** so.

When used as a main verb or a substitute verb, *do* has the full range of forms, including the present participle *doing* and the past participle *done*, as these examples show. (*Doing* and *done* are not included in the above table, which shows only the forms of the auxiliary *do*.)

The auxiliary verb *have*: ***Have** you seen today's paper?*

480 Like *do, have* is both a main verb and an auxiliary. It has the following forms:

	Positive		Negative	
	Uncontracted	Contracted	Uncontracted	Contracted
base	*have*	*'ve*	*have not,* *'ve not*	*haven't*
-s form	*has*	*'s*	*has not,* *'s not*	*hasn't*
past	*had*	*'d*	*had not,* *'d not*	*hadn't*
-ing form	*having*		*not having*	
-ed participle	*had*			

As a main verb, *have* ('possess') is sometimes constructed as an auxiliary <esp BrE>:

> I **haven't** any money. <esp BrE>

But this is increasingly rare. Nowadays both <AmE> and <BrE> prefer the *do*-construction:

> I **don't have** any money.

When used as an event verb (*see* 114) in the sense of 'take, experience, receive', the main verb *have* normally has the *do*-construction in both <AmE> and <BrE>:

Does your wife *have* coffee with her breakfast?

Did you *have* any difficulty getting here?

Did everybody *have* a good time?

481 There is also the <informal> *have got*, which is similar in function to *have* as a state verb, and where *have* is constructed as an auxiliary. It is particularly common in negative and interrogative sentences:

They **haven't got** a single idea between them!

How many students **have** you **got** in your class?

<AmE> has *gotten* as the past participle, corresponding to <BrE> *got* in certain senses: 'acquire, cause, come':

He had **gotten** stuck with a job too big for his imagination. <AmE>

<AmE> makes a distinction between *We've gotten tickets* = 'have acquired' and *We've got tickets* = 'possess'.

The auxiliary verb *be*: *What on earth **are** you doing?*

482 *Be* has eight different forms (which is more than any other English verb). *Be* is constructed as an auxiliary also when it functions as a main verb. For example, it has no *do*-construction (except in commands, *see* Note [b] below).

		Positive	Uncontracted negative	Contracted negative
base		*be*		
present	1st person singular	*am, 'm*	*am not, 'm not*	(*aren't, ain't*) [a]
	3rd person singular	*is, 's*	*is not, 's not*	*isn't*
	2nd person singular and all persons plural	*are, 're*	*are not, 're not*	*aren't*
past	1st and 3rd person singular	*was*	*was not*	*wasn't*
	2nd person singular and plural, 1st and 3rd person plural	*were*	*were not*	*weren't*
-ing form		*being*	*not being*	
-ed participle		*been*		

Note

[a] In negative questions *aren't I?*, as in *I'm right, aren't I?*, is widely used in <BrE>, but it is felt to be somewhat affected in <AmE>. In negative

declarative sentences there is no generally acceptable contracted form for *am not*. *Ain't* is a <non-standard> but frequently used construction, esp. in natural <AmE> conversation, as in *Things ain't what they used to be*. As well as serving as a contracted *are not*, *ain't* is used also for *am not*, *is not* (*Ain't it the truth?*), *has not* and *have not* (*You ain't seen nothing yet*). All these examples are taken from <very informal> AmE.

[b] The main verb *be* may have the *do*-construction in persuasive imperative sentences. *Do be quiet!* is more persuasive or emphatic than *Be quiet!* The *do*-construction is also required with negative imperatives (*see* 497): *Don't be awkward!*

The modal auxiliaries: *Can I use your phone?*

483 The modal auxiliaries do not have *-s* forms, *-ing* forms, or *-ed* participles. *Can, may, shall, will* have the special past forms *could, might, should, would*. The other modal auxiliaries (*must, dare, need, ought to, used to*) do not have such forms.

Positive	Uncontracted negative	Contracted negative
can	cannot, can not	can't
could	could not	couldn't
may	may not	(mayn't) <rare>
might	might not	mightn't
shall	shall not	shan't <rare esp. in AmE>
should	should not	shouldn't
will, 'll	will not, 'll not	won't
would, 'd	would not, 'd not	wouldn't
must	must not	mustn't
ought to	ought not to	oughtn't to
used to [see Note]	used not to	didn't use(d) to, usedn't to
need [see Note]	need not	needn't
dare [see Note]	dare not	daren't

[Note] *Used to, need,* and *dare* as auxiliaries are rare in all forms (see 484–5).

Here are some examples of modal auxiliaries as used in conversation:

| As far as I *can* see | I'm sure she's a very clever woman. |

| What Mr Johnson doesn't realize is | that not everybody else | *can* work as hard as he *can*. |

| I'm sure that Sophie *would* be awfully grateful | if you *could* see her in your office sometime. |

| What *shall* we do about this request then | – just write saying I'm very sorry I *cannot* | teach at the institute. |

| Ann *should* have had her dissertation in | at the beginning of May. |

| I did get a postcard from her | saying that the thing is now ready | and that she *will* send it by the end of June. |

| Our principal is very <u>strong</u>ly of the op<u>í</u>nion | that we <u>à</u>ll **ought** to go on t<u>é</u>aching | to the end of the <u>tèrm</u>. |

|| I think this <u>mày</u> be wh<u>ý</u> | he's so cross about the whole <u>thìng</u>. |

|| I don't mind getting <u>pìn</u> money | for proof-reading someone's <u>thèsis</u> | but they **might** <u>tèll</u> me so | bef<u>òre</u>hand. |

Dare and need: *You* ***needn't*** *worry about it.*

484 *Dare* and *need* can be constructed in two ways:

- either as main verbs with *to*-infinitive, *-s* inflection (*dares, needs*) and past forms (*dared, needed*):

  It ***needs to be said*** that your sister is not to be blamed for what happened.

- or as modal auxiliaries (with bare infinitive and without the inflected forms *dares ~ dared, needs ~ needed*):

  Our country's prestige ***need not suffer***.

  There ***need be*** no doubt about that.

The modal auxiliary construction is mainly restricted to negative and interrogative sentences, and is rare. The main verb construction can always be used, and is in fact the more common in all varieties:

  Our country's prestige ***does not need to suffer***.

  There ***does not need to be*** any doubt about that.

Used to: *They* ***used*** *not* ***to*** *come here.*

485 As an auxiliary *used* always takes the *to*-infinitive and is pronounced /ˈjuːstə/. *Used to* occurs only in the past tense:

  Brandon ***used to*** be a racing driver.

  My aunt ***used to*** come every day and play with to me.

This auxiliary may take the *do*-construction, in which case the spellings *use* and *used* both occur:

  Herb ***didn't use to smoke***. OR: Herb ***didn't used to smoke***.

In more <formal> style this construction is preferred:

  Herb ***used not to smoke***.

The interrogative construction *Used he to smoke?* is <*esp.* BrE>. The more <informal> *Did he use(d) to smoke?* is preferred in both <AmE> and <BrE>. However, a different construction is often a more natural choice, for example: *Did he smoke when you first knew him?*

Clauses

(see CGEL 10.1–33, 14.5–9)

486 Sentences are made up of clauses. A sentence may consist of one, or more than one, clause *(see* 695). There are three ways in which clauses may be described:

● In terms of the **clause elements** (subject, verb, etc.) from which they are constructed, and the verb patterns which are formed from these elements *(see* 487, 718).

● In terms of **finite clauses**, **non-finite clauses**, and **verbless clauses** *(see* 492).

● In terms of **clause function**, i.e. the function a clause performs in a sentence. We talk about nominal clauses (clauses acting as noun phrases), adverbial clauses (clauses acting as adverbial elements), etc. *(see* 495).

We shall deal with each of these in turn.

Clause elements: S, V, O, C, A

487 A clause can be analysed into five different types of clause elements:

S = Subject *(see* 705)

V = Verb (or rather verb phrase, *see* 718)

O = Object *(see* 608)

C = Complement *(see* 508)

A = Adverbial *(see* 449)

These clause elements can be shown in a diagram:

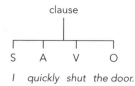

488 Among these types we may distinguish the four **main elements** of clause structure (subject, verb, complement, object) and one **modifying element** (adverbial). Adverbials differ from the other clause elements in three important ways:

- Adverbials are usually **optional**, i.e. they may be omitted (optional adverbials are given in brackets):

  (Suddenly) I felt tired.

  I (quickly) shut the door.

- Adverbials are **not restricted in number**. A clause can only have one subject, one finite verb, one complement, and one or two objects. But, there may be any number of adverbials. (This is theory, of course: in practice you will rarely find more than three adverbials in one clause.)

SV	Fran woke up.
SV[A]	Fran woke up [in the middle of the night].
[A]SV[A]	[Sometimes] Fran woke up [in the middle of the night].

- Adverbials are often **mobile**, i.e. they can occur at different places in the clause (on the positions of adverbials, *see* 451):

[A]SV[A][A][A]	[Sometimes] I stay [a couple of extra hours] [in the office] [to finish up a job].
[A]S[A]V[A][A]	[To finish up a job] I [sometimes] stay [a couple of extra hours] [in the office].

The basic verb patterns

489 If we look at the main elements in the clause (S, V, O, C), we can distinguish six basic verb patterns. (We call them 'verb patterns' rather than 'clause patterns', since it is the verb that determines the type of clause structure. For more details, *see* 718.)

- **SVC** (or sometimes **SVA**): The first verb pattern occurs with linking verbs: *be*, *appear*, *look*, *seem*, etc. Linking verbs 'link together' the subject and the complement [here in square brackets]:

  Luke's father *is* [a lawyer].

  Both boxers *became* [famous].

  The victory *seems* [a foregone conclusion].

  The guard posts *are* [along the frontier].

- **SVO**: The second verb pattern occurs with verbs that have one object, i.e. transitive verbs:

  I *like* [Hemingway's style].

- **SVOV**: The third verb pattern occurs with verbs that have an object + a verb:

  The manager *asked* [me] [to work overtime].

- **SVOO**: The fourth verb pattern occurs with verbs that have two objects (these verbs are called 'ditransitive verbs'):

  I'll *give* [you] [the report] on Monday.

- **SVOC**: The fifth verb pattern occurs with verbs that have an object and an object complement:

  We *found* [the house] [too expensive].

- **SV**: The sixth verb pattern occurs with verbs without object or complement, i.e. intransitive verbs:

  The children *laughed*.

The active-passive relation

490 There are certain relations between clause elements. One is the relation which makes it possible to change an active clause into a passive clause (*see* 613). The following verb patterns can occur in the passive (optional agents in round brackets):

Pattern	Active	Passive
SVO	Everybody rejected the idea.	The idea was rejected (by everybody).
SVOV . . .	The manager asked me to work overtime.	I was asked (by the manager) to work overtime.
SVOO	The ambulance crew gave the casualties first aid.	The casualties were given first aid (by the ambulance crew).
SVOC	Boat owners considered the bridge a menace to navigation.	The bridge was considered a menace to navigation (by boat owners).

When an active clause is changed into a passive clause, the object of the active clause is converted into the subject of the passive clause. Therefore only those patterns which contain an object can be converted into the passive. The pattern with two objects

I'll give you the report on Monday.

has two passive forms:

You'll be given the report on Monday.

The report will be given (to) you on Monday.

The complements of subjects and objects: *Ann is a teacher.*

491 The commonest verb in the pattern with linking verbs (SVC) is *be*. Since *be* links together the subject and the complement, we call it a **linking verb**. There are also other linking verbs, such as the verbs of 'appearance' and 'sensation' *look* and *feel*, and the verbs of 'becoming' *become* and *get* (*see* 719):

> My mother *looks* [so tired and worn], and I *felt* [very worried] when she rang up and said she couldn't come.
>
> Right from the beginning we *became* [very attached to each other].
>
> Let's hope the world will gradually *become* [a better place in which to live].

The verb pattern SVOC can often be expanded by a *to be* infinitive or paraphrased by a *that*-clause (*see* 724, 727):

> We found *him most helpful.*
>
> ~ We found *him to be most helpful.*
>
> ~ We found *that he was most helpful.*

The object and the complement of the SVOC verb pattern have the same relation of meaning as the subject and complement of an SVC pattern with a linking verb: *He was most helpful.*

Finite, non-finite, and verbless clauses

492 Another way of looking at a clause is to see what kind of verb phrase acts as its V element. Here we first distinguish finite clauses and non-finite clauses.

Finite clauses are clauses whose verb element is a finite verb phrase (*see* 737). In a finite verb phrase there may be just one finite verb:

> Ann *works* terribly hard. (the SIMPLE PRESENT)
>
> Ann *worked* terribly hard. (the SIMPLE PAST)

If the verb phrase consists of more than one verb, the first verb is finite:

> She *has worked* in the office for six months. (the Present Perfect)
>
> She *is working* in the office for six months. (the Present Progressive)

Normally, in <written> language, a complete sentence has at least one independent finite verb clause.

493 **Non-finite clauses** are clauses whose verb element is a non-finite verb phrase. A non-finite verb phrase consists of non-finite elements such as an *-ing* participle (*see* 578), an *-ed* participle (*see* 577), or an infinitive (*see* 575). Most non-finite clauses do not have a subject.

- *-ing* clause without a subject:

  I used to lie awake at night, **worrying about the next exam**.

- *-ing* clause with a subject:

  His remark having been represented as an insult, Mr Anderson was later forced to resign from the committee.

- *-ed* clause without a subject:

  Covered with confusion, Hannah hurriedly left the room.

- *-ed* clause with a subject:

  The job finished, we went home straight away.

- *to*-infinitive clause without a subject:

  The best thing would be **to leave straight away**.

- *to*-infinitive clause with a subject. The subject of an infinitive clause is often introduced by the preposition *for*:

  The best thing would be **for us to leave straightaway**.

- bare infinitive clause (i.e. containing an infinitive without *to*) without a subject. These are much less common than *to*-infinitive clauses:

  All I did was **ask him to leave**.

- bare infinitive clause with a subject:

  Rather than **Joan do it**, I'd prefer to do the job myself.

494 Verbless clauses contain no verb element, and often no subject:

  Dozens of tourists were stranded, **many of them children**.

  A sleeping bag under each arm, they tramped off on their vacation.

Verbless clauses are regarded as clauses because they function like finite and non-finite clauses, and because they can be analysed in terms of one or more clause elements. We can usually assume that a form of the verb *be* or some other verb has been omitted: 'many of the tourists *were* children', 'they *had* a sleeping bag under each arm'. The subject, when omitted, can usually be understood as equivalent to the subject of the main clause:

  The oranges, **when ripe**, are picked and sorted. ('when they are ripe')

  Whether right or wrong, Michael always comes off worst in an argument. ('whether he is right or wrong')

An adjective, alone or as head of an adjective phrase, can function as a verbless clause:

Anxious for a quick decision, the chairman called for a vote.

An escort of ten horsemen waited behind the coach, *half asleep in their saddles*.

The verbless clause is mobile, though it usually precedes or follows the subject of the main clause:

Even if true, this statement would be misleading.

~ This statement, *even if true*, would be misleading.

An adverb may sometimes replace an adjective functioning as a verbless clause. There is hardly any difference in meaning between these two sentences:

Nervously, the gunman opened the letter.

~ *Nervous*, the gunman opened the letter.

Clause functions

495 In terms of function, i.e. what role they have in a sentence, clauses can be divided into **main clauses** and **subclauses** (i.e. subordinate clauses; *see* 709). Subclauses are part of another clause. We can also divide clauses into nominal clauses, adverbial clauses, etc. The various functions of clauses are treated elsewhere:

- **Nominal clauses** function as subject, object, complement, prepositional complement, etc. (*see* 588). Nominal clauses can be *that*-clauses, interrogative clauses, *-ing* clauses, and infinitive clauses. In this example the first *that*-clause functions as subject and the second as object:

   [That the customer gave a false name] shows [that he was doing something dishonest.]

- **Relative clauses** (*see* 686), i.e. modifying clauses introduced by *wh*-pronouns or *that* (including 'zero-*that*'), are usually modifiers of noun phrases. In this sentence the relative clause *who live opposite our house* modifies the noun phrase head *family*:

   The family [who live opposite our house] are French.

- **Comment clauses** (*see* 499) function as sentence adverbials (*see* 461), as in this sentence where *to be honest* equates with the adverb *honestly*:

   [*To be honest*,] I'm not sure what to do.

   ~ *Honestly*, I'm not sure what to do.

- **Comparative clauses** (*see* 505) follow a comparative item such as *more* or *less*:

   This year bookshops have sold a lot more paperbacks [than they usually do].

● **Adverbial clauses** have a large number of different meanings, such as time, as in:

I used to go to the theatre [whenever I had the opportunity].

Adverbial clauses are discussed in Part Two: clauses denoting time (*see* 151), place (*see* 170), contrast (*see* 211), cause or reason (*see* 198, 204), purpose (*see* 203), result (*see* 202), and conditional clauses (*see* 207).

Cleft sentences

(*see* CGEL 18.25–30)

496 A single clause, such as

Our neighbours bought a new car last year.   [1]

can be divided into two separate parts, each with its own verb:

[It **was** our neighbours] [who **bought** a new car last year.]   [1a]

A construction like [1a] is called a **cleft sentence** (*see* 419). A sentence like [1] can be changed into different cleft sentences depending on what element is considered the most important in the sentence. This has to do with focus (*see* 399). In [1a] the subject *our neighbours* is in focus. In [1b] the object *house* is in focus:

| It was a new càr that our neighbours bought last yéar. | [1b]

In [1c] the adverbial *last year* is in focus:

| It was last yéar that our neighbours bought a new càr. | [1c]

The second part of a cleft sentence is very similar to a restrictive relative clause (*see* 687). The relative pronouns are also used in cleft sentences: e.g. *who* in [1a] and *that* in [1b] and [1c].

Besides the **it-type cleft sentence**, there is also a **wh-type cleft sentence** (*see* 420). If we want to place the object *car* of [1] in focus we can use either the *it*-type in [1b] or the *wh*-type in [2b]:

| It was a new càr that our neighbours bought last yéar. | [1b]
| What our neighbours bought last yĕar | was a new càr. | [2b]

Cleft sentences are different from sentences with **introductory *there*** (*see* 547):

There's a lovely house for sale in our village.

and **introductory *it*** (*see* 542):

It's too early to go and visit Sue at the hospital.

Commands

(*see CGEL* 11.24–30)

497 We distinguish two types: 2nd person commands and 1st and 3rd person commands.

2nd person commands: *Behave yourself.*

A command is usually a sentence with an imperative verb, i.e. the base form of the verb, without endings for number or tense:

Shut the door.

Commands are apt to sound abrupt unless they are toned down by **politeness signals** like *please* (*see* 332):

Shut the door, please.

Please *get* ready as soon as you can.

The only auxiliary verb used in commands is *do*:

Don't stay too late, Pam.

Don't be a fool.

The *do*-construction is used in such *not*-negated commands. But *do* can also occur in positive commands. If we want to make a command more **emphatic** or **persuasive**, we can say

Do sit down. [Compare: *Sit down*.]

Do tell us how you got on at your interview. [Compare: *Tell us* . . .]

In positive sentences it is only in commands that *do* can be followed by *be*:

Do be careful.

As these examples indicate, commands usually have no **expressed subject**. When the subject is missing, we can say that there is an **implied subject** *you*. This is why we call this type of command '2nd person commands'. We can see that there is an implied subject *you* when there is a reflexive pronoun *yourself/yourselves* (*see* 619):

Behave *yourself*.

or a tag (*see* 684):

Be quiet, will *you*!

However, in commands there can sometimes be an expressed subject *you*:

You just listen to me now.

You go right ahead with your plan.

This expressed *you* is stressed in commands:

'You 'put that dòwn. [Command] <impolite>

Commands with *you* can sound particularly <impolite>, as in this example. But *you* is not stressed in statements:

You 'swim wèll. [Statement]

1st and 3rd person commands: *Let's go and eat.*

498 There are also 1st person and 3rd person commands, but they are not as common as 2nd person commands. A 1st person command begins with *let me* in the singular, or *let's* in the plural (the full form *let us* is rare):

Let me have a look at your essay.

Let's go and eat. OR **Let's** go eat. <informal AmE>

In negative commands, *not* follows *let's*, but there is also an alternative construction with *do*-support <esp. BrE>:

Let's not be late for the game. ~ **Don't let's** be late for the game. <esp. BrE>

A 3rd person command has a 3rd person subject, as in

Somebody get a doctor! <informal>

Commands with *let* + a 3rd person subject are <formal>, often <elevated> in style:

Let each nation decide its own fate. <formal>

Comment clauses

(*see CGEL* 15.53–56)

499 Comment clauses comment on the truth of the sentence, the manner of saying it, or the attitude of the speaker (an emotional reaction or judgment):

The minister's proposal could, **I believe**, be a vital contribution towards world peace.

Comment clauses like *I believe* are only loosely related to the rest of the main clause they belong to, and they function as sentence adverbials (*see* 462). They are usually marked off from the other clause, in <written> English by commas:

What's more, we lost all we had.

Stated bluntly, they have no chance of recovery.

In <speech>, comment clauses are often marked off by having a separate tone unit:

| Rachel's an industrial designer | *you see*. |

| I'm not sure what to do| *to be honest*. |

Comment clauses can occur in front-, mid- or end-position. Here are some other examples of comment clauses in spoken English [– marks a pause]:

| It's the same at the board meetings too *you see* | – *I mean* he takes over the whole thing. |

| In a sense it is | a new idea | but well – *you know* | we're not prepared to do this. |

There are many types of comment clauses, such as *I see, I think, I suppose, I'm afraid, as you see, as I said, to be frank, so to say, so to speak, what's more likely, you see, you know, you bet* <familiar>. Some such items are very common as 'discourse markers' in <informal speech>, in particular *you see, you know, I mean, I think*, etc. (*see* 23).

Comparison

(*see* Section 225 and *CGEL* 7.74–90, 15.63–75)

500 Gradable adjectives and adverbs (*see* 216) have degrees of comparison: **comparative** and **superlative**. Comparison is expressed either by the endings -*er* and -*est* or by the words *more* and *most* before the adjective or adverb:

		Comparative	Superlative
Adjectives	tall	taller	tallest
	beautiful	*more* beautiful	*most* beautiful
Adverbs	soon	sooner	soonest
	easily	*more* easily	*most* easily

Comparison of adjectives

501 Comparison with the endings -*er* and -*est* is generally used with short adjectives:

● Usually one-syllable adjectives:

great ~ greater ~ greatest

Occasionally, also one-syllable adjectives occur with *more* or *most*:

more true ~ most true, more wrong ~ most wrong

- Many two-syllable adjectives, especially those ending in *-y, -ow, -le* and *-er*:

  easy ~ easier ~ easiest; also: *early, happy, healthy, pretty*, etc.

  narrow ~ narrower ~ narrowest; also: *mellow, shallow*, etc.

  able ~ abler ~ ablest; also: *feeble, gentle, humble, noble, simple*, etc.

  clever ~ cleverer ~ cleverest; also: *bitter, slender*, etc.

Two-syllable adjectives such as *common, polite, quiet* often have either type of comparison:

  common ~ commoner ~ commonest OR

  common ~ more common ~ most common

The endings sometimes involve changes in spelling (*see* 700, 703) or pronunciation (*see* 666), for example:

  pretty ~ prettier ~ prettiest, big ~ bigger ~ biggest

- Long adjectives (*awkward, possible, hopeful, useful,* etc.), including *-ed* adjectives (*interested*, etc.) and *-ing* adjectives (*interesting*, etc.) form comparison with *more* and *most*:

  I find my new work **more challenging** and **more interesting**.

  This is one of the **most beautiful** places in the area.

502 A small group of highly frequent adjectives have irregular comparison:

- *bad ~ worse ~ worst*:

  Yesterday was a **bad** day for the stock market, but today seems to be the **worst** day of the week.

- *good ~ better ~ best*:

  There'd be a **better** chance for our team to win the series with a new coach.

  To keep the children happy for the afternoon, the **best** thing to do was to run a film.

- *far ~ further ~ furthest* OR (less common, except when referring to distances) *far ~ farther ~ farthest*:

  The police never got any **further** with their investigation.

In these examples *further* is not a comparative, but means 'additional':

  Any **further** questions?

  We stayed for a **further** three weeks. (But in <informal> usage usually: **for another three weeks**.)

Old has the regular forms *older ~ oldest*, but *elder ~ eldest* are also used to denote family relations (*an elder/older sister*). *Older* is always used before a *than*-construction:

> John is nine years **older than me**.

Comparison of adverbs

503 Adverbs have the same general rules of comparison as adjectives. Adverbs of two or more syllables formed from adjectives with the *-ly* ending (*quick ~ quickly*) have comparison with *more* and *most*:

- *quickly ~ more quickly ~ most quickly*

    > The memos have to be circulated **more quickly**.

As with adjectives, there is a small group of adverbs with irregular comparison:

- *well ~ better ~ best*

    > To qualify, you have to do **better** than this.
    > The picture in the middle, that's the one I like **best**.

- *badly ~ worse ~ worst*

    > Financially, we may be **worse** hit than some of the other universities.
    > The northern regions were **worst** affected by the snow.

- (*much*) *~ more ~ most*

    > You deserve a prize **more** than anyone.
    > Chelsea is my **most** helpful colleague.

- (*little*) *~ less ~ least*

    > The test turned out to be **less** difficult than we thought.
    > The money arrived when Sophie **least** expected it.

- *far ~ further ~ furthest* OR *far ~ farther ~ farthest*

    > The sun's **further** away from the earth than the moon.
    > They seem to be **farther** apart than ever before.

Comparison of quantifiers: *Waste **less** money!*

504 The quantifiers *much, many, little* and *few* (*see 676*) also have special comparative and superlative forms when they function as determiners and pronouns:

- *much ~ more ~ most*

    > We need **more** money to buy new computers for the students.
    > Jack got **more** than he deserved.
    > **Most** of our computer equipment is ten years old.

- *many ~ more ~ most*

  We also need **more** books in the department.

  I find **most** people working in the library very helpful.

- *little ~ less ~ least*

  We now spend **less** money on periodicals than last year.

  I haven't the **least** idea what to do now.

- *few ~ fewer ~ fewest* OR *few ~ less ~ least* (On the choice of *fewer/less*, see 73.)

  We want **fewer/less**, not more restrictions.

Comparative clauses: *Ann speaks French better **than I do**.*

505 The comparative form of adjectives and adverbs is used when we want to compare one thing with another in order to point out some difference (*see* 225). For this purpose, a subclause beginning with *than* can be added after the comparative word:

> The author's most recent book is **more interesting than** his previous ones were.

In this sentence, *more interesting* may be called the **hinge element** of the comparison. The hinge element is the phrase which contains the comparative word. The following *than*-clause modifies the hinge element. It is called a 'hinge' because it belongs, in terms of meaning, both to the main clause and to the comparative subclause. The meaning of the hinge element *more interesting* complements *is* in the main clause and *were* in the subclause. But in terms of structure, the subclause does not contain a complement. Here are some more examples of comparative clauses:

> Nicole looks **much younger than** her sister does.

> Charles speaks French **less well than** he writes it.

> We're in a hurry because prices are going up **faster than** we can buy.

Comparative phrases: *Ann speaks French better than I/me.*

506 The part of the sentence following *than* may have different structures:

Ann can speak French better **than I can**.	[1]
Ann can speak French better **than I**. <formal>	[2]
Ann can speak French better **than me**. <informal>	[3]

In [1] we have the subclause *than I can* (with *speak it* omitted). Other elements of a subclause can also be omitted if they repeat the information in the main clause. If the verb is omitted, we are left with a comparative phrase as in [2] and [3] rather than a comparative clause. In <informal> English, the *than*-phrase (*than me* as in [3]) behaves like a prepositional phrase (*to me, for me,* etc.) with the following pronoun in the objective case: *me, them,* etc. (*see* 620). In <formal> English the subjective form of the pronoun (*than I, they,* etc.) is used, if the pronoun is notionally the subject of the omitted verb: *than I* [2] = *than I can speak it.* In <informal> English such clauses can be ambiguous:

He seems to like his dog more than his children.

The most likely meaning is:

He seems to like his dog more than he likes his children.

But another possible meaning is:

He seems to like his dog more than his children do.

An adverbial or adjective can follow *than* in comparative phrases:

Emma struck him as more beautiful **than ever**.

James said no more **than usual**.

There is higher unemployment in the north **than in the south**.

507 Some types of comparative phrases cannot be related to comparative clauses. One type is concerned with comparison of degree and amount:

There were **fewer** than twenty people at the meeting.

I have **better** things to do than watching television.

Another type is concerned with comparison of descriptions, where only comparison with *more* or *less* can be used:

The performance was **more good** than bad. ('The performance was good rather than bad.')

The types of structure just discussed in 505–6 are found both with 'un-equal' comparisons (*more quickly, less well*), and with 'equal' comparisons (*as quickly as you can, as much as anybody else,* etc.; *see* 230):

The voters seem to like the one candidate **as much as** the other.

Complements

(*see CGEL* 10.8, 16.20–83)

508 The term 'complement', in a general sense, means something that is necessary to complete a grammatical construction. We distinguish three types of complement: clause complements, adjective complements and prepositional complements.

Clause complements (see 491): *She is **a very good lecturer**.*

The complement of a clause can be

- a noun phrase (*see* 595):

    Dr Fonda's *a very good lecturer*.

- an adjective or adjective phrase (*see* 440):

    Dr Fonda's lectures are *interesting* and *easy to follow*.

- a nominal clause (*see* 588):

    The only trouble is (*that*) *I can't read what she writes on the blackboard*.

These examples show that the complement usually comes after the verb. If there is both an object and a complement in the sentence, the complement normally comes after the object:

All students consider her *a very good lecturer*.

The complement cannot normally be omitted. If we take away the complement, the remaining part does not make a good English sentence:

The poor service made the hotel guests absolutely furious.

(BUT NOT: *The poor service made the hotel guests.)

The object, but not the complement, can become subject if an active sentence is turned into a passive sentence (*see* 613):

She is considered *a very good lecturer*.

A complement often expresses a quality or attribute of the subject or object:

The hotel guests were *absolutely furious*.

The complement can also tell us the identity of the subject or object:

My native language is *Chinese*. ('Chinese is my native language')

Adjective complements can be *that*-clauses, *to*-infinitives and prepositional phrases (*see* 436):

I'm glad (*that*) *you think so*.	[*that*- or zero *that*-clause]
I'm glad *to hear that*.	[*to*-infinitive]
I'm glad *of your success*.	[prepositional phrase]

Prepositional complements

In the last example, the prepositional phrase *of your success* is the complement of the adjective *glad*. The prepositional phrase itself consists of a preposition (*of*) and its complement (*your success*). The complement is usually a noun phrase (*see* 595):

The committee argued *about the change in the document.*

But it can also be a *wh*-clause (*see* 590):

The committee argued *about what ought to be changed in the document.*

or an *-ing* clause (*see* 594):

The committee argued *about changing the wording of the document.*

Concord

(*see* CGEL 10.34–50)

509 **Grammatical concord** means that certain grammatical items agree with each other. Concord is therefore also called **agreement**. There are two types: concord of number (as in singular *the film is*...but plural *the films are*...) and concord of person (as in 1st person *I am* but 2nd person *you are*).

Concord of number: *she knows* ~ *they know*

Subject-verb concord

With all verbs except *be*, the question of number concord arises only in the present tense: *she knows* ~ *they know*. In the past tense there is no concord variation: *she knew* ~ *they knew*.

Be differs from other verbs in having many forms: *am, is, are* [the present tense] and *was, were* [the past tense] (*see* 482, 514). A clause acting as subject counts as singular:

To treat soldiers as hostages *is* criminal.

The modal auxiliaries differ from other verbs in having only one form (*must, can, will*, etc.): *she must know* ~ *they must know*.

Pronoun concord

A pronoun which refers back to a singular noun phrase is in the singular, and a pronoun which refers back to a plural noun phrase is in the plural (but *see* 96 on the singular use of *they*):

She lost *her life.* ~ *They* lost *their lives.*

Notional concord: *The government is/are agreed.*

510 Sometimes we find that the singular form of certain nouns, such as *family*, can be treated as plural:

> A new family *have* moved in across the street.

This is called **notional concord**, since the verb (*are*) agrees with the **idea** of plural in the **group noun** (*family*) rather than the actual singular **form** of the noun. But it is also possible to treat a group noun like *family* as singular:

> A new family *has* moved in across the street.

This is called **grammatical concord** because the basic grammatical rule says:

> singular subject + singular verb AND plural subject + plural verb

When the group is being considered as a single undivided body, the singular tends to be used, but it is often hard to see such a meaning distinction. Plural concord after a group noun is more frequent in informal speech than in formal writing. Also, plural concord is more characteristic of <BrE> than of <AmE>. Other group nouns which allow either singular or plural concord are these, many of them decision-making bodies: *association, audience, board, commission, committee, company, council, crew, department, government, jury, party, public, staff.* Here are some examples of actual usage:

> The *audience was* generous with *its* cheers and applause and flowers.
> The *audience were* clearly delighted with the performance.

> A *committee has* been set up so that in the future *it* will discuss such topics in advance.
> The *committee believe* it is essential that *their* proposal should be adopted as soon as possible.

> We have a market where the *majority* consistently *wins* what the *minority loses*.
> The *majority* of the population *are* of Scandinavian descent.

> The *government has* recognized *its* dilemma and *is* beginning to devise better school education.
> The *government want* to keep the plan to *themselves*.

> Not even the New York *public has* enough money to meet *its* needs.
> The *public are* thinking of planning *their* forthcoming annual holiday.

There is also a special case of plural concord with singular proper names which denote sports teams: *Arsenal win 3–1, England have been practising for two days.* This is regular usage in <BrE>, but not in <AmE> unless the team is in the plural: *The New York Giants win again.*

Attraction: *A large number of people disagree.*

511 The basic concord rule, singular subject + singular verb and plural subject + plural verb, is sometimes influenced by **attraction**. This means that the verb tends to agree with a noun or pronoun that closely precedes it, instead of the headword of the subject:

> A large number of **people have** asked her to stand for reelection.

> A variety of analytic **methods have** been used.

The grammatical heads of the noun phrases (*number* and *variety*) are both singular, and one would expect the verb form *has*. But the plural noun (*people* and *methods*) in the *of*-phrase modifying the head influences the form of the nearby verb. We call this feature **attraction** or **proximity**, because the last noun attracts a certain form in the verb and upsets the rule of grammatical concord. Attraction clearly works together with notional concord in many cases, in that the head noun (*number, variety, majority,* etc.) conveys the idea of 'plural'.

Concord with coordinated subjects:
Law and order is an election issue.

512 When a subject consists of two or more noun phrases coordinated by *and*, the verb is typically in the plural:

> *Monday and Tuesday* **are** very busy for me.

The coordination is taken to be a reduction of two clauses ('Monday is busy and Tuesday is busy'; *see* 515). But sometimes the verb is singular:

> *Law and order* **is** considered important in this election.

instead of

> *Law and order* **are** considered important in this election.

Here the choice of singular or plural verb depends on how we look at these qualities in the subject, whether they are seen as separate issues (*Law and order are* . . .) or as a single, complex issue (*Law and order is* . . .). A singular verb is also used when coordinated noun phrases refer to the same person or thing:

> At the party **my colleague and long-time friend**, Charles Bedford, was the guest of honour.

When two noun phrases are joined by *or* or *either* . . . *or*, the general rule is that the number of the verb is determined by the number of the last noun phrase (this is the factor of attraction or proximity; *see* 511):

> Either **the workers** or **the director is** to blame for the disruption.

> Either **the director** or **the workers are** to blame for the disruption.

But such sentences are often felt to be awkward. To avoid such concord problems, it is usually possible to use a modal auxiliary verb (which has the same form in the singular and the plural), for example:

Either *the workers or the director* **must** be blamed for the disruption.

Concord with indefinite expressions of amount:
None of them is/are here.

513 ● Indefinite expressions of amount, especially *any*, *no*, and *none*, often cause concord problems. The following cases follow the basic concord rule:

No person of that name *lives* here. [singular count + singular verb]

No people of that name *live* here. [plural count + plural verb]

So far *no money* **has** been spent on repairs. [mass noun + singular verb]

I've ordered the cement, but *none* (*of it*) **has** yet arrived. [mass noun + singular verb]

With *none of* + a plural noun phrase both a singular and a plural verb occur:

None of us **wants/want** to be killed young.

With *none of*, grammatical concord insists that *none* is singular, but notional concord invites a plural verb. A singular verb is typical of <written, formal> style, whereas a plural verb is the more natural choice in <spoken informal> English. In conversations, a plural verb is the more natural choice:

None of her boys **have** been successful in the world.

None of the people there **were** any more competent than we are.

None of my colleagues **have** said anything about it.

● The same rule also applies to *neither* and *either*:

I sent cards to Avis and Margery but *neither* of them **has/have** replied.

In fact, I doubt if *either* of them **is/are** coming.

● The plural pronoun *they* is often used in <informal> style as a replacement of pronouns ending in *-body* and *-one*:

Everyone thinks **they** have the answer to the current problems.

Has *anybody* brought **their** camera?

Anybody with any sense would have read the play in translation, wouldn't **they**?

In traditional <formal> English, the tendency has been to use *he* when the sex is not stated:

Everyone thinks **he** has the answer.

Increasingly, writers who want to avoid male dominance in language use replace *he* with *he or she* or with *s/he* in such cases (*see* 96). Nowadays the use of 'unisex' *they* is becoming more current also in <written> English:

> **Everyone** thinks **they** have the answer.

Concord of person: *I am ~ she is ~ they are*

514 As well as concord of number, there is concord of person.

- *Be* has three forms in the present tense (*see* 482).

  > *I* **am** ~ *he/she/it* **is** ~ *we/you/they* **are**

- Main verbs have only two forms in the present tense (*see* 573):

  > *He/she/our friend* etc. **likes** cooking. [3rd person singular]
  >
  > *I/you/we/they/our friends* etc. **like** cooking. [not 3rd person singular]

- Modal auxiliaries have only one form (*see* 483):

  > *I/we/you/he/she/our friend/our friends* etc. **will** cook dinner today.

Notice that *you* behaves like a plural pronoun for number concord. This is because, historically, *you* was a plural second person form: the old singular form (*thou*) is almost never used today.

Coordination

(*see CGEL* 13.1–103)

515 Coordination can occur between different grammatical units: clauses, clause elements, words. In coordination, equivalent units are linked by *and*, *or* or *but*.

Coordination of clauses: *I'm selling my car and buying a new one.*

Clauses, phrases or words may be linked together (coordinated) by the conjunctions *and*, *or*, *but*. In these examples, the conjunctions are used to link clauses:

> It's November **and** there isn't a single tourist in sight.
>
> Do you want me to send the report to you **or** do you want me to keep it?
>
> Oscar is away for a couple of days, **but** (he) will be back on Monday.

When the subjects of the two clauses refer to the same person or thing, the second subject is normally omitted, as in the last example. If the clauses have matching auxiliary verbs, they are also generally omitted:

> Laura may have received the letter **but** (she may have) forgotten to reply.

Coordination of parts of clauses

516 Coordination can be used to link parts of clauses (such as subjects, verbs, objects) rather than whole clauses. Such coordination can often be seen as cases of clause coordination in which repeated parts are omitted. For example, the sentence

> Her mother needed a chat and some moral support.

can be expanded as

> Her mother needed a chat and *her mother needed* some moral support.

But in other cases we cannot reconstruct two complete clauses:

> My closest friends are Peter and his wife.

This does not mean:

> My closest friend is Peter and my closest friend is his wife.

In addition, there are cases of coordination by *and* which may indicate a 'reciprocal' relationship:

> By the time the first crackling of spring came around, Joan and I were hopelessly in love. ('Joan was in love with me and I was in love with Joan.')
> Last night our dog and the neighbour's were having a fight. ('Our dog and the neighbour's were having a fight with *each other*.')

Since coordination in phrases has different functions, we shall treat co-ordination of phrases and smaller parts in terms of what elements are *linked*, rather than what elements are *omitted*. We deal with the omission of repeated elements in 391.

But as a coordinator is more limited than *and* and *or*. For example, it cannot normally link phrases, except in combination with a negative:

> I have been *to Switzerland*, but not *to the Alps*.

or where two adjectives or adjective phrases are coordinated:

> The weather was *warm* but rather *cloudy*.

Coordination of clause elements:
*Wash by hand **or** in the washing machine.*

517 Here are some examples of coordination within different clause elements:

> SUBJECTS: *Social security* and *retirement plans* will be important election issues.
> VERB PHRASES: Many of the laws *need to be studied* and *will have to be revised*.
> COMPLEMENTS: The laws are *rather outmoded* or *totally inadequate* and *often ambiguous*.
> ADVERBIALS: You can wash this sweater *by hand* or *in the washing machine*.

Coordination between prepositional complements:
> Our team plays in **red shirts** and **white shorts**.
> The armrest must be down during **take-off** and **landing**.

Coordination of words: *Tomorrow will be **nice and sunny**.*

518 Coordination can link two words of the same word class.

Nouns: Older people think many **boys** and **girls** look the same nowadays.

Adjectives: Tomorrow's weather will be **nice** and **sunny**.

Conjunctions: **If** and **when** she decided to tell her parents about her plans, she would do so unasked.

Sometimes words of different classes are linked, where they have a similar function:

You and **Sandra** must visit us sometime. [noun and pronoun]

The game can be played by **three** or **more** contestants. [numeral and quantifier]

Conjunctions omitted: *a sandwich, a salad and a cup of tea*

519 When more than two items are coordinated, the conjunction is normally omitted before each item except the last. In <speech>, a rising tone is normally used on all items in the list except the last:

| I'd like a ham sándwich, | a sálad | and a cup of tèa. |

In <writing>, a comma is usually used to separate all the items except the last two, but many writers put a comma also before *and* in such a list. We often omit *and* before the linking adverbs *then*, *so* and *yet*:

The car spun around again, (and) **then** violated two stop lights.

It's a small college, (and) **yet** most students love it.

Correlative coordination: *reactions of **both approval and disapproval***

520 Sometimes the coordination of two structures is made more emphatic by the addition of a word at the beginning of the first structure: *both* X *and* Y, *either* X *or* Y, *neither* X *nor* Y, etc. This is called **correlative coordination**:

The proposal produced strong reactions of **both** approval **and** disapproval.

The audience last night did not respond with **either** applause **or** boos.

The anti-trust laws are **neither** effective **nor** rational.

Another case of correlative coordination is *not* (*only*) . . . *but* . . . (*see* 234, 269).

Demonstratives

(see CGEL 6.40–44, 12.8–20)

521 The words *this, that, these* and *those* are called **demonstratives**. They can be grouped as two sets with the general meaning 'near' and 'distant' (compare the pairs *here/there, now/then* in 100):

	Singular	Plural
'near'	*this*	*these*
'distant'	*that*	*those*

- The demonstratives have number contrast for singular and plural:

    this book ~ these books
    that book ~ those books

- The demonstratives can function as determiners in noun phrases (*see* 523):

    This time Elizabeth felt nervous.

- The demonstratives can also function as pronouns, i.e. as whole noun phrases (*see* 595):

    This is a public park.
    That's another story.

In <more formal> use, *that* and *those* (but not *this* and *these*) can function as relative antecedents, i.e. the word the relative pronoun refers to (*see* 382, 686):

Richard took up a life similar to **that** (**which**) he had lived in San Francisco.

The elements which capture his imagination are **those which** make the story worth telling and worth remembering.

That cannot be an antecedent of *who* because *that* can only refer to things in this construction. For reference to people *those who* is used:

75 per cent of **those who** returned the questionnaire were in favour of the proposal.

Determiners

(see CGEL 5.10–25)

522 Determiners are words which specify the range of reference of a noun, e.g. by making it definite (*the book*), indefinite (*a book*), or by indicating quantity (*many books*). To understand the grammatical role of determiners, we have to see what determiners and nouns can occur together. Proper nouns do not normally take a determiner (*see* 667). There are three classes of common nouns relevant to the choice of determiners:

- Singular count nouns: *book, teacher, idea*, etc.
- Plural count nouns: *books, teachers, ideas*, etc.
- Mass nouns: *meat, information, money*, etc.

Determiners always precede the noun they determine, but they have different positions relative to one another. The most important group of determiners is the one that includes the articles (*a, an, the*), the demonstratives (*this, that*, etc.), and the possessives (*my, your*, etc.):

> *a* book, *the* books; *this* idea, *these* ideas, *my* idea, *my* ideas, etc.

We call this group **central determiners**, or simply **group 2 determiners** because they may be preceded by **group 1 determiners** like *all* and *half*:

> *all* the books, *all* these people, *all* my ideas, etc.
>
> *half* the time, *half* a kilo, etc.

Group 2 determiners may be followed by **group 3 determiners** like *second* and *many*:

> a *second* time, the *many* problems

The three types of determiners are listed in this table:

Group 1 determiners	Group 2 determiners	Group 3 determiners
all, both, half (see 524)	Articles: *the, a, an* (see 523)	Cardinal numerals: *one, two, three, four, . . .* (see 525)
double, twice, . . . one-third, . . . (see 524)	Demonstratives: *this, these, that, those* (see 523)	Ordinal numerals: *first, second, third*, etc. (see 525)
what, such, . . . (see 524)	Possessives: *my, your, his, her*, etc. (see 523)	General ordinals: *next, last, other*, etc. (see 525)
	Quantifiers: *some, any, no, every, each, either, neither, enough, much* (see 677)	Quantifiers: *many, few, little, several, more, less*, etc. (see 677)
	Wh-determiners: *what(ever), which(ever), whose* (see 523)	

Group 2 determiners: *the* book, *those* people, *her* money

(A) Determiners with count nouns and mass nouns

523 The following determiners can occur with all three classes of noun (singular or plural count nouns and mass nouns):

● The definite article *the* (*see* 473):

> Have you got **the book/the books/the money**?

● The possessives acting as determiners: *my, our, your, his, her, its, their* (*see* 624):

> Have you seen **my book/my books/my money**?

The genitive (*see* 530) functions like a possessive determiner. Compare:

> The teacher liked **the student's essay**.
> The teacher liked **her essay**.

● *Some* and *any* when they are stressed:

> 'There must be **some misconception** in your minds', she said.
> The defendant refused to make **any further statement**.

● The negative quantifier *no* (*see* 583):

> There was **no debate** as the Senate passed the bill.
> There were **no audience questions** after the lecture.

● The *wh*-determiners *whose, which, whichever, what, whatever* (*see* 536, 592):

> The house **whose roof** was damaged has now been repaired.
> **Whichever way** one looked at it, it was her good fortune to have a good job.
> Have you decided **what adjustments** should be made?
> We have to carry out **whatever preparations** are needed.

(B) Determiners with plural count nouns and mass nouns
(but not with singular count nouns)

● Zero article (*see* 473):

> These people need **tractors** and **help** with farming.

● Unstressed *some* /səm/ (*see* 474, 677, 698):

> I may settle for **some makeshift arrangements** for the summer.

● Unstressed *any* (*see* 677, 698):

> | Have you **any clothes** | or **any furniture** to sell? |

● *Enough* (*see* 677):

> I don't think there's **enough money** in the library to spend on books.
>
> There has not been **time enough** to institute reforms.

As the last example shows, *enough* can be placed after the headword, but this is less usual.

(C) Determiners with singular count nouns and mass nouns

The demonstratives *this* and *that* can occur with singular count nouns or mass nouns (but not with plural count nouns; *see* 521):

> **This research** requires expensive equipment.
>
> I find **that poetry** difficult to understand.

(D) Determiners with singular count nouns only

● The indefinite article *a, an* (*see* 473):

> Wait **a minute**!   What **an opportunity**!

● The quantifiers *every, each, either, neither* (*see* 75, 676):

> **Every Saturday** he gets a big kick out of football.
>
> They took the 8.30 train to the city **each morning**.
>
> **Either way** it sounds like a bad solution.
>
> It is to the advantage of **neither side** to destroy the opponent's cities.

(E) Determiners with plural count nouns only

The plural demonstrative determiners *these* and *those* can occur with plural count nouns only (*see* 521):

> 'I've been waiting to get **these things** done for months', she said.
>
> Rebecca felt it was just going to be one of **those days** when life was unbearable.

(F) Determiner with mass nouns only

The quantifier *much* can occur with **mass nouns only** (*see* 676):

> Some of the young players have so **much ability**.

Group 1 determiners: *all* the time, **twice** the number

524 When combined with other determiners, **Group 1 determiners** are placed **before Group 2 determiners**: *all the time, both the children, twice the number,* etc. There are four types of Group 1 determiners:

- *All*, *both*, *half* (*see* 677) occur before articles, possessives, or demonstratives.

All goes with plural count nouns and mass nouns:

> Through *all these years* she had avoided the limelight.
>
> During *all this time* Roy Thornton continued to paint.

With a singular count noun, *all the* + noun occasionally occurs, but *all of the* + noun or *the whole* + noun is more common:

> *All* (*of*) *the town* was destroyed by fire.
>
> ~ *The whole town* was destroyed by fire.

Both goes with plural count nouns only:

> *Both* (*the*) *books* were out of the library.

Half goes with singular or plural count nouns and mass nouns:

> The bridge was *half a mile* downstream.
>
> More than *half the audience* departed.
>
> In this village, nearly *half the children* receive no education.
>
> He stays on the island for *half the summer*.

- *Double*, *twice*, *three times*, *four times*, etc. occur with singular and plural count nouns or mass nouns denoting amount, degree, etc.:

> The party needs *double that number* of votes to win the election.
>
> The area is approximately *three times the size* of the old location.

- The fractions *one-third*, *two-fifths*, *three-quarters*, etc. usually have the construction with *of*:

> Grains and other seed food products furnish less than *one-third of the food* consumed.

- *What* and *such* occur before the indefinite article with singular count nouns:

> Victoria kept telling herself again and again *what a fool* she'd been.
>
> They had no knowledge of *such a letter*.
>
> At first glance the idea looked *such a good one*.

With plural count nouns and mass nouns *what* and *such* occur without an article:

> It's amazing *what beautiful designs* she has come up with.
>
> Our present enemies may well use *such terrible and inhumane weapons*.
>
> I could hardly believe *such good luck* was mine.

- The degree words *rather* and *quite* behave like Group 1 determiners:

    Sometimes life can be *rather a disappointing business*.

    I've known him for *quite a while*.

Group 3 determiners: *the next **few** days, a great **many** students*

525 Group 3 determiners, which include numerals and quantifiers, occur after Group 2 determiners, but before adjectives or noun phrase heads.

- **Cardinal numerals:** *one, two, three*, etc. The numeral *one* can of course occur only with singular count nouns, and all other cardinal numerals (*two, three, . . .*) only with plural count nouns (*see* 602):

    There's only (**the**) **one farm** north of here.

    (**Some**) **ten passengers** were stranded at the station.

- **Ordinal numerals** (*first, second, third*, etc.) occur only with count nouns and usually precede any cardinal numbers in the noun phrase:

    Philip had spent **the first three years** in Edinburgh.

- **General ordinals** include *next, last, other, further*, etc., which usually precede ordinal numerals:

    This was Johnson's best match in **the last two years**.

    Pamela spent **her next five days** at home.

But compare the word order of *other* with and without the definite article:

The other two projects have been scheduled for completion next year.

Two other children were seriously wounded in the highway accident.

Another is a combination of two determiners (*an + other*):

At the meeting, **another speaker** also came under criticism.

In **another four weeks** we are going on vacation. ('four weeks from now')

Quantifiers: *I said **a few**, not **few** friends.*

526 Quantifiers denote quantity or amount (*see* 676).

- *Many, several, a few, few* and *fewer* occur only with plural count nouns:

    I have corrected the **many** spelling errors in your report.

    I haven't seen my sisters for **several** years.

    Here are **a few** facts and figures. ('a small number')

    Probably only very **few** people are aware of this tradition. ('not many')

    There are **fewer** people going to church nowadays.

- *Little* (like *much*) occurs only with mass nouns:

> I advise you to use the **little** money you have to some purpose.
>
> Ruth had to work very hard with **little** help from her relatives. ('not much help')

(The adjective *little*, contrasting with *big*, is not being considered here.) Notice the different meanings of *little* and *few* compared with *a little* and *a few*:

> Can you give me a **little** help? ('some help')
>
> BUT: They gave **little** help. ('not much help')
>
> She has invited a **few** friends to the party. ('some friends')
>
> BUT: She's got **few** friends left. ('not many friends')

- The comparative determiner *more* occurs with plural nouns and mass nouns:

> We are taking **more** students this year in our department.
>
> There has been **more** activity than usual this year.

Less occurs regularly with mass nouns:

> With no drunken drivers there would be **less** anxiety and **fewer** accidents.

Many people also use *less* with plural count nouns (*less accidents*) but *fewer* is preferred in <more formal> contexts.

527 ● Some highly frequent phrases denoting number and quantity are also similar to determiners. As the table below shows, some of them can occur only with count nouns in the plural (e.g. *a large number of students*), others can occur only with mass nouns (e.g. *a large amount of money*).

Quantity phrases with count nouns in the plural:

The university had	a (great) number of a (good) number of a (large) number of a lot of <informal> lots of <informal> plenty of	foreign students.

Quantity phrases with mass nouns:

The safe contained	a great deal of a good deal of a large amount of a lot of <informal> lots of <informal> plenty of	counterfeit money.

Notice that the verb has concord with the noun following *of*, not with *plenty*, *lot* and *number* (*see* 511):

> **Plenty of** students ⎫
> **A lot of** people   ⎬ **were** at the party.
> **A great number of** guests ⎭

This concord rule also applies to introductory *there* constructions:

> There **were** ⎧ *plenty of* students ⎫
>   ⎨ *a lot of* people   ⎬ at the party.
>   ⎩ *a great number of* guests ⎭
>
> There **was** *lots of* food   on the table.

When *number* and *amount* are used in the plural, there is plural concord:

> There **were large numbers of** cars on the road this morning.
>
> Only **small amounts of** money **are** still needed for the expedition.

Exclamations

(*see CGEL* 11.31–32)

528 An exclamation is a type of sentence which is used to express the speaker's feeling or attitude. It typically occurs in <speech>:

> *What a lovely dinner* we had last night!
>
> *How well* Helen Booth is playing tonight!

The exclamation begins with the determiner *what* in noun phrases (*see* 524) or the degree word *how* with adjectives or adverbs (*see* 465). To form an exclamation, put the element of the sentence containing *what* or *how* at the beginning of the sentence (as with *wh*-questions, *see* 683), but do **not** alter the order of subject and verb:

> You have **such a** *good library.*
>
> ~ **What a** *good library* you have!
>
> She writes **such** *marvellous books.*
>
> ~ **What** *marvellous books* she writes!
>
> You are **so** *lucky* to have such a good library.
>
> ~ **How** *lucky* you are to have such a good library!
>
> She sings **so** *beautifully.*
>
> ~ **How** *beautifully* she sings!

On other types of exclamatory construction, *see* 254, 298.

Gender

(see CGEL 5.104–111)

529 English gender, in a grammatical sense, is restricted to certain pronouns (see 619) which have separate forms for masculine/feminine and personal/ non-personal, for example as shown in the table below.

Personal: masculine	*he*	*who*	*somebody*
Personal: feminine	*she*	*who*	*somebody*
Non-personal	*it*	*which*	*something*

Nouns, adjectives, and articles have no gender distinctions. Since English nouns have no grammatical gender, the choice of *he*, *she*, and *it* is based on natural distinctions of meaning. The choice between *he* and *she* depends on whether the person is male or female (see 96 for discussion of male and female reference).

Genitive

(see CGEL 5.112–126, 17.37–46, 110, 119)

Genitive of singular nouns

530 In <written> English, the genitive case of nouns in the singular is written *'s* (apostrophe + *s*). In <spoken> English, the genitive case of nouns in the singular is pronounced /ɪz/, /z/, or /s/. The pronunciation depends on the last sound of the noun (see the general pronunciation rules in 664):

a *nurse's* /ˈnɜː(r)sɪz/ skills

a *teacher's* /ˈtiːtʃə(r)z/ salary

the *chef's* /ʃefs/ favourite dish

Genitive of regular plural nouns

In <written> English the genitive of nouns which have a regular *s*-plural is indicated only by an apostrophe after the plural-*s*. In <spoken> English the genitive is not pronounced, i.e. the singular and the plural genitive sound alike, but are not written alike:

both *nurses'* /ˈnɜː(r)sɪz/ skills

all *teachers'* /ˈtiːtʃə(r)z/ salaries

the two *chefs'* /ʃefs/ favourite dishes

Genitive of irregular plural nouns

Nouns which do not form the plural with the *-s* ending have apostrophe + *s* in the genitive (*see* 637):

the *child's* /tʃaɪldz/ bike	~ the *children's* /'tʃɪldrənz/ bikes
the *woman's* /'wʊmənz/ family	~ the *women's* /'wɪmɪnz/ families

Singular names

The genitive which is indicated only by the apostrophe occurs also with singular names ending in *-s* such as *Jones*. The genitive is written either *Jones'* or *Jones's*, and usually pronounced /'dʒoʊnzɪz/. The spelling with apostrophe only is particularly common with longer names of classical origin: *Euripides' plays, Socrates' wife*.

The genitive and the *of*-construction

531 English often offers a choice when we want to express the genitive relation between nouns. In many cases we can use either the genitive or the *of*-construction:

What's *the ship's name*?	[genitive]
What's *the name of the ship*?	[*of*-construction]

Here the function of the noun in the genitive case (*ship's*) is similar to that of the noun as head of a noun phrase following *of* (*of the ship*). This is called the *of*-construction.

- **The *of*-construction** is mostly used with nouns denoting things. We can say *the leg of a table* BUT NOT **a table's leg*.

- **The *s*-genitive** is typically used with nouns denoting people. We can say *John's car* BUT NOT **the car of John*. The genitive is also commonly used in such phrases as *a day's work, today's paper, a moment's thought, the world's economy*. (On the choice of construction, *see* 106.)

Genitives in noun phrases

532 Although we have described the genitive as a case of nouns, it is better to regard it as an ending belonging to **noun phrases** (*see* 595) rather than to **nouns**. The following examples show that the whole first noun phrase, i.e. the genitive noun phrase, modifies the head of the main noun phrase:

Genitive noun phrase	Rest of the main noun phrase
some people's	opinion
every teacher's	ambition
the Australian government's	recent decision

This is seen more clearly when we compare equivalent *of*-phrases:

the opinion	*of some people*
the ambition	*of every teacher*
the recent decision	*of the Australian government*

The genitive noun phrase occupies determiner position (*see* 522) in the main noun phrase. Thus it precedes adjectives in the main noun phrase. Compare:

the longest novel

his longest novel

Charles Dickens' longest novel

But a genitive noun can also behave like an adjective, with a classifying role, as in *a women's university*. In such cases, the genitive noun can follow the adjective modifying the head of the main noun phrase:

[a famous [**women's** university] in Tokyo]

Group genitives: *an hour and a half's discussion*

533 In English we often have complex noun phrases such as

the Chairman of the Finance Committee

where the head noun (*Chairman*) is modified by a following prepositional phrase (*of the Finance Committee*; *see* 642). When we want to put such a long noun phrase in the genitive, the *-s* genitive is added to the end of the whole noun phrase (not to the head noun itself):

[[the **Chairman of the Finance Committee's**] pointed remarks]

Since the genitive ending is added to the end of the whole phrase or group, this construction is called the **group genitive**. Other examples:

The rioters must have been acting on **someone else's** instructions.

We'll see what happens in *a month or two's* time.

The lecture was followed by *an hour and a half's* discussion.

Genitives without a head noun: *at the Johnsons'*

534 The noun modified by the *-s* genitive may be omitted, if the context makes its identity clear:

My car is faster than **John's**. (i.e. 'than John's car')

But **John's** is a good car, too.

When the *of*-construction is used instead, a pronoun is usually required (*that* for singular and *those* for plural, *see* 382):

A blind person's sense of touch is more sensitive to shape and size than *that of a person with normal vision*.

The new CD-players are much better than *those of the first generation*.

Omission of the head noun is typical of expressions relating to houses, shops, etc.:

We met at *the Johnsons*'. ('at the place where the Johnsons live')

The 'double' genitive: *a friend of my wife's*

535 An *of*-construction can be combined with an *s*-genitive or possessive pronoun into a **'double' genitive**:

Shannon is a friend *of my wife's*.

This writer's style is no favourite *of mine*.

The noun in the genitive must be both definite and personal. Unlike the simple genitive, the 'double' genitive usually implies that the meaning is not unique, i.e. that 'my wife has several friends'. Compare:

He is *Leda's brother*. [suggests Leda has one, or more than one, brother]

He is *a brother of Leda's*. [suggests Leda has more than one brother]

Interrogatives

(*see* CGEL 6.36–39, 11.14–23)

536 Interrogatives are words which introduce *wh*-questions (*see* 683):

What's Mrs Brown's first name?

and interrogative subclauses (*see* 590):

I'm not sure *what* Mrs Brown's first name is.

The English interrogative words are *who, whom, whose, which, what, where, when, how, why, whether, if* ('whether'). We call them '*wh*-words' (since most of them begin with *wh*-). *Whether* and *if* are used only in interrogative subclauses.

Interrogatives in noun phrases: *What time is it?, What's the time?*

537 In the noun phrase, the interrogatives *which* and *what* can act as both determiner and pronoun:

What as determiner: *What time* is it?

What as pronoun: *What*'s the time?

The different interrogative determiners and pronouns are set out in the following table.

	Determiners	Pronouns	
	Personal and non-personal	Personal	Non-personal
Subjective case	what, which	who, what, which	what, which
Objective case	what, which	who, whom <formal>, which	what, which
Genitive case	whose	whose	
Interrogative . . . + preposition	what, which . . . + preposition	who, whom <formal> . . . + preposition	what, which . . . + preposition
Preposition + interrogative	preposition + what, which <formal>	preposition + whom <formal>	preposition + what, which <formal>

Who, **whom**, **whose**, **which**, and **what** are used both as interrogatives and as relative pronouns (*see* 690). The relative *which* can only have non-personal reference [1b], but the interrogative *which* is used with both non-personal and personal reference [2a, 2b]. Compare:

> The author **who** wrote my favourite novel is Graham Greene.
> [personal relative *who*] [1a]

> The novel **which** I like best is *The End of the Affair*. [non-personal relative *which*] [1b]

> **Which** is your favourite author? [personal interrogative *which*] [2a]

> **Who** is your favourite author? [personal interrogative *who*] [2b]

The choice of interrogative: *who* or *which*, *what* or *which*?

538 The meaning of interrogative *who*, as in [2b], is different from the meaning of interrogative *which*, as in [2a]. The difference has to do with indefinite and definite reference. The definite interrogative *which* [2a] indicates that the speaker is thinking of a definite group to choose from. *Who* [2b] and also *what* have indefinite reference, i.e. the speaker has no definite group in mind. Here are some examples:

The interrogative determiner with a personal noun

Indefinite reference:

> **What composers** do you like best?

Definite reference:

> *Which composer* do you prefer: Mozart or Beethoven?

The interrogative determiner with a non-personal noun

Indefinite reference:

> *What tax changes* are likely in the new budget?

Definite reference:

> *Which way* are you going – right or left?
> *Which Scottish university* did you go to: Edinburgh or St Andrews?

The interrogative pronoun referring to persons

Indefinite reference:

> *Who* sent you here?

Definite reference:

> *Which* is your favourite composer: Mozart or Beethoven?

The interrogative pronoun with non-personal reference

Indefinite reference:

> *What's* the name of this song?

Definite reference:

> *Which* do you prefer: classical or popular music?
> *Which* do you want: the domestic or the international airport terminal?

Which can be followed by an *of*-phrase. Compare these three sentences:

Which of the films do you like best?	[1]
Which film do you like best?	[2]
Which films do you like best?	[3]

Sentence [1] can have the same meaning as either [2] or [3]. It invites us to choose from a group: either one (singular) or more than one (plural).

The choice of interrogative: *who, whom* or *whose?*

539 The interrogative pronoun *who* is personal only:

> *Who* sent you here?

Both *who* and *whom* are used for the objective case, but *whom* is <formal>:

Who did Abigail marry?

Whom did Abigail marry? <formal>

With a preposition, the <informal> construction is to place the preposition at the end:

Who did the generals stay loyal **to**? <informal>

In the corresponding <formal> construction the interrogative follows the preposition, in which case the objective form *whom* is obligatory:

To whom did the generals stay loyal? <formal>

The possessive interrogative *whose* can function either as a determiner or as a pronoun:

Whose jacket is this? [determiner]

Whose is this jacket? [pronoun]

The noun following the determiner *whose* can be either personal or non-personal:

Whose children are they?

Whose side are you on?

The choice of interrogative: *what* versus *who* and *which*

540 As the following examples show, *what* has a wide range of uses.

What can have both personal and non-personal reference and can function both as a determiner (*What nationality is he?*) and as a pronoun (*What's his nationality?*):

[A] **What**'s your address?	[B] (It's) 18 South Avenue.
[A] **What** date is it?	[B] (It's) the 15th of March.
[A] **What**'s the time?	[B] (It's) five o'clock.
[A] **What**'s Burt doing?	[B] (He's) painting the house.
[A] **What** was the concert like?	[B] (It was) excellent.

When *what* is a pronoun and refers to a person it is limited to questions about profession and role. Contrast the three possible pronouns in:

[A] **What**'s Molly's husband?

  [B] (He's) a writer. [profession]

[A] **Which** is Molly's husband?

  [B] (He's) the man on the right with a beard. [choice from a group]

[A] **Who** is Molly's husband?

  [B] (He's) John Miller, the author of children's books. [identity]

Interrogative adverbs and conjunctions: *Where* are you going?

541 Besides interrogative determiners and pronouns, there are interrogative adverbs (*where, when, why, how*) and conjunctions (*whether, if*).

- *Where* refers to place *at* or place *to* (*see* 170):

    Where are you staying? ('At what place?')

    Where are you going for your vacation? ('To what place?')

- *When* refers to time (*see* 151):

    When are you leaving? ('At what time?')

- *Why* refers to cause, reason, and purpose (*see* 198):

    Why are you going there? ('For what reason?')

- *How* refers to manner, means, and instrument (*see* 194):

    How are you travelling? ('By what means?')

How is also an interrogative adverb of degree (*see* 215). In this function *how* can modify adverbs, adjectives and determiners:

How often do you see your friends?

How long are you staying?

How big is your boat?

How many people can it take?

Whether and *if* are interrogative conjunctions. Like the other interrogatives, they introduce indirect (*yes-no*) questions (*see* 259, 682).

Introductory *it*: *It's fascinating to read her story.*

(*see* CGEL 18.33–36)

542 The regular word order in English is subject + verb:

The colour of the car doesn't matter.   [1]

Instead of a noun phrase like *the colour of the car* we may have a clause as subject (*see* 588), such as

What colour the car is doesn't matter.   [1a]

However, [1a] is less common than [1b] with an **introductory** *it*:

It doesn't matter *what colour the car is.*   [1b]

In [1b] the subject clause (*what colour the car is*) is placed at the end of the sentence. The normal subject position at the beginning of the sentence is filled by *it*, 'introducing' the long following subject clause. [1b] contains two subjects: the **introductory subject** *it* and the **postponed subject** *what colour the car is*. Here are some more examples of sentences with introductory *it*:

It's too early *to go and visit Sue at the hospital now.*

It makes me happy *to see others enjoying themselves.*

It's easy *to understand why Bill wanted a new job.*

It made no difference *that most evidence pointed to an opposite conclusion.*

It's simply untrue *that there has been another big row in the department.*

It's no use *pretending everything is all right.*

It would be no good *trying to catch the bus now.*

543 The introductory-*it* construction is also used in the passive

● to introduce a *that*-clause:

It's not actually **been announced** yet *that the job will be advertised.*

It's actually **been suggested** *that income tax should be abolished.*

● to introduce direct or indirect speech:

It **might be asked** at this point: *'Why not alter the law?'*

● to introduce a *to*-infinitive:

In the end, **it may be decided** *not to apply for membership.*

Cases which differ from introductory *it*

544 Constructions such as *It seems that*..., *It appears that*..., *It happens that*... may look like introductory-*it* sentences, but they have no corresponding construction without *it*. For example, there is no such sentence corresponding to

It **seems that** everything is fine. (BUT NOT: *That everything is fine seems.*)

It **appeared that** the theory was not widely supported by other scientists.

It quite often **happens that** things go wrong.

Also, introductory-*it* constructions should be distinguished from sentences where *it* is a personal pronoun, as in

This may not be much of *a meal*, but *it's* what I eat.

Here *it* refers back to its antecedent, the singular noun phrase *a meal* (*see* 621).

Cases related to introductory *it*: *Her story is fascinating to read.*

545 English grammar allows us to place the emphasis on different parts of sentences. In this sentence

> **To read her story** is fascinating. [1]

To read her story is a nominal clause functioning as subject. But English prefers to avoid a clause as subject. One alternative is the introductory-*it* construction, as in [1a]:

> It's fascinating **to read her story**. [1a]

But if we want to start with *her story* as the topic of the sentence, we can say:

> **Her story** is fascinating **to read**. [1b]

In [1b] the object of the nominal clause, *her story* is 'lifted out' from the clause and 'promoted' to being subject in the main clause. The same construction can be used to 'promote' prepositional objects, such as *her* in:

> **To talk to her** was interesting.
> ~ **It** was interesting **to talk to her**.
> ~ **She** was interesting **to talk to**.

In the process, the objective pronoun *her* becomes the subjective pronoun *she*.

546 There is a similar construction for *appear, seem, be certain, be sure, be known, be said*, etc. + *to*-infinitive:

> You **seem to** have read so much.
> Our enemies **are certain to** exploit their advantage.
> My parents **are sure to** find out.
> George **was** never **known to** run or even walk fast.
> Brenda Young **is said to** be the richest woman in the world.
> The government **appears to** be facing a difficult year.

In these cases, however, the corresponding *it*-construction requires a *that*-clause. It is the subject of the *that*-clause that is 'promoted' to being subject of the main clause:

> **It appears that** the government is facing a difficult year.

Introductory *there*: *There won't be any trouble.*

(*see CGEL* 18.44–54)

547 An English sentence like this one is possible but rare:

> A storm is coming.

The natural way of saying this is to begin the sentence with an unstressed *there* and to postpone the indefinite subject (*a storm*):

There's a storm coming.

This is called a sentence with **introductory *there***, which is a very common type of construction. Here are some examples of different verb patterns (*see* 718) to show how they can be turned into sentences with introductory *there*, so long as the subject is indefinite and the verb phrase contains *be*:

There's no water [*in the house*].	(SVA)
There are lots of people getting [*jobs*].	(SVO)
There's something causing [*her*] [*distress*].	(SVOO)
There have been two bulldozers knocking [*the place*] [*flat*].	(SVOC)
There's somebody coming.	(SV)

Passive sentences also occur:

There**'s** a new novel ***displayed*** in the window.

There**'s been** a handbag ***stolen*** in the department store.

If the postponed subject [printed in **bold**] is plural, the verb is also in the plural (but *see* 548 below):

There ***are many people*** trying to buy houses in this neighbourhood.

There ***seem*** to be ***no poisonous snakes*** around here.

Were there ***any other drivers*** around to see the accident?

There ***are some friends*** I have to see.

Introductory *there* as subject: *I don't want **there** to be any trouble.*

548 Introductory *there* differs from the stressed *there* functioning as a front-placed place adverb ('*There is my car* = *My car is* 'there, see 416). Introductory *there* is unstressed and behaves in some ways like the subject of the sentence. A frequent feature of <informal conversation> is the use of the singular verb contracted form *'s* attached to the preceding *there*, also when the following postponed subject is plural. In both these examples the standard <written> and formally 'correct' construction would be *there are* (as stated in 547):

There's only four bottles left. <informal spoken>

There's better things to do than listen to gossip. <informal spoken>

Here, because of the contracted verb form, *there's* behaves as a single invariable unit for the purposes of speech processing. There is a similar tendency to use *here's*, *where's* and *how's* + plural subject in <informal

conversation> instead of the formally 'correct' plural non-contracted forms
here are, *where are* and *how are* + plural subject:

> **Here's** your keys. <informal speech>
>
> ~ **Here are** your keys. <standard written>
>
> **How's** your kids? <informal speech>
>
> ~ **How are** your kids? <standard written>

There can act as subject in *yes-no* questions (*see* 682) and tag questions
(*see* 684), where inversion of *be* and *there* takes place:

> **Is there** any more wine?
>
> There's no one else coming, **is there**?

There can also act as subject in infinitive clauses and -*ing* clauses (*see* 493):

> I don't want **there to be** any trouble.
>
> Bill was disappointed at **there being** so little to do.
>
> **There being** no further business, the meeting adjourned at 11.15. <formal>

Introductory *there* with relative and infinitive clauses: **There's** something I ought to tell you.

549 ● There is a further type of introductory-*there* sentence. As an alternative
of this sentence

> Something keeps upsetting him.

we may have:

> ~ **There's** something (that) keeps upsetting him.

It consists of *there* + a form of *be* + a noun phrase + a clause which is like
a relative clause (*see* 686). There must be an indefinite noun phrase in the
sentence, but it need not be the subject:

> **Is there** anyone in particular (that) you want to speak to?
>
> (Compare: Do you want to speak to **anyone in particular**?)

● Another common sentence pattern is introductory *there* + *be* + noun
phrase + *to*-infinitive clause. The infinitive may have a *for*-subject:

> Tonight **there**'s nothing else (for us) to do but watch TV.
>
> **There** was no one (for her) to talk to.

This pattern also occurs in the passive:

> **There** are several practical problems to be considered.

● One type of *there*-sentence is typical of <literary> contexts:

> **There** may come a time when Europe will be less fortunate.
> ('A time may come . . .')

In this construction *there* can be followed by a verb other than *be* (such as *come, lie, stand, exist, rise*). With a place adverbial in front-position, *there* may be omitted in <literary> style (*see* 416):

> On the other side of the valley (**there**) *rose a gigantic rock* surmounted by a ruined fortress. <formal, literary>

Irregular verbs

(*see CGEL* 3.11–20)

550 Most English verbs are regular, but there are over 200 main verbs that are irregular. Irregular verbs are like regular verbs in having *-s* and *-ing* forms (*see* 573). For example, the irregular verb *break* has the forms *breaks*, *breaking*, just as the regular verb *walk* has the forms *walks*, *walking*. With regular verbs we can also predict that the past tense form and past participle forms are identical and formed with the *-ed* ending added to the base:

THE BASE	PAST FORM	PAST PARTICIPLE
walk	walked	walked

With irregular verbs, however, we cannot predict their past tense or past participle forms from the base:

THE BASE	PAST FORM	PAST PARTICIPLE
break	broke	broken

We distinguish three main types of irregular verbs:

- Verbs in which **all the three principal parts** (the base, the past form, the past participle) are **identical**, for example,

  cut ~ cut ~ cut   *let ~ let ~ let*

- Verbs in which **two parts are identical**, for example,

  spend ~ spent ~ spent   *come ~ came ~ come*

- Verbs in which **all three parts are different**, for example,

  blow ~ blew ~ blown   *speak ~ spoke ~ spoken*

Within each type, the verbs are here arranged according to similarity: 'the *spend*-group', 'the *speak*-group', etc. The following list is not exhaustive (*see further GCEL* 3.11–20). For auxiliary verbs, *see* 477–85.

We give two lists which include the majority of the English irregular verbs: *the group list* and *the alphabetical list*.

The group list (*see* 551–71)

In the first list the verbs are grouped according to how the past form and past participle forms differ from the base form. For example, *put* and *cut* belong to the one group where the verbs have identical forms for base, past form and past participle: *put ~ put ~ put* and *cut ~ cut ~ cut*. *Dig* and *win* belong to another group. These two verbs are similar in that each verb has identical past tense and past participle forms and also the same vowel change: *dig ~ dug ~ dug* and *win ~ won ~ won*. This organization into groups is intended to give an idea of the different types of irregular verbs, something which is not obvious from an alphabetical arrangement.

The alphabetical list (*see* 572)

For convenient reference we also include a second list where the verbs appear in alphabetical order but with references to the group list.

In both lists we give the three parts for each verb: the base, the past tense form and the past participle. For some verbs there are alternative forms. For example, the past form of *sweat* is given both as *sweat* (irregular) and *sweated* (regular). This means that both are used, but sometimes differently depending on context, style or variety. For example, of the two forms *dreamt* and *dreamed*, the latter is usually preferred in <AmE>. Alternative forms in round brackets, such as *shone* (*shined*), indicate infrequent or special uses:

> The sun **shone** all day. BUT: He **shined** his shoes every morning.

Verbs printed in **bold** are common or very common, such as *become, begin, bring*.

The group list

All three verb parts are identical (but some verbs have alternative, non-identical forms)

The *put* group

551		
bet	bet, betted	bet, betted
bid	bid, bade	bid, bidden
broadcast	broadcast	broadcast
burst	burst	burst
bust <casual>	bust, busted	bust, busted
cast	cast	cast
cost	cost, (costed)	cost, (costed)
cut	cut	cut
fit	fit <esp AmE>, fitted	fit <esp AmE>, fitted

forecast	forecast	forecast
hit	hit	hit
hurt	hurt	hurt
input	input, inputted	input, inputted
knit	knit, knitted	knit, knitted
let	let	let
miscast	miscast	miscast
offset	offset	offset
outbid	outbid	outbid.
put	put	put
quit	quit, quitted	quit, quitted
recast	recast	recast
reset	reset	reset
rid	rid, ridded	rid, ridded
set	set	set
shed	shed	shed
shit <taboo>	shit, shat	shit
shut	shut	shut
slit	slit	slit
split	split	split
spread	spread	spread
sweat	sweat, sweated	sweat, sweated
thrust	thrust	thrust
typeset	typeset	typeset
upset	upset	upset
wed	wed, wedded	wed, wedded
wet	wet, wetted	wet, wetted

Two verb parts are identical

The *learn* group

552 These verbs can be either regular (*learned*) or irregular with a -*t* suffix (*learnt*). The regular /d/-form is especially <AmE> and the /t/-form especially <BrE>.

burn	burned, burnt	burned, burnt
dwell	dwelled, dwelt	dwelled, dwelt
learn	learned, learnt	learned, learnt
misspell	misspelled, misspelt	misspelled, misspelt

smell	smelled, smelt	smelled, smelt
spell	spelled, spelt	spelled, spelt
spill	spilled, spilt	spilled, spilt
spoil	spoiled, spoilt	spoiled, spoilt

The *spend* group

553

bend	bent	bent
build	built	built
lend	lent	lent
rebuild	rebuilt	rebuilt
rend	rent	rent
send	sent	sent
spend	spent	spent
unbend	unbent	unbent

The *read* group

554

behold <literary>	beheld	beheld
bleed	bled	bled
breed	bred	bred
feed	fed	fed
flee	fled	fled
hold	held	held
lead /iː/	led	led
mislead /iː/	misled	misled
overfeed	overfed	overfed
read /iː/	read /e/	read /e/
reread /riːˈriːd/	reread /riːˈred/	reread /riːˈred/
speed	sped, speeded	sped, speeded
uphold	upheld	upheld
withhold	withheld	withheld

The *keep* group

555 Where there are alternative regular forms (*dreamed* besides *dreamt*, etc.), the regular forms are usually preferred in <AmE>.

creep	crept	crept
deal /iː/	dealt /e/	dealt /e/
dream /iː/	dreamt /e/, dreamed	dreamt /e/, dreamed
feel	felt	felt
keep	kept	kept
kneel	knelt, kneeled	knelt, kneeled
lean /iː/	leant /e/, leaned	leant /e/, leaned
leap /iː/	leapt /e/, leaped	leapt /e/, leaped
leave	left	left
mean /iː/	meant /e/	meant /e/
meet	met	met
oversleep	overslept	overslept
sleep	slept	slept
sweep	swept	swept
weep	wept	wept

The *win* group

556 cling	clung	clung
dig	dug	dug
fling	flung	flung
hamstring	hamstrung	hamstrung
hang	hung, (hanged)	hung, (hanged)
restring	restrung	restrung
sling	slung	slung
slink	slunk	slunk
spin	spun, span	spun
stick	stuck	stuck
sting	stung	stung
strike	struck	struck
string	strung	strung
swing	swung	swung
win	won	won
wring	wrung	wrung

The *bring* group

557 **bring**	brought /ɔː/	brought /ɔː/
buy	bought	bought

catch	caught	caught
fight	fought	fought
seek	sought	sought
teach	taught	taught
think	thought	thought

The *find* group

558	bind /aɪ/	bound /aʊ/	bound /aʊ/
	find	found	found
	grind	ground	ground
	rewind	rewound	rewound
	unbind	unbound	unbound
	unwind	unwound	unwound
	wind /aɪ/	wound /aʊ/	wound /aʊ/

The *get* group

559	get	got	got, <AmE also> gotten (*see* 481)
	lose /luːz/	lost	lost
	shine	shone, (shined)	shone, (shined)
	shoot	shot	shot

The *tell* group

560	foretell	foretold	foretold
	resell	resold	resold
	retell	retold	retold
	sell	sold	sold
	tell	told	told

The *come* group

561	become	became	become
	come	came	come
	outrun	outran	outrun

overcome	overcame	overcome
overrun	overran	overrun
rerun	reran	rerun
run	ran	run

Other verbs with two forms identical

562	**beat**	beat	beaten, (beat)
	browbeat	browbeat	browbeaten
	have	had	had
	hear	heard	heard
	lay	laid [spelling irregular]	laid [spelling irregular]
	light	lit, lighted	lit, lighted
	make	made	made
	mishear	misheard	misheard
	misunderstand	misunderstood	misunderstood
	overhear	overheard	overheard
	pay	paid [spelling irregular]	paid [spelling irregular]
	remake	remade	remade
	say	said /e/	said /e/
	sit	sat	sat
	slide	slid	slid
	spit	spat, spit	spat, spit
	stand	stood	stood
	understand	understood	understood
	unmake	unmade	unmade
	withstand	withstood	withstood

All three verb forms are different

The *mow* group: The past participle can be regular (*mowed*) or irregular (*mown*).

563	hew	hewed	hewn, hewed
	mow	mowed	mown, mowed
	saw	sawed	sawn, sawed
	sew	sewed	sewn, sewed

show	showed	shown, (showed)
sow	sowed	sown, sowed
swell	swelled	swollen, swelled

The *speak* group

564	awake	awoke, awaked	awoken, awaked
	break	broke	broken
	choose /tʃuːz/	chose /tʃoʊz/	chosen /ˈtʃoʊzn/
	deepfreeze	deepfroze	deepfrozen
	freeze	froze	frozen
	speak	spoke	spoken
	steal	stole	stolen
	wake	woke, waked	woken, waked
	weave	wove	woven

The *bear* group

565	**bear** /beə(r)/	bore	borne*
	swear	swore	sworn
	tear	tore	torn
	wear	wore	worn

*Born is used in constructions with *be*. Note the spelling difference: 'She has *borne* six children and the youngest was *born* only a month ago.'

The *know* group

566	**blow**	blew	blown
	grow	grew	grown
	know	knew	known
	outgrow	outgrew	outgrown
	overthrow	overthrew	overthrown
	throw	threw	thrown

The *bite* group

| 567 | bite | bit | bitten, (bit) |
| | **hide** | hid | hidden, (hid) |

The *take* group

568

mistake	mistook	mistaken
overtake	overtook	overtaken
shake	shook	shaken
take	took	taken
undertake	undertook	undertaken

The *write* group

569

arise /aɪ/	arose /oʊ/	arisen /ɪ/
drive	drove	driven
rewrite	rewrote	rewritten
ride	rode	ridden
rise	rose	risen
stride	strode	stridden, strode
strive	strove, strived	striven, strived
underwrite	underwrote	underwritten
write	wrote	written

The *begin* group

570

begin	began, (begun)	begun
drink	drank	drunk
ring	rang, rung	rung
shrink	shrank, shrunk	shrunk
sing	sang, sung	sung
sink	sank, sunk	sunk
spring	sprang, <AmE also> sprung	sprung
stink	stank, stunk	stunk
swim	swam, swum	swum

Other verbs with all three parts different

571

cleave	cleaved, clove, cleft	cleaved, cloven, cleft
dive	dived, dove <AmE only>	dived

do	did	done
draw	drew	drawn
eat	ate \<BrE> /et/ or /eɪt/, \<AmE> /eɪt/	eaten
fall	fell	fallen
fly	flew	flown
forbid	forbad(e)	forbidden, (forbid)
foresee	foresaw	foreseen
forget	forgot	forgotten, (forgot)
forgive	forgave	forgiven
give	gave	given
go	went	gone
lie	lay	lain
outdo	outdid	outdone
overdo	overdid	overdone
overeat	overate	overeaten
oversee	oversaw	overseen
redo	redid	redone
see	saw	seen
shear /ɪə(r)/	sheared	shorn, sheared
slay	slew	slain
tread	trod	trodden, trod
undergo	underwent	undergone
undo	undid	undone
withdraw	withdrew	withdrawn

Irregular verbs in alphabetical order

572 The numbers in the rightmost column refer to sections above (551–71) where verbs are listed in groups. Verbs printed in bold are common or very common, such as *become, begin, bring.*

arise	arose	arisen	569
awake	awoke, awaked	awoken, awaked	564
be	was, were	been	482
bear	bore	borne	565
beat	beat	beaten, (beat)	562
become	became	become	561
begin	began, (begun)	begun	570

behold <literary>	beheld	beheld	554
bend	bent	bent	553
bet	bet, betted	bet, betted	551
bid	bid, bade	bid, bidden	551
bind	bound	bound	558
bite	bit	bitten, (bit)	567
bleed	bled	bled	554
blow	blew	blown	566
break	broke	broken	564
breed	bred	bred	554
bring	brought	brought	557
broadcast	broadcast	broadcast	551
browbeat	browbeat	browbeaten	562
build	built	built	553
burn	burned, burnt	burned, burnt	552
burst	burst	burst	551
bust <casual>	bust, busted	bust, busted	551
buy	bought	bought	557
cast	cast	cast	551
catch	caught	caught	557
choose	chose	chosen	564
cleave	cleaved, clove, cleft	cleaved, cloven, cleft	571
cling	clung	clung	556
come	came	come	561
cost	cost	cost	551
creep	crept	crept	555
cut	cut	cut	551
deal	dealt	dealt	555
deepfreeze	deepfroze	deepfrozen	564
dig	dug	dug	556
dive	dived, dove <AmE>	dived	571
do	did	done	571
draw	drew	drawn	571
dream	dreamt, dreamed	dreamt, dreamed	555
drink	drank	drunk	570
drive	drove	driven	569
dwell	dwelled, dwelt	dwelled, dwelt	552

eat	ate	eaten	571
fall	fell	fallen	571
feed	fed	fed	554
feel	felt	felt	555
fight	fought	fought	557
find	found	found	558
fit	fitted, <AmE> also: fit	fitted, <AmE> also: fit	551
flee	fled	fled	554
fling	flung	flung	556
fly	flew	flown	571
forbid	forbad(e)	forbidden, (forbid)	571
forecast	forecast	forecast	551
foresee	foresaw	foreseen	571
foretell	foretold	foretold	560
forget	forgot	forgotten, (forgot)	571
forgive	forgave	forgiven	571
freeze	froze	frozen	564
get	got	got, gotten <AmE>	559
give	gave	given	571
go	went	gone	571
grind	ground	ground	558
grow	grew	grown	566
hamstring	hamstrung	hamstrung	556
hang	hung, (hanged)	hung, (hanged)	556
have	had	had	562
hear	heard	heard	562
hew	hewed	hewn, hewed	563
hide	hid	hidden, (hid)	567
hit	hit	hit	551
hold	held	held	554
hurt	hurt	hurt	551
input	input, inputted	input, inputted	551
keep	kept	kept	555
kneel	knelt, kneeled	knelt, kneeled	555
knit	knit, knitted	knit, knitted	551
know	knew	known	566

lay	laid	laid	562
lead	led	led	554
lean	leant, leaned	leant, leaned	555
leap	leapt, leaped	leapt, leaped	555
learn	learned, learnt	learned, learnt	552
leave	left	left	555
lend	lent	lent	553
let	let	let	551
lie	lay	lain	571
light	lit, lighted	lit, lighted	562
lose	lost	lost	559
make	made	made	562
mean	meant	meant	555
meet	met	met	555
miscast	miscast	miscast	551
mishear	misheard	misheard	562
mislead	misled	misled	554
misspell	misspelled, misspelt	misspelled, misspelt	552
mistake	mistook	mistaken	568
misunderstand	misunderstood	misunderstood	562
mow	mowed	mown, mowed	563
offset	offset	offset	551
outbid	outbid	outbid	551
outdo	outdid	outdone	571
outgrow	outgrew	outgrown	566
outrun	outran	outrun	561
overcome	overcame	overcome	561
overdo	overdid	overdone	571
overeat	overate	overeaten	571
overfeed	overfed	overfed	554
overhear	overheard	overheard	562
overrun	overran	overrun	561
oversee	oversaw	overseen	571
oversleep	overslept	overslept	555
overtake	overtook	overtaken	568
overthrow	overthrew	overthrown	566
pay	paid	paid	562

put	put	put	551
quit	quit, quitted	quit, quitted	551
read	read	read	554
rebuild	rebuilt	rebuilt	553
recast	recast	recast	551
redo	redid	redone	571
remake	remade	remade	562
rend	rent	rent	553
reread	reread	reread	554
rerun	reran	rerun	561
resell	resold	resold	560
reset	reset	reset	551
restring	restrung	restrung	556
retell	retold	retold	560
rewind	rewound	rewound	558
rewrite	rewrote	rewritten	569
rid	rid, ridded	rid, ridded	551
ride	rode	ridden	569
ring	rang, rung	rung	570
rise	rose	risen	569
run	ran	run	561
saw	sawed	sawn, sawed	563
say	said	said	562
see	saw	seen	571
seek	sought	sought	557
sell	sold	sold	560
send	sent	sent	553
set	set	set	551
sew	sewed	sewn, sewed	563
shake	shook	shaken	568
shear	sheared	shorn, sheared	571
shed	shed	shed	551
shine	shone, (shined)	shone, (shined)	559
shit <taboo>	shit, shat	shit	551
shoot	shot	shot	559
show	showed	shown, (showed)	563

shrink	shrank, shrunk	shrunk	570
shut	shut	shut	551
sing	sang, sung	sung	570
sink	sank, sunk	sunk	570
sit	sat	sat	562
slay	slew	slain	571
sleep	slept	slept	555
slide	slid	slid	562
sling	slung	slung	556
slink	slunk	slunk	556
slit	slit	slit	551
smell	smelled, smelt	smelled, smelt	552
sow	sowed	sown, sowed	563
speak	spoke	spoken	564
speed	sped, speeded	sped, speeded	554
spell	spelled, spelt	spelled, spelt	552
spend	spent	spent	553
spill	spilled, spilt	spilled, spilt	552
spin	spun, span	spun	556
spit	spat, spit	spat, spit	562
split	split	split	551
spoil	spoiled, spoilt	spoiled, spoilt	552
spread	spread	spread	551
spring	sprang, sprung	sprung	570
stand	stood	stood	562
steal	stole	stolen	564
stick	stuck	stuck	556
sting	stung	stung	556
stink	stank, stunk	stunk	570
stride	strode	stridden, strode	569
strike	struck	struck	556
string	strung	strung	556
strive	strove, strived	striven, strived	569
swear	swore	sworn	565
sweat	sweat, sweated	sweat, sweated	551
sweep	swept	swept	555

swell	swelled	swollen, swelled	563
swim	swam, swum	swum	570
swing	swung	swung	556
take	took	taken	568
teach	taught	taught	557
tear	tore	torn	565
tell	told	told	560
think	thought	thought	557
throw	threw	thrown	566
thrust	thrust	thrust	551
tread	trod	trodden, (trod)	571
typeset	typeset	typeset	551
unbend	unbent	unbent	553
unbind	unbound	unbound	558
undergo	underwent	undergone	571
understand	understood	understood	562
undertake	undertook	undertaken	568
underwrite	underwrote	underwritten	569
undo	undid	undone	571
unmake	unmade	unmade	562
unwind	unwound	unwound	558
uphold	upheld	upheld	554
upset	upset	upset	551
wake	woke, waked	woken, waked	564
wear	wore	worn	565
weave	wove	woven	564
wed	wed, wedded	wed, wedded	551
weep	wept	wept	555
wet	wet, wetted	wet, wetted	551
win	won	won	556
wind	wound	wound	558
withdraw	withdrew	withdrawn	571
withhold	withheld	withheld	554
withstand	withstood	withstood	562
wring	wrung	wrung	556
write	wrote	written	569

Main verbs

(see CGEL 3.2–6)

The forms of main verbs

573 There are two types of verbs: main verbs and auxiliary verbs *(see* 477–85). Main verbs are either regular (such as *call, like, try*) or irregular (such as *buy, drink, set*). 'Regular' means that we can state **all** the verb forms of an English verb once we know its base form. The base is the basic, uninflected form which is given as the entry form in dictionaries. The irregular verbs are listed in 550–72. A regular English verb, such as *call*, has the following four forms:

- **the base:** *call*
- **the -s form:** *calls*
- **the -ing form:** *calling*
- **the -ed form:** *called*

The vast majority of English verbs are regular. Furthermore, all new verbs that are coined or borrowed from other languages adopt this pattern. For example, a recently coined verb *futurize* ('to implement plans based upon long-range forecasts of future developments') will have the forms *futurizes, futurizing, futurized.*

574 ● The **-s form**, also called the **3rd person singular present**, is formed in <written> English by adding *-s* or *-es* to the base *(see* 702). In <spoken> English, the *-s* form is pronounced /ɪz/, /z/, or /s/.

base	-s form
press /pres/	*presses* /ˈpresɪz/
play /pleɪ/	*plays* /pleɪz/
help /help/	*helps* /helps/

The rules for the choice of these alternatives are stated in 664; on changes in spelling, for example *try/tries, see* 701. Exceptions: *do* /duː/ ~ *does* /dʌz/, *say* /seɪ/ ~ *says* /sez/.

● The **-ing form**, or the **present participle**, is formed by adding *-ing* to the base of both regular and irregular verbs. (On changes in spelling, as in *beg* ~ *begging, see* 703.)

base	-ing form
press	*pressing*
play	*playing*
help	*helping*

● The **-ed form** of regular verbs is formed by adding *-ed* to the base. It corresponds to two forms (past and past participle) of many irregular verbs. Compare:

base	past form	past participle	
	-ed form		
press	pressed	pressed	REGULAR VERBS
play	played	played	
help	helped	helped	
base	past form	past participle	
drink	drank	drunk	IRREGULAR VERBS
know	knew	known	
hit	hit	hit	

The *-ed* form is pronounced /ɪd/, /d/ or /t/:

base	*-ed* form
pat	patted /ˈpætɪd/
praise	praised /preizd/
press	pressed /prest/

On the choice of these pronunciations, *see* 665. On changes in spelling, as in *pat ~ patted, see* 703.

The uses of the verb forms

575 The base form is used

● in all persons of the present tense except the 3rd person singular:

I/you/we/they/the students, etc. **like** fast food.

● in the imperative (*see* 497):

Look what you've done!

● in the infinitive, which may be the bare infinitive (*do*) or the *to*-infinitive (*to do*):

We'll tell them what **to do** and then let them **do** it.

● in the productive subjunctive (*see* 706):

The committee recommends that these new techniques **be** implemented at once.

576 **The -s form** is used in the 3rd person singular of the present tense (*see* 741), which is the only person where the base form is not used:

> He/She/The student/Everybody **wants** to have a good time, that's all.

577 **The -ed form** is used for both the past tense and the past participle, whereas these are distinct (e.g. *gave ~ given*) for many irregular verbs (*see* 550).

- Unlike the present tense, the past tense has only one form in all persons:

> I/You/She/We/They/The students/Everybody **wanted** to have a good time.

- The past participle is used with a form of *have* to form the perfect aspect (*see* 739):

> Ms Johnson **has asked** me to contact you.

- The past participle is used with a form of *be* to form the passive (*see* 613):

> The security guard **was given** special instructions.
>
> The plans **have been changed**.

- The past participle is used to form *-ed* participle clauses (*see* 493):

> The codes were found **hidden** in the arrested spy's computer.
>
> I also heard it **mentioned** by somebody else.

- The past participle can also become an adjective and can modify a noun:

> His **injured back** puts a stop to his career as an athlete.

The *-ing* form is used

578
- to form the progressive (*see* 739):

> Laura **is working** on a PhD thesis in information science.

- to form *-ing* participle clauses (*see* 493):

> It's a trick I learned **while recovering from the mumps**.

- The *-ing* form can also become an adjective and can modify a noun (*see* 444):

> It was a **fascinating** performance.

- The *-ing* form can also become a noun describing an action or state:

> The **telling** of stories is an important tradition in many societies.

Nationality words

(see CGEL 5.55–57, 7.25)

579 When speaking about English people **in general** we can say either *English people* or *the English* with the definite article and an adjective as head (see 448):

> *English people/The English* have managed to hold on to their
> madrigal tradition better than anyone else. [1]

When referring to some **particular** English persons we can only use the first form:

> *The English people* I met at the conference were all doctors. [2]

We call the first general type of reference, as in [1], **generic reference**, and the second specific type, as in [2], **specific reference**. Some nationality words can be used for both generic and specific reference (see 90):

> *The Australians* are said to like the outdoors. [Australians in general]

> *The Australians* I know don't particularly like the outdoors. [some specific Australians]

Nationality words

580 The following table shows the names of some countries, continents etc. and their corresponding adjectives and nouns (with specific and generic reference).

Name of country, continent, etc.	Adjective	Noun with singular reference	Noun with plural reference	Noun with generic reference (plural)
China	Chinese	a Chinese	Chinese	the Chinese
Japan	Japanese	a Japanese	Japanese	the Japanese
Portugal	Portuguese	a Portuguese	Portuguese	the Portuguese
Switzerland	Swiss	a Swiss	Swiss	the Swiss
Vietnam	Vietnamese	a Vietnamese	Vietnamese	the Vietnamese
Iraq	Iraqi	an Iraqi	Iraqis	the Iraqis
Israel	Israeli	an Israeli	Israelis	the Israelis
Kuwait	Kuwaiti	a Kuwaiti	Kuwaitis	the Kuwaitis
Pakistan	Pakistani	a Pakistani	Pakistanis	the Pakistanis
Africa	African	an African	Africans	the Africans
America	American	an American	Americans	the Americans
Afghanistan	Afghan	an Afghan	Afghans	the Afghans
Asia	Asian	an Asian	Asians	the Asians

Name of country, continent, etc.	Adjective	Noun with singular reference	Noun with plural reference	Noun with generic reference (plural)
Australia	Australian	an Australian	Australians	the Australians
Belgium	Belgian	a Belgian	Belgians	the Belgians
Brazil	Brazilian	a Brazilian	Brazilians	the Brazilians
Europe	European	a European	Europeans	the Europeans
Germany	German	a German	Germans	the Germans
Greece	Greek	a Greek	Greeks	the Greeks
Hungary	Hungarian	a Hungarian	Hungarians	the Hungarians
India	Indian	an Indian	Indians	the Indians
Norway	Norwegian	a Norwegian	Norwegians	the Norwegians
Russia	Russian	a Russian	Russians	the Russians
Argentina (the) Argentine	Argentinian Argentine	an Argentinian an Argentine	Argentinians Argentines	the Argentinians the Argentines
Denmark	Danish	a Dane	Danes	the Danes
Finland	Finnish	a Finn	Finns	the Finns
the Philippines	Philippine	a Filipino	Filipinos	the Filipinos
Poland	Polish	a Pole	Poles	the Poles
Saudi Arabia	Saudi (Arabian) [a]	a Saudi (Arabian)	Saudis, Saudi Arabians	the Saudis, Saudi Arabians
Spain	Spanish	a Spaniard	Spaniards	the Spanish
Sweden	Swedish	a Swede	Swedes	the Swedes
Turkey	Turkish	a Turk	Turks	the Turks
England	English	an Englishman [b]	Englishmen [b]	the English
France	French	a Frenchman [b]	Frenchmen [b]	the French
Holland, the Netherlands	Dutch	a Dutchman [b]	Dutchmen [b]	the Dutch
Ireland	Irish	an Irishman [b]	Irishmen [b]	the Irish
Wales	Welsh	a Welshman [b]	Welshmen [b]	the Welsh
Britain	British	a Briton [c]	Britons	the British
Scotland	Scots, Scottish [d]	a Scotsman, a Scot	Scotsmen, Scots	the Scots

Notes
[a] *Arab* is the racial and political term (*the Arab nations*, etc.). *Arabic* is used about the language and literature, as well as in *Arabic numerals* (as opposed to *Roman numerals*). *Arabia* and *Arabian* are associated with the geographical area of the Arabian peninsula (as in *Saudi Arabia*).
[b] Nouns ending in *-man, -men* refer to males. Although corresponding female nouns exist (e.g. *a Frenchwoman, two Dutchwomen*), these are rather rare. There is now a tendency to avoid such gender-linked terms which could seem <impolite>. Instead, many people prefer to use expressions such as *French people* instead of *Frenchmen, a Dutch*

woman or *a Dutch lady* instead of *a Dutchwoman*. The avoidance of nationality nouns also extends to some other nouns such as *Spaniard* and *Pole* which, although they do not signal gender, in practice are taken to refer to males rather than females. Instead, *Spanish people* and *Polish people* can be used.

[c] *Brit* is a <colloquial> variant of *Briton*, which is not very common.

[d] The inhabitants of Scotland themselves prefer *Scots* (as in *Scots law*) and *Scottish*, which denotes nationality and geographical areas (*Scottish universities*, *the Scottish Highlands*) to *Scotch*, which is commonly used in such expressions as *Scotch terrier* and *Scotch whisky*.

Negation

(*see CGEL* 10.54–70)

Not-negation: *What he says **doesn't** make sense.*

581 To make a finite clause negative, place *not* immediately after the operator (*see* 609). In <informal> English *not* is contracted to *n't* and tagged on to the previous word:

Positive clause	Negative clause
The conditions **are** satisfied by the applicant.	~ The conditions **are not** (**aren't**) satisfied by the applicant.
I **have** told the students.	~ I **have not** (**haven't**) told the students.

In these examples, the positive clause contains an auxiliary (*be*, *have*) that can serve as **operator** (i.e. first auxiliary in a verb phrase). When there is no such operator present, the auxiliary *do* has to be introduced as operator. This is called the ***do*-construction** or ***do*-support** (*see* 611). Like modal auxiliaries, *do* is followed by the bare infinitive:

Positive clause	Negative clause
Sam and Eva **like** computer games.	~ Sam and Eva **do not** (**don't**) like computer games.
What Robert says **makes** sense.	~ What Robert says **does not** (**doesn't**) make sense.

(On the constructions with *be* and *have* as main verbs in negative sentences and on the forms of the modal auxiliaries, *see* 480–5.)

Contracted negation: *She won't mind.*

582 Besides the <informal> contracted negative *n't* there are <informal> contracted verb forms *'s* for *is*, *'re* for *are*, *'ll* for *will*, etc. (*see* 478). The contracted verb forms can be tagged on to the subject (if it is a pronoun or short noun): *he'll, you're, Herb's*. Consequently, there are two forms of <informal> negation possible, one with a contracted verb, and the other with a contracted negative:

Contracted verb *+ full form of not*	*Full form of verb* *+ contracted negative*
It**'s not** their fault.	~ It **isn't** their fault.
You**'ve not** read the book, have you?	~ You **haven't** read the book, have you?
She**'ll not** mind if you stay.	~ She **won't** mind if you stay.
They**'re not** in school today.	~ They **aren't** in school today.

Both sets of contracted forms are used in <informal> English but, in general, especially with a long noun as subject, the *n't* form is more likely:

> The children **aren't** in school today.

In <formal> English, the full forms are used for both verb and negative: *It is not their fault*, etc. In questions with inversion, *not* can be placed either after the auxiliary in its contracted form *n't*, or after the subject in its full form *not*:

> Have**n't** you written to the publishers? <informal>
>
> ~ Have you **not** written to the publishers? <formal>

Negative pronouns and determiners: *There's **no** time left.*

583 *Any*-words (*see* 697) are frequently used after negation. Compare:

> We have **some** milk left. ~ We have**n't any** milk left.

Instead of the construction with *not*-negation and *any* we may equally well use *no*:

> We have**n't any** milk left. ~ We have **no** milk left.

No is a negative determiner (*see* 522). In English there are a number of negative expressions with different functions, as can be seen in the table opposite. As the table shows, *none* can be treated as either singular or plural as far as concord is concerned (*see* 513):

> **None of them has** arrived. OR **None of them have** arrived.

NUMBER	FUNCTION	COUNT		MASS
		PERSONAL	NON-PERSONAL	
singular	pronoun	*no one* *nobody*	*nothing*	*none* (of)
			none (of)	
	pronoun and determiner	*neither* (of)	*neither* (of)	
plural	pronoun	*none* (of)	*none* (of)	
singular and plural	determiner	*no*	*no*	

Other negative words: *Neither of them is correct.*

584 Besides *no* and *none* there are other negative words beginning with *n*, such as *neither, never, nowhere*:

> **neither** (determiner, pronoun, adverb of addition, *see* 234): You've given two answers. *Neither* is correct.

> **neither . . . nor** (coordinating conjunction, *see* 520): *Neither* the government *nor* the market can be blamed for the present economic situation.

> **never** (adverb of time-when or frequency): I *never* believed those rumours.

> **nowhere** (adverb of place): This tradition exists *nowhere* else in Africa.

Also, there are certain words which are negative in meaning and behaviour although they do not appear negative in form:

> **barely** ('almost . . . not'): The dormitories could *barely* house one hundred students.

> **few** ('not many'): Some people work very hard but there seem to be *few* of them left.

> **hardly** ('almost not'): There is *hardly* any butter left. ('almost no butter')

> **little** ('not much'): Nowadays, Ian seems to be doing very *little* research.

> **rarely** ('almost never'): We now know that things *rarely* ever work out in such a cut-and-dried fashion.

> **scarcely** ('almost not, almost nothing'): There was *scarcely anything* Rachel did that did not fascinate me.

> **seldom** ('not often') <rather formal>: Nature *seldom* offers such a brilliant spectacle as a solar eclipse.

The effect of negative words: Lucy *never* seems to care, *does she?*

585 The usual effect of negative words is to make the whole clause in which they occur negative (but *see* 261). Negative clauses have certain characteristics:

- After a negative item there are normally *any*-words instead of *some*-words (*see* 697).

  I had **some** doubts about his ability. [positive clause]
  ~ I didn't have **any** doubts about his ability. [negative clause = 'I had **no** doubts about his ability.']

  I **seldom** get **any** sleep after the baby wakes up.

  I've spoken to **hardly anyone** who disagrees with me on this point.

- Negative words are followed by positive rather than negative tag-questions (*see* 684):

  | She **never** seems to cáre | dòes she? |

  | That **won't** happen agàin | wìll it? |

  | You **won't** forget the shŏpping | wìll you? |

  (Compare: | You'll remember the shŏpping | wòn't you? |)

- A negative item placed at the beginning of a clause brings about the **inversion** of subject and operator, i.e. the order is operator + subject:

  Rarely in American history **has** there been a political campaign that clarified issues less.

  Never was a greater fuss made about any man than about Lord Byron.

  Only after a long argument **did** the committee agree to our plan.   [1]

There is no inversion when the negative is part of the subject:

  No one appears to have noticed the escape.

The inverted construction, as in [1], sounds rather <elevated> and <rhetorical> (*see* 417). If the negative item is **not** placed at the beginning of the clause, the word order is regular (subject + verb), and there is no *do*-construction (*see* 611). Both [1a], [1b] are more common than [1]:

  ~ The committee agreed to our plan **only** after a long argument.   [1a]

  ~ It was **only** after a long argument that the committee agreed to our plan.   [1b]

Not in phrases and in non-finite clauses

586 Sometimes the negative word *not* is attached to a noun phrase instead of the verb phrase. There is no inversion when the negated noun phrase is subject:

  This artist likes big cities. **Not all** her paintings, however, are of cities.

But inversion and the *do*-construction are required when the negated and front-placed noun phrase is object:

Not a single painting did she manage to sell.

To make non-finite clauses negative (*see* 493), we place the negative word *not* before the verb phrase, including *to* before the infinitive:

We had no opinions about Kafka, **not having** read him.

The motorist was on probation and under court order **not to drive**.

The important thing now is **not to mourn** the past but to look ahead.

Transferred negation: *I don't believe we've met.*

587 We expect to find the negative item in the clause it negates. But instead of saying

I believe we have**n't** met.   [1]

we may say

I do**n't** believe we've met.   [2]

In [2] *not* has been transferred from the subclause to the main clause. This construction, which is called **transferred negation**, occurs after verbs like *believe*, *suppose*, and *think*:

I **don't suppose anybody** will notice the improvement.

~ I **suppose nobody** will notice the improvement.

Charlotte **doesn't think** it's very likely to happen again.

~ Charlotte **thinks** it's **not** very likely to happen again.

Nominal clauses

(*see CGEL* 15.3–16)

588 Nominal clauses function like noun phrases (*see* 595). This means that nominal clauses may be subject, object, complement, or prepositional complement.

● Nominal clause as subject:

Whether I pass the test or not does not matter very much.

~ It doesn't matter very much **whether I pass the test or not**. [*it*-construction, see 542]

● Nominal clause as object:

I don't know **whether we really need a new car**.

- Nominal clause as complement:

    What our friends worry about is **whether to stay here or move elsewhere**.

- Nominal clause as prepositional complement:

    This raises the question **as to whether we should abandon the plan**.

Nominal clauses can also occasionally take an appositive function similar to that of a noun phrase in apposition (*see* 470):

    Our latest prediction, **that Norway would win the match**, surprised everybody.

    Let us know your college address, i.e. **where you live during the term**.

There are five main types of nominal clause, which will be discussed in the following sections:

- *that*-clauses (*see* 589)
- interrogative subclauses (*see* 590)
- nominal relative clauses (*see* 592)
- nominal *to*-infinitive clauses (*see* 593)
- nominal *-ing* clauses (*see* 594)

That-clauses: *I'm sure **that she'll manage somehow**.*

589 *That*-clauses can occur as subject, direct object, subject complement or adjective complement.

- *That*-clause as subject: *That we're still alive* is sheer luck.
- *That*-clause as direct object: No one can deny *that films and TV influence the pattern of public behaviour*.
- *That*-clause as subject complement: The assumption is *that things will improve*.
- *That*-clause as complement of an adjective: One can't be sure *that this finding is important*.

In <informal> use, *that* is often omitted when the *that*-clause is object, complement or postponed subject (*see* 542):

    I knew **I was wrong**. [object]

    I'm sure **we'll manage somehow**. [complement]

    It's a pity **you have to leave so soon**. [postponed subject]

Wh-interrogative subclauses: *Nobody seems to know **what to do**.*

590 Interrogative subclauses are introduced by *wh*-interrogative words, including *how* (*see* 536). They can function as subject, direct object, subject complement or adjective complement.

- *Wh*-interrogative subclause as subject: *How the book will sell* largely depends on its author.
- *Wh*-interrogative subclause as direct object: I don't know *how Eve managed to do it.*
- *Wh*-interrogative subclause as subject complement: This is *how John described the accident.*
- *Wh*-interrogative subclause as complement of an adjective: I wasn't certain *whose house we were in.*

Wh-clauses can have all the functions of *that*-clauses. In addition, *wh*-clauses can be prepositional complement (which *that*-clauses cannot be):

None of us were consulted about **who should have the job.**

When the *wh*-element is a prepositional complement, the preposition can be in either initial position <formal> or final position <informal>:

Thomas couldn't remember **on which** shelf he kept the book. <formal>

~ Thomas couldn't remember **which** shelf he kept the book **on**. <informal>

An infinitive *wh*-clause can be formed with all *wh*-words except *why*:

Nobody knew **what to do**. ('what they were supposed to do')

They discussed **where to go**. ('where they should go')

Charlie explained to me **how to start the motor**. ('how one should start the motor')

Yes-no interrogative subclauses: *She wondered whether Stan would call.*

591 *Yes-no* interrogative subclauses are formed with *if* or *whether*:

Olivia wondered **if/whether Stan would call**.

Do you know **if/whether the shops are open today**?

The alternative question (*see* 242) has *if/whether . . . or*:

Do you know **if/whether the shops are open or not**?

Only *whether* can be directly followed by *or not*:

Whether or not Wally lost his job was no concern of mine.

Nominal relative clauses: *What we need is something to get warm.*

592 Nominal relative clauses are also introduced by different *wh*-words. They have the same functions as noun phrases:

- Nominal relative clause as subject:

  What we need is something to get warm. ('the thing that we need . . .')

  Whoever owns this boat must be rich. ('the person who owns . . .')

- Nominal relative clause as direct object:

  I want to see **whoever deals with complaints**. ('the person that . . .')

  You'll find **what you need** in this cupboard. ('the things that . . .')

  I can go into a shop and buy **whatever is there**.

- Nominal relative clause as subject complement:

  Home is **where you were born, reared, went to school and**, most particularly, **where grandma is**.

- Nominal relative clause as object complement:

  You can call me **what(ever) names you like**.

- Nominal relative clause as complement of a preposition:

  You should vote for **which(ever) candidate you like the best**.

Nominal relative clauses are introduced by a *wh*-determiner or *wh*-pronoun (*see* 523), as in this proverb:

Whoever laughs last, laughs longest.

This sentence can also be put in the form:

~ **Those who** laugh last, laugh longest.

Whoever is here replaced by the demonstrative pronoun *those* and the relative pronoun *who*. *Who* alone hardly occurs in this nominal relative function.

As we see above, a nominal relative clause can be introduced by a *wh*-word ending in *-ever*, e.g. *whatever*. These words have general or inclusive meaning. Thus the pronoun *whatever* means roughly 'anything which'. Other expressions containing relative clauses can be used instead, such as *anyone who, the person who* instead of *whoever*:

Whoever told you that was lying.

~ **Anyone who** told you that was lying.

~ **The person who** told you that was lying.

Nominal *to*-infinitive clauses: *I was glad **to be able to help***.

593 Nominal *to*-infinitive clauses have a number of different functions in the clause:

- Nominal *to*-infinitive clause as subject:

  To say there is no afterlife would mean a rejection of religion.

- Nominal *to*-infinitive clause as direct object:

    We want **everyone to be happy**.

- Nominal *to*-infinitive clause as subject complement:

    The minister's first duty will be **to stop inflation**.

- Nominal *to*-infinitive clause as complement of an adjective:

    I was very glad **to help in this way**.

The subject of a *to*-infinitive is normally introduced by *for*. A pronoun subject here has the objective form:

   What I wanted was **for them to advance me the money**.

Nominal *-ing* clauses:
I don't like **people telling me how to do things**.

594 Nominal *-ing* participle clauses have the same range of functions as nominal *to*-infinitive clauses. In addition, they can act as complement of a preposition:

- Nominal *-ing* participle clause as subject:

    Telling stories was one thing my friend was well-known for.

- Nominal *-ing* participle clause as direct object:

    I don't mind **people telling me how to do things better**.

- Nominal *-ing* participle clause as subject complement:

    What William likes best is **playing practical jokes**.

- Nominal *-ing* participle clause as prepositional complement:

    Jessica sparked off the opposition by **telling a television audience it was gossip**.

    Anna is quite capable of **telling her employers where they are wrong**.

When the *-ing* clause has a subject, there is sometimes a choice between two constructions. The genitive case of nouns and the possessive form of pronouns are typical of <formal> style:

   Winston was surprised at **his family's** reacting so sharply. <formal>

   Winston was surprised at **their** reacting so sharply. <formal>

In <informal> style, the uninflected form of nouns and the objective case of personal pronouns are more common:

   Winston was surprised at **his family** reacting so sharply. <informal>

   Winston was surprised at **them** reacting so sharply. <informal>

Noun phrases

(*see CGEL* Chapter 17)

595 A noun phrase is called a noun phrase because the word which is its head (i.e. main part) is typically a noun. In the following two sentences there are several noun phrases [printed in italics]:

> [On *Tuesday*] [*a German passenger liner*] rescued [*the crew of a trawler*]. [*It*] found [*them*] drifting [on *a life raft*] after [*they*] had abandoned [*a sinking ship*].

Here are the noun phrases with a description of their grammatical functions:

1. *Tuesday* is a prepositional complement (*see* 654) in the prepositional phrase *On Tuesday*, which functions as a time-when adverbial.
2. *a German passenger liner* is the subject of the first sentence.
3. *the crew of a trawler* is the object. This noun phrase contains another noun phrase, *a trawler*, which is prepositional complement in the prepositional phrase *of a trawler*.
4. *It* is a personal pronoun referring to *a German passenger liner* and functioning as the subject of the second sentence.
5. *them* is a plural personal pronoun referring to *the crew of a trawler*. The reason why the plural *them* can refer to the singular *crew* is that this is a group noun (*see* 510).
6. *a life raft* is the prepositional complement in the prepositional phrase *on a life raft*, which functions as a place adverbial.
7. *they* is a plural personal pronoun referring to *the crew of a trawler* and functioning as subject of the subclause beginning with *after*.
8. *a sinking ship* functions as the object of *had abandoned*.

596 A head noun can be accompanied by determiners (*a, the, his*, etc.) and one or more modifiers: *passenger* modifies *liner* and *German* modifies *passenger liner*. This type of modification is called **premodification** because the modifiers stand **before** the head noun. When there is modification **after** the head, it is called **postmodification**. An example of this is in *the crew of a trawler*, where the head *crew* is postmodified by the prepositional phrase *of a trawler*. Often there exists a choice between the two types of modification: we could also say *the trawler's crew*, using premodification (*see* 650) instead of *the crew of a trawler*, using postmodification (*see* 641).

Pronouns such as *it* and *them* typically have a function equivalent to that of a whole noun phrase. In this book, in fact, we regard pronouns as the heads (and often the only words) of noun phrases. The structure of the English noun phrase can be written:

The brackets indicate that the determiners and modifiers can be left out. But determiners are more essential to noun phrase structure than modifiers. The only situation in which a noun phrase has no expressed determiner is where it has a 'zero article' (*see* 473). Here are some examples of noun phrases:

Determiner	Premodification	HEAD	Postmodification
the		BOOKS	
a	*good*	BOOK	
some		BOOKS	*to read*
all those	*good*	BOOKS	*I want to read*
a	*sinking*	SHIP	
a	*German*	PASSENGER LINER	
the		CREW	*of a trawler*

The different parts of noun phrase structure are treated separately in this part of the grammar: determiners in 522, premodifiers in 650 and postmodifiers in 641. Apart from nouns, pronouns (*see* 661) and adjectives (*see* 448) may act as head of a noun phrase.

Number

(*see CGEL* 5.73–103)

Singular and plural number: *this problem ~ those problems*

597 In English, there is singular number (denoting 'one') and plural number (denoting 'more than one'). Number is a feature of nouns (*book/books*), demonstrative pronouns (*this/these*, *see* 521), and personal pronouns (*she/they*, *see* 619). It is also shown through concord with singular or plural forms of the verb (*see* 575).

The regular plural of nouns is formed by adding -*s* or -*es* to the singular (*see* 635).

● **Count nouns** can be singular or plural (*see* 58), as in:

> *one daughter ~ two daughters*
> *a fast train ~ fast trains*
> *this problem ~ these problems*

But many nouns do not have plural number. They include **mass nouns** (also called **non-count nouns** or **uncountables**) and **proper nouns** (also called **names**).

● **Mass nouns** such as the following are singular only (*see* more examples in 62 and 68): *advertising, advice, applause, cash, evidence, food, furniture, garbage, homework, hospitality, information, knowledge, luggage, machinery, money, music, pollution, refuse, rubbish, traffic, trash, waste, weather*:

> Our *advertising is* mainly concentrated on the large national newspapers.
>
> People who distrust credit cards say '*Cash is* King.'
>
> There *is* hardly any *evidence* against her.
>
> Our city is known for its fine *food*, good *music* and colourful *hospitality*.
>
> *This information is* of course confidential.
>
> *Is* this your *money*? – No, *it's* my sister's.

● **Proper nouns** such as *Margaret, Stratford, Mars, the Mississippi, Broadway* are also singular only:

> The Mississippi River is 2,350 miles from mouth to source.

For some exceptions, such as *the Wilsons* (= the Wilson family), *the West Indies, see* 671.

Singular nouns ending in -s: What's the big **news**?

598 There are some nouns which require special comment, such as singular nouns ending in -*s*.

● *News* is always singular:

> *That's* good *news*!
>
> Instead of being depressed by *this news*, she was actually relieved by *it*.

● **Subject names in** -*ics* are singular: e.g. *classics* ('classical languages'), *linguistics, mathematics, phonetics, statistics*:

> *Statistics is* not as difficult as some people think.

Here, *statistics* = 'the science of using information discovered from studying numbers'. But when *statistics* = 'figures' it is treated as a plural:

> The official *statistics show* that 6 per cent of the population are unemployed.

- **Names of games** ending in *-s* are singular, e.g. *billiards, darts, dominoes, fives, ninepins*:

  Billiards is my favourite game.

- **Proper nouns** ending in *-s* are singular, e.g. *Algiers, Athens, Brussels, Flanders, Marseilles, Naples, Wales. The United Nations (the UN)* and *the United States of America (the USA)* have a singular verb when considered as single units:

  The United States has appointed a new ambassador to Japan.

- **The names of some diseases** ending in *-s* are usually treated as singular, e.g. *measles, German measles, mumps, rickets, shingles.* Similarly *AIDS* (which is an acronym of 'acquired immune deficiency syndrome'):

  AIDS is an illness which destroys the natural system of protection that the body has acquired against disease.

Plural-only nouns: *How much are **those sunglasses**?*

599 There are some nouns which occur only in the plural (sometimes only in certain senses), for example *people, police, trousers.*

- *People* as the plural of *person*:

  There *are* too *many people* in here.

But *people* has the plural *peoples* when it is a group noun, in the sense of 'men and women of a particular country, race', etc.:

  The *peoples* of Central Asia speak many different languages.

  This country has been settled by *peoples* of many heritages.

- *Police*:

  The *police have* dropped the case.

  Several *police were* injured.

But 'a member of the police force' = *policeman, police officer*: 'Why don't you ask a *policeman*?'

- *Cattle*:

  Holstein *cattle are*n't a beef breed and *they* are rarely seen on a ranch.

600 • Some nouns denoting **tools** or **instruments** consisting of two equal parts joined together are treated as plural:

  [A] Have you seen my *scissors*? [B] Here *they are*.

To express one or more items of such nouns we can use *a pair of, two pairs of*:

I'd like *a pair of scissors*, please.

Other nouns that behave like *scissors*: *binoculars, glasses, pincers, pliers, tongs, scales* [for weighing], *shears, tweezers*.

● Nouns for **articles of dress** consisting of two parts are also treated as plural:

[A] Where *are* my *trousers*? [B] *They are* in the bedroom where you put *them*.

But such plural nouns can be 'turned into' ordinary count nouns by means of *a pair of* or *pairs of*:

I need to buy *a* new *pair of trousers*.

How many *pairs of blue jeans* do you have?

Other nouns that behave like *trousers* are: *briefs, jeans, pants, pajamas* <AmE>, *pyjamas* <BrE>, *shorts, slacks, tights, trunks*:

My *pants* were soaking wet.

Amy was dressed in a tight-fitting pair of *slacks*.

601 There are many nouns which, in a given sense, only occur in the plural, for example *contents* (as in *the contents of a book, the contents of a cupboard, a list of contents*, etc.):

The *contents* of this 195-page document *are* not known to many.

The minister has to work through the *contents* of a bulging briefcase in the evenings.

The singular form *content* denotes what is contained by a text or by a particular substance:

The *content* of a text frequently influences its style.

The average nickel *content* of the alloy is about 2.5 per cent.

Here are some other examples of plural-only, or mainly plural, nouns:

arms ('weapons'): Arms *were* distributed widely among the civilian population.

ashes: After the fire many a ranch-house lay as a square of blackened ashes. (BUT: *cigarette ash*)

funds ('money'): Our *funds are* too scarce to permit this plan. (BUT: *a fund* 'a source of money': The family set up a *fund* for medical research.)

oats: The *oats were* sown early this year. (BUT: *corn, barley* are singular.)

odds: The *odds are* not very strongly in favour of a tax cut.

outskirts: They met in a place on the *outskirts* of the city.

premises ('building'): The butler discovered the residential *premises were* on fire.

quarters, headquarters: The proposal aroused violent opposition in some *quarters.* ['circles'] (BUT: the third *quarter* of the year 2002 = 'three-month period')

spirits ('mood'): She got home in high *spirits,* relaxed and smiling. (BUT: These people have retained their pioneering *spirit.*)

stairs: She was about to mount a wide flight of marble *stairs.*

steps: They stood on the *steps* of the ambassador's home.

surroundings: The *surroundings* of their house *are* rather unattractive.

thanks: My warmest *thanks are* due to your organization.

To make *thanks* singular one can use expressions like these:

A *vote of thanks was* proposed to the retiring manager. <formal>

And now, let's give a *big thank-you* to our hostess! <informal>

Numerals

(*see* CGEL 6.63–69)

Cardinals and ordinals

602 The **cardinal numerals** (*one, two, three,* etc.) and the **ordinal numerals** (*first, second, third,* etc.) are shown in the following list. The ordinals are normally preceded by another determiner, usually the definite article (*see* 525):

[A] How many people are taking part in the competition?

[B] There are **ten** on the list, so you are **the eleventh**.   [1]

They have **five children** already, so this will be **their sixth child**.   [2]

Numerals can be used either as pronouns [1], or as determiners [2]. Cardinal numerals also function as nouns, when they name a particular number, e.g. (playing with dice):

You need a **six** or two **threes** to win the game.

	Cardinals		Ordinals
0	zero		
1	one	1st	first
2	two	2nd	second
3	three	3rd	third
4	four	4th	fourth
5	five	5th	fifth
6	six	6th	sixth
7	seven	7th	seventh
8	eight	8th	eighth
9	nine	9th	ninth
10	ten	10th	tenth
11	eleven	11th	eleventh
12	twelve	12th	twelfth
13	thirteen	13th	thirteenth
14	fourteen	14th	fourteenth
15	fifteen	15th	fifteenth
16	sixteen	16th	sixteenth
17	seventeen	17th	seventeenth
18	eighteen	18th	eighteenth
19	nineteen	19th	nineteenth
20	twenty	20th	twentieth
21	twenty-one (etc.)	21st	twenty-first (etc.)
24	twenty-four (etc.)	24th	twenty-fourth (etc.)
30	thirty	30th	thirtieth
40	forty	40th	fortieth
50	fifty	50th	fiftieth
60	sixty	60th	sixtieth
70	seventy	70th	seventieth
80	eighty	80th	eightieth
90	ninety	90th	ninetieth
100	a/one hundred	100th	hundredth
101	a/one hundred and one (etc.)	101st	hundred and first (etc.)
120	a/one hundred and twenty	120th	hundred and twentieth (etc.)
200	two hundred	200th	two hundredth
1,000	a/one thousand	1,000th	thousandth
2,000	two thousand (etc.)	2,000th	two thousandth (etc.)
100,000	a/one hundred thousand	100,000th	hundred thousandth

In English texts, alphabetic forms are considerably more common than digit forms for numerals lower than ten (*one, two, three ... ten*). Digit forms are more common than alphabetic forms for numerals over ten (*11, 12, 13*, etc).

0 = *zero, nought, naught, oh, nil, nothing, love*

603 The numeral 0 is spoken or written out in different ways: *zero, nought, naught, oh, nil, nothing,* and *love*.

- *Zero* /ˈzɪərəʊ ‖ ˈzɪrəʊ/, the most common alphabetical form referring to the numeral *0*, is used especially in mathematics and for temperature (*see* 606):

    This correlation is not significantly different from **zero**.

    Her blood pressure was down to **zero**.

    The temperature dropped and stood at **zero** in the daytime.

- *Nought* /nɔːt/ ‖ *naught* /nɔːt/ occurs chiefly as the name of the numeral *0*:

    To write 'a million' in figures, you need a one followed by six noughts ‖ naughts.

- Read as /əʊ/, sometimes written *oh*, used for example in telephone and fax numbers. In <AmE> telephone numbers are more often read as 'zero' than 'oh':

    Dial 7050 ['seven oh five oh'] and ask for extension 90. ['nine oh'] <esp BrE>

    Who used to play Agent 007? ['double oh seven']

    Flight 105 ['one oh five']

- *Nil* or *nothing* is used in contexts such as these (especially football scores):

    The visitors won 4–0. ['four nil, four nothing, four to nothing', *see* 606 below]

    Now the party's influence was reduced to *nil*.

    The training promises to be arduous and the pay will be *nil*.

- *Love* is used in tennis, table tennis, badminton and squash:

    The champion leads by 30–0. ('thirty love')

In general use, zero is replaced by the negative determiner *no* or the pronoun *none*:

    There were *no* survivors from the air disaster.

    None of the passengers or crew survived.

Hundred, thousand, million, billion

604 *One* or *a* must be used with *hundred*, *thousand*, *million* and *billion* when they are spoken or written out:

100	*one hundred* OR *a hundred*
1,000	*one thousand* OR *a thousand*
1,000,000	*one million* OR *a million*
1,000,000,000	*one billion* OR *a billion* OR *one thousand million*

These numerals have the singular form following both singular and plural numbers or quantifiers. But all four have the -s plural when they denote an indefinite number:

four *hundred* soccer fans   BUT: *hundreds of* soccer fans

ten *thousand* books   BUT: *thousands of* books

several *million* yen   BUT: *millions of* yen

The actor got *ten million* dollars for appearing in that film.

BUT: [A] How many children are born each year?

        [B] I don't know – *millions and millions*.

Hundreds of thousands of people had to be evacuated during the monsoon.

Fractions, decimals, superscripts, etc.

605 Fractions, decimals, superscripts, etc. are written and read out as follows:

Fractions

$\frac{1}{2}$ (a) *half*: They stayed (for) half an hour. OR They stayed for a half hour

$\frac{1}{4}$ *a quarter*: They stayed (for) a quarter of an hour

$\frac{1}{10}$ *a/one tenth*: a tenth of the population

$\frac{3}{4}$ *three quarters* OR *three fourths*: three quarters of an hour

$1\frac{1}{2}$ *one and a half*: one and a half hours, an hour and a half

$3\frac{2}{5}$ *three and two fifths*: three and two fifths inches

$\frac{3}{568}$ *three over five six eight* [in mathematics]

Decimals

0.9   *nought point nine* <esp BrE> OR *zero point nine* <esp AmE>

2.5   *two point five*

3.14   *three point one four*

Superscripts

10^2 *ten squared*

10^3 *ten cubed*

10^4 *ten to the power of four*

Arithmetic

$4 + 4 = 8$ *four plus four equals eight* OR *four and four makes/is eight*

$5 \times 2 = 10$ *five multiplied by two equals ten* OR *five times two makes/is ten*

$6 \div 2 = 3$ *six divided by two equals/makes/is three*

Temperatures

606 −15°C   *fifteen (degrees) below (zero)* OR *minus fifteen (degrees Celsius)*
    85°F   *eighty-five (degrees Fahrenheit)*

Currency

   25c   *twenty-five cents* OR *a quarter*
   $4.75   *four dollars seventy-five* OR *four seventy-five*
   20p   *twenty pence* OR *twenty p* /piː/
   £9.95   *nine pounds ninety-five (pence)* OR *nine ninety-five*
   €52.70 *fifty-two euros (and) seventy cents*

Sports scores

   5–1   *five to one* OR *five one*
   3–0   *three to nil* OR *three nil* OR *three (to) nothing* <BrE> OR *three (to) zero* OR
        three blank <AmE>
   2–2   *two all* OR *two two* OR <AmE> *two up* (i.e. it's a tie or a draw)

Approximate numbers

Approximate numbers are specified in numerous ways, such as these:

approximately (*about, around, roughly*) $1,500

some forty books

fifty *or so* people

about eleven*ish* ~ about eleven o'clock

a fifty*ish* woman ~ a woman about fifty years of age

300-*odd* demonstrators ~ slightly over 300 demonstrators

Dates and times of the clock

Years

607 1996 *(the year) nineteen ninety-six* OR *(the year) nineteen hundred and ninety-six* <more formal>
    2000 *the year two thousand*
    2010 *(the year) two thousand (and) ten* OR *(the year) twenty ten*

Decades

Decades can be written: *the 1990s* OR *the 90s* OR *the '90s*. They are also written, and read out, as *the nineteen nineties* OR *the nineties*.

The plural *twenties* denotes an age or a period between 20 and 29; similarly with *thirties* (30–39), *forties* (40–49), etc.:

He looked like a man *in his early/mid/late forties*.

Dates <written>:

Our daughter was born

> *on 18 August 2001.* <esp. BrE>
> *on August 18, 2001.* <esp. AmE>
> *on August 18th, 2001.* <esp. AmE>

The alternative written forms are *18/8/01* (day + month) <in BrE> BUT *8/18/01* (month + day) <in AmE>.

Dates <spoken>:

Our daughter was born

> *on the eighteenth of August, two thousand (and) one.*
> *on August the eighteenth, two thousand (and) one.*
> *on August eighteenth, two thousand (and) one.*

Times of the clock

Times of the clock are read out in full as follows:

at 5	*at 5 (o'clock)*
at 5.15 ‖ 5:15	*at five fifteen* OR *at a quarter past five* OR *at a quarter after five* <AmE>
at 5.30 ‖ 5:30	*at five thirty* OR *at half past five*
at 5.45 ‖ 5:45	*at five forty-five* OR *at a quarter to six* OR *at a quarter of six* <AmE>
at 5.50 ‖ 5:50	*at five fifty* OR *at ten (minutes) to six*
at 6.10 ‖ 6:10	*at ten (minutes) past six* OR *at ten minutes after six* <AmE> OR *at six ten* [for instance in referring to a timetable]

Objects

(see CGEL 10.7–8, 27–32, 16.25–67)

608 The object of a clause can be a noun phrase *(see 595):*

Can you see *that white boat* over there?

But the object can also be a nominal clause (*see* 588):

> Now we can see *that too little has been spent on the environment*.

The object usually refers to the person, thing, etc., affected by the action of the verb:

> Anna kissed *him* gently on the cheek.

> George parked *his car* outside an espresso bar.

The object normally follows the verb phrase. English typically has **SVO order** (subject + verb + object) in both main clauses and subclauses:

> After the chairman announced *the takeover bid*, the stock exchange council banned *dealings in the company's shares*.

But on variations of word order, *see* fronted topic (411), exclamations (528), *wh*-questions (683) and relative clauses (687).

The object of an active sentence can usually be turned into the subject of a passive sentence (*see* 613):

> ACTIVE: A dog owner found *little Nancy* yesterday morning.

> PASSIVE: *Little Nancy* was found yesterday morning (by a dog owner).

When a clause has two objects, the first is an **indirect object** and the second a **direct object**. The indirect object is typically personal, as in these examples: *me, the patient*.

> 'Nobody gives [*me*] [flowers] anymore', Georgina said.

> Lucy bought [*the patient*] [fruit, meat and cheese].

The indirect object is often equivalent to a prepositional phrase with *to*:

> Nobody gives [flowers] [*to me*] anymore.

or a prepositional phrase with *for* (*see* 730):

> She bought [fruit, meat and cheese] [*for the patient*].

However, an alternative prepositional construction is not always possible, as in these sentences:

> We all wish [*you*] [better health].

> Isabelle leaned down and gave [*John*] [a real kiss].

Operators

(*see CGEL* 2.48–50, 3.21–30, 34, 37)

What is an operator?

609 Auxiliary verbs have different meanings and functions in the verb phrase (*see* 735). But they have one important feature in common: they all occur before the main verb. When finite (*see* 737), they are placed first in the finite verb phrase. We call the first auxiliary of a verb phrase the **operator**. Compare the following interrogative sentences with the matching declarative ones (the operator is printed in **bold**):

> *Will* she *be* back after the weekend?
>> ~ She *will be* back after the weekend.
>
> *Were* they *showing* any comedy films?
>> ~ They *were showing* some comedy films.
>
> *Was* he *lecturing* on English grammar?
>> ~ He *was lecturing* on English grammar.
>
> *Have* I *been asking* too many questions?
>> ~ I *have been asking* too many questions.
>
> *Would* a more radical decision *have been* possible?
>> ~ A more radical decision *would have been* possible.

In each question, the first auxiliary (operator) of the finite verb phrase is placed first, and isolated from the rest of the verb phrase, no matter how complex the phrase is.

Be acts like an operator even when it is a main verb, and so the term 'operator' will be used also in cases like this one:

> *Is* she a good student?

In <BrE> also *have* sometimes acts like an operator even when it is a main verb:

> *Have* you any money?

However, there is an alternative *do*-construction, which is used in both <AmE> and <BrE> (*see* 611):

> *Do* you *have* any money?

Operators in interrogatives and negatives

610 Operators are important in English because they are generally used in the construction of interrogative and negative sentences. In *yes–no* questions the operator stands before the subject. This is called **inversion** of subject and operator:

> *You have* met the new students. [declarative]
>
> *Have you* met the new students? [interrogative: *yes–no* question]

In negative statements the operator stands before *not*. In <informal> English, the auxiliary is combined with the negative contraction *n't* (*see* 582):

I **will** **not** be going to the seminar tomorrow.

> ~ I **won't** be going to the seminar tomorrow.

Chris **is** **not** playing so well this season.

> ~ Chris **isn't** playing so well this season.

Chloe **has** **not** got the whole-hearted consent of her parents.

> ~ Chloe **hasn't** got the whole-hearted consent of her parents.

Adverbs with mid-position, such as *always*, *never* (*see* 458), usually take the same position as *not*, just after the operator:

> Things **will** **never** **be** the same again.

> That sort of attitude **has** **always** **appealed** to me.

Such adverbs are also found before the operator, especially for contrast:

> I submit that this is the key problem of international relations, that it **always** **has** been, that it **always** **will** be.

The *do*-construction: *Do you know the way?*

611 In a verb phrase which has no auxiliary verb there is no word that can act as operator, for example:

> Connor **knows** the way.

> You **need** some advice.

> The delegates **arrived** yesterday.

In such cases, we have to introduce the special **'dummy' operator** *do* in *yes–no* questions (*see* 682) and *not*-negation (*see* 581). This is called **the do-construction** or *do*-**support**. *Do* as operator is followed by the infinitive of the main verb:

Yes–no questions	Not-negation
Does Connor **know** the way?	Connor **doesn't** **know** the way.
Do you **need** any advice?	You **don't** **need** any advice.
Did the delegates **arrive** yesterday?	The delegates **didn't** **arrive** yesterday.

Other constructions with an operator

612 Apart from *yes–no* questions and *not*-negatives, there are some other constructions which also require an operator, including the 'dummy' operator *do*. Such constructions are:

- **Emphatic sentences** (*see* 300):

    Dò *be* quiet! (More emphatic than *Be quiet!*)

    I dìd *enjoy* that meal last night! ('I really enjoyed that meal')

- **Tag questions** (*see* 684):

    | Charles Perry won the men's dòubles lást year | dìdn't he? |

    | Paige has got a very distinctive accent as we̊ll | hàsn't she? |

- **Wh-*questions*** where the *wh*-element is **not** the subject:

When **did** you come back from Spain?	[*when* = adverbial]
How long **did** Grace stay in Egypt?	[*how long* = adverbial]
What **did** she do so long in Athens?	[*what* = object]
Who **did** you want to speak to?	[*who* = prepositional complement]

But no operator and no *do*-construction are needed when the *wh*-element is subject:

    Who is this in the picture?

    Which guests are coming by train?

    What took you so long?

    Who met you at the airport?

    (BUT: Who did you meet at the airport? [*who* = object])

- **Subject-operator inversion** occurs also in statements when a negative expression is placed first in the sentence (*see* 417):

    Only after a long delay **did** news of Livingstone's fate **reach** the coast.
    <rather formal>

An *it*-type cleft sentence (*see* 496) would be more natural in most contexts:

    It was only after a long delay that news of Livingstone's fate reached the coast.

Passives

(*see CGEL* 3.63–78)

613 The term **passive** is the name of verb phrases which contain the construction *be* + past participle (*see* 739): *is accepted, has been shown, will be covered, might have been considered*, etc. The passive is not very common in <informal speech> but a regular feature in <formal, especially scientific

written> texts, as in the following extract from a paper on odontology (with passive verb phrases in *italics*):

It *is* generally *accepted* that, when it *is exposed* in the oral cavity, any natural or artificial solid surface *will* quickly *be covered* by thin organic films. It *has been shown* in several studies that these films contain material of salivary origin.

The opposite of **passive** is **active**. Here are some pairs of examples of different verb types to show the contrast between active clauses and their corresponding passive clauses:

Everyone *rejected* the bold idea.

~ The bold idea *was rejected* (by everyone).

The ambulance crew *gave* the casualties first aid.

~ The casualties *were given* first aid (by the ambulance crew).

Boat owners *considered* the bridge a menace to navigation.

~ The bridge *was considered* a menace to navigation (by boat owners).

The committee *asked* Mr Pearson to become director of the institute.

~ Mr Pearson *was asked* (by the committee) to become director of the institute.

Turning actives into passives

614 To change an active clause into a passive clause:

1. Replace the active verb phrase by the matching passive one.
2. Make the object of the active clause the subject of the passive clause.
3. Make the subject of the active clause **the agent** of the passive clause. The agent is the noun phrase which occurs after the preposition *by* in the passive clause. The agent is an optional part of the passive construction: *by* + agent can usually be omitted altogether, as indicated by round brackets in the examples in 613.

These three changes can be pictured as follows:

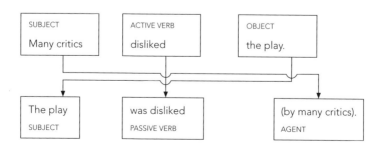

345

615 The effect of the change into the passive is to reverse the positions of the noun phrases acting as subject and object in the active sentence. With verbs like *give*, which can have two objects, it is usually the first object (the indirect object) that becomes subject of the passive clause:

> The department *gave* [Mrs Barry] [no authority to take such a decision].
>
> ~ [Mrs Barry] *was given* [no authority to take such a decision].
>
> Our school *did not give* [science subjects] [enough time].
>
> ~ [Science subjects] *were not given* [enough time].

But there is also another passive construction where the direct object is made subject and *to* is added before the object:

> ~ [Enough time] *was not given* [to science subjects].

Most active sentences which have a noun phrase or pronoun as object can be made passive. However, a few verbs which take an object do not have a passive: they include *have* (as in *I have a small car*), and *hold* (as in *This jug holds one pint*). Also, the passive is sometimes not possible when the object is a clause.

Passives without agents: *Nobody was injured in the crash.*

616 The *by*-phrase containing the agent of a passive clause (and corresponding to the subject in an active clause) is only required in specific cases. In fact, only about one out of five English passive clauses has an expressed agent. The passive is especially associated with <impersonal> style, such as <scientific and official writing>. Here the question of who is the agent (i.e. who performs the action described by the verb) is often unimportant and need not be stated:

> The question *will be discussed* at a meeting tomorrow.

The passive may be a convenient construction to choose also when we do not know who the performer of an action is:

> A police officer *was killed* last night in a road accident.

The *get*-passive: *I hope you didn't get hurt.*

617 As we have seen in the examples given so far, the passive auxiliary is normally *be*. There is also a passive with *get*:

> The boy *got hurt* on his way home from school.
>
> It's upsetting when a person *gets punished* for a crime they didn't commit.

The *get*-passive is found in <informal> style, and normally in constructions without an agent.

Passives with prepositional verbs and non-finite verb phrases:
This matter will have to be dealt with.

618 The passive also occurs with prepositional verbs (e.g. *deal with, ask for, believe in, cater for, look at, stare at, talk about, wonder at; see* 632). The prepositional object, i.e. the noun phrase following the preposition of the active sentence, then becomes the subject of the passive sentence:

> The members also **talked about** other possibilities at the meeting.
> ~ Other possibilities **were** also **talked about** at the meeting. [1]
> Someone **will have to deal with** this matter right away.
> ~ This matter will **have to be dealt with** right away. [2]
> I just don't like people **staring at** me.
> ~ I just don't like **being stared at**. [3]
> An improvement in relations between our countries **is to be hoped**
> **for** as a result of the conference. [4]

As the examples [3] and [4] show, the passive can also occur in non-finite verb phrases. Compare:

> I want everybody **to understand** this.   [active **to**-infinitive]
> ~ I want this **to be understood** by everybody.   [passive **to**-infinitive]
> Without anybody **asking** her, Joan did the
>   job herself.   [active **-ing** clause]
> ~ Without **being asked**, Joan did the job herself [passive **-ing** clause]

Personal and reflexive pronouns

(*see CGEL* 6.15–31)

The range of forms

619 Personal pronouns (e.g. *she, they*) and reflexive pronouns (e.g. *herself, themselves*) are related. Both distinguish between personal and non-personal gender and, within personal gender, between masculine and feminine (*see* 529):

	Singular	Plural
1st person	*I ~ myself*	*we ~ ourselves*
2nd person	*you ~ yourself*	*you ~ yourselves*
3rd person	*he ~ himself* *she ~ herself* *it ~ itself*	*they ~ themselves*

For the 2nd person the same form is used in the singular and plural of personal and possessive pronouns (*you, your, yours*), but there is a separate plural of reflexive pronouns: *yourself* (singular) and *yourselves* (plural). *We*, the 1st person plural pronoun, denotes 'I plus one or more others' (*see* 97).

620 Five personal pronouns have both subjective and objective forms:

> *I ~ me, we ~ us, he ~ him, she ~ her, they ~ them* (but *you* and *it* have only one form)

Some personal pronouns also have two genitive forms:

> *my ~ mine, our ~ ours, you ~ yours, her ~ hers, their ~ theirs* (but *his* has only one form)

The genitives of the personal pronouns are usually called **possessive pronouns** (*see* 623). The following table gives all the forms of personal and reflexive pronouns.

		Personal pronouns				Reflexive pronouns
				Possessives		
		subjective case	objective case	acting as determiner	acting as pronoun	
1st person	singular	I	me	my	mine	myself
	plural	we	us	our	ours	ourselves
2nd person	singular plural	you		your	yours	yourself yourselves
3rd person	singular masculine	he	him	his		himself
	singular feminine	she	her	her	hers	herself
	singular non-personal	it		its		itself
	plural	they	them	their	theirs	themselves

Personal pronouns

621 Personal pronouns, as we see from this table, are classified according to

- **person:** 1st, 2nd, 3rd person
- **number:** singular, plural
- **gender:** masculine, feminine, non-personal
- **case:** subjective, objective, genitive (or possessive)

The choice of person, number and gender is decided by meaning, which is supplied either by context outside language, or by the sort of noun phrase to which the pronoun 'refers' (or 'points back'; *see* 375). Pronouns generally point back to a noun phrase, as in this example and in [1] and [2] below:

My brother is out, but *he* will be returning soon.

But a personal pronoun in a subclause can also 'point forward' to a noun phrase in the following main clause, as *it* pointing forward to *the plane* in [3] below. Compare the different order in the following three alternative sentences.

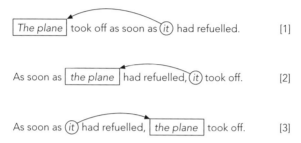

In last the especially in <formal written> English that the personal pronoun precedes the noun phrase, as in [3].

It is especially in <formal written> English that the personal pronoun precedes the noun phrase, as in [3].

Subjective and objective forms

622 The choice of subjective and objective case is made on the basis of grammatical position. The simplest rule to use is that the **subjective form** is the one used **in subject position** with finite verbs, and the **objective form** is the form used **in all other positions**.

Subjective case:

She was very helpful.

Objective case:

I found *her* very helpful.	[*her* = direct object]
She gave *him* her home number.	[*him* = indirect object]
I have to speak to *them* about it.	[*them* = prepositional complement]
She is five years older than *him*.	[*him* = prepositional complement]
[In a telephone conversation]	
[A] Who's that? [B] It's *me* – Àgnes.	[*me* = subject complement]

In the last two examples, *older than him* and *it's me* are <informal> English. It is sometimes stated that the subjective form is the correct one here. But *older than I* and *it's I* sound rather stilted, and are avoided in <informal> use (*see* 506).

Possessives

623 There are two kinds of possessives, each with its separate function. *My, your, her,* etc. act as determiners before noun heads. *Mine, yours, hers,* etc. act as pronouns, i.e. as independent noun phrases. In pronoun function, the possessive is stressed. Compare the two corresponding genitive noun constructions (*see* 530) in the right-hand column:

Determiner function:	This is **her** book.	~ This is **Joan's** book.
Pronoun function:	This book is ˈ**hers**.	~ This book is ˈ**Joan's**.

Possessives as determiner: *Have you changed your mind again?*

624 Unlike many other languages, English uses determiner possessives with reference to parts of the body and personal belongings:

> Hannah broke **her** leg when she was skiing in Austria.
>
> Don't tell me they've changed **their** minds again!
>
> Don't lose **your** balance and fall into the water!
>
> I can't find **my** glasses.

The definite article is usual in prepositional phrases related to the object:

> She took the little girl by **the** hand. [The hand belongs to the little girl.]
>
> Something must have hit me on **the** head. [The head is mine.]

In passive constructions, the prepositional phrase is related to the subject:

> He was shot in **the** leg during the war.

Possessives as pronoun: *Is that paper yours?*

625 The forms *mine, hers, theirs,* etc., can act in all the main positions where a noun phrase is possible:

- A possessive as subject:

  > **Yours** is an international company, **mine** is just a small local firm.

- A possessive as subject complement:

  > Is that my copy or **yours**?

- A possessive as object:

  > Philip wanted a bike, so I let him borrow **yours**.

- A possessive as prepositional complement:

  > This is a special policy of **theirs**, is it?
  >
  > What business is it of **hers**? (compare 535)

● A possessive is also used in comparisons after *than* and *as*:

Your car looks faster than **ours**. ('our car')

Reflexive pronouns: *Have you locked **yourself** out?*

626 Reflexive pronouns are used as objects, complements, and (often) prepositional complements where these elements have the same reference as the subject of the clause or sentence. Notice that in some cases the reflexive pronoun receives nuclear stress, and in other cases not:

We have to find **ourselves** a new home.

Have you locked **yourself** out?

Bradley works too hard. He'll burn **himself** out.

I hope Ella enjoyed **herself** at the party.

Most authors start by writing novels about **themselves**.

This is a word the aborigines use among **themselves**.

Jack certainly has a high opinion of **himself**.

Carolyn got a seat all by **herself**.

The indefinite pronoun *one* (see 680) has its own reflexive, as in

One mustn't fool **oneself**.

It's just a journey one does by **oneself**.

Reflexives are also used in imperative and non-finite constructions, where they point back to the element which is understood to be the subject of the verb:

Make **yourself** at home.

I've asked everyone to help **themselves**. [On concord here, see **96**.]

But the ordinary personal pronouns are used in many prepositional phrases denoting place:

He turned around and looked **about him**.

Have you any money **on you**?

We examined all the documents **in front of us**.

Personal or reflexive pronoun:
*someone like **you** ~ someone like **yourself***

627 The reflexive pronouns (*myself, ourselves*, etc.) are sometimes used as alternatives to the objective forms of personal pronouns (*me, us*, etc.). This happens after *as for, but for, except for, like*, and in coordinated noun phrases:

As for **me/myself**, I don't mind what you decide to do.

For someone like **me/myself**, one good meal a day is quite enough.

The picture Molly showed us was of **her/herself** and Brian on the terrace.

Emphatic use: *I'll do it* **myself.**

628 The reflexive pronouns also have an emphatic use where they follow a noun phrase or another pronoun, and reinforce its meaning:

> I spoke to the manager *himself*.
>
> The question was how Louise *herself* was to achieve this goal.
>
> If the premises *themselves* were improved, the college would be much more attractive.
>
> Ellie's getting a divorce: she *herself* told me.

We can also postpone the reflexive pronoun to the end of the sentence (*see* 428):

> She told me so *herself*.
>
> He'll be here *himself*.
>
> Without being asked, Joe fixed the lock *himself*.

Alternative constructions: *my* **own** *room* ~ *a room* **of my own**

629 After a possessive determiner, *own* can be used for reflexive or emphatic meaning: *my own, your own, his own* etc.:

> John cooks **his own** dinner. ('John cooks dinner for **himself**')
>
> We'll have to make **our own** decisions.
>
> The government is encouraging people to buy **their own** homes.

The intensifying adverb *very* can be added before *own* for added emphasis:

> Do you like the soup? The recipe is **my very own**.

The combination possessive + *own* can also occur in an *of*-phrase (*compare* 535):

> I'd love to have a house **of my own**.
>
> It's so much easier for students to work in a room **of their own**.

Phrasal and prepositional verbs

(*see CGEL* 16.3–16)

Phrasal verbs: *Go on!*

630 Verbs may form combinations with adverbial particles such as *down, in, off, on, out, up*:

> Aren't you going to **sit down**?
>
> When will they **give in**?

My interview *went off* very smoothly.

The plane has just *taken off*.

Did Ryan *catch on* to what you were saying?

We expect this project to *go on* another three years.

The doctor thinks by the end of next week you could *get out* in the air a little.

Drink up quickly.

It's a pity their marriage did *break up*, and whose fault was it?

I usually *get up* quite early and *get on* with my òwn work.

I stood there for another ten minutes but Alexandra didn't *turn ùp*.

Such verb–adverb combinations are called **phrasal verbs**, and they are usually <informal>. Most adverbs in phrasal verbs are place adverbs identical in form to prepositions (*down*, *in*, *up*, etc.; *see* 192). Verbs can also combine with prepositional adverbs which function like prepositional phrases (*see* 654):

They *walked past* (the place). [1]

She *ran across* (the street). [2]

In [1] and [2], the noun phrases are omitted by ellipsis. Like these, some phrasal verbs retain the individual meanings of the verb and the adverb (for example *sit down*). Other phrasal verbs are idiomatic: the meaning of the combination cannot be built up from the meanings of the individual verb and adverb, as in *catch on* ('understand'), *give in* ('surrender'), *turn up* ('appear, arrive').

Alternative adverb positions: *Turn on* the light! ~ *Turn* the light *on*!

631 Many phrasal verbs can take an object:

The new government was unable to *bring about* immediate expansion.

The president decided to *break off* diplomatic relations immediately.

The union *called off* the strike.

I'll *get out* my old pair of skis.

We've got to *find out* what's going on here.

Daniel couldn't *get over* the fact that Natasha died.

Robert's parents were forced to *make up* the deficit.

Georgia is *bringing up* her brother's children.

The enemy *blew up* the bridge.

With most phrasal verbs, the adverb can either come before or follow a noun object:

They *turned on* the light. ~ They *turned* the light *on*.

But when the object is a personal pronoun it always has to come before the adverb:

> They **turned** it **on**. (BUT NOT: *They **turned on** it.)

In some cases phrasal verbs with objects look identical to verbs followed by a prepositional phrase. Compare:

> They **ran** 'over the c\`at. ('knocked down and passed over')
> [phrasal verb]

> They **ran over** the bri\`dge. ('crossed the bridge by running')
> [verb + preposition]

Prepositional verbs: *Will you* **attend to** *that?*

632 A verb may also form a fixed combination with a preposition (*see* 744), for example:

> The article also **hinted at** other possibilities.
>
> Brandon has **applied for** a new job.
>
> The mayor announced that he would not **run for** re-election.
>
> Would you like to **comment on** the situation?
>
> I don't **object to** this proposal in principle.

The noun phrase following the preposition is called the **prepositional object**. Here are some other examples of prepositional verbs:

> The plan must be flexible enough to **allow for** technological breakthroughs.
>
> The new hospital is equipped to **care for** all patients.
>
> Zoe said she was not adequately trained to describe or **enlarge on** these difficult questions.
>
> What is called a plan for action **amounts to** doing nothing.
>
> At the meeting Katie told Bill not to bother about the contract – she would **attend to** that.
>
> These statements can be interpreted to **conform to** our own point of view.
>
> We must give small shops a chance to **compete with** large supermarkets.
>
> The personal pronouns are normally unstressed because they **refer to** what is prominent in the immediate context.
>
> The minister stated categorically that we should under no circumstances **resort to** the use of such weapons unless they are first used by our enemies.

Notice that prepositional verbs are commonly 'stranded' at the end of the sentence (*see* 659) when they are part of prepositional verbs:

That's exactly what I'm *hoping for*.

Jordan had a poor salary but he didn't need much to *live on*.

Phrasal and prepositional verbs compared:
call her *up* BUT *call on* her

633 Phrasal and prepositional verbs may seem very similar, for example:

Matthew *called up* his wife to tell her he'd met some old friends and could be home late. [1]

Megan went to the hospital to *call on* a friend after a serious operation. [2]

But **phrasal verbs**, such as *call up* in [1], and **prepositional verbs**, such as *call on* in [2], are different in several ways:

● The adverb in a phrasal verb [1] is usually stressed and has nuclear stress in end-position. The preposition in a prepositional verb [2] is normally unstressed. Compare:

All young men were *called up* | for military service. [1]

We'll *call on* you | as soon as we arrive. [2]

● The preposition in a prepositional verb must come before the prepositional object. Compare the phrasal verb [3] with the prepositional verb [4]:

We'll *call up* our friends. [3]

~ We'll *call* our friends *up*.

~ We'll *call* them *up*.

We'll *call on* our friends. [4]

~ We'll *call on* them. (BUT NOT: *We'll *call* our friends *on*.)

● Only the prepositional verb allows an adverb to be placed between the verb and the preposition:

They *called* early *on* their friends. (BUT NOT: *They *called* early *up* their friends.)

Unlike some languages, English allows the prepositional object to become the subject of a passive sentence (*see* 613). Compare:

Some employees *looked upon* the manager almost as a saint.

~ The manager was *looked upon* almost as a saint (by some employees).

Phrasal-prepositional verbs: *This noise is hard to put up with!*

634 In <informal> English, some verbs can combine as an idiom with both an adverb and a preposition, for example:

> What a preposterous idea! She'll never **get away with** it. ('succeed')
>
> We shouldn't **give in to** their arguments so easily. ('yield')
>
> You shouldn't **break in on** a conversation like that. ('interrupt')
>
> Alex **walked out on** the project. ('abandoned')
>
> I'm trying to **catch up on** my own work. ('bring . . . up to date')
>
> Samantha seems to **put up with** almost anything. ('tolerate')

We call these combinations **phrasal-prepositional verbs**. Like prepositional verbs, some phrasal-prepositional verbs can be turned into the passive by changing the prepositional object into the subject of the clause (*see* 618):

> They thought such tendencies would increase rather than be **done away with**. ('be abolished')

We cannot insert an adverb between the preposition and the object, but we can do so between the adverb and the preposition:

> Oddly enough Andrew **puts up** willingly **with** that manager of his.

In relative clauses, and other fronting constructions where the prepositional object is front-placed, the adverb and preposition stay after the verb. (Compare the 'stranded' preposition with prepositional verbs, *see* 659. The front-placed object and the stranded preposition are printed in **bold**.)

> Is this **something** the police are **checking up on**? ('investigating')
>
> You don't realize **what** I've had to **put up with**. ('tolerate')

Here are some more examples of phrasal-prepositional verbs in <informal> English:

> The robbers managed to **make away with** most of the bank's money. ('escape with')
>
> You should never **look down on** people in trouble. ('have a low opinion of')
>
> Now let's **get down to** some serious talk. ('give some serious attention to')
>
> Why don't you just **drop in on** the new neighbours? ('call on' <casual>)
>
> You can't just **back out of** an agreement like that!
>
> The first thing you've got to do, to be happy, is to **face up to** your problems. ('confront')
>
> What does it all **add up to**? ('amount to')
>
> Somebody's got to **stand up for** those principles! ('defend')

Plurals

(see CGEL 5.73–103)

Regular plurals: one **dog** ~ many **dogs**

635 Most nouns are count nouns: they can occur in both the singular, denoting 'one', or in the plural, denoting 'more than one' (see 58). Most count nouns have the regular -s plural, which is formed by adding an -s to the singular: one dog ~ two dogs. In some cases, spelling changes occur when -s is added (see 702). For the pronunciation of the -s ending, see 664.

In most compounds the ending is added to the last part: district attorney ~ district attorneys. So also: breakdowns, check-ups, grown-ups, stand-bys, take-offs, etc. But in a few compounds where the head noun comes first, the ending follows the first part: editors-in-chief, lookers-on (BUT: onlookers), mothers-in-law, notaries public, runners-up, passers-by. A few compounds have both the first and the last part in the plural, as in woman writer ~ women writers.

Irregular plurals

Voicing + -s plural: knife ~ knives

636 Some singular nouns which end in the voiceless /f/ or /θ/ sound (spelled -f and -th) change to the corresponding voiced sound /v/ or /ð/ in the plural before the regular /z/ ending.

- Most nouns ending in -f have the regular plural /fs/: beliefs, chefs, chiefs, cliffs, proofs, roofs, safes, etc. But some nouns ending in -f(e) have voiced plurals pronounced /-vz/ and spelled -ves:

calf ~ calves	half ~ halves
knife ~ knives	leaf ~ leaves
life ~ lives	loaf ~ loaves
shelf ~ shelves	thief ~ thieves
wife ~ wives	wolf ~ wolves

There is also voicing in plural reflexive pronouns: herself ~ themselves (see 619).

- Nouns ending in a consonant before -th have the regular plural: month /mʌnθ/ ~ months /mʌnθs/. With a vowel before the -th, the plural is also often regular, as with cloths, deaths, faiths. But there is voicing in mouth /maʊθ/ ~ mouths /maʊðz/, path ~ paths. In some cases we find both regular and voiced plurals: oath /oʊθ/ ~ oaths /oʊθs/ or /oʊðz/. Similarly: truths, wreaths.

- House /haʊs/ has voicing in the plural: /haʊzɪz/, but the spelling is regular: houses.

Change of vowel in the plural: *foot ~ feet*

637 The following nouns form the plural by a vowel change instead of an ending: *foot* /fʊt/ ~ *feet* /fiːt/ (on *six foot/feet two inches*, see 638), *tooth* /tuːθ/ ~ *teeth* /tiːθ/, *goose* /guːs/ ~ *geese* /giːs/, *man* /mæn/ ~ *men* /men/, *mouse* /maʊs/ ~ *mice* /maɪs/ (for the hand-held device used with a computer, both *mice* and the regular *mouses* occur), *woman* /ˈwʊmən/ ~ *women* /ˈwɪmɪn/; *child* /tʃaɪld/ has the plural *children* /ˈtʃɪldrən/.

No plural ending: *one sheep ~ many sheep*

638 Most animal nouns form a regular plural: *bird ~ birds, hen ~ hens, rabbit ~ rabbits*, etc. But some animal nouns can be used both with a singular and a plural meaning without change in form (called 'zero plural').

- Some animal nouns are always unchanged: *one sheep ~ many sheep, one deer ~ two deer*. Similarly: *grouse, moose, plaice, salmon*. These nouns are usually unchanged: *trout* (e.g. *a lot of fine trout*), *carp, pike*.

- The following nouns occur with both the regular and the unchanged plurals: *herring* (*several herring/herrings*), *antelope, fish, flounder*.

- *Dozen* and *foot* have no plural form in many expressions of quantity:

    He scored a **dozen** goals (BUT: He scored **dozens of** goals.)

    [A] How tall is Travis?

    [B] He's **six foot eight** (OR **six feet eight** OR **six feet eight inches**, abbreviated in writing: **6 ft. 8 in.**)

- Plural expressions like *five days* do not have a plural *-s* when they modify a noun (*see 651*): *a five-day week, a six-cylinder engine, an eight-month-old baby*.

- *Series* and *species* can be used as either singular or plural: *one series/ two series* of lectures.

Foreign plurals: *one analysis ~ several analyses*

639 Some nouns borrowed from foreign languages (including Latin and Greek) keep their foreign plurals, instead of adopting regular English plurals. Other foreign nouns can have both a regular plural and a foreign plural.

Nouns ending in -*us* (Latin). Only regular plurals occur in, for example, *bonus ~ bonuses, campus ~ campuses, circus ~ circuses*. The foreign plural *-i* pronounced /aɪ/ is used in *stimulus ~ stimuli* /ˈstɪmjʊlaɪ/, *alumnus ~ alumni, bacillus ~ bacilli*. Both plurals are used in *cactus ~ cactuses/cacti, focus*

~ focuses/foci, radius ~ radiuses/radii, terminus ~ terminuses/termini, syllabus ~ syllabuses/syllabi. Corpus, denoting a collection of texts to be used in linguistic analysis, has another Latin plural: *corpora*, besides the regular *corpuses*.

Nouns ending in -*a* (Latin): The regular plural occurs in *area ~ areas, arena ~ arenas*, etc. The foreign plural in *-ae* (pronounced /iː/) is used in *alumna ~ alumnae, alga ~ algae, larva ~ larvae*. Both plurals occur in *formula ~ formulas/formulae, antenna ~ antennas/antennae*. Foreign plurals tend to be more common in technical usage, whereas the *-s* plural is more natural in everyday language. We find *formulas* in general use, as in *the formulas of politicians, milk formulas*. But *formulae* is often used in mathematics: *algebraic formulae*. Similarly, *antennas* is found in general uses and in electronics (*directional antennas*), but *antennae* in biology. *Schema* has Greek plural: *schemata* besides the regular *schemas*.

Nouns ending in -*um* (Latin): Only the regular plural occurs in *album ~ albums, gymnasium ~ gymnasiums, museum ~ museums*, etc. Usually regular are also *forum ~ forums, stadium ~ stadiums, ultimatum ~ ultimatums*. The foreign plural in *-a* /ə/ is used in *curriculum ~ curricula, stratum ~ strata*. Both the regular and the foreign plural occur in *memorandum ~ memorandums/memoranda, symposium ~ symposiums/symposia*.

Medium always has the plural *media* in the *mass media* sense where newspapers, magazines, radio and television are considered as a group: *the national media, a media event. Media* and also *data* 'information, facts' are often used as if they were singular mass nouns:

> The media **are/is** giving a biased account of this story.
>
> **These** data **show/This** data **shows** that the hypothesis was right.

Nouns ending in -*ex* and -*ix* (Latin): The foreign plural *-ices*, pronounced /-ɪsiːz/, is used in *index ~ indices, codex ~ codices*. Both regular and foreign plurals occur in *apex ~ apexes/apices, appendix ~ appendixes/appendices, matrix ~ matrixes/matrices*.

640 **Nouns ending in -*is*** (Greek): The regular plural occurs in *metropolis ~ metropolises*. The foreign plural *-es* /-iːz/, is used in *analysis ~ analyses, axis ~ axes, basis ~ bases, crisis ~ crises, diagnosis ~ diagnoses, ellipsis ~ ellipses, hypothesis ~ hypotheses, oasis ~ oases, parenthesis ~ parentheses, synopsis ~ synopses, thesis ~ theses*.

Nouns ending in -*on* (Greek): Only regular plurals are used in *demon ~ demons, neutron ~ neutrons, proton ~ protons*. The foreign plural *-a* /ə/ is used in *criterion ~ criteria, phenomenon ~ phenomena*. Both plurals are used in *automaton ~ automatons/automata*.

Postmodifiers

(see CGEL 17.9–64)

Different types of postmodifiers

641 A noun can be modified by another word (often an adjective) placed before the noun: *the red house*. Such words are called **premodifiers**. A noun can also be modified by a following phrase or a clause, often a relative clause: *the house which is red*. Modifiers after the noun head are called **postmodifiers** (*see* 596).

We have the following types of postmodifiers [noun phrase heads are printed in SMALL CAPITALS, modifiers printed in **bold**]:

- Relative clauses (*see* separate entry 686):

  The parents wanted to meet *the* BOY *who was going out with their daughter*.

- Non-finite clauses equivalent to relative clauses (*see* 643):

  They wanted to meet *the* BOY *going out with their daughter*.

- Prepositional phrases (*see* 642, 654):

  A *nice young* WOMAN *in jeans* was watching me.

- Appositive clauses (*see* 646):

  There is no getting away from the FACT *that inflation is causing hardship*.

- Adverbs (*see* 648):

  Where is *the* WAY *out*?

- Adjectives (*see* 649):

  There's NOTHING *new* about these techniques.

- Clauses of time, place, manner and reason (*see* 647):

  In Stratford-on-Avon we visited *the* HOUSE *where Shakespeare lived*.

Two or more postmodifiers can modify the same noun:

Have you seen the HOUSE [*in Stratford-on-Avon*] [*where Shakespeare lived*]?

Prepositional phrases as postmodifier: *a week **of hard work***

642 Prepositional phrases (*see* 654) are by far the most common type of postmodifier in English. Prepositional phrases can often be expanded to relative clauses (on *of*-phrases, *see also* 106, 531):

Is this *the* ROAD **to Paris**? ('Is this the road **that leads to Paris**?').

These are *economic* ACTIONS **beyond the normal citizen's control**. ('... actions which are beyond...')

This message is scarcely *a* CAUSE **for regret**.

The government seems to have *no* CONTROL **over capital movement**.

There must be *a better* WAY **of doing it**.

Non-finite clauses as postmodifier

643 All three types of non-finite clause (*-ing* participle clauses, *-ed* participle clauses, and *to*-infinitive clauses) can function as postmodifiers similar to relative clauses. Here are some examples:

● **-ing *participle clauses:* the GIRL *sitting opposite me***

> PEOPLE **working in the IT business** are often young. ('who are working in the IT business')
>
> Do you know any of *those* PEOPLE **sitting behind us**?
>
> A MAN **wearing a grey suit** left the office.
>
> Last Friday I got *a* LETTER **saying that there was trouble afoot**.

The participle clause does not have tense (*see* 128, 392), so that it can be interpreted, according to context, as past or present. But the *-ing* participle clause need not carry the meaning of the progressive aspect (*see* 132, 740):

> All ARTICLES **belonging to the college** must be returned. ('all articles that belong...'; a progressive form *'that are belonging' could not be used here.)

644 ● **-ed *participle clauses:* the SUBJECT *discussed in the book***

> The QUESTION **debated in Parliament yesterday** was about the new tax. ('that was debated in Parliament')
>
> We have seen *the* DAMAGE *to the pine* **done by the deer**. ('that *has been done/had been done/was done* by the deer')

The participle clause (*done by the deer*) corresponds in meaning to a passive relative clause, but the participle clause contains none of the distinctions that can be made by tense and aspect.

645 ● **to-*infinitive clauses:* the best THING *to do***

> If you can't think of *a* THING **to do**, try something – anything.
>
> I've got SOMETHING **to say to you**.

The *to*-infinitive clause is often preceded by *next*, *last*, ordinal numerals or superlatives:

> The next TRAIN **to arrive** was from Chicago. ('the train which arrived next')
>
> Mr Knowles is the last PERSON **to cause trouble**. ('the person who would be the last to cause trouble')
>
> Amundsen was the first MAN **to reach the South Pole**. ('the man who reached the South Pole first')

In many infinitive clauses, the head of the noun phrase is the implied object or prepositional object of the infinitive verb:

> The best PERSON **to consult** is Wilson. ('the person that you should consult')
>
> There are plenty of TOYS **to play with**. ('toys which they can play with')

In these cases, a subject preceded by *for* may be added:

> The best PERSON **for you to consult** is Wilson.
>
> There are plenty of TOYS **for the children to play with**.

(On other infinitive clauses, such as *the time to arrive*, see 728.)

Appositive clauses as postmodifier:
*Have you heard the NEWS **that our team won**?*

646 Appositive clauses are nominal clauses which have a relation to the head similar to that between two noun phrases in apposition (*see* 470). They can be *that*-clauses (*see* 589) or *to*-infinitive clauses (*see* 593):

> We will stick to my IDEA **that the project can be finished on time**.   [1]
>
> It is reported that there has been a PLOT **to overthrow the government**.   [2]

The noun phrase can be related to a subject + *be* + complement construction:

> My idea is *that the project can be finished on time*.   [1a]
>
> The plot was *to overthrow the government*.   [2a]

The head of an appositive clause is an abstract noun such as *fact, idea, reply, answer, appeal, promise*:

> We were delighted at the NEWS **that our team had won**.
>
> We gratefully accepted John's PROMISE **to help us**.
>
> The mayor launched an APPEAL to the public **to give blood to the victims of the disaster**.

The examples of appositive clauses given so far have been restrictive (*see* 687). There are also non-restrictive appositive clauses. (On the distinction between restrictive and non-restrictive meaning, *see* 110.)

> His main ARGUMENT, **that scientific laws have no exceptions**, was considered absurd.

> His last APPEAL, **for his son to visit him**, was never delivered.

Clauses of time, place, manner, and reason

647 There are a number of postmodifying clauses which denote adverbial relations: time (*see* 151), place (170), manner (194) and reason (198).

Finite clauses introduced by a *wh*-word, such as *when, where, why*

TIME: Can you give me a TIME **when you will be free**?
PLACE: The Smiths wanted to take a vacation in a PLACE **where people could speak English**.
REASON: There's no REASON **why you should have to do a thing like that**.

Finite clauses introduced by *that* or *zero* (i.e. with *that* left out)

TIME: I'll never forget the TIME (**that**) **we've had together here**.
PLACE: That's hardly a PLACE (**that**) **one wants to go for a holiday**.
MANNER: The WAY (**that**) **you suggested to solve the problem** didn't work.
REASON: The REASON (**that**) **I'm asking** is that I need your advice.

To-infinitive clause

TIME: I'll have plenty of TIME **to deal with this problem**.
PLACE: That's probably the best PLACE **to go** (**to**) **for trout-fishing**.
MANNER: There's really no other WAY **to do it**.
REASON: I have no REASON **to believe Alex can finish his thesis this year**.

Adverbs as postmodifier: *Can you find the road* **back**?

648 Some adverbs are used as postmodifiers of nouns (*see also* 468):

> Can you find the ROAD **back**?

> The PEOPLE **outside** started to shout.

> Have you written your paper for the SEMINAR **tomorrow** ('tomorrow's seminar')?

Adjectives as postmodifier: *There's something **odd** about him.*

649 Adjectives which modify a noun usually stand before the noun: *an odd person*. But in some constructions, e.g. with a pronoun like *something, anyone* or *everyone*, they follow the noun (*see* 443):

> There was SOMETHING **odd** about his behaviour.
>
> ANYONE **keen on modern jazz** should not miss this opportunity.

Premodifiers

(*see CGEL* 17.94–120)

Different types of premodifiers

650 Modifiers which are placed after determiners (*see* 522) but **before the head** of a noun phrase are called **premodifiers**. There are different types of premodifiers [the head is printed in SMALL CAPITALS and the premodifier in **bold**]:

- **Adjectives** as premodifiers (see 440):

> We had a **pleasant** HOLIDAY this year.
>
> There are plenty of **bright** PEOPLE here.

An adjective can itself be modified by degree adverbs (*see* 459):

> We had a **very pleasant** HOLIDAY this year.
>
> There are a number of **really quite bright young** PEOPLE here.

- **-*ing* participles** as premodifiers:

> a **beginning** STUDENT, the **developing** COUNTRIES, a **continuing** COMMITMENT

- **-*ed* participles** as premodifiers:

> a **retired** TEACHER, **reduced** PRICES, **wanted** PERSONS, the **defeated** ARMY

- **Nouns** as premodifiers:

> Are the **removal** EXPENSES paid by your company?
>
> The **passenger** LINER dropped anchor in the harbour.

Compounds as premodifier: *camera-ready* copy

651 Compounds often function as premodifiers of nouns. A compound is a combination of words which function as a single adjective or noun:

We've just bought a **brand-new** CAR.

Do you have to submit **camera-ready** COPY?

That's an absolutely **first-class** IDEA!

These are all **hard-working** STUDENTS.

Is that a **new-style** CARDIGAN?

Emma has some pretty **old-fashioned** NOTIONS.

There are also modifiers which consist of more than two words, e.g. *out of date*. They are not hyphenated when they occur as complements (after the verb in a clause):

This dictionary is *out of date*.

But they are often hyphenated when they are placed as modifiers before a noun:

an **out-of-date** DICTIONARY

a **ready-to-wear** SUIT

thick **red-and-white-striped** WALLPAPER

Sequences of three, four, or even more nouns can occur in a noun phrase, e.g.:

a Copenhagen airline ticket office

These are formed either through noun premodification or through noun compounds, or through a combination of both. We can show the way in which this example is built up as follows:

airline ticket ('a ticket issued by an airline')

airline ticket office ('an office which sells *airline tickets*')

Copenhagen airline ticket office ('an *airline ticket office* in Copenhagen')

The structure of this noun phrase can be indicated by bracketing:

a [Copenhagen [[airline ticket] office]]

More than one premodifier: *the **American spring medical** conference*

652 When a noun head has two or more premodifiers, these tend to occur in a certain order. We deal with them in a right-to-left order, i.e. starting from the head (printed in SMALL CAPITALS, modifiers in **bold**). The item that comes next before the head is the type of classifying adjective which means 'consisting of', 'involving', or 'relating to':

A **medical** CONFERENCE will be held here next year.

Next closest to the head is the noun modifier:

We always attend the **spring medical** CONFERENCE.

Before the noun modifier comes the adjective derived from a proper noun:

I mean the **American spring medical** CONFERENCE.

However, most noun phrases have a simpler structure with no more than two modifiers, for example:

oriental CARPETS

Scandinavian furniture DESIGNS

653 Before these modifiers we can find a variety of other modifiers, such as colour-adjectives (*deep-red*), adjectives denoting age or size (*young, large*) and participles (*printed*):

deep-red *oriental* CARPETS

a **young** *physics* STUDENT

a **large** *lecture* HALL

printed *Scandinavian furniture* DESIGNS

the **European** *Wind Energy* ASSOCIATION

These premodifiers can themselves be preceded by other modifiers:

expensive *deep-red oriental* CARPETS

a **very, very** *young physics* STUDENT

a *large* **enough** *lecture* HALL

attractive *printed Scandinavian furniture* DESIGNS

the **Brussels-based** *European Wind Energy* ASSOCIATION

Notice the middle position of *little, old* and *young* when they are unstressed:

My grandmother lives in a 'nice *little* 'VILLAGE.

This is indeed a '**fine** *red* 'WINE.

Alexander looks like a '**serious** *young* 'MAN.

Prepositional phrases

(*see CGEL* Chapter 9)

Complements of prepositions

654 A prepositional phrase consists of a preposition (*see* 657) followed by a prepositional complement. The complement is usually a noun phrase, but can also be another element:

● Preposition + a noun phrase (*see* 595):

As usual, Ann's bright smile greeted me **at** *the breakfast table*.

- Preposition + a *wh*-clause (*see* 590):

  She came *from* what she called 'a small farm' of two hundred acres.

- Preposition + an *-ing* clause (*see* 594):

  Warren tried to shake off his fears *by* looking at the sky.

- Preposition + an adverb:

  You can see the lake *from* here.

655 There are two types of nominal clauses which cannot be the complement of a preposition: *that*-clauses (*see* 589) and *to*-infinitive clauses (*see* 593). With such clauses, the preposition is omitted:

  I was surprised *at* the news.

  I was surprised *that things changed so quickly.* (at is omitted)

  I was surprised *to hear you say that.* (at is omitted)

By contrast, a *wh*-clause can be preceded by a preposition:

  I was surprised *at* what happened next.

  I agree *with* what you say, Amy.

Sometimes, the addition of *the fact* (*see* 646) can serve to convert the *that*-clause construction into a form suitable for a prepositional complement. Compare:

  I think everybody's aware *of* these problems.

  ~ I think everybody's aware *that there are problems.*

  ~ I think everybody's aware *of* the fact that there are problems.

The functions of prepositional phrases

656 Prepositional phrases have many different grammatical functions. Here are the main functions:

- **Prepositional phrases as adverbial** (*see* 449):

  We may need you to do some work *in the evening*.

  To my surprise, the doctor phoned the next morning.

  Finally I went back *to my old job*.

- **Prepositional phrases as modifier in a noun phrase** (*see* 596):

  Chelsea felt she had no CHANCE *of promotion*.

  CONGRATULATIONS *on your article*.

  We've rented this COTTAGE *in the country* for peace and quiet.

  The NOISE *from the sitting-room* was deafening.

  The world has to reduce its OUTPUT *of greenhouse gases*.

- **Prepositional phrases as verb complement**:

> We are passionately COMMITTED *to the development of Africa*.
>
> You don't seem particularly WORRIED *about the situation*.

- **Prepositional phrases as complement of an adjective** (*see* 437):

> How can you remember when that novel came out? I'm terribly BAD *at dates*.

A prepositional phrase may occasionally function as subject, complement, etc.:

> *Before lunch* is when I do my best work.

Prepositions and prepositional adverbs

(*see CGEL* 9.65–66)

Simple prepositions

657 Prepositions are very frequent words like *at, for* and *by* that are placed before a noun phrase (*by his work*), an *-ing* clause (*by working hard*), etc. to form a prepositional phrase (*see* 654). The most common English prepositions are simple, i.e. they consist of one word. Here are the most common simple prepositions:

about	above	after
along	around	at
before	below	beside
between	by	down
for	from	in
into	of	off
on	over	past
since	till	through
to	under	until
up	with	without

In the following examples, the brackets [ ] enclose prepositional phrases:

> Do you know anything more definite [*about* her]?
>
> Temperatures hardly rose [*above* freezing] [*for* three months].
>
> When Miranda went to see Bill [*after* the accident] he was [*in* bed] [*with* a drip feed].

As Joan Bradley was walking [*up* the street] the van stopped [*beside* her] and one [*of* the men] lifted her [*into* it] and shut the door.

One prepositional phrase can be included in another:

The fire was discovered [*at* about five [*past* seven]].

A new scheme may be announced [*before* the end [*of* this month]].

[*After* walking [*up* the lane]] they made a sharp turn [*to* the right] [*past* some buildings].

It must be a nasty surprise [*for* motorists] going [*along* a moorland road] [*at* the end [*of* the night]] to suddenly find a kangaroo jumping out [*at* them].

This is one [*of* the cheapest ways [*of* reducing our output [*of* greenhouse gases]]].

Complex prepositions

658 There are also prepositions consisting of more than one word, so-called **complex prepositions**. Here are some two-word prepositions:

along with	as for	away from
because of	due to	except for
instead of	out of	outside of
preliminary to	together with	up to

There are also three-word prepositions:

as distinct from	by means of	in case of
in comparison with	in front of	in relation to
in terms of	on account of	on behalf of
on top of	with reference to	with regard to

Here are some examples of both simple and complex prepositions:

[*Because of* family circumstances] Michael was kept [*in* the hospital] [*for* a time].

Certain trades are [*in* many communities] closed areas [*of* employment], [*except for* a lucky few].

The boy said the blast knocked him [*out of* bed] and [*against* the wall].

It's [*up to* the government] to take action [*against* this ecological disaster].

Decide what the place is worth [*to* you] [*as* a home] [*in comparison with* what it would cost] to live [*in* town].

The training has not been enough [*in relation to* the need].

I grinned, feeling supremely [*on top of* things].

Stranded prepositions: *What's she looking at?*

659 Normally a preposition comes before its complement:

I came *in my brother's car*. [1]

But there are cases where this does not happen, as in this *wh*-question:

Which car did you come *in*? [1a]

In *wh*-questions, relative clauses and exclamations, the preposition can stand either at the end, as in [1a], or at the beginning, as in [1b]:

~ *In which car* did you come? [1b]

Prepositions which are deferred to the end of the sentence are called **stranded prepositions**. 'Stranding', as in [1a], is associated with <informal English, spoken or written>, whereas 'non-stranding', as in [1b], is associated with <careful public writing>, such as academic prose. Here are some examples:

● **In relative clauses** (*see* 688):

That's a job you need special training *for*. [<informal> with stranding and zero *that*]

~ This is a post *for which* one needs special training. <formal>

The means *through which* the plan may be achieved are very limited. <formal>

● **In *wh*-questions** (*see* 683, including indirect questions, *see* 259):

Who do you work *for*?

~ *For whom* do you work? <formal>

What were you referring *to*?

I asked her *which company* she worked *for*.

● **In exclamations** (*see* 528):

What a difficult situation he's *in*!

With what amazing skill this artist handles the brush! <formal>

There are some clauses where there are no alternative positions for the preposition. In nominal *wh*-clauses, passive clauses, and most infinitive clauses, the preposition must occur at the end:

● *wh*-clauses (*see* 590, 592):

What I'm convinced *of* is that the world's population will grow too fast.

● Passive clauses (*see* 618):

The old woman was cared *for* by a nurse from the hospital.

● Infinitive clauses (*see* 593):

> *Our new manager* is an easy man to work **with**.

Prepositional adverbs: *A police car just went* **past**.

660 A prepositional adverb is an adverb which behaves like a preposition with the complement omitted (*see* 185, 192):

> I walked **past the entrance**.   [**past** = preposition]
>
> I got a quick look at their faces   [**past** = prepositional adverb]
> as we went **past**.

Prepositions consisting of one syllable are normally unstressed, but prepositional adverbs are stressed. Compare:

> She stayed **in the house** all dày. ~ She stayed ìn.

Pronouns

(*see* CGEL 6.1–13)

661 Pronouns are words like *I, you, me, this, those, everybody, nobody, each other, who, which*. A pronoun can function as a whole noun phrase, for example in being subject or object of a clause: *I love you*. Many of them act as substitutes (*see* 375) or 'replacements' for noun phrases in the context. A singular noun phrase is replaced by a singular pronoun and a plural noun phrase is replaced by a plural pronoun:

> [A]: **What sort of car** is **this**?   [B]: **It**'s called a hatchback.
>
> [A]: **What cars** are **those**?   [B]: **They**'re called hatchbacks.

Since a pronoun functions as a whole noun phrase, it does not normally have any determiners or modifiers. But many words can function both as determiners (which require a head) and as pronouns (which do not require a head).

> **Which** bike is yours?   [**Which** is a determiner]
>
> **Which** is yours?   [**Which** is a pronoun]
>
> **This** bike is mine.   [**This** is a determiner]
>
> **This** is my bike.   [**This** is a pronoun]

Some items, e.g. *she, herself, they, one another, each other*, cannot be determiners but are pronouns only:

> **She** had to support **herself** while attending college.
>
> At first **they** didn't recognize **one another**.
>
> The members of the family were separated from **each other** for several months.

662 Pronouns are treated under different headings in this part of the grammar:

> Demonstratives: *this, that, these, those* in 521.
>
> Interrogatives: *who, which, what, where,* etc. in 536–41.
>
> Negatives: *none, nobody, no one, nothing,* etc. in 581–7 (negation) and 675–80 (quantifiers).
>
> Personal and reflexive pronouns: *I, my, mine, myself,* etc. in 619–29.
>
> Reciprocal pronouns: *each other* and *one another* in 685.
>
> Relative clauses: *who, whom, whose, which, that* in 686–94.
>
> Quantifiers: *some, any, someone, everything, anybody, each, all, both, either, much, many, more, most, enough, several, little, a little, few, a few, less, least,* etc. in 675–80.

Pronunciation of endings

(*see CGEL* 3.3–10, 5.80, 5–113, 7.80)

The five endings of English

663 English has very few grammatical endings (inflections). The only five endings regularly used are *-s, -ed, -ing, -er, -est.* But some of them are used for more than one word-class. Here we deal with rules for the pronunciation of grammatical endings, whether they are added to nouns, verbs, or adjectives.

The *-s* ending: *She works hard.*

664 The *-s* ending has three different grammatical functions:

- **plural of nouns:** *Amy stayed for two **weeks**.* (*see* 635)
- **genitive of nouns:** *It was a **week's** work.* (*see* 530)
- **3rd person singular present tense of verbs:** *She **works** hard.* (*see* 574)

However, the rules for pronouncing the ending are the same in all functions:

Function	Pronunciation		
	/ɪz/-ending	/z/-ending	/s/-ending
Plural of nouns	horse ~ horses	dog ~ dogs	cat ~ cats
Genitive of nouns	George ~ George's	Jane ~ Jane's	Ruth ~ Ruth's
3rd person singular of verbs	catch ~ catches	call ~ calls	hit ~ hits

- The pronunciation is /ɪz/ after bases ending in voiced or voiceless sibilants: /z/, /s/, /dʒ/, /tʃ/, /ʒ/, /ʃ/. Examples of plurals, genitives and 3rd person singular present tense:

/tʃ/: *church ~ churches*	/s/: *prince ~ prince's*
/dʒ/: *Reg ~ Reg's*	/ʒ/: *barrage ~ barrages*
/z/: *praise ~ praises*	/ʃ/: *wash ~ washes*

- The pronunciation is /z/ after bases ending in a vowel and voiced consonants other than /z/, /dʒ/, /ʒ/:

  boy ~ boys /bɒɪ/ ~ / bɒɪz/   *pig ~ pig's*   *read ~ reads*

- The pronunciation is /s/ after bases ending in voiceless sounds other than /s/, /tʃ/, /ʃ/:

  month ~ months /mʌnθ/ ~ / mʌnθs/   *week ~ week's*   *tick ~ ticks*

Note the irregular pronunciations of the verbs *do* and *say* in the 3rd person singular present tense:

do ~ does /duː/ ~ /dʌz/ (stressed), /dəz/ (unstressed)

say ~ says /seɪ/ ~ /sez/

The *-ed* ending (see 574): *She worked hard.*

665 The *-ed* ending of regular verbs has three spoken forms:

- /ɪd/ after bases ending in /d/ and /t/:

pad ~ padded	/pæd/ ~ /ˈpædɪd/
pat ~ patted	/pæt/ ~ /ˈpætɪd/

- /d/ after bases ending in vowels and voiced consonants other than /d/:

mow ~ mowed	/moʊ/ ~ /moʊd/
praise ~ praised	/preɪz/ ~ /preɪzd/

- /t/ after bases ending in voiceless sounds other than /t/:

press ~ pressed	/pres/ ~ /prest/
pack ~ packed	/pæk/ ~ /pækt/

The *-er, -est* and *-ing* endings

666 Normally the endings *-er, -est, -ing*, pronounced /ə(r)/, /ɪst/, and /ɪŋ/, are simply added to the base (*see* 501). But note these special changes of pronunciation:

- Syllabic *l* is no longer syllabic before *-er* and *-est*:

  simple /'sɪmpl/ ~ *simpler* /'sɪmplə(r)/ ~ *simplest* /'sɪmplɪst/

- Three adjectives ending in /ŋ/ change /ŋ/ to /ŋg/ before *-er* and *-est*:

  long /lɒŋ/ ~ *longer* /'lɒŋgə(r)/ ~ *longest* /'lɒŋgɪst/

Also in: *strong* ~ *stronger* ~ *strongest, young* ~ *younger* ~ *youngest*.

But no change in *sing* /sɪŋ/ ~ *singing* /'sɪŋɪŋ/.

- Whether or not speakers pronounce final *r* in words like *pour* and *poor*, the *r* is always pronounced before *-ing, -er* and *-est*:

  The rain is *pouring* /'pɔːrɪŋ/ down.
  It would be *fairer* /'feərə(r)/ to take a vote.

Proper nouns and names

(*see CGEL* 5.60–72)

The unique reference of proper nouns

667 Proper nouns have **unique reference**, and usually have no article in English (*see* 92). The following list gives examples of article usage with some classes of proper nouns.

Proper nouns without an article: *Professor Dale*

668 *Personal names* (with or without titles) have no article:

> *Miranda, Paul, Helen Lee, Shakespeare, Mr and Mrs Johnson, Lady Macbeth,*
> *Dr Clark, Judge Powell* <mainly AmE>, *Professor Dale*

Contrast names with 'unique' descriptions, for which *the* is needed:

> *President Roosevelt* (BUT: *the President of the United States*)
> *Lord Nelson* (BUT: *the Lord* = 'God'; see 83)

Family terms with unique reference often behave like proper nouns:

> Hello *Mother/Mummy/Mum/Ma*! (The last three terms are <familiar>.)
> *Father/Daddy/Dad* will soon be home. (The last two terms are <familiar>.)

669 *Calendar items* have no article.

- Names of festivals and public holidays: *New Year's Day, Independence Day, Anzak Day, Canada Day*

- Names of the months and the days of the week: *January, February, Monday*

- Names of seasons may have the article omitted <esp. BrE>: I last saw her *in (the) spring*. BUT: *in the spring of 1999* (see 83).

670 *Geographical names* usually have no article.

- Names of continents: (*North*) *America*, (*mediaeval*) *Europe*, (*Central*) *Australia*, (*East*) *Africa*

- Names of countries, counties, and states: (*modern*) *Brazil*, (*Elizabethan*) *England*, (*eastern*) *Kent*, (*northern*) *Florida*

- Cities and towns: (*downtown*) *Washington*, (*suburban*) *Long Island*, (*ancient*) *Rome*, (*central*) *Tokyo*. BUT: *The Hague, the Bronx; the City, the West End, the East End* (*of London*)

- Lakes: *Lake Michigan, Lake Ladoga,* (*Lake*) *Windermere, Loch Ness*

- Mountains: *Mount Everest, Vesuvius,* (*Mount*) *Kilimanjaro*. BUT: *The Matterhorn*

- In combinations of name and common noun denoting buildings, streets, bridges, etc., the second noun usually has the main stress: *Hampstead 'Heath*. But names ending in *Street* have the main stress on the first noun: *'Oxford Street*.

Madison 'Avenue	Westminster 'Bridge
Park 'Lane	Leicester 'Square
Russell 'Drive	Greenwich 'Village
Reynolds 'Close	Kennedy 'Airport
Portland 'Place	Harvard Uni'versity

BUT: *the Albert 'Hall, the Haymarket* (a street name in London), *the George Washington Memorial Parkway, the Massachusetts Turnpike, the University of London*

Proper nouns with the definite article: *the Wilsons*

671 **Plural names** take the definite article: *The Netherlands* (BUT: *Holland*), *the West Indies, the Bahamas, the Alps, the Canaries, the Channel Islands, the Hebrides, the British Isles, the Himalayas, the Midlands, the Pyrenees, the Rockies, the Wilsons* ('the Wilson family')

672 *Some geographical names* take the definite article.

Rivers: *the Amazon, the (River) Avon, the Danube, the Ganges, the Mississippi, the Nile, the Rhone, the Thames*

Seas: *the Atlantic (Ocean), the Baltic (Sea), the Mediterranean, the Pacific*

Canals: *the Panama Canal, the Erie Canal, the Suez Canal*

673 Some *institutions* and other facilities take the definite article.

Hotels, pubs and restaurants: *the Grand (Hotel), the Hilton, the Old Bull and Bush*, etc.

Theatres, cinemas, etc.: *the Apollo Theatre, the Globe, the Odeon, the Hollywood Bowl*. BUT: *Drury Lane* (theatre), *Covent Garden* (opera house)

Museums, libraries: *the Huntingdon (Library), the British Museum, the National Gallery, the Smithsonian Institution, the Uffizi*

674 *Newspapers* usually take the definite article: *The Daily Express, The Independent, The New York Times, The Observer*. The article is dropped after genitives: *today's Times*. Magazines and periodicals normally have no article: *English Today, Language, Nature, Newsweek, New Scientist, Scientific American, Time*.

Quantifiers

(see CGEL 5.10–25, 6.45–62)

The grammatical functions of quantifiers

675 Quantifiers are words such as *all, any, some, nobody*, which denote quantity or amount (*see* 70). They can function both as determiners (*some people*) and pronouns (*some of the people*).

- Words like *some, no* and *any* can function as determiners (i.e. **Group 2 determiners**, *see* 523): *some friends*.

- Words like *all* can function as determiners and can precede *the, this*, etc. in the noun phrase (i.e. **Group 1 determiners**, *see* 524): *all the time*.

- Words like *few* can function as determiners and can follow *the, these*, etc. (i.e. **Group 3 determiners**, *see* 525): *the few facts*.

Determiners: *fewer* jobs, *less* income

676 The table opposite shows five groups of quantifiers (A–E) and their grammatical functions as determiner or pronoun (alone or with an *of*-phrase).

(N = noun)	Count				Mass	
	Singular		Plural		Singular	
	Determiner function	Pronoun function	Determiner function	Pronoun function	Determiner function	Pronoun function
Group A: Words with inclusive meaning (see 80)	all N	all (of N)	all N	all (of N)	all N	all (of N)
	every N	every one (of N)				
	each N	each (of N)				
			both N	both (of N)		
	half N	half (of N)	half N	half (of N)	half N	half (of N)
Group B: *Some-* and *any*-words (see 697)	some N	some (of N)	some N	some (of N)	some N	some (of N)
	any N	any (of N)	any N	any (of N)	any N	any (of N)
	either N	either (of N)				
Group C: Words denoting degrees of quantity and amount (see 70)			many N	many (of N)	much N	much (of N)
			more N	more (of N)	more N	more (of N)
			most N	most (of N)	most N	most (of N)
			enough	enough (of N)	enough N	enough (of N)
			few N	few (of N)	little N	little (of N)
			a few N	a few (of N)	a little N	a little (of N)
			fewer N	fewer (of N)	less N	less (of N)
			less N	less (of N)	less N	less (of N)
			fewest N	fewest (of N)	least N	least (of N)
			several N	several (of N)		
Group D: Unitary	one N	one (of N)				
Group E: Negative words	no N	none (of N)	no N	none (of N)	no N	none (of N)
	neither N	neither (of N)				

677 ●

Group A determiners (*see* 75). In the following examples, Group A determiners are printed in **bold**, and noun phrase heads in SMALL CAPITALS:

All the WORLD will watch the World Cup on TV. (BUT: *the whole world* is more usual than *all the world*.)

Every STUDENT must attend ten of the meetings *each* YEAR.

Both ANSWERS are acceptable.

All, *both* and *each* can also occur after their heads. If the head is subject, they have the mid-position of adverbs (*see* 451):

All his FRIENDS were on vacation.	~ *His friends* were *all* on vacation.
Both of THEM love dancing.	~ *They both* love dancing.
Each of the ROOMS have a telephone.	~ *The rooms each* have a telephone.

● *Group B determiners* (*see* 697). *Some* and *any* can be used as determiners with singular count nouns when they are stressed (on unstressed *some*, *see* 523):

There was ʹ*some* ʹBOOK or other on this topic published last year.

I didn't have ʹ*any* ʹIDEA they wanted me to make a speech.

In <familiar> style, stressed *some* means '*a wonderful*' etc.:

That's ʹ*some* ʹCAR you've got there!

However, *some* and *any* are usually used with plural nouns and mass nouns:

It's unfair to mention *some* PEOPLE without mentioning all.

His resignation has been expected for *some* TIME.

● *Group C determiners* (*see* 80):

The company lost *many* MILLIONS *of dollars*.

It's been spending too *much* MONEY on speculation.

The chairman asked for *more* INFORMATION.

The student was *a few* MINUTES late for the interview.

There are far *fewer* FACTORIES going to come to our part of the country.

It has been said that good writing is the art of conveying meaning with the greatest possible force in *the fewest possible* WORDS.

Why is it that some people pay *less* INCOME TAX than any of us?

Enough can occur both before and after its head:

There hasn't been *enough* TIME to institute reforms.

There hasn't been TIME *enough* to institute reforms.

- *The group D determiner* one:

One is used as an indefinite determiner in such expressions as *one day, one morning, one night*:

> **One** DAY Katie will change her mind. ('at an indefinite time')

One is also a numeral (*see* 602): *One ticket, please* and a pronoun (*see* 680): *How does one deal with such problems?*

- *Group E determiners*:

> They had **no** KNOWLEDGE of secret negotiations.
>
> There were **no** CONDITIONS laid down in the contract.

Pronouns with an of-construction: *all of* the time

678 ● As the table in 676 shows, most of the quantifiers can also be followed by an *of*-phrase, e.g. *all the people ~ all of the people*:

> You can fool **all the** PEOPLE **some of the** TIME, and **some of the** PEOPLE **all the** TIME, but you cannot fool **all the** PEOPLE **all of the** TIME. (Abraham Lincoln in a speech made in 1858)
>
> You see so **much of this** STUFF in the newspapers nowadays.

Both of is normally followed by a pronoun or a definite noun phrase:

> Do sit down, **both of** YOU.
>
> People seem to have money to spend on entertainment and food, **both of** WHICH are expensive.
>
> **Both of those** STORIES originated in newspaper reports.

- The *of*-phrase may be omitted if the quantifier acts as a substitute for an earlier noun phrase (*see* 379):

> [A] I don't know **which book** to buy. [B] Why don't you buy **both**?
>
> [A] Would any of you like **some** [B] Yes, I'd love **some**.
>   **more soup**?
>
> **Many of them** are competent people, but **a few** are not.
>
> I've got **most of the data** now for my conference paper, but **some** is still missing.

- *Every* and *no* cannot act as pronouns. Instead we use *every one* and *none*:

> [A] Did you say you pay **no** INTEREST on this loan? [B] Yes, **none** at all.
>
> **None of the new** LAPTOPS have been sold.

(On verb concord after *none of*, *see* 513. The corresponding determiner construction would be: *No laptop has/No laptops have been sold.*)

Pronouns ending in -body, -one, -thing

679 The following quantifier pronouns are singular and have either personal or non-personal reference:

	Personal reference	Non-personal reference
GROUP A	everybody, everyone somebody, someone	everything something
GROUP B GROUP E	anybody, anyone nobody, no one	anything nothing

There are two sets of pronouns with personal reference: one set ending in *-body* (*everybody, somebody, anybody, nobody*) and another set ending in *-one* (*everyone, someone, anyone, no one*). Both sets with personal reference have a genitive form: *everybody's, everyone's,* etc. There is no difference of meaning between the two sets. Here are some examples:

> *Everybody* says Dr Barry is an unusual woman.
>
> *Everybody* made *their* contribution to the good cause. (On concord here, *see* 513.)
>
> We chatted about the news, and so did *everyone* else in the department.
>
> I first heard this thing mentioned by *somebody* else.
>
> *Someone* must have seen what happened.
>
> Are you writing this paper in collaboration with *someone*?
> (on *some*-forms in questions, *see* 243)
>
> If *anybody* rings I'll say you're too busy to come to the phone.
>
> We wouldn't be on speaking terms with *anyone* if we made this proposal.
>
> Is there *anyone* we can give a lift?
>
> Money isn't *everything*.
>
> Give me *something* to do that's in line with what I like doing.

One: *Are there any good ones?*

680 *One* is a numeral (*see* 602) and a pronoun. The pronoun *one* has three uses:

- The pronoun *one* can follow certain other quantifiers and can be followed by *of* (*see* 678):

> What is happening in this country now concerns *every one of us*. (with *every* and *one* written as separate words)
>
> There are many ways of making an omelette, *only one of* WHICH is right.

With *each* and *any, one* is optional:

> The doctors came to **each** (**one**) in turn and asked how the patients felt.

- As a pronoun, *one* (with the plural form *ones*) may substitute for an indefinite noun (*see* 380):

> I want A MAP of Tokyo – but **a really good one**.

> We haven't got A TEXTBOOK of our own. We use **English and American ones**.

- As an indefinite personal pronoun, *one* means 'people in general' (*see* 98). In this use *one* has a genitive form *one's* and a reflexive form *oneself*:

> I've always believed in having the evenings free for doing **one's hobbies**.

> This is just a journey **one** does by **oneself**.

Questions

(*see CGEL* 11.4–23)

Different types of questions

681 There are direct and indirect questions:

> 'How did you get on at your interview?', Sarah asked.   [direct question]

> Sarah asked me **how I got on at my interview**.   [indirect question]

Indirect questions are always signalled by an interrogative word such as *how* or *what*. But direct questions need not contain an interrogative word (on interrogative words, *see* 536; on indirect questions, *see* 259).

We also distinguish between *yes–no* questions, *wh*-questions and tag questions (*see* 241).

Yes–No questions: *Did you find the file?*

682 The answer to a *yes–no* question is *yes* or *no*, which explains its name. To make a statement into a *yes–no* question, put the operator (*will, is,* etc.) before the subject (the operator is printed in SMALL CAPITALS):

> Jane WILL be in the office later today.

> ~ WILL Jane be in the office later today?

Yes–no questions usually have **rising intonation** (*see* 40):

> WILL you be around at lúnch time?

> Is Bill márried?

> HAVE you replíed to the letter?

> DOES Joan still live in Austrália?

The last example has the 'dummy operator' *does* (*see* 611). A form of *do* has to be used here because there is no operator in the corresponding statement:

~ Joan still lives in Australia.

Wh-questions: *How are you feeling today?*

683 *Wh*-questions begin with an interrogative word: *who, what, when*, etc. (*see* 536) and normally have **falling intonation**. Starting from a statement, this is how to form *wh*-questions: Put the sentence element which contains the *wh*-word at the beginning of the sentence. If the element containing the *wh*-word is object, complement or adverbial, place the operator (i.e. the first auxiliary in a verb phrase or the finite verb *be*) in front of the subject.

● *Wh*-element is object:

They bought a Volvo.	~ **Which car** DID they bu̱y?
John asked a question.	~ **What question** DID John ask?

The operator normally comes just after the *wh*-element. In these examples the *do*-construction has to be used, because the corresponding statements have no operator.

● *Wh*-element is complement:

The subject of the lecture is lexicology.

~ **What**'s the su̱bject of the lecture?

● *Wh*-element is adverbial:

They'll leave tomorrow. ~ **When** WILL they le̱ave?

● *Wh*-element is subject. If the element containing the *wh*-word is the subject, the verb phrase remains the same as in the corresponding statement, and no inversion or *do*-construction is necessary (*see* 611):

Jane said she might be late. ~ **Who** said tha̱t?

Who's ca̱lling?

What made you decide to take an MBA̱?

See 659 on cases where the *wh*-element is a prepositional complement:

What's she li̱ke?

Tag questions: *Anna's a doctor, **isn't she**?*

684 Tag questions are tagged on to the end of a statement (*see further* 245):

Anna's a doctor, **isn't she**?	[1]
Anna isn't a doctor, **is she**?	[2]

Tag questions are shortened *yes–no* questions and consist of operator plus pronoun, with a negative (*isn't she* in [1]) or without a negative (*is she* in [2]). The choice of operator depends on the preceding verb phrase. The pronoun repeats or refers back to the subject of the statement. Usually the tag question is in a separate tone unit:

| Tom is yòunger than you | ísn't he? |

| She had a rèst | dídn't she? |

| That would be dìfficult | wóuldn't it? |

| You are staying hère | áre you? |

Reciprocal pronouns

(*see CGEL* 6.31)

685 We can bring together two sentences such as *Ann likes Bob* and *Bob likes Ann* into a reciprocal structure:

EITHER: Ann and Bob like *each other*.

OR: Ann and Bob like *one another*.

Each other and *one another* are both reciprocal pronouns:

We looked at *each other*. ~ We looked at *one another*.

Each other is the more frequent alternative, but when more than two people or things are involved, *one another* is often preferred:

Their children are all quite different from *each other*.

People have to learn to trust *one another*.

The reciprocal pronouns can be used in the genitive:

They exchange favours – they literally scratch *each other's* backs.

They are two people who have chosen to share *one another's* lives in an intimate and committed relation.

Relative clauses

(*see CGEL* 6.32–35, 17.10–25)

The grammatical function of relative clauses

686 The main function of a relative clause is to modify a noun phrase (*see* 595):

They read every BOOK *that they could borrow in the village*.

Here the relative clause is *that they could borrow in the village*. The relative pronoun *that* points back to the head of the noun phrase (*book*), which is called the **antecedent** (printed in SMALL CAPITALS).

The term **relative clause** is used for various types of subclauses which are linked to the main clause. The linking is achieved with a back-pointing element (*see* 84), usually a relative pronoun (but *see* 592 on nominal relative clauses). The relative pronouns are *who, whom, whose, which, that*, and zero (a 'zero pronoun' is not expressed). Although a zero pronoun is not pronounced, it still 'exists' in that it fills a grammatical position in the clause. These two sentences are alternatives:

> The RECORDS *which he owns* are mostly classical.
> [The relative pronoun *which* functions as object of *owns*]

> ~ The RECORDS *he owns* are mostly classical.
> [The zero relative pronoun functions as object of *owns*]

The choice of relative pronouns

687 There are several relative pronouns to choose from. The choice depends on different factors.

- The choice of relative pronoun depends on whether the clause is **restrictive** or **non-restrictive** (*see* 110).

Restrictive relative clause:

> | My sister *who lives in Nagóya* | will be thìrty next year. | [i.e. I have two or more sisters]

Non-restrictive relative clause:

> | My síster | *who lives in Nagóya* | will be thìrty next year. | [i.e. I have only one sister]

- The choice of relative pronoun also depends on whether the head of the noun phrase (i.e. the antecedent) is **personal** or **non-personal**.

Personal antecedent:

> This is the message we want to communicate to the MEN AND WOMEN *who will soon be going to help the hunger-stricken areas*.

Non-personal antecedent:

> We need to find a HOUSE *which is big enough for our family*.

- The choice of relative pronoun also depends on what role the pronoun has in the relative clause: whether it is **subject**, **object**, etc. This determines the choice between *who* and *whom*.

Relative pronoun as subject:

> Have you met the MAN *who is going to marry Diana*? [1]

Relative pronoun as object (note that the object, when it is a relative pronoun, is fronted, i.e. is placed before the subject, not after the verb):

> Have you met the MAN *whom Diana is going to marry*? <formal> [2]

Instead of the <rather formal> *whom* in [2], we can also have *who* [2a] or, more common, zero (i.e. *who* omitted), as in [2b]:

> Have you met the MAN *who Diana is going to marry*?
> <less formal, rare> [2a]

> Have you met the MAN *Diana is going to marry*? <informal> [2b]

Relative pronouns as prepositional complement

688 There is an even greater choice of constructions when the relative pronoun acts as prepositional complement (*see* 659):

> Do you know the MAN *Diana is engaged to*? <informal>

> ~ Do you know the MAN *who Diana is engaged to*? <less formal, rare>

> ~ Do you know the MAN *whom Diana is engaged to*? <formal, rare>

> ~ Do you know the MAN *to whom Diana is engaged*? <very formal>

Once again, the relative pronoun is fronted, and the preposition may or may not precede. However, the construction preposition + relative pronoun may be the only one available, as in

> Maurice wrote me a LETTER *in which he said*: 'I'm not interested in how long a bee can live.'

In other cases, the construction with the end-placed, 'stranded' preposition (*see* 659) may be the only one available:

> The PLAN *they've come up with* is an absolute winner.

The uses of relative pronouns

689 The uses of relative pronouns are given in this table:

	Restrictive and non-restrictive		Restrictive only
	personal	non-personal	personal and non-personal
subjective	who	which	that
objective	who(m)		that, zero
genitive	whose	of which, whose	

We will now discuss the use of three forms of relative pronouns: *wh*-pronouns, *that*, and zero.

Wh-relative pronouns

690 The **wh-relative pronouns** are *who, whom, whose* and *which*. They reflect the personal/non-personal gender of the antecedent (printed in SMALL CAPITALS):

- **who, whom** *for personal*:

    There's a MAN outside *who wants to see you.*

- **which** *for non-personal*:

    I want a WATCH *which is absolutely waterproof.*

But this distinction does not exist with ***whose***. If a pronoun is in a genitive relation to a noun head, the pronoun can have the form *whose* for both personal and non-personal antecedents:

My FRIEND *whose car we borrowed* is Danish.

They came to an old BUILDING *whose walls were made of rocks.*

In the examples where the antecedent is non-personal (such as CARS, BUILDING), there is some tendency to avoid the use of *whose* by using the *of*-phrase, but this construction can be awkward and <formal>:

~ They came to an old BUILDING *the walls of which were made of rocks.* <formal>

That and zero as relative pronouns

691 *That* is used with both personal and non-personal reference. However, it cannot follow a preposition, and is not usually used in non-restrictive relative clauses. The zero relative pronoun (i.e. with no pronoun expressed) is used like *that*, but it cannot be the subject of a clause.

- *That* as subject cannot be left out:

    The POLICE OFFICER *that caught the thief* received a commendation for bravery.

- But *that* as object or prepositional complement can be left out:

    The MAN (*that*) *he caught* received a jail sentence.

    This is the kind of PROBLEM (*that*) *I can live with.*

Restrictive relative clauses

692 All the relative pronouns can be used in restrictive relative clauses, particularly *that* and the zero relative, but also *who* (*whom, whose*) and *which*.

We can now complete the picture of the possible choices among all the relative pronouns in restrictive clauses by six sets of examples.

- Relative pronoun as subject and with personal antecedent:

    He is the sort of PERSON *who* always answers letters.

    ~ He is the sort of PERSON *that* always answers letters.

- Relative pronoun as subject and with non-personal antecedent:

    This author uses lots of WORDS *which* are new to me.

    ~ This author uses lots of WORDS *that* are new to me.

- Relative pronoun as object and with personal antecedent:

    Our professor keeps lecturing on AUTHORS *who* nobody's ever read.

    ~ Our professor keeps lecturing on AUTHORS *that* nobody's ever read.

    ~ Our professor keeps lecturing on AUTHORS nobody's ever read.

    ~ Our professor keeps lecturing on AUTHORS *whom* nobody's ever read. <formal>

- Relative pronoun as object and with non-personal antecedent:

    I need to talk to you about the E-MAIL *which* you sent me.

    ~ I need to talk to you about the E-MAIL *that* you sent me.

    ~ I need to talk to you about the E-MAIL you sent me.

- Relative pronoun as prepositional complement and with personal antecedent:

    I know most of the BUSINESSMEN *that* I'm dealing *with*.

    ~ I know most of the BUSINESSMEN I'm dealing *with*.

    ~ I know most of the BUSINESSMEN *with whom* I am dealing. <formal>

    ~ I know most of the BUSINESSMEN *whom* I am dealing *with*. <formal, rare>

    ~ I know most of the BUSINESSMEN *who* I am dealing *with*. <rare>

- Relative pronoun as prepositional complement and with non-personal antecedent:

    Is that the ORGANIZATION *which* she referred *to*?

    ~ Is that the ORGANIZATION *that* she referred *to*?

    ~ Is that the ORGANIZATION she referred *to*?

    ~ Is that the ORGANIZATION *to which* she referred? <formal>

Non-restrictive relative clauses

693 Only *wh*-pronouns are usually used in non-restrictive clauses. The meaning of a non-restrictive relative clause is often very similar to the meaning of a coordinated clause (with or without conjunction), as we indicate by paraphrases of the examples (on intonation and punctuation here, *see* 111):

> Then I met a GIRL, *who* invited me to a party.
>
> ~ Then I met a girl, and she invited me to a party.
>
> Here is JOHN SMITH, *who* I mentioned to you the other day.
>
> ~ Here is John Smith: I mentioned him to you the other day.

In non-restrictive clauses *which* is sometimes followed by a noun, and therefore functions as a relative determiner instead of a relative pronoun:

> The fire brigade is all too often delayed by traffic congestion, and arrives on the scene more than an hour late, by *which* TIME there is little chance of saving the building.

Sentence relative clauses

694 The sentence relative clause is a special type of non-restrictive clause. It does not point back to a noun but to a whole clause or sentence. The relative pronoun in sentence relative clauses, which have the function of sentence adverbial (*see* 461), is *which*:

> THE COUNTRY IS ALMOST BANKRUPT, *which is not surprising*. ('and this is not surprising')
>
> WE'VE GOT FRIDAY AFTERNOONS OFF, *which is very good*. ('and that is very good')

Sentences

(see CGEL 10.1, 11.1–2, 13.3)

Clauses and sentences

695 Sentences are units made up of one or more clauses (*see* 486). Sentences containing just one clause are called **simple**, and sentences containing more than one clause are called **complex**. Here are two simple sentences:

> Sue heard an explosion.
>
> She phoned the police.

● They may be joined into a complex sentence by **coordination** (*see* 515), i.e. combining the two clauses by *and*:

> Sue heard an explosion and (she) phoned the police.

● The two simple sentences can also be joined into a complex sentence by **subordination** (*see* 709), i.e. making one clause into a **main clause** and the other into a **subclause**:

> When Sue heard an explosion, she phoned the police.

Four kinds of sentence

696 A simple English sentence, i.e. a sentence consisting of only one clause, may be a statement, a question, a command, or an exclamation.

Statements are sentences in which the subject generally comes before the verb (but *see* fronted topic, 411):

> I'll speak to the manager today.

Questions (*see* 681) are sentences which differ from statements in one or more ways:

- The operator is placed immediately before the subject:

  > *Will* you see him now?

- The sentence begins with an interrogative word (*see* 536):

  > *Who* do you want to speak to?

- The sentence has subject + verb order but with rising intonation in \<spoken\> English (*see* 40, 244) and ending with a question mark in \<written\> English:

  > You'll speak to the mánager today?

Commands (*see* 497) are sentences with the verb in the imperative, i.e. the base form of the verb (*see* 573). In \<written\> English, command sentences do not normally end with an exclamation mark, but with a full stop (period):

> Call him now.

Commands usually have no expressed subject but sometimes take the subject *you* (*see* 497):

> (You) speak to the manager today.

Exclamations (*see* 528) are sentences which begin with *what* or *how*, without inversion of subject and operator. In \<written\> English, exclamations usually end with an exclamation mark (!):

> *What* a noise they are making in that band!

Communication in complete sentences is typical of \<formal\> or \<written\> language. In \<speech\> and \<informal writing\> it is common to use less fully structured units with the verb and other parts are omitted (*see* 254, 299): *What a noise!, Careful!, More coffee anyone?*

Some-words and any-words

(*see CGEL* 6.59–62, 10.60–63)

697 *Some* and *any* can function both as determiners (*see* 522) and pronouns (*see* 661). In both functions the choice between *some* and *any* depends on the grammatical context: *some* is the normal word in positive statements, and *any* is the normal word after negatives and in *yes–no* questions:

Ann has bought **some** new records.	[positive statement]
Ann hasn't bought **any** new records.	[after a negative]
Has Ann bought **any** new records?	[**yes–no** question]

There are a number of other items which behave like *some* and *any* in this respect. Therefore we need to distinguish two classes of words, which we call *some*-words and *any*-words:

- **Some-words** are: *some, someone, somebody, something, somewhere, sometime, sometimes, already, somewhat, somehow, too* (adverb of addition)

- **Any-words** are: *any, anyone, anybody, anything, anywhere, ever, yet, at all, either*

698 The following table illustrates the contrasts between matching *some-* and *any*-words.

Some-words	*Any-words*	
Positive statements	After negatives	Questions
DETERMINER They've had *some* lunch.	They haven't had *any* lunch.	Have they had *any* lunch?
PRONOUN He was rude to *somebody*.	He wasn't rude to *anybody*.	Was he rude to *anybody*?
PLACE ADVERB They've seen her *somewhere*.	They haven't seen her *anywhere*.	Have they seen her *anywhere*?
TIME-WHEN ADVERB I'll see you again *sometime*.	I won't *ever* see you again.	Will I *ever* see you again?
FREQUENCY ADVERB He *sometimes* visits her.	He doesn't *ever* visit her.	Does he *ever* visit her?
DEGREE ADVERB She was *somewhat* annoyed.	She wasn't *at all* annoyed.	Was she *at all* annoyed?

There are similar contrasts between between *already* and *yet*, between *still* and *any more* or *any longer*, and between *somehow* and *in any way*:

The guests have arrived **already**.

~ The guests haven't arrived **yet**. ~ Haven't the guests arrived **yet**?

She's *still* at school.

~ She isn't at school *any longer*. ~ She is *no longer* at school.

In negative clauses, *any*-words follow *not* and its shortened form *n't*, and also other negative words such as *nobody, no, scarcely,* etc. (*see* 585):

Nobody has **ever** given her **any** encouragement.

When *any*-words are stressed and have inclusive meaning (*see* 77) they can occur also in positive statements:

Ànyone can do that!

Phone me 'any time you like.

Any customer can have a car painted **any** colour that he wants so long as it is black. [Henry Ford on the Model T Ford, 1909]

Any-words in other contexts

699 There are also other grammatical contexts where *any*-words occur:

- In *yes–no* interrogative subclauses:

  I sometimes wonder whether examinations are **any** use to **anyone**.

- In conditional clauses (*see* 210):

  If there is **anything** we can do to speed up the process, do let us know.

- After verbs with negative implication, such as *deny, fail, forget, prevent*:

  Some historians DENY that there were **any** Anglo-Saxon invasions **at all**.

  I'm sorry that my work PREVENTS me from doing **anything** else today.

- After adjectives with negative implication, such as *difficult, hard, reluctant*:

  I think it's DIFFICULT for **anyone** to understand what the senator means.

  I really feel RELUCTANT to take on **any** more duties at this time.

- After prepositions with negative implication, such as *against, without*:

  Mrs Thomas can hold her own AGAINST **any** opposition.

  The bill is expected to pass WITHOUT **any** major opposition.

- With comparisons (*see* 500) and constructions with *as* and *too*:

  Naomi sings this very difficult part BETTER THAN **anyone** else.
  ('Nobody sings this part better.')

  It's TOO late to blame **anyone** for the accident.

Spelling changes

(see CGEL 3.5–10, 5.81, 5.113, 7.79)

700 There are some changes in the spelling of endings of nouns, verbs, adjectives, and adverbs. It will be convenient to deal with all such spelling changes here in one place. They involve three types of change: replacing, adding, and dropping letters.

Replacing letters: carry ~ carries

701 *Changing* **y** *to* **ie** *or* **i**. *Y* is kept after a vowel, as in *play ~ played, journey ~ journeys*, but in bases ending in a consonant + *y*:

- *y* becomes *ie* in verbs before 3rd person singular present *-s* (see 574): they *carry ~* she *carries*

- *y* becomes *ie* in nouns before plural *-s* (see 635): one *copy ~* several *copies*

- *y* becomes *i* in adjectives before comparative *-er* or *-est* (see 500): *early ~ earlier ~ earliest*

- *y* becomes *i* in adverbs before the *-ly* used to form adverbs from adjectives (see 464): *easy ~ easily*

- *y* becomes *i* in verbs before *-ed* (see 574): they *carry ~* they *carried*

In three verbs there is a spelling change from *y* to *i* also after a vowel: *lay ~ laid, pay ~ paid, say ~ said*. In *said* there is also a change of vowel sound: /seɪ/ ~ /sed/.

Changing **-ie** *to* **-y**. Before the *-ing* ending (see 574), *-ie* is changed to *-y*: *they die ~ they are dying*

Adding letters: box ~ boxes

Adding e to nouns and verbs ending in sibilants

702 Unless already spelled with a final silent *e*, bases ending in sibilants receive an additional *e* before the *-s* endings. The sibilants are /z/, /s/, /dʒ/, /tʃ/, /ʒ/, /ʃ/. The added *e* occurs

- in the plural of nouns: one *box ~* two *boxes*, one *dish ~* two *dishes*

- in the 3rd person singular present of verbs: they *pass ~* she *passes*, they *polish ~* he *polishes*

Adding *e* to nouns ending in -*o*

Some nouns ending in -*o* have the plural spelled -*oes*, such as: *echoes, embargoes, goes, heroes, noes, potatoes, tomatoes, torpedoes, vetoes.* Many nouns ending in -*o* can have either -*oes* or -*os*, for example: *archipelagoes* or *archipelagos, cargoes* or *cargos.* The plural -*os* spelling is always used after a vowel (*radios, rodeos, studios,* etc.) and in abbreviations: *hippos* (~ *hippopotamuses*), *kilos* (~ *kilograms*), *memos* (~ *memorandums*), *photos* (~ *photographs*), *pianos* (~ *pianofortes*).

An additional -*e* is also added in two irregular verbs ending in -*o*: they *do* /duː/ ~ she *does* /dʌz/, they *go* /goʊ/ ~ she *goes* /goʊz/

Doubling of consonants: *hot ~ hotter ~ hottest*

703 Final consonants are doubled when the preceding vowel is stressed and spelled with a single letter

- in adjectives and adverbs before -*er* and -*est*:

big ~ bigger ~ biggest	BUT: *quiet ~ quieter ~ quietest*
hot ~ hotter ~ hottest	BUT: *great ~ greater ~ greatest*

- in verbs before -*ing* and -*ed*:

drop ~ dropping ~ dropped	BUT: *dread ~ dreading ~ dreaded*
stop ~ stopping ~ stopped	BUT: *stoop ~ stooping ~ stooped*
per'mit ~ per'mitting ~ per'mitted	BUT: *'visit ~ 'visiting ~ 'visited*
pre'fer ~ pre'ferring ~ pre'ferred	BUT: *'enter ~ 'entering ~ 'entered*

Normally there is no doubling when the vowel is unstressed (as indicated by the examples in the righthand column), but in <BrE> -*l* is doubled also in an unstressed syllable:

cruel ~ crueller ~ cruellest <BrE>	BUT: *crueler ~ cruelest* <AmE>
travel ~ travelling ~ travelled <BrE>	BUT: *traveling ~ traveled* <AmE>

Dropping letters: *hope ~ hoping ~ hoped*

704 If the base ends in silent -*e*, the *e* is dropped

- in adjectives and adverbs before -*er* and -*est*:

  brave ~ braver ~ bravest
  free ~ freer /'friːə(r)/ ~ *freest* /'friːɪst/

- in verbs before -*ing* and -*ed*:

  create ~ creating ~ created
  hope ~ hoping ~ hoped
  shave ~ shaving ~ shaved

Compare the spelling of

> hope ~ hoping ~ hoped   with *hop ~ hopping ~ hopped*
>
> stare ~ staring ~ stared   with *star ~ starring ~ starred*

Verbs ending in *-ee*, *-ye*, *-oe*, and often *-ge*, do not drop the *e* before *-ing* (but they drop it before *-ed*):

> agree ~ agreeing   BUT: *agreed*
>
> dye ~ dyeing   BUT: *dyed* (Compare *die ~ dying*)
>
> singe ~ singeing /ˈsɪndʒɪŋ/   BUT: *singed* (Compare *sing ~ singing* /ˈsɪŋɪŋ/)

Subjects

(*see* CGEL 10.6, 10.18–26)

705 ● The subject of a clause is generally a noun phrase (*see* 595): either a full noun phrase, a name or a pronoun:

> *The secretary* will be late for the meeting.
>
> *Jane* will be late for the meeting.
>
> *She* will be late for the meeting.

The subject can also be a non-finite clause (*see* 593):

> *Playing football* paid him a lot more than working in a factory.

or a finite nominal clause (*see* 589):

> *That there are dangers to be dealt with* is inevitable.

Starting a sentence with such a long clause makes it 'top-heavy' and it is more common to have a construction with introductory *it* (*see* 542):

> ~ It is inevitable *that there are dangers to be dealt with*.

● The subject normally occurs before the verb in statements:

> *They have* had some lunch.

In questions, the subject occurs immediately after the operator (*see* 609):

> *Have they* had any lunch?

● The subject has number and person concord with the finite verb (*see* 509):

> I'*m* leaving. ~ *The teacher is* leaving.

With modal auxiliaries there is no difference in the form of the verb:

> I *must* leave. ~ *The teacher must* leave.

● The most typical function of a subject is to denote the actor, i.e. the person, event, etc. causing the happening denoted by the verb:

> *Joan* drove Ed to the airport.

● When an active sentence is turned into a passive sentence (*see* 613), the subject of the active sentence becomes the agent of the passive. The agent is introduced in a *by*-phrase, but the agent need not be expressed (*see* 616):

> *Everybody* rejected the proposal.
>
> ~ The proposal was rejected (*by everybody*).

Subjunctives

(*see CGEL* 3.58–62)

Productive subjunctives

706 After a verb like *demand* or *insist* followed by a *that*-clause as complement we may find two different verb constructions:

> Mary insists that John *left* before she did.　　　　　　[1]
>
> Mary insists that John *leave* immediately.　　　　　　[2]

The reason is that *insist* has two different meanings: in [1] it means 'declare firmly' and the verb in the *that*-clause is the normal past form (*left*); in [2] it means 'demand insistently' and the following verb is in the subjunctive, which is **the uninflected base form** (*leave*). We call this second construction the 'mandative' subjunctive, or **the productive subjunctive** (to mark it as different from subjunctives that are formulaic expressions like *Come what may*, *see* 708). The subjunctive is used after governing expressions which express will (or volition). They are verbs like *insist*, adjectives like *insistent* and nouns like *insistence*.

● Here are some **verbs** which govern a subjunctive in the following *that*-clause: *advise, ask, beg, decide, decree, demand, desire, dictate, insist, intend, move, order, petition, propose, recommend, request, require, resolve, suggest, urge, vote.*

Examples:

> Some committee members *asked* that the proposal *be read* a second time.
>
> Public opinion *demanded* that an inquiry *be held*.
>
> Ann *suggested* that her parents *stay* for supper.
>
> Employers have *urged* that the university *do* something about grade inflation.
>
> Then I called her up and *proposed* that she *telephone* her lawyer.

● **Adjectives** which are often followed by a verb in the subjunctive can have a personal subject. Examples are: *anxious, determined, eager*:

> She was *eager* that the family *stay* together during the storm.

Adjectives with a subjunctive verb can also have an impersonal *it*-construction, for example *advisable, appropriate, desirable, essential, fitting, imperative, important, necessary, preferable, urgent, vital*:

> It is *important* that every member *be informed* about these rules.

● **Nouns** which take a following verb in the subjunctive are, for example, *condition, demand, directive, intention, order, proposal, recommendation, request, suggestion*:

> The Law Society granted aid on the *condition* that he *accept* any reasonable out-of-court settlement.

> Further offences will lead to a *request* that the official *be transferred* or *withdrawn*.

The use of the uninflected base form means there is lack of the usual concord between subject and finite verb in the 3rd person singular present. Also, there is no distinction between present and past tenses (*see* 740). The use of the subjunctive is more common in <AmE> than in <BrE>, and in <written, formal> than in <spoken> English.

Alternatives to the subjunctive

707 ● There is an optional construction, **putative *should*** (*see* 280), which in <BrE> is more common than the subjunctive. Compare the following *should*-constructions [1a, 2a] as alternatives to the subjunctive construction [1, 2]:

> Public opinion *demanded* that an inquiry *be held*. [1]
>
> ~ Public opinion *demanded* that an inquiry *should be held*. [1a]
>
> Ann *suggested* that her parents *stay* for supper. [2]
>
> ~ Ann *suggested* that her parents *should stay* for supper. [2a]

● <BrE> has in fact a third option, the indicative, which is rarer in <AmE>:

> The inspector has *demanded* that the vehicle *undergoes* rigorous trials to test its efficiency at sustained speeds.

> It is *essential* that more decisions *are taken* by majority vote.

● To avoid the somewhat <formal> subjunctive [3a] there is the further possibility of a construction with *for* + infinitive [3b]:

> It is *important* that every member *be informed* of these rules. [3a]
>
> It is *important for every member to be informed* of these rules. [3b]

Formulaic and *were*-subjunctives

708 ● The subjunctive constructions discussed so far are fully productive and quite common, especially in <written AmE>. There is also a **formulaic subjunctive**, but is used only in certain set expressions. It consists of the base form of the verb:

> ***Come*** what may, I'll be there. ('whatever happens')
>
> Heaven ***help*** us! (an exclamation of despair)

● There is also another type of construction, the ***were*-subjunctive** (*see* 277), where *were* is used (instead of the expected *was*):

> If I ***were*** you, I wouldn't do it.

The *were*-subjunctive occurs in clauses expressing a hypothetical condition (especially *if*-clauses) or after verbs such as *wish*. Usually the expected form *was* can also be used, and is more common in <informal> style:

> If the road ***were/was*** wider, there would be no danger of an accident.
>
> Sometimes I wish I ***were/was*** someone else!

Subordination

> (*see CGEL* Chapter 14)

What is subordination?

709 Two clauses in the same sentence may be related either by **coordination** or **subordination**. Compare these two sentences:

> Joan arrived at the office by ten but no one else was there. [coordination]
>
> Joan arrived at the office by ten before anyone else was there. [subordination]

In coordination, the two clauses are 'equal partners' in the same structure:

710 A subclause can also have another subclause inside it, which means that the first subclause behaves as a 'main clause' with respect to the second subclause. For example, the sentence *I know that you can do it if you try* is made up of three clauses, each within the other:

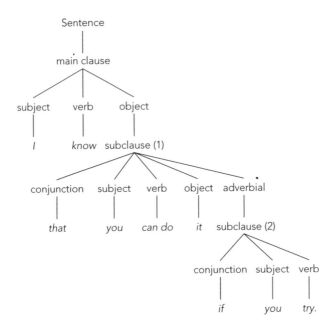

Subclauses can have various functions in their main clause. They may be subjects, objects, adverbials, prepositional complements, postmodifiers, etc.

Finite, non-finite and verbless subclauses

711 A main clause is almost always a finite clause. A subclause, on the other hand, can be a finite, non-finite, or verbless clause:

- A finite subclause (*see* 492)

    This news came *after the stockmarket had closed.*

- A non-finite subclause (*see* 493)

    No further discussion arising, the meeting was brought to a close.

- A verbless subclause (*see* 494):

    Summer vacation then only weeks away, the family was full of excitement.

All three types of clause (finite, non-finite, and verbless) may of course themselves have subclauses inside them. Here is a non-finite clause containing a finite subclause:

[Driving home [after I had left work]], I accidentally went through a red light.

Here is a verbless clause containing a non-finite subclause:

[Never slow [to take advantage of an opponent's weakness]], the Australian moved ahead confidently to win the fourth set.

Signals of subordination

712 A subclause is not usually capable of standing alone as the main clause of a sentence. Subclauses are usually marked as subclauses by some signal of subordination. The signal may be

- *that*, which is often omitted ('zero *that*'):

    I hope (*that*) *the department will cooperate on this project.*

- another subordinating conjunction, for example *before, if, when* (*see* 207):

    I wouldn't have been at all surprised *if the entire roof had collapsed.*

- a *wh*-word (*see* 536):

    I asked Jessica *why she wanted to move to another university.*

- inversion, which is <rather formal> and can always be replaced by an *if*-clause (*see* 278):

    Had I been a royal princess, they couldn't have treated me better.

    ~ *If I had been a royal princess*, they couldn't have treated me better.

- lack of a finite verb, but for example a *to*-infinitive, as in:

    I hope *to phone you back at the very beginning of next week.*

Apart from *that*-clauses with *that* omitted (including relative clauses, *see* 691), there is only one type of subclause that contains no expressed signal of subordination. This is a comment clause (*see* 499):

He must be at least sixty years old, *I suppose.*

It can be related to the main clause of a *that*-clause:

~ I suppose (that) he must be at least sixty years old.

The various uses of subordinating conjunctions are discussed in Part Two (*see* 360). Some subordinating conjunctions (*after, as, before, but, like, since, till, until*) also function as prepositions (*see* 654). Compare:

I haven't seen Bill *since the end of the war.*   [*since* = preposition]
I haven't seen Bill *since the war ended.*   [*since* = conjunction]

Simple subordinating conjunctions

713 We can distinguish between **simple**, **compound**, and **correlative** conjunctions.

Here are some simple subordinating conjunctions: *after, although, as, because, before, however, if, like* <familiar>, *once, since, that, though, till, unless, when, whenever, where, wherever, whereas, whereby, whereupon, while, whilst* <especially BrE>.

After we had arrived at the airport we had to wait for over two hours.

Although extensive inquiries were made at the time, no trace was found of any relatives.

A stranger came into the hall *as the butler opened the front door.*

The party opposed the aircraft *because* they were out of date.

The election result was clear *before* polling closed.

Paul seemed a bit moody, *like he used to be years ago.* <familiar> [many people prefer *as* to *like* here]

Once you begin to look at the problem there is almost nothing you can do about it.

I'm ashamed *that I can't remember my new colleague's first name.*

Hadn't we better wait *till Samantha arrives?*

You can't be put on probation *unless you are guilty.*

You will not be transferred *until they get someone to take your place.*

You have to crack the head of an egg *when you take it out of the* pan – otherwise it goes on cooking.

She said I could use her notebook computer *whenever I wanted.*

I don't know *where to start.*

Wherever I go I hear you've been very successful.

They need some facts and figures *whereby they can assess alternative strategies.*

After the adjournment, the lawyer requested Parker to visit him, *whereupon Parker burst into tears.* <formal and rare>

I've got a colleague taking my classes *while I'm away,* you see.

We must realize that *whilst God could erect a cocoon around us to protect us,* our faith would be worthless if he did. <*whilst* is especially BrE and rare>

Compound subordinating conjunctions

714 Compound subordinating conjunctions contain more than one word, although one of these words may be omitted if it is *that.* We can distinguish the following types:

- *Compound conjunctions ending with* **that**, *where* **that** *cannot be omitted:* except that, in order that (in order to *with infinitives),* so that, such that.

    The horse reared and threw the officer from the saddle, *except that one booted foot caught in the stirrup.*

    Did you consider the fact that your brother possibly died *in order that you can live?* <formal and rare>

Dr Bird's research is important **in that** *it confirms the existence of a relationship between smoking and cancer.*

I try to have a look at the student files **so that** *I know what everybody's doing.*

We're all trying to pull our wits together to submit papers **such that** *the university will pay our fares to the congress next year.* <rather formal>

● *Compound conjunctions ending with* **that,** *where* **that** *may be omitted.* Most of these compound conjunctions are <rather formal>: *assuming (that), considering (that), granting (that), granted (that), now (that), provided (that), providing (that), supposing (that).*

By the end of next year, **assuming (that)** *a general business recovery gets under way*, interest rates should begin to edge upwards again.

Granting (that) *there are only a few problems to be solved*, these problems make great demands.

The grass in the meadows was growing fast, **now (that)** *the warm weather was here.*

The government will endorse increased support for public education, **provided (that)** *such funds can be received and expended.*

715 ● *Compound conjunctions ending with* **as:** *as far as, as long as, as soon as, insofar as, inasmuch as* <very formal>, *so as + to-*infinitive, *so far as, so long as.*

As far as *we were aware*, the party had not officially opposed the bill's passage.

Like Caesar he has only one joke, **so far as** *I can find out.*

This is a solution most people try to avoid, **as long as** *they can see an alternative approach to the problem.*

Librarians perform a teaching and research role **inasmuch as** *they instruct students formally and informally and advise and assist faculty in their scholarly pursuits.* <formal>

Insofar as *science generates any fear*, the fear stems chiefly from the fact that new unanswered questions arise. <formal>

Our politicians generally vote **so as to** *serve their own constituency.*

● *Compound subordinating conjunctions ending with* **than,** e.g. *rather than* + a non-finite clause:

It was an audience of at least a couple of thousand who came to hear music **rather than** *go to the beach.* (See 310 on the use of the base form *go* here.)

● *Other compound subordinating conjunctions: as if, as though, in case*

It began to look **as if** something was going to happen.

Shannon hesitated, **as though** hunting for words and ways of putting them.

A man like Jess would want to have a ready means of escape **in case** it was needed.

Correlative subordinating conjunctions

716 Correlative conjunctions consist of two markers: one marking the main clause, and the other marking the beginning of the subclause. These conjunctions include: *if ... then, no sooner ... than, as ... as, so ... as, whether ... or, the ... the.* The second marker, if it is *that*, is sometimes omitted: *so ... (that), such ... (that).*

If it is true that new galaxies are forever being formed, **then** the universe today looks just as it did millions of years ago.

No sooner were the guards posted **than** the whole camp turned in for a night of sound sleep. <rather formal>

I can be **as** stubborn **as** she can.

We are getting **such** high yields per acre **that** many farmers are being forced to buy new harvesting machines.

The more you jog, **the** more you get hooked by the habit of taking regular exercise. (*See* 233.)

Whether ... or ... is an exception: here both words mark alternatives in a subclause:

She didn't care **whether** she won **or** not.

The functions of subclauses

717 Subclauses may function grammatically as subject, object, complement, or adverbial in a main clause.

Subject: What I like doing most in my spare time is playing around with my computer.

Direct object: It may interest you to know **that Sue and I are engaged.**

Indirect object: I gave **whoever it was** a drink.

Subject complement: The idea is **that we meet and work at George's place in the mornings.**

Object complement: I can't imagine John **overcome with grief.**

Adverbial: When we moved to the new town my wife worried that she might not be able to find another job.

Other functions:

> *Postmodifier in a noun phrase:* The friend *who shared Kate's room* was an art student.
>
> *Complement of a preposition:* Their loyalty will depend on *which way the wind is blowing*.
>
> *Complement of an adjective:* The curtain was now ready *to go up*.

Nominal clauses (*see* 588) can function as subject, object, complement, or complement of a preposition, i.e. in general they can have the same function as noun phrases. (On these and other types of subclauses, *see* 495.)

Verb patterns

(*see CGEL* 16.18–85)

Six basic verb patterns

718 The part of a clause following the verb phrase depends on the verb for its basic structure. For example, we can use the verb *find* with these different contexts:

I found Sophie in the library.	['discover']
I found Sophie a new job.	['obtain']
I found Sophie to be a very competent person.	['judge']

We distinguish six basic verb patterns in English:

- **SVC** Linking verbs with subject complement (719–20):

    She *is* [a doctor].

- **SVO** Verbs with one object (721–6):

    She *wants* [some help].

- **SVOV** ... Verbs with object + verb (727–9):

    She *wants* [you] [to help].

- **SVOO** Verbs with two objects (730–2):

    She *gave* [her sister] [some records].

- **SVOC** Verbs with object and object complement (733):

    She *found* [the task] [impossible].

- **SV** Verbs without object or complement (734):

    The door *opened*.

Within each basic verb pattern, we can distinguish a varying number of subpatterns. It is not possible to list here all the verbs which can occur in each pattern. For this you will need to consult a dictionary. The patterns are given in the active, but where passives (*see* 613) are common, we also include passive examples.

Linking verbs with subject complement: *Sorry I'm late.*

719 A **linking verb** (also called 'copular verb') has a following complement consisting of a noun phrase, an adjective etc. The most common linking verb is *be*. In the following examples, verbs are printed in *italics* and complements and objects are indicated by [brackets].

> Sorry I*'m* [late].
>
> *Was* Scott [a personal friend of yours]?

Among other linking verbs there are two groups: **current linking verbs** and **resulting linking verbs**.

- **Current linking verbs** (such as *appear, feel, look, remain, seem*) are like *be* in that they indicate a state:

> Mr Brown always *appears* [calm and collected].
>
> I never *lie* [awake] at night.
>
> I hope this will *remain* [a continuing tradition].
>
> That did not *seem* [a good idea] to me.
>
> You *sound* [a bit dubious].
>
> I'd love to go on with this job as long as I can *stay* [alive on it].
>
> The things that are poisonous we don't eat, so we don't know if they *taste* [nice] or not.

- **Resulting linking verbs**, such as *become* and *get*, indicate that the role of the verb complement is a result of the event or process described in the verb:

> The situation *became* [unbearable].
>
> Quite unexpectedly, Patricia's parents *fell* [sick] and died.
>
> Why did Mr MacGregor *get* [so angry]?
>
> We have to learn to *grow* [old] because we are all going to *grow* [old].
>
> Our neighbour said she'd seen her dog *turn* [nasty] just once.

720 - The complement of a linking verb can be a noun phrase or adjective phrase, as in the examples above, or else a nominal clause (*see* 588):

> The answer *is* [that we don't quite know what to do now].

- The complement of a linking verb can also be an *-ed* adjective (such as *puzzled*, *depressed*) or *-ing* adjective (such as *amusing*, *interesting*):

    Some of the spectators **looked** [rather puzzled].

    Dr Barry's lectures **were** [not very clear] but [rather amusing].

- With some verbs, *to be* can occur between the linking verb and the complement:

    There doesn't **seem to be** [any trouble with this car].

    Everybody **seems** (**to be**) [very depressed] at the moment.

    What the team did **proved** (**to be**) [more than adequate].

- As a linking verb, *be* is often followed by an adverbial, particularly an adverbial of place:

    I'd like to **be** [in town] for a few weeks.

Verbs with one object

The object is a noun phrase: *Did you* phone *the doctor?*

721 The object of verbs with one object (ordinary transitive verbs) can be a noun phrase:

    Let me just **finish** [the point].

    Where did you **hear** [that rumour]?

    Do you **believe** [me] now?

    Did you **phone** [the doctor]?

    This event **caused** [great interest] in our little village.

- The verb may be a phrasal verb, i.e. verb + adverbial particle + object (*see* 630). When the object is a full noun phrase, it may be placed either before or after the adverbial particle:

    They **blew up** [the bridge]. ~ They **blew** [the bridge] **up**.

If the object is a pronoun, it may only be placed before the particle:

    ~ They **blew** [it] **up**.

In the passive:

    ~ The bridge/It **was blown up**.

- The verb may be a prepositional verb, i.e. verb + preposition + object (*see* 632):

    Then the president **called on** [the governor] to explain why.

As Natasha was going up the stairs, Mr Middleton accidentally **bumped into** [her].

Andrew **came across** [someone whose name he had forgotten].

● The verb may be a phrasal-prepositional verb, i.e. verb + adverbial particle + preposition + object (*see* 634):

The statement was firm enough to **do away with** [all doubts].

Like other verbs in this pattern, prepositional verbs and phrasal-prepositional verbs can also appear in the passive:

Then the governor **was called on** to explain why.

Things like that **would** increase rather than **be done away with**.

The object is an infinitive: *We* agreed *to stay overnight.*

722 The object of a transitive verb is often a *to*-infinitive:

We *agreed* to stay overnight.

The company has *decided* to bring out a new magazine.

Don't *expect* to leave work before six o'clock.

I'd *like* to discuss two points in your paper.

I've been *longing* to see you.

Ed brought a manuscript I had *promised* to check through.

Other verbs which take a *to*-infinitive as object include (*can't*) *afford, ask, dislike, forget, hate, hope, learn, love, need, offer, prefer, refuse, remember, try, want.*

Help can be used with a to-infinitive or a bare infinitive (i.e. without *to*):

After her mother died Elizabeth came over to *help* (to) settle up the estate.

The object is an -*ing* form: *I* enjoyed *talking to you.*

723 One group of transitive verbs is followed by an -*ing* form:

We ought to *avoid* wasting money like this.

Obviously there would be just a few people one would *enjoy* talking to at the party.

I believe most people *dislike* going to the dentist.

Why did you *stop* talking?

Other such verbs are *admit, confess, deny, finish, forget, hate, keep, like, loathe, love, prefer, remember,* (*can't*) *bear,* (*can't*) *help,* (*can't*) *stand,* (*not*) *mind.*

The object is a *that*-clause:
I agree that the prospects are pretty gloomy.

724 ● The object of the verb can be a *that*-clause (where *that* is often omitted):

I *agree* (that) the economic prospects are pretty gloomy at the moment.

After school I *discovered* (that) I hadn't got any saleable skill.

I always *thought* (that) you two got on well together.

Passive with introductory *it* (*see* 543):

It would still have to be *agreed* that these acts were harmful.

Other verbs which take a *that*-clause are: *admit, announce, bet, claim, complain, confess, declare, deny, explain, guarantee, insist, mention, object, predict, promise, reply, say, state, suggest, warn, write.*

● After *believe, hope, say, suppose* and *think*, the *that*-clause can be replaced by *so*:

[A] Is it worth seeing the manager about the job?

[B] I *believe* so./I don't *believe* so.

Not may replace a negative *that*-clause:

[A] Does that symbol stand for 'cold front'?

[B] No, I don't *think* it does.
~ No, I don't *think* so.
~ No, I *think* not.

725 The verb may have a *that*-clause with **putative *should*** (*see* 280) or a **subjunctive** verb (*see* 706). *That* is rarely omitted in these constructions:

The prosecuting attorney *ordered* that the store detective (should) be summoned for questioning.

The lawyer *requested* that the hearing (should) be postponed for two weeks.

The officer *suggested* that the petitioner (should) be exempt only from combatant training.

Other verbs which can have this construction are *ask, command, decide, demand, insist, intend, move, prefer, propose, recommend, require, urge.*

The object is a *wh*-clause: *I wondered why we didn't crash.*

726 ● Some verbs take a finite clause introduced by a *wh*-word (*see* 536), such as *how, why, where, who, whether* or *if*:

The department *asked* if/whether it could go ahead with the expansion plans.

We flew in rickety planes so overloaded that I *wondered* why we didn't crash.

Other verbs with a *wh*-clause as object are, for example, *care, decide, depend, doubt, explain, forget, hear, mind, prove, realize, remember, see, tell, think*. The verbs *know, notice* and *say* usually occur in negative sentences:

> We **don't know** if these animals taste nice or not.

● Some verbs like *forget, know, learn, remember* and *see* can take an infinitive clause introduced by a *wh*-word:

> I don't **know** what to do next.
>
> She **forgot** where to look.

Verbs with object + verb

Verb with object + infinitive: *Have you* heard *Juliet sing?*

727 Many transitive verbs have an object which is followed by another non-finite verb.

● A few verbs (*hear, help, let, make*) have an object + infinitive without *to*:

> Have you **heard** [Professor Cray] [lecture on pollution]?
>
> Just **let** [me] [finish], will you?
>
> Danielle's letter **made** [me] [think].

Help occurs with or without *to*:

> Will you **help** [me] [(to) write the invitations to the party]?

The *to*-infinitive is always used in the passive:

> The former Wimbledon champion **was made** [to look almost a beginner].

● Most verbs which take an object + infinitive have the *to*-infinitive:

> Henrietta **advised** [Bill] [to get up earlier in the morning].
>
> When Joe Scott was 15 his parents **allowed** [him] [to attend classes at the Academy of Fine Arts].
>
> Can I **ask** [Dr Peterson] [to ring you back]?
>
> I **want** [you] [to get back as soon as possible].

Passive examples are common:

> [Bill] **was advised** by Henrietta [to get up earlier in the morning].
>
> [Mr Bush] **is** not **allowed** [to drive a car], but I saw him driving a car!

Some other verbs in this pattern are: *believe, force, order, permit, require, teach, tell, urge*.

Verb + object + -ing form: *We got the machine working.*

728   In the end we *got* [the machine] [working].

I can't *imagine* [Burt] [interrupting anybody].

The announcement *left* [the audience] [wondering whether there would be a concert].

I *resent* [those people] [spreading rumours about us].

Other verbs in this pattern include *catch, find, hate, like, love, (don't) mind, prefer, see, stop.*

Verb + object + -ed form: *We finally got the engine started.*

729   I must *get* [my glasses] [changed].

We've just *had* [our house] [re-painted].

I like your hair — you've *had* [it] [curled]!

Verbs with this construction include the perceptual verbs *feel, hear, see, watch,* the volitional verbs *like, need, want* and the causative verbs *get* and *have.*

Verbs with two objects

Both objects are noun phrases

730 ● The verb has an indirect object + a direct object:

Let me *give* [you] [an example of this].

Did you manage to *teach* [the students] [any English]?

I'll *write* [Pam] [a little note].

With a verb like *offer* this construction can be replaced by a direct object + *to* + noun phrase:

They *offered* [my sister] [a fine job].

~ They *offered* [a fine job] [to my sister].

Passive:

My sister *was offered* a fine job.

~ A fine job *was offered* to my sister.

Other verbs which can take the alternative construction with *to* include *bring, give, hand, lend, owe, promise, read, send, show, teach, throw, write.*

- Verbs like *buy, find, get, make, order, save, spare,* which can take the construction with an indirect object + a direct object, can have an alternative construction with direct object + *for* + noun phrase:

  I'll *buy* [you all] [a drink]. ~ I'll *buy* [a drink] [for you all].

  Can I *get* [you] [anything] ~ Can I *get* [anything] [for you]?

- Some verbs with two objects, such as *ask* and *cost,* cannot be replaced by prepositional constructions with *to* or *for*:

  The interviewer *asked* [me] [some awkward questions].

In the passive, only the second object (in this example *some awkward questions*) can appear alone:

  I *was asked* some awkward questions.

There is no corresponding passive with *cost*:

  It's going to *cost* [me] [a fortune] to buy all these course books.

Verb + object + *that*-clause:
The pilot informed *us that the flight was delayed.*

731 Verbs like *tell* have an indirect object + a *that*-clause (*see* 589), where *that* is often omitted:

  I *told* [him] [I'd ring again].

Other such verbs are: *advise, assure, bet, convince, inform, persuade, promise, remind, show, teach, warn, write.*

So can substitute for the *that*-clause after *tell*:

  [A] Did you *tell* [her] [that I am busy both evenings]?

  [B] Yes, I *told* [her] [so].

Verb + object + *wh*-clause: We asked *him what he was going to do.*

732 Verbs like *tell, teach* and *ask* can have an object + a finite or non-finite *wh*-clause (*see* 590):

  Perhaps you'd like to *tell* [us] [what you want].

  Nobody *taught* [the students] [how to use the machines].

  The president *asked* [each department] [whether it could go ahead with the expansion plans].

Passive:

  [Each department] *was asked* [whether it could go ahead with the expansion plans].

Verbs with object and object complement

733 Verbs such as *call*, *find* and *consider* have an object and an object complement and are called **complex-transitive verbs**.

- The complement following the object is a noun phrase in:

    Would you *call* ['Othello'] [a tragedy of circumstance]?

With some verbs, *to be* may be inserted before the complement:

    We *found* [Mrs Oliver] (*to be*) [a very efficient secretary].

    All fans *considered* [Phil] (*to be*) [the best player on the team].

Passive:

    ~ [Phil] *was considered* (*to be*) [the best player on the team].

Other such verbs: *appoint*, *elect*, *imagine*, *make*, *name*, *suppose*, *think*, *vote*.

- The complement is more likely to be an adjective with verbs like *declare*, *find*, *judge*, *keep*, *leave*, *make* and *wash*:

    If you do that it will *make* [Jo] [very angry].

    I had to quit because I *found* [my work in the office] [so dull].

- With verbs such as *believe*, *feel*, *imagine*, *suppose* and *think*, *to be* is usually inserted before an adjective complement:

    Many students *thought* [the exam] (*to be*) [rather unfair].

    We *believed* [the accused] (*to be*) [innocent].

Passive:

    ~ [The accused] *was believed to be* [innocent].

Verbs without object or complement

734 Verbs which have no object or complement are called **intransitive verbs**:

    Eliza's heart *sank*.

    Don't ever *give up*. ('surrender')

Intransitive verbs are usually followed by one or more adverbials:

    You are *teaching* at a college, aren't you?

    The Argentinian *leads* by three games to one.

    Do you *go* to Dr Miller's lectures?

    He used to *come in* late in the morning.

Verb phrases

(see CGEL 3.21–56, 4.2–40)

735 Verb phrases can consist of just the main verb (*see* 573):

> Betsy **writes** dozens of e-mails every day.

Verb phrases can also contain one or more auxiliary verbs before the main verb. Auxiliary verbs such as *be, have, might* are 'helping verbs' and help the main verb to make up verb phrases:

> She **is writing** long e-mails to her boyfriend.
>
> She **has been writing** e-mails all morning.
>
> Those e-mails **might** never **have been written**, if you hadn't reminded her.

There are two types of auxiliaries: **primary auxiliary verbs** and **modal auxiliary verbs**.

Main verbs		*write, walk, frighten, etc.* and also *do, have, be*
Auxiliary verbs	Primary auxiliaries	*do, have, be*
	Modal auxiliaries	*can, could, may, might, shall, should, will, would, must, used to, ought to, dare, need*

736 There are three **primary auxiliary verbs**: *do, have,* and *be.* As the table shows, these verbs can also act as main verbs.

- *Do* helps to form the *do*-construction (also called *do*-support, *see* 611):

  > Betsy **didn't write** many e-mails.

- *Have* helps to form the perfect aspect:

  > She **has** written only one e-mail.

- *Be* also helps to form the progressive aspect:

  > She **was** interviewing somebody or other when it suddenly started to rain.
  >
  > You must **be** joking!

- *Be* also helps to form the passive:

  > It has **been** shown in several studies that these results can **be** verified.

The **modal auxiliary verbs** (*see* 483) help to express a variety of meanings, for example intention (*see* 141), future time (140) and ability (287):

> I was teaching classics and then thought I **will** cease to teach classics.
> I **will** go abroad and teach English.
>
> If we **can** catch that train across there we**'ll** save half an hour.

Finite and non-finite verb phrases

737 There are two kinds of verb phrase: finite and non-finite.

- **Finite verb phrases** may consist of just a finite verb:

  He *worked* very hard indeed.

In finite verb phrases consisting of more than one verb, the finite verb is the first one (*was* and *had* in these examples):

He **was** *working* for a computer company at the time.

The enemy's attack **had** *been planned* for fifteen years.

The finite verb is the element of the verb phrase which has present or past tense. In the given examples *working* and *been planned* are non-finite verb forms, but they function in finite verb phrases: *was working* and *had been planned*.

Finite verb phrases occur as the verb element of main clauses and most subclauses (*see* 709). There is usually person and number concord between the subject and the finite verb. **Concord** of person is particularly clear with *be* (*see* 509): *I am ~ you are ~ he is*. With most finite main verbs, there is no concord contrast except between the 3rd person singular present and all other persons: *she reads ~ they read*. Modal auxiliaries count as finite verbs, although they have no concord with the subject: *I/you/he/ they can do it*.

738 The non-finite forms of the verb are:

- **the infinitive:**   (*to*) *call*
- **the -*ing* participle:** *calling*
- **the -*ed* participle:**   *called*

Many irregular verbs (*see* 550) have different forms for the past tense (*did*, *went*, etc.) and -*ed* participle (*done*, *gone*, etc.). Regular verbs, however, have the same -*ed* form for both functions: *worked* (past tense) and *worked* (-*ed* participle). The -*ed* participle (or 'past participle') is so called because of its -*ed* ending with regular verbs.

Compare finite and non-finite verb phrases:

- **Finite verb phrases**

  Con **works** in a laboratory.

  She's **working** for a degree in physics.

  She'll **be working** with overseas students.

- **Non-finite verb phrases**

  I actually like *to get up* early in the morning.

  Liz heard the door *open*.

  When *asked* to help she never refused.

  My father got a degree through *working* in the evenings.

  Having bought this drill, how do I set about using it?

Combinations of verbs

739 When a verb phrase consists of more than one verb, there are certain rules for how the verbs can be combined. There are four basic verb combinations:

(A) **Modal** – a modal auxiliary followed by a verb in the infinitive:

We [*can*] [*do*] nothing else.

(B) **Perfect** – a form of *have* followed by a verb in the *-ed* participle form:

I [*have*] never [*heard*] of him since.

(C) **Progressive** – a form of *be* followed by a verb in the *-ing* form:

We [*are*] [*getting*] on well together.

(D) **Passive** – a form of *be* followed by a verb in the *-ed* participle form:

He [*was*] never [*forgiven*] for his mistake.

These four basic combinations may also combine with each other to make up longer strings of verbs in one single verb phrase. The order is then alphabetical: A + B + C + D:

A + B	He *must have typed* the letter himself.
A + C	He *may be typing* at the moment.
A + D	The letters *will be typed* by Mrs Anderson.
B + C	He *has been typing* all morning.
B + D	The letters *have been typed* already.
C + D	The letters *are being typed*, so please wait a moment.
A + B + C	He *must have been typing* the letters himself.
A + B + D	The letters *must have been typed* by the secretary.

As we can see in the figure opposite, the verbs in the middle of the phrase serve both as the second part of the previous combination and as the first part of the following combination:

Verb phrases

must	have	been	typing
A: Modal +	Infinitive		
	B: Have +	Past participle	
		C: Be +	-ing form

Tense and aspect

740 By **tense** we understand the correspondence between the form of the verb and our concept of time (past, present, or future). English has two simple tenses: the present tense (*see* 116) and the past tense (*see* 123).

- **The present tense:** How *are* you today?
- **The past tense:** Fine thanks, but yesterday I *felt* awful.

Aspect concerns the manner in which a verbal action is experienced or regarded, for example as complete or in progress. English has two marked aspects: the progressive aspect (*see* 132) and the perfect aspect (*see* 125).

- **The perfect aspect:** I've never *felt* better, thanks.
- **The progressive aspect:** How *are* you *feeling* today?

741 The present and past tenses can form combinations with the progressive and perfect aspects. The letters in [square brackets] denote the basic combinations (*see* 739).

Present time

- **The simple present:** Our teacher *uses* a blackboard and *writes* illegible things on it.
- **The present progressive** [C]: What's he *writing* now?

Past time

- **The simple past:** I *wrote* a letter and *got* an answer almost by return post.
- **The past progressive** [C]: I could neither read what our teacher *was writing* nor hear what he *was saying*.
- **The present perfect** [B]: Some people I meet at this party *have written* at least one book – if not two.
- **The present perfect progressive** [B + C]: He *has been writing* books on the Beatles since 1967.

- **The past perfect** [B]: The Secretary of State said he *had spoken* to both sides, urging restraint.
- **The past perfect progressive** [B + C]: That's what people *had been saying* for a long time.

The passive (*see* 613) is formed by adding combination type [D], for example:

- **The passive simple past** [D]: This book *was written* for people who have a sense of humour.
- **The passive past perfect** [B + D]: The attack on this small friendly nation *had been planned* for fifteen years.

There is no future tense in English corresponding to the time/tense relation for present and past, but there are several expressions available for expressing future time (*see* 140), notably the modal auxiliary *will*.

The operator in the verb phrase

742 We have now described structures and contrasts of the verb phrase, in terms of modals, tense, aspect, and active-passive. There are also other constructions where the verb phrase plays an important part. For these constructions, the first auxiliary verb of the verb phrase has a special function as operator (*see* 609–12).

- In *yes–no* questions (*see* 682) the auxiliary verb functions as operator (printed in **bold**):

  Will you be staying long?

- In negation with *not* (*see* 581) the auxiliary verb functions as operator. Compare:

  I *have* received some letters this morning.

  ~ I *haven't received* any letters this morning.

  She *speaks* fluent French but she *doesn't speak* a word of English.

- Emphasis is frequently produced by *do* as operator (*see* 264, 300, 611):

  One change was likely to happen. Whether it *did* happen,
    I just don't know.

- The *do*-construction can be used in imperatives (*see* 497):

  Do be careful.

- The operator can stand alone (without the main verb) when it acts as a substitute form (*see* 384):

  [A] *Have* you seen these photographs? [B] Yes I *have*, thanks.

Word-classes

(see CGEL 2.34–45)

743 We can make a distinction between major word-classes and minor word-classes. Check the references here for further information about word classes given elsewhere in this grammar.

Major word-classes

744 The major word-classes are also called **open class words**. Major word-classes are 'open' in the sense that new members can easily be added. We cannot make a complete inventory of all the nouns in English, because no one knows for sure all the nouns used in English today, and new nouns are continually being formed. The four major word-classes, ordered according to overall frequency in English texts, are:

- **Nouns:** *belief, car, library, room, San Francisco, Sarah, session,* etc. (see 57, 597).
- **Main verbs:** *get, give, obey, prefer, put, say, search, tell, walk,* etc. (see 573).
- **Adjectives:** *afraid, blue, crazy, happy, large, new, round, steady,* etc. (see 440).
- **Adverbs:** *completely, hopefully, now, really, steadily, suddenly, very,* etc. (see 464).

Minor word-classes

745 Words that belong to the minor word-classes are also called **closed-class words**. Minor word-classes are 'closed' in the sense that their membership is limited in number, and they can be listed. A minor word-class cannot easily be extended by new additions: for all practical purposes, the list is closed. Minor word-classes (such as determiners, pronouns, and conjunctions) change relatively little from one period of the language to another. Minor word-classes are:

- **Auxiliary verbs:** *can, may, should, used to, will,* etc. (*see* 477)
- **Determiners:** *a, all, the, this, these, every, such,* etc. (*see* 522)
- **Pronouns:** *anybody, she, some, they, which, who* etc. (*see* 661)
- **Prepositions:** *at, in spite of, of, over, with, without,* etc. (*see* 657)
- **Conjunctions:** *although, and, because, that, when,* etc. (*see* 515, 709)
- **Interjections:** *ah, oh, ouch, phew, ugh, wow,* etc. (*see* 299)

746 Many English word-forms belong to more than one word-class. Some examples:

- *Love* is both a verb, as in *Do you **love** me?* and a noun, as in *What is this thing called **love?***
- *Since* is both a conjunction, as in ***Since** the war ended, life is much better* and a preposition, as in ***Since** the war life is much better.*
- *Round* belongs to five word-classes:

  preposition: Jill put her arms **round** Jack.

  adverb: All the neighbours came **round** to admire our new puppy.

  adjective: That's a nice **round** sum.

  noun: The champion was knocked out in the second **round**.

  verb: The cattle were **rounded** up at the end of the summer.

Zero

747 We use the term 'zero' in grammar to mark the position where an item has been omitted. In the following examples, Ø marks the position of the zero item:

- **Zero *that*** as a relative pronoun (*see* 686):

  Joan is the person Ø I like best in the office.

  ~ Joan is the person **that** I like best in the office.

- **Zero *that*** as a subordinating conjunction (*see* 712):

  I hope Ø you'll be successful in your new job.

  ~ I hope **that** you'll be successful in your new job.

- **Zero article** with mass nouns and plural count nouns (*see* 523):

  The possession of Ø *language* is a distinctive feature of the human species.

  My best subject at school was Ø *languages*.

Index

- References are to section numbers, not pages.
- Functions or meanings appear in ordinary type (e.g. proportion, female, purpose).
- Individual words and phrases treated in the Grammar are printed in italics (e.g. *proper*, *because of*).
- Grammatical terms are entered in small capitals (e.g. PROPER NOUN).
- References to language varieties are given in angle brackets, e.g. <spoken>, <AmE>.